DUMBARTON OAKS STUDIES

XXIV

PRIVATE RELIGIOUS FOUNDATIONS
IN THE BYZANTINE EMPIRE

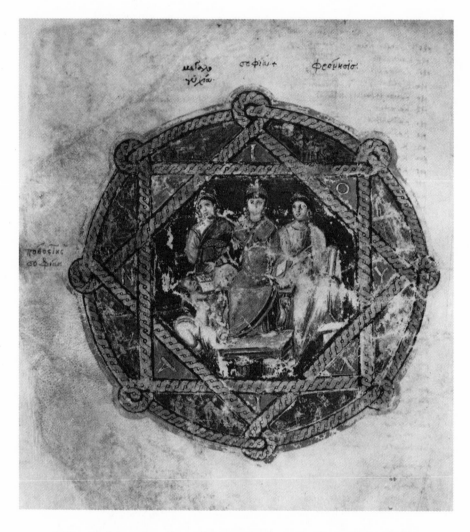

Juliana Anicia as founder and patroness, from the Vienna Dioscorides,
Vindo. med. gr. 1, fol. 6v (Österreichische Nationalbibliothek)

PRIVATE RELIGIOUS FOUNDATIONS
IN THE BYZANTINE EMPIRE

JOHN PHILIP THOMAS

DUMBARTON OAKS RESEARCH LIBRARY AND COLLECTION

WASHINGTON, D.C.

Library of Congress Cataloging-in-Publication Data

Thomas, John Philip.
Private religious foundations in the Byzantine Empire.

(Dumbarton Oaks studies ; 24)
Bibliography: p. 277
Includes index.
1. Byzantine Empire—Religious and ecclesiastical
institutions. 2. Byzantine Empire—Church history.
3. Orthodox Eastern Church—Byzantine Empire—History.
I. Title. II. Series.
BX300.T47   1987   250'.9495   87-8870
ISBN 0-88402-164-5

Contents

Acknowledgments

This book has been ten years in progress and is offered gratefully to the scholarly world with acknowledgment of the individuals and institutions that have facilitated my work on it. Though I cannot claim to have been his student, it is hard to see how this book could have been written without the benefit of the late Emil Herman's distinguished bibliography. My fondly remembered mentor, the late Robert Lee Wolff, guided me through the preparation of the Harvard doctoral dissertation (completed in 1980) that has served as the foundation for this book. Peter Topping and Alexander Kazhdan, who read and commented upon that dissertation, have indirectly helped me improve the book. To Giles Constable I owe the idea for the book; to Dumbarton Oaks, four years of support as a research associate. Numerous colleagues, fellows, and visitors to Dumbarton Oaks during those years have read portions of this manuscript, including Patricia Karlin-Hayter, Robert Ousterhout, Natalia Teteriatnikov, Leslie MacCoull, and Frank Trombley. To them, too, I owe thanks, absolving them and the others who have helped me for the faults of this book. Some important revisions were made at the National Humanities Center in Research Triangle Park, North Carolina, during the 1984–85 academic year. Final work on the manuscript was done at The Citadel, Charleston, South Carolina, with the assistance of a grant from the Citadel Development Fund.

Hingham, Massachusetts

Abbreviations

The following is a list of all abbreviations employed in the notes to refer to journals, original sources, and collections of sources. The list also includes a small number of secondary sources referred to in the notes by acronyms, but not the much larger number of such works referred to after first citation by shortened titles.

AASS	*Acta Sanctorum Bollandiana* (Brussels, 1643–1770, 1894–; Paris and Rome, 1866, 1887)
AB	*Analecta Bollandiana*
ACO	*Acta Conciliorum Oecumenicorum*, ed. E. Schwartz, 4 vols. (Strasbourg, Berlin, and Leipzig, 1914–)
AHDO	*Archives d'histoire du droit oriental*
AKK	*Archiv für katholisches Kirchenrecht*
ATR	*Anglican Theological Review*
B	*Basilica*, ed. H. J. Scheltema and H. Van der Wal, *Basilicorum Libri LX* (Groningen, 1955–)
BA	*The Biblical Archaeologist*
BASP	*Bulletin of the American Society of Papyrologists*
BCH	*Bulletin de correspondance hellénique*
BF	*Byzantinische Forschungen*
BGU	*Aegyptische Urkunden aus den staatlichen Museen zu Berlin, Griechische Urkunden*, 11 vols. (Berlin, 1895–1968)
BIFAO	*Bulletin de l'Institut Français d'Archéologie Orientale*
BKU	*Aegyptische Urkunden aus den staatlichen Museen zu Berlin, Koptische Urkunden*, 3 vols. (Berlin, 1902–68)
BM Copt.	Walter Ewing Crum, *Catalogue of the Coptic Manuscripts in the British Museum* (London, 1905)
BNJ	*Byzantinisch-neugriechische Jahrbücher*
BSAA	*Bulletin de la société archéologique d'Alexandrie*
BSC	*Byzantine Studies Conference, Abstracts of Papers*
BZ	*Byzantinische Zeitschrift*

C. Ant.	Concilium Antiochenum (ca. 326), canones ed. R&P 3 (Athens, 1853)
C. Carth.	Concilium Carthaginiensis (419), canones ed. R&P 3 (Athens, 1853)
C. Chalc.	Concilium Chalcedonense (451), canones ed. R&P 2 (Athens, 1852)
C. Const.	Concilium Constantinopolitanum (536), Acta, ed. Mansi, Vol. 8 (Florence, 1762)
C. Const. I et II	Concilium Constantinopolitanum primum et secundum (861), canones ed. R&P 2 (Athens, 1852)
C. Gang.	Concilium Gangrense (ca. 362), canones ed. R&P 3 (Athens, 1853)
C. Laod.	Concilium Laodicenum (ca. 340), canones ed. R&P 3 (Athens, 1853)
C. Nicaen. II	Concilium Nicaenum secundum (787), canones ed. R&P 2 (Athens, 1852)
C. Trull.	Concilium Trullanum (692), canones ed. R&P 2 (Athens, 1852)
CH	Church History
CJ	Codex Justinianus, ed. P. Krüger, Corpus juris civilis, Vol. 2, 10th ed. (Berlin, 1929)
CLT	A. A. Schiller, Ten Coptic Legal Texts (New York, 1932)
CMH	Cambridge Medieval History, ed. J. B. Bury and others, 8 vols. (Cambridge, 1913–66)
CO	Walter Ewing Crum, Coptic Ostraca from the Collections of the Egypt Exploration Fund (London, 1902)
Const. Apost.	Didascalia et Constitutiones Apostolorum, ed. F. X. Funk (Paderborn, 1905)
CPR	Corpus papyrorum Raineri, 4 vols. (Vienna, 1895–1958)
CSCO	Corpus scriptorum christianorum orientalium (Paris, Louvain, 1903–)
CSEL	Corpus scriptorum ecclesiasticorum latinorum (Vienna, 1866–)
CSHB	Corpus scriptorum historiae Byzantinae (Bonn, 1828–97)
CTh	Codex Theodosianus, ed. Th. Mommsen, P. Meyer and others (Berlin, 1905)

DACL	Dictionnaire d'archéologie chrétienne et de liturgie, ed. F. Cabriol and H. Leclercq (Paris, 1907–53)
DDC	Dictionnaire de droit canonique, ed. R. Naz (Paris, 1935–)
Dig.	Digest, ed. Th. Mommsen, Corpus juris civilis, Vol. 1 (Berlin, 1928)
DOP	Dumbarton Oaks Papers
EA	Ekklesiastike Aletheia
EEBS	Hepeteris Hetaireias Byzantinon Spoudon
EO	Echos d'Orient
FIRA	Fontes iuris Romani ante-Justiniani, ed. S. Ri cobono and others, 2nd ed. (Florence, 1940–43)
GOTR	Greek Orthodox Theological Review
GRBS	Greek, Roman and Byzantine Studies
HJ	Historisches Jahrbuch
IF	Indogermanische Forschungen
Inst.	Institutiones, ed. P. Krüger, Corpus juris civilis, Vol. 1 (Berlin, 1928)
IRAIK	Izvestiia Russkago Archeologicheskago Instituta v Konstantinople
JBL	Journal of Biblical Literature
JEA	Journal of Egyptian Archaeology
JGR	K. E. Zachariä von Lingenthal, Jus graeco-romanum, 7 vols. (Leipzig, 1856–84)
JHS	Journal of Hellenic Studies
JÖBG	Jahrbuch der österreichischen byzantinischen Gesellschaft
Jones, LRE	A. H. M. Jones, The Later Roman Empire 284–602: A Social and Administrative Survey, American edition, 2 vols. (Norman, Okla., 1964)
JSAH	Journal of the Society of Architectural Historians
JTS	Journal of Theological Studies
KRU	Walter Ewing Crum, Koptische Rechtsurkunden des achten Jahrhunderts aus Djême (Theben), (Leipzig, 1912)
KTE	P. V. Ernstedt, Koptskie teksty Gosudartsvennogo Ermitazha (Moscow-Leningrad, 1959)
KTM	P. V. Ernstedt, Koptskie teksty Gosudarstvennogo Muzeva izobrazitelnikh iskussty imeni A. S. Pushkina (Moscow-Leningrad, 1959)

Mansi	J. D. Mansi, *Sacrorum conciliorum nova et amplissima collectio*, 31 vols. (Florence and Venice, 1759–98)
MB	K. A. Sathas, *Mesaionike Bibliotheke. Biliotheca graeca medii aevi*, 7 vols. (Vienna and Paris, 1872–94)
MDAI Cairo	*Mitteilungen des deutschen archäologischen Instituts*
MGH, AA	*Monumenta Germaniae historica, Auctores antiquissimi*, 15 vols. (Berlin, 1877–1919)
MH	*Medievalia et Humanistica*
MIÖG	*Mittheilungen des Instituts für österreichische Geschichtsforschungen*
MM	F. Miklosich and F. Müller, *Acta et diplomata graeca medii aevi sacra et profana*, 6 vols. (Vienna, 1860–90)
MTZ	*Münchener theologische Zeitschrift*
NJ	Justinian, *Novellae*, ed. R. Schoell and W. Kroll, *Corpus juris civilis*, Vol. 3, 5th ed. (Berlin, 1928)
NPB	Angelo Mai and J. Cozza-Luzi, *Nova patrum bibliotheca*, 10 vols. (Rome, 1852–1905)
N Val	Valentinian III, *Novellae*, ed. Th. Mommsen, *Codex Theodosianus* (Berlin, 1905)
OC	*Orientalia Christiana*
OCP	*Orientalia Christiana Periodica*
Ostrogorsky, HBS	George Ostrogorsky, *History of the Byzantine State* (New Brunswick, N.J., 1969)
P. Amh.	B. P. Grenfell and A. S. Hunt, *The Amherst Papyri*, 2 vols. (London, 1900–01)
P. Antin.	*The Antinoopolis Papyri*, 3 vols. (London, 1950–67)
P. Bad.	*Veröffentlichungen aus den badischen Papyrus-Sammlungen*, 6 vols. (Heidelberg, 1923–38)
P. Bal.	Paul Kahle, *Bala'izah, Coptic Texts from Deir el-Bala'izah in Upper Egypt*, 2 vols. (London, 1954)
P. Basel	E. Rabel and W. Spiegelberg, *Papyrusurkunden der öffentlichen Bibliothek der Universität zu Basel*, 2 vols. (Berlin, 1917)
P. Berl. Inv.	Unpublished papyri of the *BGU* series
P. Cairo Masp.	Jean Maspero, *Catalogue général des antiquités égyptiennes du Musée du Caire. Papyrus grecs d'époque byzantine*, 3 vols. (Cairo, 1911–16)

P. Copt. Ryl.	Walter Ewing Crum, *Catalogue of the Coptic Manuscripts in the Collection of the John Rylands Library, Manchester* (Manchester-London, 1909)
P. Flor.	G. Vitelli and D. Comparetti, *Papiri Fiorentini*, 3 vols. (Milan, 1906–15)
P. Fouad	A. Bataille and others, *Les Papyrus Fouad I* (Cairo, 1939)
P. Grenf. 2	B. P. Grenfell and A. S. Hunt, *New Classical Fragments and Other Greek and Latin Papyri* (Oxford, 1897)
P. Lond.	F. G. Kenyon and H. I. Bell, *Greek Papyri in the British Museum*, 7 vols. (London, 1893–1974)
P. Michael.	D. S. Crawford, *The Greek Papyri in the Collection of Mr. G. A. Michailidis* (London, 1955)
P. Mon.	A. Heisenberg and L. Wenger, *Veröffentlichungen aus der Papyrussammlung der koniglichen Hof- und Staatsbibliothek zu München: Byzantinische Papyri* (Leipzig-Berlin, 1914)
P. Ness.	C. J. Kramer, *Excavations at Nessana*, 3 vols. (Princeton, 1958)
P. Oxy.	B. P. Grenfell, A. S. Hunt, and others, *The Oxyrhynchus Papyri*, 50 vols. (London, 1898–)
P. Princ.	A. C. Johnson and others, *Papyri in the Princeton University Collection* (Baltimore and Princeton, 1931–42)
P. Ross. Georg.	G. Zereteli and P. V. Ernstedt, *Papyri russischer und georgischer Sammlungen*, 5 vols. (Tiflis, 1925–35)
PG	J. P. Migne, *Patrologiae cursus completus. Series graeco-latina*, 161 vols. (Paris, 1857–66)
PL	J. P. Migne, *Patrologiae cursus completus. Series latina*, 221 vols. (Paris, 1844–55)
PLRE	A. H. M. Jones, J. R. Martindale and J. Morris, *The Prosopography of the Later Roman Empire*, 2 vols. (Cambridge, 1971–)
PO	*Patrologia Orientalis*, 39 vols. (Paris, Turnhout, 1904–)
Ps-Ath.	Wilhelm Riedel and Walter Ewing Crum, *The Canons of Athanasius of Alexandria, The Arabic and Coptic Versions* (London-Oxford, 1904)
Ps–Basil	Canons of Pseudo-Basil, ed. Wilhelm Riedel, *Die Kirchenrechtsquellen des Patriarchats Alexandrien* (Leipzig, 1900), pp. 231–83

PSBA	*Proceedings of the Society of Biblical Archaeology*
PSI	G. Vitelli and M. Norsa, *Papiri greci e latini*, 14 vols. (Florence, 1912–57)
R&P	G. A. Rhalles and M. Potles, *Syntagma ton theion kai hieron kanonon*, 6 vols. (Athens, 1852–59)
RAC	*Rivista di archeologia cristiana*
RB	*Revue bénédictine*
REB	*Revue des études byzantines*
REG	*Revue des études grecques*
RH	*Revue historique*
RHE	*Revue d'histoire ecclésiastique*
RHPR	*Revue d'histoire et de philosophie religieuses*
RIDA	*Revue internationale des droits de l'antiquité*
SB	F. Preisigke, F. Bilabel, and others, *Sammelbuch griechischer Urkunden aus Aegypten*, 11 vols. (Strassburg, 1915–26; Heidelberg, 1931–55; Wiesbaden, 1958–)
SBN	*Studi bizantini e neoellenici*
SCH	*Studies in Church History*
SOAW	*Sitzungsberichte der österreichische Akademie der Wissenschaften. Philosophisch-historische Klasse*
ST	Walter Ewing Crum, *Short Texts from Coptic Ostraca and Papyri* (London, 1921)
Stud. Pal.	C. Wessely, *Studien zur Palaeographie und Papyruskunde*, 11 vols. (Leipzig, 1901–24)
T&M	*Travaux et Mémoires*
Trinchera, SGM	Francisco Trinchera, *Syllabus graecarum membranarum* (Naples, 1865)
VC	Walter Ewing Crum, *Varia Coptica* (Aberdeen, 1939)
VV	*Vizantiiskii Vremennik*
ZRVI	*Zvornik rodoba Vizantioloshkog instituta*
ZSR	*Zeitschrift der Savigny-Stiftung für Rechtswissenschaft*

Introduction

The pioneering work of Ulrich Stutz introduced the concept of the *Eigen-kirche*, or "proprietary church," to the scholarly world of the late nineteenth century.[1] His work has stimulated a series of regional studies and much controversy in regard to his theory of a Germanic origin for proprietary churches.[2] In the field of Byzantine studies, however, an able Austrian scholar, Josef von Zhishman, had already anticipated Stutz's work with his *Das Stifterrecht in der morgenländischen Kirche* (Vienna, 1888). Zhishman's work was fundamental and is still of great value. He wrote too soon, however, to take advantage of the important and extensive evidence from papyri uncovered at Oxyrhynchus, Aphrodito, and elsewhere in Egypt in the early decades of this century.[3]

Artur Steinwenter, a renowned Coptic legal scholar, wrote a brilliant article in 1930 which for the first time outlined the uses of the papyri for the study of proprietary churches and monasteries.[4] Thanks to Steinwenter, it is now clear that not only the "founder's right" studied by Zhishman but actual private religious foundations existed in the early Byzantine Empire. Stutz's theory of a Germanic origin for the *Eigenkirche* thus is no longer tenable, for it is evident that the proprietary churches of Byzantium and of medieval Europe developed from the private religious foundations already in existence in late Roman times.[5]

This book is an attempt to bridge the work of Steinwenter and Zhishman and to serve as a foundation for a yet unwritten institutional history of the Greek Orthodox church in the Byzantine era. Zhishman's approach to his subject was admirably systematic in presentation and constitutional in outlook. My own presentation is more analytical and relies primarily on a continuous historical narrative. This book, then, should

[1] Ulrich Stutz, *Die Eigenkirche als Element des mittelalterlich-germanischen Kirchenrechtes* (Berlin, 1895) and *Geschichte des kirchlichen Benefizialwesens von seinen Anfangen bis auf die Zeit Alexanders III* (Berlin, 1895).

[2] Consult the bibliography in H. E. Feine, *Kirchliche Rechtsgeschichte*, Vol. 1: *Die katholische Kirche* (Weimar, 1950), 131–41.

[3] Discussed below in Chapter 3.

[4] Artur Steinwenter, "Die Rechtsstellung der Kirchen und Klöster nach den Papyri," *ZSR* 50 *k.a.* 19 (1930), 1–50.

[5] Feine, without a full knowledge of the Byzantine sources, argues against this view in "Ursprung, Wesen und Bedeutung des Eigenkirchentums," *MIÖG* 58 (1950), 195–208. See now also Richard Puza, "Gründer einer Gemeinde und Stifter einer Kirche oder eines Klösters in der christlichen Antike," *AKK* 151 (1982), 58–72, esp. 69.

be of interest to any student of the Byzantine church or of its role in Byzantine history.

In its own way, this is pioneering work, like that of Stutz, Zhishman, and Steinwenter. My task has been made considerably easier by the many splendid articles of the late Emil Herman (mostly in *Orientalia Christiana Periodica*), which have laid the groundwork for most of what we know about the institutional structure and internal operations of the Byzantine church.[6] Nevertheless, students of Byzantine history are well aware that evidence for certain periods is so scarce that frequently it is impossible to do more than offer reasonable conjectures as guides to interpretation. All too often I have had to allow some major interpretations to stand on only one or two testimonies in the sources. On the other hand, I have no doubt that I have failed to exhaust the potential illustrative material for many well-attested developments. The fact that there is scarcely any topic in Byzantine historiography that is not in some way important for the understanding of private religious foundations means that this study cannot be exhaustive. My work will doubtless need emendation and expansion by other scholars; but a significant body of evidence has now long been available for the study of these foundations, so it is time to begin to appreciate their importance for Byzantine civilization.

This study concerns the private ownership of ecclesiastical institutions; yet, in any society, an individual's right to ownership of any form of property is rarely absolute. What, then, was the nature and extent of private ownership of religious institutions in the Byzantine Empire? Did a private benefactor own his foundation outright, or was he, as its founder, or by virtue of his relationship to the founder, merely the beneficiary of a complex of legal rights in it? There are no simple answers to these questions because the legal relationship of a private patron and his foundation varied considerably, depending upon the vigor of governmental and ecclesiastical legislation, throughout the long history of the Byzantine Empire.

It may be useful to start with a definition to initiate discussion. In the broadest sense, private religious foundations can be held to encompass

---

[6]Emil Herman, "Les bénéfices dans l'église orientale," in *DDC* 2 (Paris, 1937), cols. 706–35; "Zum kirchlichen Benefizialwesen im byzantinischen Reich," *SBN* 5 (1939), 657–71; "Das bischöfliche Abgabenwesen im Patriarchat von Konstantinopel vom IX. bis zur Mitte des XIX. Jahrhunderts," *OCP* 5 (1939), 434–513; "Ricerche sulle istituzioni monastiche bizantine. Typika ktetorika, caristicari e monasteri 'liberi'," *OCP* 6 (1940), 293–375; "Die Regelung der Armut in den byzantinischen Klöstern," *OCP* 7 (1941), 406–60; "Die kirchlichen Einkünfte des byzantinischen Niederklerus," *OCP* 8 (1942), 378–442; "Le professioni vietate al clero bizantino," *OCP* 10 (1944), 23–44; "'Chiese private' e diritto di fondazione negli ultimi secoli dell'impero bizantino," *OCP* 12 (1946), 302–21; "La 'stabilitas loci' nel monachismo bizantino," *OCP* 21 (1955), 115–42; "The Secular Church," in *CMH* 4 (2nd ed.), pt. 2 (Cambridge, 1966), 104–33.

all those churches, monasteries, and philanthropic institutions (e.g., *no-sokomeia*, or "hospitals," *gerokomeia*, or "old age homes," and *orphan-otropheia*, or "orphanages") founded by private individuals (usually lay-men) and retained for personal administration, independent of the public authorities of the state and church. In actual practice, the matter was considerably more complicated, since clerics and monks are known to have founded religious institutions in the capacity of private property owners, and emperors and other public officials might as readily endow private foundations as public ones, depending upon their personal pref-erences. The modern historian looks in vain for a contemporary Byzan-tine definition, and there is certainly no systematic legal exposition of the status of these foundations. Even on the more limited question of the rights and duties of private benefactors, such testimony as does exist arises chiefly from litigation or restrictive legislation.[7] Yet there can be no doubt about the existence of private religious foundations in the sense encompassed by the definition above, thanks to explicit contemporary references. The fifth-century *Codex Theodosianus* terms the churches *privatae ecclesiae*, and a law of Emperor Alexius Comnenus (1081–1118) calls the monasteries *monasteria kosmika*.[8] Only rarely, however, do we have the benefit of such explicit designations, and the modern historian must face the vexing problem of identifying probable private religious foundations on the basis of somewhat arbitrary criteria.

I have relied upon three broad indicators of private ownership. The strongest indication is a testimony of a sale or purchase of a religious institution by a private individual. Such testimonies, although not com-mon, occur with sufficient frequency throughout Byzantine history (until the patriarchate proscribed sales in 1325) to confirm the continued ex-istence of private foundations. Testimony to significant financial assist-ance provided by a benefactor to a religious institution is another impor-tant indicator. The difficulty is that it is often hard to distinguish private foundations, properly speaking, from those institutions that (like most modern churches) were only lay-assisted. Obviously, provision of oper-ating expenses or of clerical salaries is more significant than the gift of a mosaic or votive offering. The last of the three indicators is the fact of a private act of foundation, particularly when coupled with the exercise of benefactors' rights by the founder or (even more significantly) by his or her heirs. This is significant because until the late eleventh century few benefactors were willing to erect a church or monastery without obtain-ing compensatory benefits.

It is important to remember in this connection that the designation of

---

[7] See the discussion below in Chapter 9.
[8] *CTh* 16.5.14; Alexius Comnenus, *De jure patriarchae* (*JGR* 3.408.12).

a foundation by one of our sources as "independent" did not mean, as it does now and even in Byzantium after the eleventh century, an autonomous, self-governing institution.[9] Rather, these foundations are to be understood as "independent" in the sense of being under private administration, that is, not a "public" institution controlled by the ecclesiastical hierarchy. It is also important not to confuse the spiritual jurisdiction over private institutions that was often claimed (and sometimes actually exercised) by the ecclesiastical hierarchy with the right to administer these institutions. The latter the founders nearly always reserved for themselves, their heirs, or designees.

This is far from the only instance in which the technical vocabulary of our sources deserves close attention. Given the linguistic conservatism of Byzantine high culture, it is not surprising to find a fair amount of continuity of usage throughout the life of the empire. Naturally the modern investigator must be alert for the masking of important changes by the persistence of traditional nomenclature. In my experience, however, the Byzantine sources give every indication of being very careful about the usage of terms that served to distinguish certain types of institutions and their statuses, personal rights and responsibilities, official dignities and ranks, sundry incomes, fees, and emoluments. Careful philological study of these terms promises rich rewards for future investigation. In anticipation of this work, I have been hesitant to employ uniform English equivalents in this study without reference to the Greek originals. Here, it seems, it is English and not Byzantine Greek which serves to obscure crucial distinctions. As an aid to the non-specialist reader, I have provided a lengthy glossary of the most important technical terms and the strictly functional English equivalents I have used for them in this study.

In the absence of a proper institutional history of the Greek Orthodox church in Byzantine times, it has been necessary for me to treat private foundations in a very general context. It need hardly be said that the achievement of this institutional history is still a long way off, and this study ought not be taken as a claimant to that honor. Yet given its admittedly broad focus, students of the church in the western Middle Ages may well miss cross-references to the essentially parallel history of its ecclesiastical institutions. For this shortcoming I must plead my own inexpertise. Nevertheless, I have benefited enormously from my knowledge of the course of ecclesiastical history in the West, which more than once has given me an indication of what to look for in the less well explored Byzantine sources. I hope that my present work will yield reciprocal dividends for the study of the church in the West.

[9] See the discussion below in Chapter 8.

CHAPTER ONE

The Origins of Private Religious Foundations in the Later Roman Empire

A GREAT number, if not an actual majority, of the ecclesiastical institutions of the Byzantine Empire owed their foundation to private initiative. This apparently was the case even in Constantinople, where the number of imperial religious foundations was exceptionally high.[1] These private religious foundations should be distinguished carefully from other ecclesiastical institutions.

Among the oldest churches, predating official recognition of Christianity, were the ancient foundations of the early Christian communities. The sources refer to them in late Roman times as *katholikai ekklesiai*.[2] These included the bishop's (or "cathedral") church and its immediate dependencies in each diocese. They appear in cities, towns and occasionally in the countryside throughout Byzantine history, yet they were much rarer than one might expect from their importance as the empire's public churches.[3]

Imperial foundations such as Hagia Sophia, Holy Apostles, and the numerous churches built by Justinian (527–565) in Constantinople and elsewhere constitute an intermediate category of foundations to be dis-

---

[1] The tenth-century itinerary *Patria Konstantinoupoleos*, ed. Th. Preger, *Scriptores originum Constantinopolitanarum* (Leipzig, 1907), attributes ninety religious institutions to the emperors and their families, but twenty-two of the attributions to Constantine and his mother Helena must be considered extremely doubtful. The *Patria* notes fifty-five foundations by laymen, but only eight by monks and members of the ecclesiastical hierarchy. *De antiquitatibus Constantinopolitanis*, ed. Anselmo Banduri, *Imperium orientale* (Paris, 1711) records sixty-four imperial foundations, including thirteen attributed to Constantine and Helena, forty-one private foundations, and only three patriarchal or monastic foundations, with six unattributed. Precise figures for Constantinople await tabulation from R. Janin, *La géographie ecclésiastique de l'empire byzantin*, Pt. 1: *Le siège de Constantinople et le patriarcat oecuménique*, Vol. 3: *Les églises et les monastères*, 2nd ed. (Paris, 1969). For some preliminary figures, see Peter Charanis, "The Monk as an Element of Byzantine Society," *DOP* 25 (1971), 61–84, esp. 65–68.

[2] On these public churches, see W. E. Crum, "A Use of the Term 'Catholic Church'," *PSBA* 27 (1905), 171–72; Stephan Zorell, "Die Entwicklung des Parochialsystems bis zum Ende der Karolingerzeit," *AKK* 82 (1902), 74–98.

[3] Herman, "Secular Church," 118; seconded by Jean Lassus, *Sanctuaires chrétiens de Syrie* (Paris, 1947), 253.

tinguished from both public and private churches yet sharing features of each.[4] They were in the first instance personal benefactions, whether erected with funds from the private fortune of the emperors or from state revenues, yet they tended to assume a public character with the passage of time. Although the church authorities enjoyed wide discretionary authority over them, the reigning emperor exercised the right to nominate candidates for clerical ordinations in them, as private founders and their families did for their foundations.[5]

The private religious foundations that are the subject of this study had their origins in the age before the conversion of Emperor Constantine (306–337) to Christianity. Since for most of this period Christians were a proscribed sect,[6] it is not to be expected that the sources will be readily employable for determining the institutional origins of these foundations. The fairly abundant pre-Constantinian Christian literature hardly ever sheds more than incidental light on the question, helpful inscriptions are few, and the evidence afforded by archeology often poses as many problems as it resolves. Still, a tentative outline of the probable evolution of private religious foundations can be attempted.

ARCHITECTURAL CONTEXT OF CHRISTIAN WORSHIP

Perhaps the greatest difficulty facing the investigator is disentangling the origins of what emerge as the distinctly separate public and private foundations of the post-Constantinian era. Their origins before the Constantinian conversion are hard to distinguish precisely because the *katholikai ekklesiai* could hardly be conceived of as "public" institutions before the official recognition of Christianity.[7] Consequently, in the era before Constantine, all Christian churches were necessarily private foundations, yet some more so than others.

[4] For these imperial foundations, see Gilbert Dagron, *Naissance d'une capitale: Constantinople et ses institutions de 330 à 451* (Paris, 1974), 397–408; L. Voelkl, "Die konstantinischen Kirchenbauten nach den literarischen Quellen des Okzidents," *RAC* 30 (1954), 99–136, and *Die Kirchenstiftungen des Kaisers Konstantin im Lichte des römischen Sakralrechts* (Cologne, 1964); G. T. Armstrong, "Constantine's Churches: Symbol and Structure," *JSAH* 33 (1974), 5–16, "Imperial Church Building and Church-State Relations, A.D. 313–363," *CH* 36 (1967), 3–17, and "Imperial Church Building in the Holy Land in the Fourth Century," *BA* 30 (1967), 90–102; Janin, *Géographie*, Vol. 3, pp. 41–50, 455–70; Eusebius, *De vita Constantini* 2.45–6, 3.29, ed. Ivar Heikel (Leipzig, 1902); Procopius, *De aedificiis* 1.8.5, ed. Jakob Haury (Leipzig, 1913; rev. 1964).

[5] *NJ* 3.2.1 (535).

[6] For the legal status of Christians at this time, see G. E. M. De Ste. Croix, "Why Were the Early Christians Persecuted?" *Past and Present* 26 (1963), 6–38.

[7] For the vexing problem of their legal status before the conversion of Constantine, see Giuseppe Bovini, *La proprietà ecclesiastica e la condizione giuridica della chiesa in età*

The development of the institutional infrastructure of Christianity could not have occurred without the generous participation of the laity at all times. Denied ready access to the synagogues, the first Christian apostles resorted to meetings in private residences. Before too long, the regular meeting of the Christian community acquired the designation of *ekklesia*.[8]

An injunction believed to be of Christ himself commanded stability of residence: "Into whatever city (*polis*) or village (*kome*) you may enter, inquire who is worthy in it, and there remain until you depart. Entering into the house (*oikia*), greet it. If indeed be the house worthy, let your peace come upon it; but if it be not worthy, let your peace return unto you."[9] By no later than A.D. 57, certain Christian communities had made it a practice to hold their meetings in particular private residences.[10] Thus, the apostle Paul wrote several times of the *ekklesia* at the house (*oikos*) of Prisca and Acquila at Ephesus. Other lay benefactors figure prominently in the Pauline epistles, such as Phoebe, the *prostasis* (patroness) of the *ekklesia* at Cenchreae, the port city of Corinth. Paul also mentioned Nymphas of Laodiceia and Philemon of Colossae as hosts of Christian assemblies in their private residences.

Christian scripture does not indicate the next step of institutionalization until the pseudo-Pauline epistle *Ephesians* (A.D. 80–90) adopts architectural terminology to form a metaphor for the spiritual community: "No more are you strangers and sojourners, but fellow citizens of the saints and kinsmen (*oikeioi*) of God, having been built on the foundation of the apostles and prophets, Christ Jesus himself being the cornerstone in whom all the building being fitted together grows into a holy shrine (*naos hagios*) in the Lord, in whom also you are being built into a dwelling place (*katoiketerion*) of God in spirit."[11] As this scriptural citation indicates, it was becoming possible for the Christian communities of the empire to associate themselves with the architectural setting of their meeting places rather than seeing themselves as an essentially spiritual community meeting wherever might chance to be convenient. This institutionalization was not accomplished without a certain amount of am-

---

precostantiniana (Milan, 1948), 3–70; Gerda Krüger, *Die Rechtsstellung der vorkonstantinischen Kirchen* (Stuttgart, 1935); Elisabeth Herrmann, *Ecclesia in re publica: Die Entwicklung der Kirche von pseudostaatlicher zu staatlich inkorporierter Existenz* (Frankfurt, 1980).

[8] For the general development, see Harold Turner, *From Temple to Meeting Place: The Phenomenology of Places of Worship* (The Hague, 1979); Stephen Walke, "The Use of *Ecclesia* in the Apostolic Fathers," *ATR* 32 (1950), 39–53; and J. Y. Campbell, "The Origin and Meaning of the Christian Use of the Word *Ekklesia*," *JTS* n.s. 49 (1948), 130–42.

[9] Matt. 10:11–13; cf. Mark 6:10–11, Luke 9:4–5, ed. E. Nestle and K. Aland, *Novum testamentum graece*, 26th ed. (Stuttgart, 1979).

[10] Rom. 16:1-3, I Cor. 16:19, Col. 4:15, Phil. 2.

[11] Eph. 2:19–22.

bivalence that was to persist for centuries.[12] Christian apologetic literature such as the *Octavius* of Minucius Felix could deny, even in the early
third century A.D., that Christians had any use for temples or altars.
Clement of Alexandria also maintained the quaintly conservative position "It is not the place (*topos*) but the assemblage (*athroisma*) of the
elect that I call an *ekklesia*."

Even long after the official recognition of Christianity, Isidore of Pelusium echoed Clement in maintaining that the community of true believ-
ers was the real church, not some elaborately decorated building. In fact,
however, a rudimentary institutional infrastructure had developed by no
later than the middle second century.[13] Justin Martyr wrote in his *Apologia* of meetings each Sunday at established sites where Christians gathered in the cities and in the countryside. More informal arrangements
may well have persisted, too, as Justin himself later claimed (ca. 165) in
alleging before imperial examiners that he held meetings only in his residence above the baths of Myrtinus in Rome. Post-Constantinian apocryphal literature recalls this era by postulating wealthy Christian converts who hosted the apostles in their homes or turned their residences
over to them for use as churches.[14]

The apocryphal tradition reads conversion of private dwellings back
too far, but in so doing shows an awareness of the next stage in institutionalization, the acquisition of property for renovation for ecclesiastical
services. These renovated private dwellings are known as *domus ecclesiae*, and at this point the evidence afforded by archeology becomes important.[15] The *domus ecclesiae* of Dura-Europos is one of the earliest and
certainly the best known of these churches. Based on a private structure

[12] Minucius Felix, *Octavius* 10, 32, ed. C. Halm, *CSEL* 2 (Vienna, 1867); Clement of
Alexandria, *Stromata* 7.5 (*PG* 9, col. 437); Isidore of Pelusium, *Epistolae* 2.246 (*PG* 78,
col. 685); cf. *Martyrium S. Iustini et sociorum*, Rec. B, 3.1, ed. Herbert Musurillo, *The
Acts of the Christian Martyrs* (Oxford, 1972).

[13] Justin Martyr, *Apologia* 1.67, ed. J. K. T. von Otto (Jena, 1876); *Martyrium S. Iustini*,
Rec. A, 3.

[14] E.g., *Acta Pauli et Theclae* 7, ed. León Vouaux, *Les Actes de Paul et ses lettres apo-
cryphes* (Paris, 1913); *Vita et martyrium sanctae Caeciliae* 26 (*PG* 116, col. 180); [Ps-]
Clement of Rome, *Recognitiones* 4.6, 10.71, ed. Bernhard Rehm (Berlin, 1965).

[15] F. V. Filson, "The Significance of the Early House Churches," *JBL* 58 (1939), 105–12;
Hans-Josef Klauck, "Die Hausgemeinde als Lebensform im Urchristentum," *MTZ* 32
(1981), 1–15, with references to the early Christian sources in notes 44–48, and *Hausgemeinde und Hauskirche im frühen Christentum* (Stuttgart, 1981); Joan Petersen, "House-
Churches in Rome," *Vigiliae Christianae* 23 (1969), 264–72; Richard Krautheimer, *Early
Christian and Byzantine Architecture*, 3rd ed. (Baltimore, 1979), 27–38; J. P. Kirsch, "La
domus ecclesiae cristiana del III secolo a Dura-Europos in Mesopotamia," in *Studi dedicati
alla memoria di Paolo Ubaldi* (Milan, 1937–45), 73–82, and "Origine e carattere degli
antichi titoli cristiani di Roma," in *Atti del III congresso nazionale di studi romani*, ed. C.
G. Paluzzi (Bologna, 1934), Vol. 1, pp. 39–47; K. Gamber, *Domus Ecclesiae: Die ältesten
Kirchenbauten Aquilejas* (Regensburg, 1968).

erected early in the third century, the *domus ecclesiae* itself would appear to date after renovations undertaken ca. 231. The building itself was destroyed in 257, providing a valuable terminus ante quem for the initiation of this stage in ecclesiastical institutionalization. The archeological evidence and the available literary sources provide no clue as to who purchased or administered *domus ecclesiae* such as this one at Dura. Thus it is unclear whether the *domus ecclesiae* is the distant ancestor of the post-Constantinian private churches or of public religious foundations. Perhaps it served as progenitor of both.

It is clear, however, that by A.D. 250–260 Christian bishops owned landed property, specifically burial grounds known as *koimeteria*, for these were seized by the imperial government in Valerian's persecution of 257–260 and restored by his son and successor, Gallienus (260–268).[16] The bishops suddenly assumed an important role in the latter half of the third century, supplementing what to all appearances seems once to have been the exclusive role of the laity in the provision of places for Christian worship. An admittedly late account by the fourth-century bishop Gregory of Nyssa records the foundation of a church by Gregory Thaumaturgus, bishop of Cappadocian Caesarea (d. ca. 270).[17] This was a community undertaking, but under the leadership of the bishop, and for the creation of a church *ek ton themelion*, as many of our sources describe it, or "from the ground up," so to speak.

Indeed, the "Peace of the Church," as the long interval (260–303) between the persecutions of Valerian and Diocletian is called, saw the replacement of old churches (presumably *domus ecclesiae*) with new buildings of more spacious dimensions in the cities of the empire.[18] Ironically it is the vehement anti-Christian polemicist Porphyry whose *Kata Christianon logoi* of 268 is the earliest text to mention the erection of buildings intended from the start to serve as Christian churches.[19] The Christian communities had come full circle. Once their leaders had criticized the pagans for their temples, but now they were erecting structures that rivaled them.

The novelty of the episcopal role is apparent from the difficulties encountered at Antioch when Paul of Samosata, who had erected a church

[16] Eusebius of Caesarea, *Historia ecclesiastica* 7.11.10, 7.13; with Christopher Haas, "Imperial Religious Policy and Valerian's Persecution of the Church, A.D. 257–260," *CH* 52 (1983), 133–44.

[17] Gregory of Nyssa, *Epistola 25* (*PG* 46.3, cols. 1093–1100); for Gregory Thaumaturgus, see Eusebius, *Historia ecclesiastica* 7.14.

[18] Eusebius, *Historia ecclesiastica* 8.1.5.

[19] Porphyry, *Kata Christianon logoi*, Fr. 76, ed. Adolf von Harnack, *Abhandlungen der königlich preussischen Akademie der Wissenschaften, Philosophisch-historische Klasse* (Berlin, 1916); cf. Krautheimer, *Byzantine Architecture*, 38.

to serve as his episcopal see, was deposed for heresy and refused to give up possession of the church.[20] The Christian community sought the assistance of Emperor Aurelian (270–275) and got it, specifically a *prakteon* ordering the transferral of the building to "those with whom the bishops of the [Christian] doctrine in Italy and Rome should communicate in writing." This was a very important decision, as our source Eusebius, bishop of Caesarea, seems only dimly to have realized, for it established the principle that the Christian community could exercise a valid claim to the ownership of its meeting place. Had Aurelian (or the bishops) decided to support Paul, it is hard to see how a distinct system of what were to become the public churches could have established itself independently of private religious foundations.

As it was, there remained considerable opportunity for confusion. An inscription of Tiberius Polycharmos, patron of the Jewish synagogue in Stobi, datable to 279, tellingly demonstrates this by analogy.[21] This benefactor evidently enlarged the synagogue considerably through the expenditure of his own fortune, "without touching in any way the sacred [funds]." Yet Polycharmos reserved for himself and his heirs rights of ownership (*despoteia*) over the upper chambers of the addition. Consistent with this division of responsibility, Polycharmos pledged in this inscription to undertake the repair of the roof tiles of the upper chambers.

When the catastrophe of Diocletian's persecution struck, the transition from *domus ecclesiae* to churches erected *ek ton themelion* had not yet been completed. Indeed, at Rome the bishops continued to acquire private dwellings for conversion into *domus ecclesiae* long after the persecution had ended.[22] So also at Constantinople, where the partisans of Bishop Gregory Nazianzus (379–381) converted a small private dwelling into the church of St. Anastasia because the church of Hagia Sophia was for a time in the hands of his opponents.[23] The onset of persecution then found many Christian communities still worshiping in *domus ecclesiae*, as at the small African town of Abitinae, where the local authorities discovered a priest Saturninus holding a religious service in 304 in the *domus* of Octavius Felix.[24] At Cirta the authorities confiscated and inventoried the contents of another church in a *domus*.[25] By 310 the hard-

---

[20] Eusebius of Caesarea, *Historia ecclesiastica* 7.30.19.

[21] N. Vulić, "Inscription grecque de Stobi," *BCH* 56 (1932), 291–98; for the Stobi synagogue, see Ernst Kitzinger, "A Survey of the Early Christian Town of Stobi," *DOP* 3 (1946), 81–162, esp. 141–42, with bibliography at 159–60.

[22] For which see J. P. Kirsch, *Die römischen Titelkirchen im Altertum* (Paderborn, 1918).

[23] Sozomen, *Historia ecclesiastica* 7.5, ed. J. Bidez and J. C. Hansen (Berlin, 1960); cf. Socrates, *Historia ecclesiastica* 5.7 (*PG* 67), with Janin, *Géographie*, Vol. 3, p. 22.

[24] *Passio SS. Dativi, Saturnini presb. et aliorum*, ed. Pio Franchi de' Cavalieri, *Note agiografice* (Vatican City, 1935), 49–71, at 51.

[25] *Gesta apud Zenophilum*, ed. Karl Ziwsa, *S. Optati Milevitani libri VII, CSEL* 26 (Vienna, 1893), 185–97.

pressed Christians of Palestine were reverting to the practice of their ancestors by once again resorting to the renovation of *oikoi* to serve as churches.[26]

Not only private property owners but also the corporate Christian church (called the *corpus Christianorum*) suffered confiscations as a result of the edicts of persecution. An Egyptian papyrus of 304 shows a lector of the "former church of the village of Chysis" declaring that said church had neither money, slaves, nor possessions, either from gifts or testamentary bequests.[27] Yet a slightly earlier papyrus speaks of the donation of land to a church as "an old custom," confirming that some churches had already become property-owning institutions.[28]

The imperial legislation issued in 311–313 to end the persecution and mandating the return of confiscated property to the Christians reflects the mixed pattern of ownership of Christian ecclesiastical institutions at the turn of the century. The original edict of toleration of Galerius (305–311), issued in 311, encourages the Christians to build their churches once again but makes no provision for the return of confiscated property.[29] Maxentius (306–312), however, seems to have anticipated his imperial colleagues by restoring confiscated properties to the Christians of Rome in a letter given to their bishop Miltiades (311–314).[30] The text of Licinius' (308–324) instructions to the governor of Bithynia, issued in June 313 and popularly known as the "Edict of Milan," is especially important because it shows an awareness of the distinction between Christian places of assembly owned by private individuals and those that belonged to the Christian communities corporatively: "Since the aforementioned Christians are known to have had not only those places in which they have been accustomed to assemble, but also other possessions of their corporative right (*ius corporis*)—that is, of the churches, not of individual persons—we command all these to be returned by the law which we have expressed above, absolutely without any ambiguity of meaning or disputation, to the aforementioned Christians, that is, to their corporation and their places of assembly (*conventicula*)."[31]

[26] Eusebius of Caesarea, *Liber de martyribus Palaestinae* 13.1, ed. E. Schwartz (Leipzig, 1908), 947.

[27] *P. Oxy.* 33.2673 (A.D. 304).

[28] *P. Oxy.* 12.1492 with Giuseppe Ghedini, "Ho topos nel P. Oxy. 1492," *Aegyptus* 2 (1921), 337–38; cf. *P. Oxy.* 8.1162.2, and Clement of Alexandria, *Stromata* 7.5.

[29] Eusebius, *Historia ecclesiastica* 8.17.1,9; Lactantius, *De mortibus persecutorum* 34, ed. S. Brandt and G. Laubmann, CSEL 27.2 (Vienna, 1897).

[30] Augustine, *Breviculus collationis cum Donatistis* 3.34, and *Contra partem Donati post gesta* 17, ed. M. Petschenig, CSEL 53 (Vienna, 1910); Optatus, *De schismate* 1.16–17, ed. Karl Ziwsa, CSEL 26 (Vienna, 1893).

[31] Lactantius, *De mortibus persecutorum* 48.7–9, with section 9 quoted here, of which Eusebius, *Historia ecclesiastica* 10.5.11, preserves a similar text in Greek; for the edict itself, see Herbert Nesselhauf, "Das Toleranzgesetz des Licinius," HJ 74 (1955), 44–61.

The *nomos* of Maximinus Daia (309–313), also of 313, notes that the orders of Diocletian and his colleagues for the abolition of Christian assemblies had served as a pretext for the confiscation of private property belonging to Roman citizens by zealous officials.[32] Even though the ownership of Christian churches at that time happened to be divided between private patrons and incorporated Christian communities, it is easy to appreciate how the officials charged with carrying out the edicts of persecution might have thought this a distinction of little importance. Now, however, Maximinus Daia chose to reaffirm Galerius' edict permitting the construction of new churches and also to command the restoration of houses (*oikiai*) and estates (*choria*) to the "ancient [legal] jurisdiction of the Christians."

A *diataxis* of Constantine to Anulinus, proconsul of Africa, is consonant with other imperial legislation of 313, ordering the return of possessions once belonging to the *katholikai ekklesiai*.[33] This is the first mention in the legal sources of the *katholikai ekklesiai*, soon to assume their role as the public churches of the empire. Another imperial directive of Constantine recorded by Eusebius of Caesarea notes the ownership of *martyria* (martyr's shrines) by the (public) churches, and likewise orders their return.[34] In 318 a certain Paul, priest of a community of Marcionite Christian sectaries, appears in an inscription as the founder of a church at Lebaba, a Syrian village.[35] Taken together, these sources show the emergence of a rudimentary system of public churches just as Christianity was receiving official recognition and support from the emperor.

For their part, private benefactors were not inactive, even at the height of the great persecution. The site plans for the Anastasius *martyrion* near Salona (ca. 305–310) show an example of what was to become a typical post-Constantinian private religious foundation, with the martyr's remains placed under the apse and the sarcophagi of the founder and his family under the nave.[36]

IMPACT OF THE CONVERSION OF CONSTANTINE

With the conversion of Constantine to Christianity, there was a dramatically increased need for places of worship according to the new state-

---

[32] Eusebius, *Historia ecclesiastica* 9.10.8.

[33] Eusebius, *Historia ecclesiastica* 10.5.15–17; for relations between Constantine and the Christians, see Timothy Barnes, *Constantine and Eusebius* (Cambridge, Mass., 1981).

[34] Eusebius of Caesarea, *De vita Constantini* 2.37, 39, 40.

[35] Wilhelm Dittenberger, *Orientis graeci inscriptiones selectae*, Vol. 2, No. 608 (Leipzig, 1905).

[36] Ejnar Dyggve and Rudolf Egger, *Forschungen in Salona*, Vol. 3 (Vienna, 1939), esp. 10–16; André Grabar, "Les monuments paléochrétiens de Salone et les débuts du culte des martyrs," in *Disputationes Salonitanae* 1970, ed. Zeljko Rapanić (Split, 1975), 69–74.

supported creed. Even before the end of the persecutions, Pope Marcellus (308–309) is said to have had to draw upon the resources of his church at Rome to build new structures to serve the needs of recent converts.[37] The shortcoming naturally was acute in the new capital of Constantinople, where the pre-Constantinian Christian community was probably quite small.[38] Constantine took vigorous action to remedy the deficiencies. He erected several new churches himself on a lavish scale at Constantinople, Nicomedia, and Jerusalem.[39] Taking full account of the existing stock of churches, he ordered that the bishops should enlarge or completely rebuild these with the aid of the provincial governors and funds from the treasury. In Palestine this effort was not limited to the great cities, for even such lesser towns as Mambre and Heliopolis received churches at this time thanks to Constantine's generosity.

The direct involvement of the emperor in the construction of *katholikai ekklesiai*, sometimes distinguished further as *basilicae* (imperial churches), was bound to lead to misunderstandings and controversy. Nor were problems long in coming. Optatus of Mileve preserved a letter of Constantine to the bishops of Numidia (330) in which the emperor expresses his frustration at the refusal of Donatist Christian sectaries to relinquish the "basilica of the *ecclesia catholica*" which he had erected for his namesake city of Constantina (formerly Cirta), declaring that "though they had been warned to give up what was not theirs, they refused to do so."[40] To compensate the orthodox bishops, the emperor decided to accede to their request to turn over a public building "with all its rights" to the ownership (*dominium*) of the *ecclesia catholica* to serve as the site of a new church. Doubtless the Donatists thought themselves equally entitled to the earlier *basilica* on the strength of a prior imperial bequest.

Constantine was not the only emperor to discover that a *basilica* once entrusted to the ecclesiastical hierarchy might be impossible to recover. In 385 Emperor Valentinian II (375–392), at the instigation of his mother, Justina, attempted to lay claim to the Basilica Porciana in Milan so it could be put at the disposal of his mother's retinue and her Arian Gothic bodyguard. Bishop Ambrose (374–397), with the backing of the orthodox faithful of his diocese, successfully opposed the emperor's

---

[37] *Liber Pontificalis*, ed. Louis Duchesne (Paris, 1886), Vol. 1, p. 164.

[38] Janin, *Géographie*, Vol. 3, p. xi.

[39] Eusebius, *De vita Constantini* 2.45–46, 3.25, 48, 50–51, 58, 4.57; Socrates, *Historia ecclesiastica* 1.16; Sozomen, *Historia ecclesiastica* 2.3; cf. the important comments by G. Dagron, *Naissance*, 388–409; G. J. M. Bartelink, "'Maison de Prière' comme dénomination de l'église en tant qu'édifice, en particulier chez Eusèbe de Césarée," *REG* 84 (1971), 101–18, provides a valuable philological study of the terminology.

[40] *Epistula Constantini de basilica catholis erepta*, ed. Karl Ziwsa, *S. Optati Milevitani libri VII*, CSEL 26 (Vienna, 1893), 213–16.

claims. A letter written by Ambrose to his sister Marcellina recounts the events and recalls the bishop's exchange of correspondence with the emperor: "You have no right to violate the house of a private individual, so do you think you can take away the house of God? It is asserted that everything is permitted for the emperor, that everything is his. I respond: Oh emperor, do not oppress yourself with the notion that you have any imperial right in those things that are divine. . . . The palaces belong to the emperor, the churches to the priest. Authority is committed to you over public, not sacred buildings." [41]

Perhaps it is significant that these two successful defiances of imperial wishes for the employment of *basilicae* occurred in the western half of the Roman Empire. In the east, and during most of the course of Byzantine history, the emperors generally were able to put imperial churches at the disposal of partisans of their own favored creeds of Christianity. There is even a possibility that some sort of imperial right of patronage in churches such as Hagia Sophia provided the basis for the frequent dismissals of patriarchs by the emperors in Byzantine history.

If *katholikai ekklesiai* and imperial churches could not always be distinguished, the distinction between simple private churches and secular dwellings was even murkier. The tangled affair of Ischyras, a priest of the Meletian Christian sect in the Egyptian village of Irene Secontaruri, was one of the scandals employed by Eusebius, bishop of Nicomedia, and other enemies of Athanasius, bishop of Alexandria (328–373), to discredit the latter in the eyes of Constantine. The allegation was that one of Athanasius' partisans, a certain Macarius, had used violence to stop Ischyras from conducting a religious service and had broken a chalice in the process. What actually happened cannot be reconstructed, since only Athanasius' defense survives in his *Apologia contra Arianos*.[42] In it Athanasius flatly denies that Ischyras ever received proper ordination as a cleric of any sect and that he ever had a church in which to minister: "He found no one to believe him, except his own relatives. For he never had a church, nor was he ever considered a clergyman by those who lived but a short distance from his own village. . . . The church that he says he has never was a church at all, but quite a small private house belonging to an orphan by the name of Ision. . . . He is not a priest of the *katholike ekklesia*, nor does he have a church, nor has a cup ever been broken, but he falsified and fabricated everything." [43]

---

[41] Ambrose, *Epistola* 20 (*PL* 16, col. 1038B, cf. 1042A). For the controversy, see Andrew Lenox-Conyngham, "The Topography of the Basilica Conflict of A.D. 385/6 in Milan," *Historia* 31 (1982), 353–63.

[42] Athanasius, *Apologia contra Arianorum*, ed. H. G. Opitz, *Athanasius Werke* (Berlin, 1940), Vol. 2, Pt. 1, pp. 87–168; cf. Sozomen, *Historia ecclesiastica* 2.23.1; in general, L. W. Barnard, "Athanasius and the Meletian Schism in Egypt," *JEA* 59 (1973), 181–89.

[43] Athanasius, *Apologia* 74.3–4, 76; trans. adapted from Archibald Robertson, *Select Writings and Letters of Athanasius, Bishop of Alexandria* (London, 1891), 139–40.

Athanasius' account, accepted at face value, would serve to show how simple a matter it was for anyone to promote himself as a priest and point to any convenient private residence as his *domus ecclesiae*. On the other hand, it certainly is possible that Athanasius was being less than forthright here, and that Ischyras indeed was a dissident priest superintending a modest village church. In that event, it would stand as an interesting testimony to early rivalry between private foundations and the bishop's *katholikai ekklesiai*. Whatever the actual facts in the case, it should be noted that Ischyras eventually was able to obtain an imperial grant from Constantius II (337–361) in 339 for the construction of a church. Athanasius, to his credit, dutifully includes the letter of award in his defense of his conduct in the affair.[44]

Even if the claims of Ischyras were completely fabricated, there are other examples of private oratories, or *eukteria*, usually of wealthy Christian families, that are attested by later sources.[45] Some of these were completely private, in the fullest sense of the word, closed to all but the families and the household of their owners. Yet the more extended households, especially those on great estates, might well have had an oratory that would come to assume a quasi-public character due to the scarcity of churches in the countryside in the fourth century. Since their owners would have to secure the services of priests on occasion, these private chapels soon became a matter of concern to the ecclesiastical authorities, just as Ischyras' supposed church in the house of the orphan Ision came to the attention of Athanasius. Other sources and archeological evidence indicate that there were also transformations of rooms or buildings that remained constitent parts of private dwellings into family oratories.[46]

CASE STUDIES IN THE CONSTRUCTION, PATRONAGE, AND MANAGEMENT OF PRIVATE CHURCHES

To a certain extent, the Constantinian imperial foundations provided *exempla* which very wealthy private benefactors would follow in subsequent generations. Late and unreliable sources allege that some churches in Constantinople owed their foundations to such benefactors even in Constantine's day.[47] These attributions should be rejected as spurious,

---

[44] Athanasius, *Apologia* 85.7.

[45] *NJ* 58 (537), 131.8 (545); Lassus, *Sanctuaires*, 146, fig. 62, a chapel associated with the Byzantine palace of Qasr ibn Wardan in Syria; the house of Eusebia in Sozomen, *Historia ecclesiastica* 9.2.1–13.

[46] R. Goodchild, "A Byzantine Palace at Apollonia (Cyrenaica)," *Antiquity* 34 (1960), 246–58, esp. 252–53; A. W. Meates, *Lullingstone Roman Villa, Kent* (London, 1955), esp. 130–47.

[47] *Patria Konstantinoupoleos* 3.6, 16, 99 (ed. Preger, pp. 216, 218, 249), with commentary by Janin, *Géographie*, Vol. 3, pp. 259, 409, 492. The reputed founders are all unknown to *PLRE*, Vol. l.

especially when the sources use the name of a city district to account for the origin of a church located in that quarter (for example, the invention of a patrician Probus as the founder of a church of St. John the Baptist in a quarter of Constantinople known as ta Probou). None of the individuals alleged to have founded churches in the capital in the Constantinian era is attested elsewhere in the sources for the period. It seems more likely at this time that domestic residences continued to be converted into *domus ecclesiae* by private patrons as well as ecclesiastical prelates, and that family chapels slowly evolved into oratories which were still privately owned but open for public worship on the model of the diocesan *katholikai ekklesiai*.

Such transformations were presumably accomplished in a variety of ways. An unusual case connected with the rediscovery of the relics of forty soldiers who suffered martyrdom under Licinius illustrates one way this chanced to happen.[48] A certain Eusebia, a deaconess and partisan of Macedonius I (341–360), a former bishop of Constantinople, kept the remains of these martyrs in her own house outside the capital. Macedonius was important for his role in introducing monasticism to the capital as well as his sponsorship of diocesan philanthropic institutions.[49] As a firm opponent of Arianism, he lost the confidence of Constantius II and was deposed in favor of Eudoxius (360–369). Macedonius' followers continued to play an important part in the monastic life of the capital even though they suffered condemnation as heretics at the Council of Constantinople in 381. When Eusebia saw her own death approaching, she reached an agreement with some Macedonian monks. She promised to bequeath her house to them in exchange for a promise to bury her next to the relics. It was agreed that there should be an *eukterios oikos* (oratory) there in order to render due honor to the martyrs. All the arrangements were to remain secret, and the oratory itself was located underground.

Some years later, Flavius Caesarius (consul in 397) buried his wife, who had also been a partisan of Macedonius, next to the tomb of Eusebia, once her intimate friend. Still later, Caesarius purchased the site from the Macedonian monks so that he might be buried next to his wife. Evidently Caesarius had no idea that the site contained a Macedonian oratory, only that he was buying a Macedonian monastery (he himself was orthodox), which the monks sold, and he then demolished, without

---

[48] Sozomen, *Historia ecclesiastica* 9.2; cf. G. Dagron, "Les moines et la ville: Le monachisme à Constantinople jusqu'au concile de Chalcédoine (451)," *T&M* 4 (1970), 229–76, at 246–47.

[49] Sozomen, *Historia ecclesiastica* 4.2.3, 4.20.2, 4.26, 7.7, 8.1; Socrates, *Historia ecclesiastica* 2.42; with commentary by Dagron, "Monachisme," 239, 244–49, and *Naissance*, pp. 441–42.

qualms. The consul then erected his own private church dedicated to St. Thrysus on the site of the older building.

Sometime after Caesarius' death, a priest named Polychronius recalled that there had once been a Macedonian oratory on the site and resolved to investigate its origins. The priest had been a household servant of Caesarius and now probably served in the church of St. Thrysus. He was fortunate enough to find one of the aged Macedonian monks still living who revealed the secret of the existence of the relics of the forty martyrs. The lapse of time and the extensive alterations to the site prevented the old monk from determining the precise location of the relics. Polychronius had witnessed the burial of Caesarius' wife, however, and with the assistance of some clues provided by the monk he was able to excavate and uncover the underground oratory and the prized relics. Empress Pulcheria took a personal interest in the excavations. She declared a holiday upon the rediscovery of the relics and supplied a costly casket for their rededication in the church of St. Thrysus. Sozomen, the church historian, was present for the occasion, which he says occurred during the tenure of Proclus (434–447) as archbishop of Constantinople.

The account, even if not strictly accurate in all details, nevertheless indicates that by the 390s many of the distinctive features of Byzantine private religious foundations—such as the construction, sale, and purchase of church buildings—were already socially and religiously acceptable. To the very end of the Byzantine Empire, this reliance upon private philanthropy for the expensive construction of ecclesiastical foundations was normative.

Even individuals in religious life might be dependent upon private philanthropy for the means to erect these expensive foundations. This was true especially of monasteries, which in their origins were exclusively private foundations.[50] The Syrian monk Isaac, for example, convinced Flavius Saturninus (consul in 383) to donate land and build a monastery for him in Constantinople in 382.[51] Likewise it was the Egyptian landowner Petronius who founded the monastery of Teveu for Pachomius (ca. 340), even though an official of the bishop of Panopolis had encouraged Pachomius in the endeavor.[52]

---

[50] See Karl Suso Frank, *Grundzüge der Geschichte des christlichen Mönchtums* (Darmstadt, 1975), esp. 15–17, 36–37, and Vera von Falkenhausen, "Monasteri e fondatori di monasteri a Costantinopoli tra Costantino Magno e Giustiniano I," *Corsi di cultura sull'arte ravennate e bizantina* 26 (1979), 151–55; for the female ascetics discussed below, see Elizabeth Clarke, "Ascetic Renunciation and Feminine Advancement: A Paradox of Late Ancient Christianity," *ATR* 63 (1981), 240–57.

[51] *Vita S. Isaacii, AASS* May, Vol. 7, cols. 251C–252C; cf. Dagron, "Monachisme," 232–33.

[52] *Vita prima S. Pachomii* 80–81, ed. François Halkin, *Subsidia Hagiographica* 19 (1932), 1–96, at 54.

Melania the Elder, heiress of a wealthy Roman family, built a monastery for herself in Jerusalem, where she lived for twenty-seven years until ca. 410.[53] She also was the source of philanthropic distributions to other churches and monasteries which were disbursed through a trust administered by her relatives and stewards. Her granddaughter Melania the Younger was advised by African bishops not to distribute alms casually to monasteries, but instead to "give to each monastery a house (*oikia*) and an income (*prosodon*)" in order to assure permanent benefits for the recipient institutions.[54] Melania followed this advice in founding two great monasteries in Thagaste, for which she provided a "sufficient income." Later, when she founded a monastery on the Mount of Olives outside Jerusalem, Melania provided an example of humility by declining the office of *hegoumene* (abbess) for herself though she retained the right to choose the foundation's director.[55] Olympias, another wealthy benefactress active at the beginning of the fifth century, built a monastery adjacent to Hagia Sophia in Constantinople which she populated with her relatives and chambermaids.[56] Olympias, unlike Melania the Younger, assumed the direction of this foundation herself, and was succeeded in that office in turn by two of her relatives.

For their part, imperial and ecclesiastical authorities followed the lead of Constantine and Macedonius and played their own roles in the construction of new foundations. Even so, the role of private philanthropy remained paramount. It is doubtful whether the institutional church could ever have raised such monumental structures as the principal churches of Constantinople independent of the benefactions of the emperors and wealthy private individuals. The number of patriarchal churches in the capital always remained small.[57] It also appears that a decision by the imperial authorities in the 390s to cut back on all forms of direct and indirect subsidies to the churches and the clergy may also have played a part in opening the field to private benefactors at this time.

Private religious foundations were even more important in the rural areas of the empire. John Chrysostom, archbishop of Constantinople (398–404), pointedly urged the great landowners to undertake the task of providing places of worship for the agricultural laborers on their estates.[58] Here, as in the medieval West, it is likely that the pagan masses of the countryside first attended services at the oratories on the estates of

[53] Palladius, *Historia Lausiaca* 46.5, 54.2, ed. Cuthbert Butler (Cambridge, 1898–1904).

[54] Gerontius, *Vita S. Melaniae junioris* 20, 22, ed. Denys Gorce (Paris, 1962).

[55] Gerontius, *Vita* 41.

[56] *Vita S. Olympiadis* 6, 12, ed. Anne-Marie Malingrey, *Jean Chrysostome: Lettres à Olympias*, 2nd ed. (Paris, 1968).

[57] *De antiquitatibus* 35E, ed. Banduri, and *Patria Konstantinoupoleos* 3.65 (p. 239), provide some examples of patriarchal foundations.

[58] John Chrysostom, *In acta apostolorum homilium XVIII* (PG 60, cols. 147–50).

their employers.[59] Thus the rural private church became one of the principal vehicles for the propagation of the Christian faith in the countryside.

Of course the ecclesiastical authorities were concerned, as Athanasius had been in the Ischyras affair, that the correct credal version of Christianity be preached in the countryside. A law of Emperor Valens (364–378), probably from the year 377, complains that religious dissidents, expelled from the (public) churches of the empire, were finding refuges for holding their religious services in the residences and on the estates of private landowners.[60] A subsequent law of Theodosius I (379–395) indicates that it was common practice by 381 for outlawed sectaries to establish churches in residences and on private estates where they hoped to be beyond the reach of the law.[61] A law of Gratian (375–383) issued at Trier in 378 demonstrates that the authorities in the Western Roman Empire were also aware of this problem.[62] By 388 the government of the Eastern Roman Empire was already making a distinction between public and private churches in legislation prohibiting heretical assemblies: "We command that the Apollinarians and all other followers of diverse heresies shall be prohibited from all places, from the walls of cities, from the congregation of honorable men, from the communion of the saints. They shall not have the right to ordain clerics, they shall forfeit the privilege of assembling congregations either in public or private churches."[63]

While the use of legal sources in connection with the assemblies of religious dissidents on private estates leads to many vexing problems of interpretation, they do indicate the existence of private churches in the countryside as early as 377. Theodosius I prayed in a rural oratory, probably of private origin, that happened to be near his army's encampment on the eve of the battle of Aquileia in 394.[64] Although these oratories were apparently not uncommon by this time, there were still not enough of them to satisfy conscientious church authorities. The fact that the sources frequently give attention to oratories associated with heterodox groups should not obscure the fact that contemporaneous orthodox chapels (such as the one visited by Theodosius I) also existed. Yet serious consideration ought to be given to the possibility that the expulsion of religious dissidents from the public churches of the empire gave an un-

---

[59] Cf. Elie Griffe, *La Gaule chrétienne à l'époque romaine*, Vol. 3 (Paris, 1965), 291–96, and W. Seston, "Note sur les origines religieuses des paroisses rurales," *RHPR* 15 (1935), 243–54.

[60] *CTh* 16.6.2.1.

[61] *CTh* 16.5.8, cf. 16.5.12 (383), 16.2.33 (398).

[62] *CTh* 16.5.4 (378).

[63] *CTh* 16.5.14, trans. Clyde Pharr, *The Theodosian Code* (Princeton, 1952), p. 453.

[64] Theodoret, *Historia ecclesiastica* 5.24, ed. L. Parmentier (Leipzig, 1911; rev. ed. Berlin, 1954).

intended boost to the development of sectarian private churches in the countryside.

Of course the mere fact that a private individual, orthodox or heterodox, founded a church did not mean that the building, once erected, would remain in the full proprietorship of the founder and his family. The extent of the rights that a founder exercised in his or her church seems to have been a matter of personal discretion. Since these foundations were not yet regulated either by civil or canon law, and the technical considerations of ownership and responsibility for their supervision did not interest our literary sources, proprietary rights must be inferred from the study of individual foundations over the course of several generations.

The case of a church of St. Theodore in Constantinople is instructive.[65] Apparently there already was a tiny church dedicated to this saint located next to a great palace owned by the patrician Sporacius (consul in 452) when the latter structure was spared the ravages of a devastating fire that swept the capital. Sporacius attributed the preservation of his palace to the agency of St. Theodore, and proceeded to build a grand new church in his honor on the site of the first church. The *Anthologia Palatina* preserves Sporacius' dedicatory inscription for this church. Another inscription in the same collection shows that his nephew Antolius, whom Sporacius had brought up as if he were his own son, buried him in St. Theodore's. Later, the honor of burial within a church became an exceptional privilege, usually reserved for the institution's founders and chief benefactors.[66]

Despite its private origin, this church of St. Theodore eventually came to be asssociated closely with the cathedral church of Hagia Sophia, with which it shared a common clergy along with two other dependent churches by the year 535. As this was one of the churches destroyed in the Nika revolt of 532 and subsequently rebuilt, it is possible that the change in its status from a private to a public institution occurred at that time. Yet the fact that Emperor Anastasius (491–518) ordered the Theopaschite addition to the hymn of the Trisagion chanted in St. Theodore's in 512 suggests that this church had become a public charge well before its destruction in the Nika revolt. Perhaps this was occasioned by the demise of Sporacius' family line sometime before the early sixth century.

[65] Janin, *Géographie*, Vol. 3, pp. 152–53; Chrysippus, *Laudatio S. Theodori*, *AASS* November, Vol. 4, pp. 70–71; *Anthologia Palatina* 1.6–7, ed. Hugo Stadtmüller (Leipzig, 1894); *NJ* 3.1 (535), esp. lines 33–38; *Chronicon paschale*, ed. L. Dindorf, *CSHB* (Bonn, 1832), Vol. 1, p. 623; Theophanes, *Chronographia* a.m. 6005, ed. Karl De Boor (Leipzig, 1883–85), p. 159; *Patria Konstantinoupoleos* 3.30 (pp. 225–26).

[66] The *ktetorikon dikaion ensoriasthesomenon*, for which see Zhishman, *Stifterrecht*, 63.

In any case, Emperor Maurice (582–602) restored it at the end of the century when it was damaged again, this time by fire.

The church of the Theotokos ton Chalkoprateion, one of those that shared a common clergy with St. Theodore's and Hagia Sophia, had always been an imperial foundation at the disposal of the diocesan authorities.[67] It was one of the four important foundations initiated by Empress Pulcheria. Apparently she left it uncompleted at her death in 453, and it was left to Empress Verina, wife of Leo I (457–471), to bring the work on it to a conclusion. Significantly, title did not pass to Pulcheria's relatives, the surviving members of the Theodosian house. Instead, this church remained an imperial rather than a private responsibility. Leveled twice by earthquakes, it was rebuilt by Justin II (565–578) and by Basil I (867–886).

The praetorian prefect Rufinus (392–395), the powerful minister of Arcadius (395–408), erected an important group of ecclesiastical buildings on his estate in the suburbs of Chalcedon.[68] These included a great church dedicated to Sts. Peter and Paul (for which Rufinus brought relics from Rome) and a substantial monastery with its own oratory. A magnificent palace adjoined the ecclesiastical buildings. Rufinus' contemporary Claudian, the pagan poet, severely censured him for arrogance in erecting this grandiose monument to his own fame. Yet Rufinus' ambitious undertaking foreshadowed the preferences of subsequent generations of benefactors. Only an occasional Byzantine dared to criticize such ostentatious displays of philanthropy.[69]

Rufinus' sudden disgrace and death in 395 cut short the completion of his plans. It is uncertain whether he was even buried in the church as he had intended. The Egyptian monks he had settled in the monastery departed for home, and the whole estate lay vacant for some time. Rufinus'

---

[67] Janin, *Géographie*, Vol. 3, p. 237; *NJ* 3.1 (535), lines 19–33; Theodore Lector, *Ecclesiastica historia* 1.5, ed. G. C. Hansen (Berlin, 1971); Nikephoros Kallistos, *Ecclesiastica historia* 14.2, 15.14 (*PG* 146, col. 1061A, *PG* 147, 41D); *Patria Konstantinoupoleos* 3.32 (pp. 226–27); Theophanes Continuatus, *Chronographia*, ed. I. Bekker, *CSHB* (Bonn, 1838), p. 339.

[68] For Rufinus, see *PLRE*, Vol. 1, pp. 778–81; Jules Pargoire, "Rufinianes," *BZ* 8 (1899), 429–77; Janin, *Géographie*, Vol. 2: *Les églises et les monastères des grands centres byzantins* (Paris, 1975), 36–40; Claudian, *In Rufinum* 2.447–49, ed. Maurice Platnauer (London, 1922); Callinicus, *Vita S. Hypatii* 8.4–7, 12.5, 12.13, 34.2, ed. G. Bartelink (Paris, 1971); Zosimus, *Historia nova* 5.8, ed. L. Mendelssohn (Leipzig, 1887); *CTh* 9.40.17 (399); Sozomen, *Historia ecclesiastica* 8.17; *Vita S. Auxentii* (*PG* 114, col. 1408); *C. Const.* (536), *Acta*, ed. ACO 3, p. 48; Procopius, *Bellum Persicum* 1.25.21, 30, ed. J. Haury (Leipzig, 1905–13; rev. 1962), *Bellum Vandalicum* 2.9.13, ed. J. Haury (Leipzig, 1905; rev. 1962).

[69] Among the few, Jerome, *Epistola* 130, ed. I. Hilberg, *CSEL* 56 (Vienna, 1918), p. 183; also, John Chrysostom, *In Matthaeum homilium L* (*PG* 58, col. 509), cf. *In acta apostolorum homilium XXIX* (*PG* 60, col. 217).

wife and daughter had sought ecclesiastical sanctuary. When assured by
Rufinus' rival Eutropius that no harm was intended them, they departed
for Jerusalem as exiles. They certainly did not inherit Rufinus' property,
most of which reportedly went to Eutropius, his successor as Arcadius'
chief minister.

When Eutropius in turn suffered disgrace and exile, an extant law of
Arcadius (399) ordered that all of his property was to be confiscated by
the treasury. That the religious foundations, located in the heart of Rufinus' former domains, shared the vicissitudes of the bulk of his property
seems to offer the best explanation for their subsequent history. Empress
Eudoxia placed the great church at the disposal of Archbishop Theophilus of Alexandria for the famous Synod of the Oak in 403, at which John
Chrysostom was deposed and sent into exile. Meanwhile, St. Hypatius
and an intrepid band of companions had settled in the ruins of the monastery and undertook some repairs.

Earlier attempts to revive monastic life in the monastery abandoned
by Rufinus' Egyptians had been unsuccessful. The treasury must have
been willing to tolerate the existence of Hypatius' community. The Hy-
patians rehabilitated the memory of Rufinus as the creator of the original
foundation (Hypatius' biographer, Callinicus, calls him *makarios*, "the
blessed one"), showing the deference toward the founder that would become a notable Byzantine tradition. In 431 Hypatius made bold to erase
the name of Patriarch Nestorius (428–431) from the diptychs in the basilica in defiance of the bishop of Chalcedon, his ecclesiastical superior.
Urbicius, *cubicularius* of Theodosius II, made an offer in 434 to undertake the renovation of the monastery. Hypatius accepted gratefully, but
he himself remained the director of the institution. By the end of his life
in 446 Hypatius must have appeared to be well on his way to establishing
the independent status of his monastery as a private foundation. He received legacies and pondered the legal rights of the monastery to inherit
the property of a rich man who had died in its care.

The subsequent history of the monastery is obscure, but it was visited
by St. Auxentius in 451 and by St. Sabas in 513. Its *hegoumenos* (spiritual director) was among the signatories of a synod at Constantinople in
536. Rufinus' estate next emerges in the full light of history as the hereditary possession of Justinian's famous general Belisarius. Here the general's wife, Antonina, succeeded in disgracing her enemy, the praetorian
prefect John of Cappadocia. The prefect took refuge in a church on the
estate in 541, quite possibly the basilica of Sts. Peter and Paul erected by
Rufinus. It would appear, then, that Hypatius' efforts to establish an independent monastery came to naught, and that the treasury firmly rees-
tablished imperial authority over the whole estate. Justinian may have
given the property to Belisarius as a reward for his loyal services, perhaps

in 535 when he pensioned his Vandal opponent Gelimer with an estate in Galatia. The monastery appears once again in Byzantine history under Patriarch Theophylact (933–956), who found it necessary to rebuild it from ruins.

The career of Juliana Anicia, one of the last descendants of the Theodosian house, deserves special mention for her work in the erection of several important churches in Constantinople and its suburbs.[70] She was the daughter of Anicius Olybrius (d. 472), one of the last, ephemeral rulers of the Western Roman Empire, and Placidia, daughter of Valentinian III (425–455). Since she was born after the Theodosian dynasty had ceased to rule in either half of the empire, her benefactions are all the more remarkable as expenditures from her evidently considerable private resources.

Juliana's grandmother Licinia Eudoxia, daughter of Theodosius II and spouse of Valentinian III, had begun the construction of the church of St. Euphemia in Constantinople in 462. Licinia died before anything but the foundations could be completed. Her daughter Placidia and son-in-law Olybrius completed the construction and provided properties for its support. Juliana herself took an interest in furnishing and beautifying this family church which was located near the palatial residence of her father. Several dedicatory inscriptions preserved in the *Anthologia Palatina* commemorate her labors, acclaiming the church as the work of three generations. The most detailed of these reads as follows: "I am the House of the Trinity, and three generations built me. First Eudoxia, daughter of Theodosius, having escaped from war and the barbarians, erected and dedicated me to God in acknowledgement of her rescue from distress. Next her daughter Placidia with her most blessed husband adorned me. Thirdly, if perchance my beauty was at all deficient in splendor, munificent Juliana invested me with it in memory of her parents, and bestowed the height of glory on her mother and father and her mother's illustrious mother by augmenting my former adornment. Thus was I made."[71] These inscriptions, then, provide a unique documentation for this period of a long-standing family association with a religious foundation.

Juliana was also responsible for the construction of a church of St. Stephen in Constantinople, probably during the reign of Anastasius (491–518). Here she placed the relics of St. Stephen that her great-

---

[70] For Juliana Anicia, see *PLRE*, Vol. 2, pp. 635–36; Frank Clover, "The Family and Early Career of Anicius Olybrius," *Historia* 27 (1978), 169–96; Janin, *Géographie*, Vol. 2, p. 21; Vol. 3, pp. 124–26, 274–76 405–6; *Patria Konstantinoupoleos* 3.60 (p. 238); *Anthologia Palatina* 1.10,12–17, esp. 12; Marcellinus, *Chronicon* A.D. 439, ed. Th. Mommsen, *MGH, AA* 11, p. 80; Jules Pargoire, "A propos de Boradion," *BZ* 12 (1903), 449–93, esp. 489.

[71] *Anthologia Palatina* 1.12, trans. W. R. Paton, *The Greek Anthology*, Vol. 1 (London, 1916), 13.

grandmother Aelia Eudocia, spouse of Theodosius II, had brought back with her from Jerusalem in 439.[72] These relics had reposed temporarily in the church of St. Lawrence founded by Pulcheria, Eudocia's sister-in-law. It is possible, as has been suggested, that Juliana exercised a sort of right of "pious spoliation" by translating these relics discovered by her great-grandmother some sixty years earlier.

Juliana Anicia also founded a church of St. Polyeuktos as well as numerous other churches not identified specifically by the sources. A remarkable dedicatory illustration to a manuscript of Dioscorides in Vienna (see Frontispiece) salutes her as the founder of a church of the Theotokos in Honoratae, a suburb of the capital.[73] The manuscript illumination portrays a seated Juliana, flanked on either side by personifications, on the right by Phronesis (Prudence) and on the left by Megalopsychia (Magnanimity). On the lower left are two smaller personifications, Eucharistia Technon (Gratitude of the Arts), who kisses the right foot of the patroness, and Pothos tes Philoktistou (Desire for Devotion to Building) who holds an open book, upon which Juliana drops some coins. Juliana herself holds a book or diptych. All these figures are within an octagon, itself framed by an eight-pointed star. In the points of the star are found the letters of the patroness' name. The star is found within a circle, with the interstices filled with scenes of putti engaged in building construction activities. A reference in the *Chronographia* of Theophanes to this church dates its foundation to 512.

Juliana died in 527, leaving behind two sons and several granddaughters. An interesting postscript to her career is the fact that the *curopalates* Peter, brother of Emperor Maurice (582- 602), transformed the old residence of Areobindus and Juliana into a church of her beloved Theotokos. By then it appears that the remarkable family of Theodosius had finally died out, some nine generations and well over two hundred years after it had become prominent in the political life of the later Roman Empire.

Juliana's foundations serve to illustrate the transmission of ecclesiastical institutions and the changes in administration and ownership that might occur during their extremely long existences. Some churches in Constantinople had institutional lives of over a thousand years.[74] Since no patron's family would ever span more than a fraction of this time no

---

[72] *Patria Konstantinoupoleos* 3.59 (p. 237); Janin, *Géographie*, Vol. 3, p. 275; K. Holum and G. Vikan, "The Trier Ivory, Adventus Ceremonial, and the Relics of St. Stephen," *DOP* 33 (1979), 113–33.

[73] Theophanes, *Chronographia* a.m. 6005, ed. De Boor, pp. 157–58; O. M. Dalton, *Byzantine Art and Archaeology* (Oxford, 1911), 460; Ioannis Spatharakis, *Corpus of Dated Illuminated Greek Manuscripts to the Year 1453* (Leiden, 1981), Vol. 1, pp. 5–6.

[74] Obviously including Hagia Sophia, Hagia Irene, and Holy Apostles, but also St. Menas (Janin, *Géographie*, Vol. 3, p. 333), and Theotokos of Blachernai (Janin, *Géographie*, Vol. 3, p. 161).

matter how prolific its progeny and how tenaciously it held on to its property rights, it is not surprising to see many changes in the administration of particular churches over the centuries. The offices of the emperor, the patriarch, and the local metropolitan or bishop did not depend on a particular family or dynasty for survival, so the incumbents of these positions often were the beneficiaries when the founder's line ceased. Moreover, when disaster (whether man-made or natural) struck, the emperor was often the only one with the resources to attempt the work of reconstruction, as Justinian did after the Nika revolt in 532 and Basil I was to do after a severe earthquake in 870.

IMPERIAL TAX POLICY AND ITS RELATIONSHIP TO CLERGY ON PRIVATE ESTATES

Initially the emperors had played an active role in sponsoring the erection of new churches as well as in rebuilding existing structures. Yet these were not the only ways that the emperors chose to promote the development of the institutional infrastructure of Christianity. Constantine and his successors granted many privileges to the church and its ministers, foremost among them being some important tax exemptions.[75] Constantine relieved the urban clergy of the obligation to pay the *collatio lustralis*, a particularly vexing tax that fell on urban craftsmen of all sorts. His exemption of the rural clergy from *capitatio*, the head tax, was probably even more significant in terms of the number of clergy affected. Constantine also established the principle that clergy should always be exempt from compulsory labor services known as *munera sordida*. Since the vast majority of clergy throughout late Roman and Byzantine times seem to have supported themselves at least in part by agriculture and crafts, a partial or total tax exemption could make the difference between a difficult and a comfortable existence for these individuals.[76]

The existence of tax exemptions practically insured a significant increase in the numbers of aspiring clergy, a fact of which Constantine himself was aware.[77] His son Constantius II (337–361) confirmed the

---

[75] *Leges saeculares* 117, ed. S. Riccobono, FIRA 2, p. 794; CTh 16.2.2 (319); and A. H. M. Jones, *The Later Roman Empire 284- 602*, American edition, 2 vols. (Norman, Oklahoma, 1964), 65, 431, 912, 1178, n. 52, and 1382, n. 101; for discussions of clerical immunities, see Clémence Dupont, "Les privilèges des clercs sous Constantin," *RHE* 62 (1967), 729–52, Otto Grashof, "Die Gesetzegebung der römischen Kaiser über die Güter und Immunitäten der Kirche und des Klerus nebst deren Motiven und Principien," *AKK* 36 (1876), 3–51, and Barnes, *Constantine*, 50.

[76] For the agricultural and commercial activities of the clergy, see Herman, "Professioni vietate," 23–44, and Ewa Wipszycka, *Les ressources et les activités économiques des églises en Egypte du IVe au VIIIe siècle* (Brussels, 1972), 154–73.

[77] CTh 16.2.6 (326).

clergy's immunity from *collatio lustralis* and *munera* while also extending exemption from *capitatio* and *munera* to their wives, children, and servants.[78] Emboldened perhaps by these concessions, the fathers of the Council of Ariminium (359) petitioned the emperor for the elimination of *munera* attached to church lands liable to the *iuga*, the land tax.[79] The emperor granted this request as well, but he ruled that individual landowning clerics had to pay the *iuga* on their own property and sustain the *munera* attached thereto. This petition makes clear that the church did not enjoy automatic exemption from property taxes on the lands it owned.[80] Moreover, clerics who were fortunate to own land of their own had to pay the *iuga* also, even if as individuals they were exempt from *capitatio*.

Although the pagan Emperor Julian (361–363) canceled these tax exemptions for the duration of his short reign, it appears that his Christian successors restored them promptly after his death.[81] Theodosius I affirmed clerical exemption from the *capitatio* in a law of 381.[82] Yet by 398 it appears that the imperial government had begun to reconsider what must have been a very costly policy of tax immunities for clerics of all sorts as well as their families and dependents. A law of Arcadius from that year orders internal recruitment for ordination to the clergy for churches in villages or on private estates so that these clerics would continue to meet the obligation of their *capitatio*.[83] The law leaves to the discretion of the local bishop the number of clergy who ought to be ordained to serve the needs of each locality, and clearly indicates that universal clerical exemption from *capitatio* was no longer being extended.

It is remarkable that such an abrupt change of policy would have occurred without comment by one of the many interested contemporary observers of ecclesiastical affairs. Perhaps certain categories of clergy, such as those who staffed the churches on private estates, had never enjoyed the tax immunities of their fellow urban clergymen, despite the picture of universal exemption given by earlier laws. Alternatively, the rural clergy simply may not have been very numerous until the proliferation of churches on private estates, which was occurring at the very time this law was issued.

The fiscal interests of the state probably prompted this reversal of policy—if such it was—concerning the payment of *capitatio* and the insistence on local recruitment. These were complementary provisions, for

[78] *CTh* 16.2.8 (343), 16.2.10 (346), 16.2.14 (356), 16.2.15.1 (360).
[79] *CTh* 16.2.15 (360); but cf. *CTh* 11.1.1 with Jones, *LRE*, 1373, n. 65.
[80] *CTh* 16.2.40 (412), 11.1.33 (423); Theodoret, *Historia ecclesiastica* 4.7; Jones, *LRE*, 361.
[81] Sozomen, *Historia ecclesiastica* 5.5.
[82] *CTh* 16.2.26 (381).
[83] *CTh* 16.2.33 (398).

surely a clergy recruited locally from the peasantry would have posed the fewest problems in administering the collection of the *capitatio*.[84] As a result, the local bishop's choices for clerical appointments to many of the churches within his spirtual jurisdiction narrowed considerably.

A law of Theodosius II (409) refines the government's policy, forbidding an individual enrolled on the tax lists for *capitatio* to become a cleric without the express permission of his *dominus* (landlord).[85] The tenor of this law is in accord with the socially conservative views of contemporary church authorities, but it meant a further abridgment of the local bishop's choices for appointments since it foreclosed the possibility that he could choose a candidate (even locally) without securing the prior approval of the owner of the estate. It surely was a short step from these laws to the right of the landlord to nominate the clergy for ordination to churches on his estate—a right that received legal recognition by the mid- sixth century.[86] John Chrysostom, for one, thought it a fair bargain that the landlord should employ a cleric of his own choosing in exchange for the construction of a new church.[87] Evidently others agreed with him, for there is no record of protests from the ecclesiastical authorities in the East as the choice of clergy for these churches slipped out of their control.[88]

A certain number of clerics continued to enjoy exemption from the *capitatio* even in the fifth century.[89] Those ordained in excess of this number had to pay the tax and also perform the *ruralia obsequia*, a form of *munera*, although they were allowed to offer substitutes to discharge the latter responsibility. The idea of restricting the number of clergy in any given locality was not a new one. Constantine himself feared an unregulated increase and directed that replacements should occur on a one-to-one basis as older clerics died.[90] Arcadius' law of 398 left the decision to the local bishop. It would have been difficult to lay down a universal formula by legislative fiat, since local needs must have varied greatly in accordance with population and the number of existing facilities. Constantine's inflexible formula quickly became impractical as the number

---

[84] Perhaps by the intermediary of a landlord having the right of self-taxation, or *autoprageia*, for which see Jones, *LRE*, 358, 407, 780.

[85] *CJ* 1.3.16 (409); A. H. M. Jones, "The Roman Colonate," *Past and Present* 13 (1958), 1–13, esp. 6.

[86] Officially recognized by Justinian in *NJ* 57.2 (537) and 123.18 (546).

[87] John Chrysostom, *Homilium XVIII* (*PG* 60, col. 148).

[88] Cf. the strict limitations imposed on founders' rights in Ostrogothic Italy by Pope Gelasius, *Epistolae* Nos. 14.4, 25, 34, 35, ed. Andreas Thiel, *Epistolae romanorum pontificum genuinae* (Braunsberg, 1868); for Gelasius' attitudes on the appointment of clerics to private estate churches, see *Epistolae* Nos. 14.4, 20–22, 41 (ed. Thiel), and *Epistola* No. 10, ed. S. Loewenfeld, *Epistolae pontificum romanorum ineditae* (Leipzig, 1885).

[89] *CJ* 1.3.16 (409).

[90] *CTh* 16.2.6 (326).

of Christians expanded, and the perceived need for clerical manpower continued to increase down to Justinian's time and even beyond.

The emperors of the late fourth century also took stock of the value of other revenues lost as a result of generous tax exemptions accorded to the clergy by their predecessors. A law of Gratian dated to 379 limits the amount of tax-free income that clerics could earn before they became subject, like lay craftsmen, to the *collatio lustralis*.[91] The authorities were certainly not eager to see slaves and *coloni* (peasants attached to the land they worked) elevated to the priesthood in order to escape the tax rolls by reason of clerical exemption. Two laws of Valentinian III forbade acquisition of exemption in that way.[92] Far from defending the rights of slaves and *coloni* to aspire to clerical status, the church authorities were already on record in favor of a policy of friendship and cooperation with the landlords. They fully supported rights of ownership or patronage over slaves, *coloni*, and others of "ignoble birth," in part because the church feared the double claim on the loyalty of clerics bound both to its service and that of their masters.[93]

This understanding helps account for such legislation as a law of Theodosius II dated to 434. This law upholds the right of the church to inherit the property of clerics and monks who die intestate without surviving relatives, but excepts those who had been liable to the tax-rolls, subject to *ius patronatus* (patron's right), or of curial (civic councillor) status.[94] The self-asserted logic of this distinction is that in the latter cases the property of the deceased belonged to his patron, the *dominus* of the *possessio* (or the *curia* in the case of decurions), and so was not transferable on the death of the incumbent to his church. This law then serves as an indication that many clergy serving in rural private churches were simply *coloni* who had to work land rented to them by their landlords in order to earn a living.

The laws of Arcadius and Theodosius II remained definitive on the status of the clergy until Justinian took up the problem again over a century later in 546. An earlier law in which he permitted even runaway slaves to become monks under certain conditions demonstrates that this emperor was determined to favor the interests of religion over the property rights of the landlords.[95] The law of 546 is very much in the same spirit.[96] It orders that slaves who became priests "with the knowledge of their lord and the absence of his opposition" also became free men by

[91] *CTh* 13.1.11 (379); this law applied only to clerics in Gaul, Italy, and Illyricum.
[92] *N Val* 13.8 (445), 35.3 (452).
[93] See Leo the Great, *Epistola* 4 (*PL* 54, col. 611).
[94] *CTh* 5.3.1 (434) = *CJ* 1.3.20.
[95] *NJ* 5.2.1 (535); contrast to Zeno's *CJ* 1.3.36 (484).
[96] *NJ* 123.17 (546).

virtue of their ordinations. Slaves could even become priests and free men without the knowledge of their masters, but in that case there was to be a probationary period of a year during which their masters could claim them and return them to their servile status. Similarly, *enapographoi* (peasants bound to the soil) had the right to become clerics, even contrary to the will of their masters, provided that they continued to fulfill their agricultural obligations. Here Justinian was reversing Theodosius II's requirement that the lord of the estate should approve all promotions of his dependents to the clerical state. Justinian left Arcadius' law intact, however, since the *enapographos*, given his contractual obligations, could only serve as a cleric close to his own landholding.

Evidently Justinian was attempting to break the stranglehold on clerical appointments that lay landlords exercised in his day, while previous emperors had aided and abetted its creation in the fiscal interests of the treasury. The new legislation gave local bishops more latitude to make their own appointments, and is consistent with the rest of Justinian's ecclesiastical legislation which sought to strengthen the rights of the episcopacy over private benefactors and their foundations in the dioceses.[97] The practical effect, however, is open to question, since it would have taken a determined bishop to provide the moral support necessary to maintain a priest in his tenure of a private church against the will of the owner of the estate.[98]

IDEALIZED PORTRAIT OF AN ESTATE CHURCH

Although the actual balance of authority between the local bishop and the landlord church owner in the countryside may be a matter for conjecture, one of the homilies of John Chrysostom presents a valuable, if extremely idealized, image of a rural private church ca. A.D. 400.[99] In the homily Chrysostom reproved his audience of landowners for providing such amenities as markets, baths, and taverns for peasants while omitting to erect churches for them, implying thereby that estate churches were not yet an ordinary fixture of rural settlements. If we are to believe Chrysostom, the church nearest to some estates might be quite far away, though surely not the thousands of *stadia* (or multiples of 125 miles) that he claimed in the homily. His homily sets as an explicit goal that no estate would henceforth be without a church of its own in order to promote

[97] See B. Granić, "Die rechtliche Stellung und Organisation der griechischen Klöster nach dem justinianischen Recht," *BZ* 29 (1929), 6–34.

[98] This was true especially since Justinian recognized the right of patrons to present candidates for ordination by the local bishops in *NJ* 57.2 (537). For conditions attached to this right, see the discussion below in Chapter 2.

[99] John Chrysostom, *Homilium XVIII* (PG 60, cols. 147–50).

Christianization of the countryside and to serve as a safeguard against heresy.

The apparent reluctance of property owners to undertake the construction of these churches is noteworthy. Justinian's legislation on the subject in the sixth century indicates that this reluctance would persist for some time to come.[100] Chrysostom himself openly admitted that the costs would probably exceed any profits, at least in material terms, but he suggested that the non-material rewards would be quite substantial and worthwhile. Foremost among these would be an increased respect for law and order among the landlord's peasants. The church itself would serve as an everlasting memorial of the benefactor, who would enjoy the honor of recognition as its founder. A considerable prestige would attach to the estate which had the only church in the area. Peasants from neighboring estates would travel some distance to attend services there. The property owner would find the church conveniently located for his own use at morning and evening services. The peasants could attend each morning before commencing their work in the fields. The priest himself would provide an example of piety to all by working with his own hands in the fields. He would be a dinner companion and spiritual director to the landowner as well as a molder of peasant behavior and a guard of the estate. In Chrysostom's vision, "The farm having a church is like God's paradise: there is no shouting there, no tumult, no enemies at variance, no heresies; you can see that all are friends holding the same beliefs in common!"[101] Even the ordinarily unruly peasant assemblies and the foremen would be respectful out of deference to the priest.

Chrysostom's homily urges all men of good will to the task, not only the great proprietors of his audience but the smaller ones too. They should recruit a priest, a deacon, and a sacerdotal college, then provide *apomoirai* (portions) and *aparchai* (first fruits) as a sort of "dowry" for the church. If the owner could not meet all the costs of construction, he should at least make a beginning by laying the foundations or making a small house in the form of a church, that is, a *domus ecclesiae*. Subsequent owners of the estate would then embellish this foundation, reserving the founder's glory for the original benefactor. An individual who could not undertake construction all by himself was urged to persuade his neighbors to help in a joint project. Thus all men of means had a role to play.

THE PROBLEM OF SECTARIAN CHURCHES ON PRIVATE ESTATES

Chrysostom's homily shows an acute awareness of competition between official orthodoxy and proscribed religious sectaries for the hearts and

---

[100] *CJ* 1.3.45 (530); *NJ* 131.7, 10 (545); cf. Zeno's law, *CJ* 1.2.15 (474–491).
[101] John Chrysostom, *Homilium XVIII* (PG 60, col. 148, lines 6–9).

minds of the rural population of the empire.[102] In part this competition resulted from the way in which the imperial government attempted to enforce its religious policies. Except where an entire province stood in opposition to these policies (as Monophysite Egypt did in the fifth and sixth centuries), it was a simple enough matter for the state to lend its support to the "orthodox" faction of the clergy and expel the previous, now discredited, incumbents from the easily accessible public churches of the empire.[103] It was a much more difficult matter to root out the "heretical" clergy stationed in private churches on estates. There the arm of the law was weak. As a matter of fact, the imperial government ordinarily depended upon powerful private property owners to perform some governmental functions such as conscription for the army and tax collection.[104] This essential weakness of the government led to the issuance of a major part of the ecclesiastical legislation of the Theodosian Code which is dedicated to laws against various Christian sectaries.[105]

Generally speaking, this legislation assumes that the landowner was ignorant of the fact that there was a heretical *conventiculum* (meeting place) on his estate. In the eyes of the law, the property owner enjoyed the benefit of the doubt.[106] The heretical church, having been denied legal existence, could be viewed only as a completely secular structure employed for illegal purposes.[107] Although the religious sectaries themselves may have considered that they held their churches corporatively, the imperial legislators were incapable of recognizing this for ideological reasons.[108]

This outlook makes the legal sources difficult to use as a tool for determining the ownership of the religious edifices mentioned in them. It is, for example, problematic whether a *conventiculum* (that is, *ecclesia*) was privately owned by a landlord who sponsored its *conventus* (assembly), whether the sectarian community itself owned the building, or whether the place of worship was subordinated in conventional pattern

---

[102] For background, see W. H. C. Frend, "Town and Countryside in Early Christianity," *SCH* 16 (1979), 25–42.

[103] Athanasius, *Historia Arianorum* 54, ed. H. G. Opitz, Vol. 2, Pt. 1, pp. 183–230, Sozomen, *Historia ecclesiastica* 4.20, 7.5, 8.1, and Socrates, *Historia ecclesiastica* 2.38, 3.11, provide examples of such displacements.

[104] Jones, *LRE*, 362, 615, 805.

[105] *CTh* 16.5: *De haereticis*, discussed by Lucio de Giovanni, *Chiesa e Stato nel Codice Teodosiano: Saggio sul libro XVI* (Naples, 1980), 81–106.

[106] Note, for example, *CTh* 16.5.21 (392), 16.5.34 (398), 16.5.57 (415).

[107] Synesius, *Epistola* No. 67, ed. A. Garzya (Rome, 1979), echoes this attitude of the law, dismissing the Arian churches as nothing more than private dwellings; so also Augustine, *Enarrationes in Psalmos XXI*, 2.31, ed. D. E. Dekkers and I. Fraipont (Turnhout, 1956), p. 133, in condemning Donatists for usurping *tituli Christi* for the protection of private residences.

[108] *CTh* 16.5.57.2 (415); also Justinian's emendation of the word *ecclesiae* in *CTh* 16.5.65.3 (428) to *conventicula, quae ipsi audacter ecclesias nuncupare conantur* in *CJ* 1.5.5.

to a local (in this case "heretical") bishop. As it is, the legislation chooses to portray large estates worked by *conductores* (short-term leaseholders) and administered by *procuratores* (the owner's property managers) and other domain officials, often in opposition to the expressed wishes of the *possessores*.[109] This may have been true in some cases, but the picture is at variance with John Chrysostom's contemporary testimony to the estate owner's interest in the close surveillance of his property.

In more candid moments, the imperial legislation reports property owners who offered preexisting private churches to persecuted dissidents; others simply refused to expel clerics and communities of cobelievers already living on their properties.[110] Yet the law's emphasis on the makeshift, secret, and irregular character of their meetings is surely misleading. The sectarian communities employed all of the ordinary *copiae*, *potestates*, and *facultates* of orthodox communities, as is clear from the explicit prohibition of their exercise.[111] These churches had developed hierarchies, including lectors, deacons, priests, and even bishops in some cases, as well as established sources of income.[112] In short, everything suggests that the churches of the sectaries were modeled on those of the orthodox. In some cases, as with the Arians, Nestorians, and Monophysites, they had once been the "orthodox" churches, and in the minds of their local adherents they continued to be so regarded in defiance of whatever credal variant the imperial authorities happened to be supporting at the time.[113]

Since the commencement of official disfavor did not cause the sectaries to adopt a radically different form of organization, there would appear to be much to learn from an examination of these "heretical" churches in the way of clues to the organization of analogous "orthodox" churches. Indeed, the legal sources confirm John Chrysostom's testimony that similar orthodox churches existed on private landholdings.[114] One need not take seriously the assertion of a law of Leo I that churches on

[109] *CTh* 16.5.21 (392), 16.5.34 (398), 16.5.36 (399), 16.6.4.1 (405), 16.5.40.7 (407), 16.5.54.5–6 (414), and 16.5.57 (415).

[110] For heretical assemblies in private churches, see *CTh* 16.5.14 (388) and 16.5.30 (402).

[111] *Facultas obtinendarum ecclesiarum*: *CTh* 16.1.3 (381); *copia fabricandarum ecclesiarum*: *CTh* 16.5.8 (381), cf. 16.5.12 (383) and 16.5.65 (428); *potestas instituendorum clericorum*: *CTh* 16.5.14 (388), cf. 16.5.12 (383); *copia colligendarum congregationum*: *CTh* 16.5.12 (383), cf. 16.5.14 (388) and 16.5.65 (428); *licentia celebrandi conventus*: *CTh* 16.5.66.2 (435), cf. 16.5.12 (383) and 16.5.30 (402); *donatio in ecclesiae*: *CTh* 16.5.65.3 (428).

[112] *CTh* 16.5.19 (389), 16.5.65 (428), cf. 16.5.52.5 (412), 16.5.57.2 (415), and *NJ* 42.3.2 (536).

[113] See *The Sixth Book of the Select Letters of Severus of Antioch*, ed. E. W. Brooks, Vol. 2 (London, 1903–4), passim, e.g., pp. 24, 45, in which the Monophysite patriarch of Antioch habitually refers to his party as the "orthodox" while castigating the official (Chalcedonian) party as the "heretics."

[114] *CTh* 16.2.33 (398), 16.5.14 (388); cf. *CJ* 1.5.10 (466–472?).

properties transferred from orthodox persons to sectaries would simply collapse and fall into ruins from disuse.[115] That there was little or no structural incompatibility is apparent from the fact that imperial legislation usually awards a sectarian *aedificium* (building) to the local catholic church.[116]

The geographical scope of the anti-heretical legislation is noteworthy. Violations of imperial ordinances are foreseen in the following localities: the *urbs* (city), *oppidum* (town), *vicus* (village), *civitas* (city), private *domus* (house), *fundus* (large family estate), *privata possessio*, *villa*, *suburbanum* (all suburban estates), *praedium* (a private estate), or *ager* (farm).[117] As might be expected, rural hiding places dominate the list. Theodosius I tried to set up a network of *inquisitores* (investigators) in a law of 382 in order to enforce the ban on these illegal assemblies.[118] He encouraged informers to come forward without fear of the usual odium being attached to them on account of their accusations. This apparently was an ineffective measure, for a year later this emperor turned again to property owners "who esteem the cult of true observance" to expel those holding illegal services behind the walls of private dwellings.[119]

Theodosius' sons decided to rely upon local officials for enforcement of the laws. Arcadius enlisted the services of the *rectores provinciarum* (provincial governors) in a law of 404, while Honorius depended upon the *defensores curialium* (municipal advocates) in his law of 408.[120] A later law of Honorius (414) supposes that the indignant *dominus* of an estate, informed of what was going on behind his back through the accusation of the *iudices* (provincial governors), would sternly reprove his local subordinates or replace them.[121]

Despite all these enactments, the task of eliminating the institutional infrastructure of dissident religious sects proved no easier than convinc-

---

[115] *CJ* 1.5.10.3 (466–472?).

[116] *CTh* 16.5.57.2 (415), 16.5.65 (428), 16.5.54.5–6 (414).

[117] In order of appearance, *domus*: *CTh* 16.6.2.1 (377), 16.5.8 (381), 16.5.12 (383), 16.5.33 (397), 16.5.34 (398), 16.5.35 (399), 16.5.36 (399), 16.5.30 (402), 16.2.37 (404), 16.6.4.1 (405), 16.6.7 (413), 16.5.54 (414), 16.5.57 (415), 16.5.58 (415); *fundus*: *CTh* 16.6.2.1 (377), 16.5.8 (381), 16.5.21 (392), 16.5.36 (399); *ager*: *CTh* 16.5.4 (378), 16.5.8 (381), 16.5.9.1 (382), 16.5.12 (383), 16.6.7 (413); *oppidum*: *CTh* 16.5.4 (378), 16.5.7 (381); *urbs*: *CTh* 16.5.7 (381), 16.5.14 (388), 16.5.19 (389), 16.5.20 (391), 16.5.34 (398), 16.5.58 (415); *civitas*: *CTh* 16.5.8 (381), 16.5.34 (398), 16.5.45 (408), 16.5.58 (415); *privata possessio*: *CTh* 16.5.8 (381), 16.2.33 (398?); *villa*: *CTh* 16.5.12 (383), 16.5.66.2 (435); *suburbanum*: *CTh* 16.16.5.19 (389), 16.5.66.2 (435); *vicus*: *CTh* 16.2.33 (398); *praedium*: *CTh* 16.6.4.1 (405), 16.5.40.7 (407), 16.5.54.5 (414), 16.5.58.4 (415). This list incidentally provides a chronological documentation of the geographic spread of private churches.

[118] *CTh* 16.5.9.1 (382).

[119] *CTh* 16.5.11 (383).

[120] *CTh* 16.4.6 (404) and 16.5.45 (408).

[121] *CTh* 16.5.54.6 (414).

ing them that their beliefs were erroneous. Meanwhile, the imperial legislation reveals a gradual change of focus from the landlord's agents to the landowner himself as the likely culprit in the transgressions.[122] Accordingly, the imperial legislators modified the particularly savage penalties once imposed upon the *procuratores* and *conductores* as time passed on.[123]

The survival of religious dissidents over the centuries in the bosom of the empire proves that the government's repressive measures were never a complete success, and it is likely that private churches continued to provide havens for these sectaries. The *Historia arcana* of Procopius of Caesarea, for example, testifies not only to the survival but also the astounding prosperity of some Arian communities of the empire in the early sixth century.[124] This was well over a hundred and fifty years after the triumph of the Nicaean creed under Theodosius I. According to Procopius, the Arians preserved some of their churches intact throughout this period as well as their endowments of *oikiai* (houses), *komai* (villages), and *chorai* (estates). Even many orthodox peasants reportedly depended for their livelihoods upon lands owned by these churches. These Arian churches survived unmolested by the emperors before Justinian's time, despite laws forbidding their legal existence and even an explicit bar against an Arian making a will or inheriting property.[125] The Montanists also survived in Phyrgia despite similar repressive legislation.[126]

It was no simple task to uproot entire communities of sectaries in the countryside. The peasants had a strong devotion to their traditional beliefs and were determined to fight, if necessary, to defend them.[127] Constantius II had discovered this earlier when, at the urging of Bishop Macedonius of Constantinople, he sent four detachments of troops to Paphlagonia to aid his efforts to convert a Novatian community at Mantinium. Nearly a half century later, a proud Paphlagonian peasant recalled for the church historian Socrates how the Novatians, armed with improvised weapons and suffering great losses, had destroyed the imperial army almost to a man.

Justinian also encountered armed resistance, although most of the sec-

---

[122] *CTh* 16.5.57.1–2 (415) and 16.5.58 (415) mark this new emphasis on the *dominus* of the *domus* or *possessio*.

[123] Compare *CTh* 16.5.36 (399) and 16.6.4.1 (405) with the more moderate provisions of *CTh* 16.5.57.1–2 (415) and 16.5.54.5–6 (414).

[124] Procopius, *Historia arcana* 11.14–23, ed. Jakob Haury (Leipzig, 1906; rev. 1963).

[125] Earlier repressive legislation against the Arians includes *CTh* 16.5.8 (381), 16.5.11–13 (383–384). *CJ* 1.5.12 (527) and *NJ* 45 (537) are prominent among Justinian's own more general laws against religious sectaries; cf. Procopius, *Historia arcana* 11.15.

[126] Earlier repressive legislation against the Montanists includes *CTh* 16.5.34 (398), 16.5.57 (415), 16.5.65 (428); cf. Procopius, *Historia arcana* 11.23.

[127] Procopius, *Historia arcana* 11.21–22; Socrates, *Historia ecclesiastica* 2.38.

taries simply fled their ancestral lands to find new refuges elsewhere.[128] The Montanists of Phyrgia burned themselves in their churches at the approach of the imperial army. The Arians could be uprooooted only by the confiscation of their church properties and the dispossession of their agricultural dependents on these lands. Despite the difficulties of the undertaking, Justinian must have realized that legal disabilities alone would not suffice to wipe out the Arian and Montanist sectaries. Only a determined attack upon the economic infrastructure of their communities could accomplish the government's goals.

The legal status of these sectarian churches is ambiguous, as it probably was to contemporaries as well. According to a law of Theodosius II dated to 415, the churches of the Montanists existed on private possessions but still had their own *donarii* (votive offerings):[129]

> If, indeed, any person should receive the aforesaid persons [Montanists] for the purpose of holding the forbidden meetings, he shall undoubtedly understand that he will be deprived of the property in which he allowed such meetings to be held and the accursed mysteries to be performed, whether such property was a house or a landholding. . . . Moreover, if any of their buildings should now exist, which ought not to be called churches but funeral grottoes, such property with its votive offerings shall be adjudged to the venerable churches of the orthodox sect. This must be accomplished in such a way that the property of private persons shall not be molested, so that under the pretext of property belonging to the Montanists, despoliation and plunder may not be perpetrated against private persons.

This peculiar situation of a church located on private property but possessing its own *donarii* might well have been the norm for private churches, whether sectarian or orthodox, which were closely associated with great estates.

Unlike the Montanist churches depicted in this law, the Arian churches do not seem, according to Procopius' account, to have been ordinary private institutions. Yet the legal limbo in which these churches existed must have obscured their status. Procopius may not have had a clear idea of their organization and administration or have cared to convey it to his readers if he did. If these churches were independent, they must have become so by being communally owned and managed. At this late date, they certainly could not have remained public churches of the official

---

[128] Procopius, *Historia arcana* 11.20,23; cf. the penalties enjoined against the Montanists in *CTh* 16.5.57.1 (415).

[129] *CTh* 16.5.57 (415), trans. Clyde Pharr, p. 461.

diocesan organization, for it is unlikely that any government, however indulgent or inefficient, would have tolerated continued control of *katholikai ekklesiai* by an illegal sect.

The ambiguous status of these churches helps to explain the difficulty that the imperial legislators faced in determining responsibility for illegal religious assemblies, since the place of *conventus* was both a *domus* (in strict legal title) of the *dominus* of the estate and an *ecclesia* of the sectaries. The usual close association of private churches with the estates of their founders (notable in Chrysostom's homily) and the unwillingness of the legislators to recognize the existence of sectarian churches combined to create this conceptual difficulty. The law of Theodosius II quoted above shows the inevitable results of this self-imposed confusion.

The private nomination of clergy and provision of financial support must have been more conducive to the maintenance of sectarian communities than the episcopal nomination and provisioning that was the rule in the public churches of the empire.[130] The emperors themselves might have unwittingly aided the survival of dissident religious communities by severely limiting the local bishop's choices for clerical ordinations to estate residents approved by the landlord. Presumably the local bishop could always refuse to ordain a heterodox candidate not of his own choosing, but determining orthodoxy may not have been a simple matter. The correspondence of Severus, Monophysite patriarch of Antioch (512–518), illustrates the constant pressures he was under to ordain candidates, even unqualified ones, as favors to powerful laymen.[131] Severus remarked that rebuffed petitioners made themselves enemies to the Monophysite cause. If such a conscientious prelate as Severus found it so difficult to resist these pressures for appointments to a public church, it is easy to imagine the predicament facing rural bishops in the matter of appointments to private estate churches.

---

[130] For the provisioning of the clergy in the cathedral churches of the empire and their dependencies, see Herman, "Secular Church," 121–25, and A. H. M. Jones, "Church Finance in the Fifth and Sixth Centuries," *JTS* n.s. 11 (1960), 84–94.

[131] Severus of Antioch, *Epistolae* 1.8, 17, 33; 7.6, ed. Brooks.

CHAPTER TWO

The Regulation of Private Religious Foundations under Justinian and His Immediate Predecessors

U NTIL the mid-fifth century private benefactors enjoyed nearly complete liberty in the construction, endowment, and management of their foundations. Slowly this began to change, with the Council of Chalcedon (451) marking the beginning of a new era of strict regulation of these increasingly important and numerous institutions.[1] The guiding principles of the council's legislation on this subject were that a founder's grant, once made, was irrevocable and that all religious foundations, including private ones, must be subordinated to the authority of the local bishop.[2] Hereafter no one was to found a monastery or an oratory without the prior approval of the local bishop. Estate and other rural churches were to be subject to the oversight of the local bishop too. Monks likewise were to submit to the spiritual authority of their local bishop, and their monastery, once consecrated by him, could not be converted to any secular purpose.

Despite this legislation, conversions of monasteries and philanthropic institutions into secular dwellings continued to plague the ecclesiastical authorities down through the centuries.[3] Unscrupulous laymen converted religious foundations into hostels, taverns, and factories, as well as private residences. Yet for structural reasons churches were less attractive prospects for conversion projects, and so secularization of these institutions does not seem to have occurred to any significant extent. The persistence of the secularizations of the other facilities indicates that prop-

[1] See Leo Ueding, "Die Kanones von Chalkedon in ihrer Bedeutung für Mönchtum und Klerus," in A. Grillmeier and H. Bacht, eds., Das Konzil von Chalkedon: Geschichte und Gegenwart, Vol. 2 (Würzburg, 1953), 569–676.

[2] No foundations without episcopal approval: C. Chalc., c. 4 (R&P 2.226); subordination of all clergy to the local bishops: c. 8 (R&P 2.234), cf. c. 17 (R&P 2.258); founder's bequest of a monastery irrevocable once made: c. 24 (R&P 2.271).

[3] C. Trull., c. 49 (R&P 2.423); C. Nicaen. II (787), c. 13 (R&P 2.612); Alexius Studites, Hypomnema B' (1028) (R&P 5.30).

erty owners were often stubbornly disposed to treat their foundations with the arbitrary proprietor's discretion permitted by law in most other respects. The canonical legislation of Chalcedon remained, however, as an emphatic expression of opinion of the ecclesiastical hierarchy that private religious foundations had a special legal character and purpose which necessarily limited the property rights of their owners.

The council's restrictions on the property rights of the founders could hardly be said to be onerous, and serve to emphasize how completely arbitrary the power of the patrons of religious institutions had been before the mid-fifth century. Classical Roman law traditionally had taken a more radical position with respect to the sacral character of pagan temples. The jurist Papinian asserted that it was not possible for an individual to own consecrated property.[4] Marcian declared that sacred property was incapable by definition of belonging to an individual, and remained sacred even if the temple erected on it ceased to stand.[5] Some eighty years after Chalcedon, Emperor Justinian endorsed these principles of classical law by incorporating them in his legal handbook, the *Institutes*.[6] These rules did not reflect actual circumstances, however, or even recognized legal practice, as the discussion of Justinian's regulation of private foundations will illustrate. The more limited Chalcedonian principles, though also ineffective in practice, were to prove more influential as the standard against which future reformers would judge the practices of their own times.

Although Chalcedon certainly strengthened the hand of the local bishop in his relationships with private foundations located within his diocese, the prelate still had to use his authority with discretion. A story preserved in John Moscus in his *Pratum spirituale* illustrates the point. The patriarch of Constantinople Gennadius (458–471) wanted to correct the notorious conduct of a certain Charisius, a lector in the oratory of St. Eleutherius, a private foundation.[7] Gennadius summoned the lector and personally reproved him, but Charisius persisted in his old ways. The patriarch then found himself obliged to send his *apokrisiarios* (personal envoy) to the oratory with instructions to appeal to St. Eleutherius himself either to reform the lector or strike him down. Despite the recent affirmation of his powers of spiritual supervision over all the clerics of his diocese, the patriarch did not venture to dismiss Charisius from his

---

[4] *Dig.* 18.1.73.
[5] *Dig.* 1.8.6.3.
[6] *Inst.* 2.1.7–8; 3.23.5.
[7] John Moschus, *Pratum spirituale* (PG 87.3, cols. 3008–9). For the foundation of this church, reportedly by the patrician Basileios during the reign of Arcadius, see *Patria Konstantinoupoleos* 3.192 (p. 275); cf. Janin, *Géographie*, Vol. 3, pp. 115–16.

post, but the lector's sudden death spared Gennadius the necessity of such a drastic intervention in a private foundation.

The ecclesiastical authorities' position vis-à-vis the private foundations, however, was somewhat stronger after Chalcedon. Pope Leo the Great, in a letter to Empress Pulcheria dated June 9, 451, could use only moral suasion to bring about the deposition of the Monophysite archimandrite Eutyches from his leadership of a monastery in the suburbs of Constantinople.[8] After the council, the imperial government joined forces with the hierarchy in a determined campaign to compel acceptance of the new orthodoxy by all religious foundations. For his part, Emperor Marcian forbade the foundation of Eutychian churches or monasteries and outlawed their use of existing facilities.[9] His law followed in the tradition of successive emperors since the last quarter of the fourth century who had tried to prevent the founders of private churches from putting them at the disposal of outlawed religious sectaries.

Emperor Leo I, in a law that dates to 466–472, reaffirmed the existing restrictions by forbidding the sale or transfer of *praedia* (rural estates) or of other properties that contained churches or oratories of the orthodox faith to any member of a heterodox sect, on pain of confiscation of the property by the treasury.[10] The law poses no objection, however, to similar transactions between orthodox property owners, and so it implicitly acknowledges the legality of private ownership of religious institutions. Another law of Leo I, dated 459, lent the support of the government to Chalcedon's provision that oratories could be founded only with the approval of the local bishop.[11] According to the law, there was now no shortage of such churches, and so public buildings were not to be subject to arbitrary conversions for service as ecclesiastical institutions.

This legislation served as a prelude to the first general law governing the construction of private churches that was enacted by Emperor Zeno (474–491).[12] His law requires that a founder granting property for the foundation of an oratory or philanthropic institution submit legally correct acts of donation which would bind him and his heirs to his announced intentions. Zeno gave permission to the bishops and their financial stewards, the *oikonomoi*, to take the initiative from the heirs, if necessary, and to compel fulfillment of the promised foundation. Through this law the government was declaring its interest in seeing private religious construction projects carried through to completion. This

---

[8] Leo the Great, *Epistola* 84 (*PL* 54, col. 922).
[9] *CJ* 1.5.8 (455).
[10] *CJ* 1.5.10 (466–472?).
[11] *CJ* 1.3.26 (459).
[12] *CJ* 1.2.15 (474–491).

concern took precedence over the founder's private property rights, an important step in the abridgment of these traditional rights of disposition over private foundations.

In a western document of 471 the Catholic Goth Flavius Valila listed the sources of revenue which he assigned for the church of the Blessed Virgin that he had erected on his estate at Cornuta near modern Tivoli.[13] This carefully considered document provides for the support of the assigned clergy, for the lighting of the church, and for necessary repairs and building maintenance. Valila intended that revenues from his landed property should supply the necessary funds. Under a legal device known as the *donatio mortis causa*, Valila reserved some of the land and its revenue for his own use until death, when the church was to receive the entire estate.[14] Valila set aside specific lands whose revenues would support the officiating clergy, thus separating their maintenance from that of the church as a whole. His list of the movable property donated to the church includes the usual church furnishings as well as agricultural implements for the exploitation of the estate. Valila excluded clerics, bishops, and his relatives and descendants alike from any right to alienate these dedications from the church. In many respects, then, this document anticipates the requirements that Justinian was to enact into law two generations later.

LEGISLATION OF JUSTINIAN

Justinian, acting initially through his quaestor Tribonian (d. ca. 542), elaborated and systematized the regulation of private foundations as no emperor before or after him ever did.[15] Naturally he was much indebted to the precedents supplied by his imperial predecessors, the canons of Chalcedon, and the contemporary practices of conscientious benefactors. His own regulations would remain authoritative until the late ninth century.

Neither the civil nor the ecclesiastical authorities of the empire ever attempted to outlaw the private ownership of churches. The theoretical principle borrowed from pagan classical law and embraced by Justinian in his *Institutes* to the effect that "what belongs to divine law is among

---

[13] Ed. with commentary by Ulrich Stutz, *Benefizialwesens*, 53–54, and also Luigi Bruzza, *Regesto della chiesa di Tivoli* (Rome, 1880), Doc. 1.

[14] For the *donatio mortis causa*, see *CJ* 1.2.14.1 (470) and W. W. Buckland, *Textbook of Roman Law*, 2nd ed. (Cambridge, 1950), 257–58.

[15] For Justinian's ecclesiastical legislation, see Gustav Pfannmüller, *Die kirchliche Gesetzgebung Justinians* (Berlin, 1902); August Knecht, *System des justinianischen Kirchenvermögensrechts* (Stuttgart, 1905); Hamilcar Alivisatos, *Die kirchliche Gesetzgebung des Kaisers Justinian I.* (Berlin, 1913); for Tribonian's role in the formation of Justinian's legislation, see Tony Honoré, *Tribonian* (London, 1978), esp. 243–56.

no man's property" remained without practical effect.[16] Leo I's legislation had the effect of confirming the rights of private property owners to buy and sell ecclesiastical foundations among themselves. In 545 Justinian himself issued a law that tightened up some of the provisions of Leo's law by including Jews, Samaritans, and pagans on the list of those ineligible to purchase property that contained a private church.[17] By this same law he also forbade rental of such properties to the groups enumerated, and he changed the recipient of confiscations from the treasury to the local orthodox church.

Leo's law, and Justinian's emendation of it, provide the background for consideration of two important laws of Justinian that deal specifically with private churches. The first of these laws, issued in 537, places severe restrictions on the employment of oratories in private houses.[18] The emperor objected to the private celebration of the liturgy. Accordingly, he banned these oratories, but lessened the significance of this prohibition by permitting private individuals to summon clergy from the regular churches (provided the local bishop gave his permission) to celebrate the liturgy within the residences in special rooms set aside for prayer. This arrangement preserved the local bishop's rights of spiritual supervision in accordance with the canonical prescription of Chalcedon.[19] Justinian feared that without such supervision, these most private spiritual retreats would be used by sectarian dissidents.

In Justinian's second law on the subject, issued in 545, he made his intentions clearer by forbidding anyone to perform the holy liturgy, either in his own house, or on a *proasteion* or *chorion*, or to allow others to do so, except, of course, the clergy subordinate to the local bishop.[20] Justinian thereby extended the scope of his earlier law to cover rural as well as urban localities. Since the novel that contains this law also includes Justinian's revision of Leo I's law on the transfer of estates containing churches, it is clear that the emperor had no intention of banning private churches outright. Justinian was not trying to prevent regular services in private churches either. His intention was simply to subordinate these churches to the local bishops through their control of the officiating clergy. Justinian certainly did intend to prevent private individuals from sponsoring religious services closed to public scrutiny and from maintaining their own clergy without effective supervision by the bishops. It is hardly likely that he intended to place the same restrictions

[16] *Institutes* 2.1.7.
[17] *NJ* 131.14.1–2 (545).
[18] *NJ* 58 (537).
[19] C. *Chalc.*, c. 8 (R&P 2.234) and Theodore Balsamon, *Commentaria ad C. Chalc.*, c. 8 (R&P 2.236), both suggesting possible abuses by laymen in their capacity as founders or patrons as a motivation for this canon.
[20] *NJ* 131.8 (545); cf. C. *Chalc.*, c. 17 (R&P 2.258).

on those urban and rural private churches that were open for public worship under the watchful eyes of the orthodox bishops.

In a law of 538 Justinian acknowledged that landlords were still building illegal churches for religious dissidents despite repeated legal prohibitions.[21] Monophysite sources present an even more vivid picture of widespread contempt for the laws.[22] Justinian and his Chalcedonian partisans condemned these churches as "robbers' lairs" and "dens of iniquity." The emperor nevertheless hoped to curb the problem by insisting that the prospective founder obtain the approval of the local orthodox bishop before commencing construction. The emperor must have realized that private foundations were too important to ban outright, despite the dangers that illegal employment posed for the good order of the church. His legislation sought to prevent future abuses and to channel indispensable private philanthropy in useful directions.

Justinian's difficulties with the Monophysites at the time of his first law on the subject in 537 had an important influence on his decision to ban oratories in private houses. The fathers of the council held in Constantinople in May 536 had petitioned the emperor to expel the Monophysites from the capital, complaining bitterly that they were conducting services illegally in the public churches, in private homes, and on *proasteia*.[23] Four months later Justinian obligingly issued a novel complying with all their requests.[24] Empress Theodora's protection and maintenance of Severus of Antioch and other Monophysite leaders in the imperial palace itself probably convinced Justinian that the problem was grave and that new laws were needed.[25]

Although Justinian had no objection to the sale, rental, and transfer of properties containing churches and oratories among orthodox landowners, he was vehemently opposed to secularization of religious facilities. A law dated to 535 singles out the Egyptians (although noting violations elsewhere) for this offense with respect to monasteries.[26]

The requirement for founders to obtain the permission of their local bishop before initiating the construction of a church or monastery was the cornerstone of Justinian's program for regulating private founda-

---

[21] *NJ* 67.1 (538); cf. *NJ* 131.14.2 (545).

[22] E.g., John of Ephesus, *Lives of the Eastern Saints*, ed. and trans. E. W. Brooks, *PO* 17 (Paris, 1923), Fifth History: Lives of Simeon and Sergius, pp. 106–7; Twelfth History: Lives of Mary and Euphemia, p. 177; *PO* 18 (Paris, 1924), Thirty-First History: Lives of Elijah and Theodore, p. 583.

[23] *C. Const.* (536), *Acta* (Mansi, Vol. 8, col. 1006C).

[24] *NJ* 42 (536), esp. 3.2.

[25] John of Ephesus, *Lives*, *PO* 18 (Paris, 1924), Twenty-Fifth History: Life of John of Hephaestopolis, p. 531; Forty-Seventh History: Of the Refugees in Constantinople, pp. 676–84; Forty-Eighth History: Lives of the Five Patriarchs, p. 686.

[26] *NJ* 42 (536), esp. 3.2.

tions. In support of the mandate of Chalcedon, Justinian issued a law in 538 (renewed in 545) which sets out the prescribed ritual observances.[27] The bishop was to say a prayer on the site, fix a cross there, and arrange for a procession. All of this would serve to make the erection of a church or monastery a matter of public knowledge and official scrutiny.[28] In time, the establishment of the cross came to symbolize the bishop's spiritual jurisdiction over the building, though it did not, of course, give him any property right in it.

Despite Justinian's best intentions, ecclesiastical dissidents were not deterred by this requirement. After the condemnation of the Monophysites at the Council of Constantinople in 536, they lost control of many of their existing churches and monasteries, especially in the large cities like Alexandria. There a notable named Dorotheus lodged an appeal with the governor of Egypt, Aristomachus, asking permission to build new churches for communities of Monophysite monks.[29] Surprisingly, Aristomachus gave Dorotheus permission to do as he wished, effectively undermining Justinian's law. In another case, a militant Syrian Monophysite monk named Sergius defiantly erected a monastery at Qlwfyte without the permission of the local Chalcedonian bishop.[30] Sergius' opponents reported him to the bishop, who sent his agents to arrest him and demolish the monastery. Sergius vowed to rebuild the monastery thirty times, if necessary, and ultimately he was successful in defying the local authorities and establishing his foundation on a permanent basis.

Like his predecessor Zeno, Justinian was concerned about insuring that the heirs of a benefactor would carry out testamentary plans for the construction of religious foundations. Justinian confirmed Zeno's regulation in a law of his own issued in 530, and he also established time limits for the completion of construction.[31] At first these were three years for an oratory and one year for a philanthropic institution, but in 545 the emperor thought it necessary to extend the limit for oratories to five years.[32] Justinian obliged the heirs to buy or lease a building to serve as a temporary home for a philanthropic institution if they could not meet the time limit.

Justinian ordered the local magistrates to assist the bishops and their

---

[27] NJ 67.1 (538), cf. C. Chalc., c. 4 (R&P 2.226); confirmed by NJ 131.7 (545).

[28] Cf. NJ 123.32 (546), which forbids laymen to conduct religious processions without the participation of the local bishop.

[29] History of the patriarchs of Alexandria, ed. and trans. B. Evetts, PO 1 (Paris, 1907), pp. 457–58.

[30] John of Ephesus, Lives, PO 17 (Paris, 1923), Fifth History: Lives of Simeon and Sergius, pp. 106–7.

[31] CJ 1.3.45 (530).

[32] NJ 131.10 (545).

oikonomoi whom Zeno had already deputed for the responsibility of seeing to it that the heirs fulfilled their legal obligation.[33] Moreover, if the metropolitans and archbishops suspected that the bishop and the benefactor's heirs were in collusion to frustrate the completion of a foundation, Justinian ordered that they, too, should assume responsibility for the fulfillment of the testamentary bequest.[34] The authorities could summon the reluctant heirs to court if necessary, where they might be compelled to pay double the original bequest from the founder's estate.[35] Justinian was even willing to allow the local bishop to undertake the task of construction himself and to exclude the founder's family from participation in the frequently profitable financial administration of the institution.[36] Yet only a flat refusal to proceed with construction, maintained over a long period of time, would justify this drastic overriding of the traditional rights of the founder's family.

In the absence of a testamentary bequest of property, it was frequently necessary to purchase land on which to build a new religious foundation.[37] Mare the Solitary, a Monophysite ascetic and favorite of Empress Theodora, purchased a *proasteion* (suburban estate) in the vicinity of Constantinople as the site for a *martyrion* that he intended to build with imperial assistance.[38] Thomas the Armenian, another Monophysite monk, purchased land adjacent to the Euphrates River for the erection of his monastery.[39] The famous Palestinian abbot St. Sabas purchased land for a *xenodocheion* (guesthouse) at Jericho with money he had inherited from his mother, Sophia.[40] St. Nicholas of Hagios Sion was compelled to buy land for a church that he wished to erect at Pinara in order to overcome opposition to his plans.[41]

IMPERIAL FOUNDATIONS

Justinian and Theodora, and, to a lesser extent, their predecessors as well, were great benefactors in their own right. Although a detailed ex-

---

[33] *CJ* 1.3.45.2 (530).

[34] *CJ* 1.3.45.6 (530).

[35] *CJ* 1.3.45.7 (530).

[36] *CJ* 1.3.45.1b (530).

[37] For a contrary view, see B. Granić, "L'acte de fondation d'un monastère dans les provinces grecques du Bas-Empire au Ve et au VIe siècle," in *Mélanges Charles Diehl*, Vol. 1 (Paris, 1930), 101–5, at 104.

[38] John of Ephesus, *Lives*, PO 18 (Paris, 1924), Thirty-Sixth History: Life of Mare the Solitary, p. 639.

[39] John of Ephesus, *Lives*, PO 17 (Paris, 1923), Twenty-First History: Life of Thomas the Armenian, p. 296.

[40] Cyril of Scythopolis, *Vita Sabae*, Ch. 25, ed. Eduard Schwartz, *Kyrillos von Skythopolis* (Leipzig, 1939), p. 109.

[41] *Vita Nicolai Sionitae*, Ch. 69, ed. Gustav Anrich, *Hagios Nikolaos*, Vol. 1 (Leipzig, 1913), p. 50.

amination of imperial foundations is beyond the scope of this study, there is still much to learn from the circumstances attending the erection of these institutions since they continued to form a paradigm for the benefactions of private individuals. Zachariah of Mitylene provides an account of Bishop Thomas of Amida's construction of a church at Dara under the orders of Emperor Anastasius (491–518).[42] Anastasius obliged Thomas to submit an account of his expenditure of imperial funds on the project, and in return he sent the bishop a receipt from the treasury acknowledging proper use of the money and promising immunity from investigation for embezzlement. Evidently this procedure remained the usual way in which the emperor's subordinates received documentation of the faithful and honest performance of their duties, judging from the incidental mention of such receipts in a late eleventh-century monastic foundation charter.

The monastic hagiographer Cyril of Scythopolis recorded Justinian's own arrangements for the construction of a church of the Theotokos at Jerusalem in the early 530s.[43] The emperor assigned a certain Theodorus, a *mechanikos* (architectural engineeer) for the actual construction of the church. The *trakteutai* (tax clerks) of the praetorian prefect's office in Palestine were to supply the gold necessary to meet the costs. Peter, archbishop of Jerusalem, had the final authority over the project, but Barachos, bishop of Bakatha, was charged with immediate oversight of the construction. Thus the emperor seems to have adopted for himself the system of administrative oversight that he was requiring of others at this time in his law regulating private foundations.

Justinian and Theodora also took an interest in assisting the private foundations of their ecclesiastical favorites. The imperial couple's activities in this area resulted in foundations that defy easy categorization of ownership. According to one version of the foundation of the Chora monastery of Constantinople, Justinian allowed the monk Theodore (reputedly the maternal uncle of Theodora) to tour imperial properties in the capital to pick out a site for the monastery.[44] Theodore selected a property that had once belonged to the *illustris* Charisius and that already contained a small private church. Mare the Solitary was another beneficiary of imperial favor who seems to have possessed the equivalent

[42] Zachariah of Mitylene, *Syriac Chronicle* 7.6, trans. F. J. Hamilton and E. W. Brooks (London, 1899). For later Byzantine parallels, see Gregory Pakourianos, *Typikon*, ed. Paul Gautier, "Le Typikon du sébaste Grégoire Pakourianos," *REB* 42 (1984), 5–145, at pp. 127–29, lines 1777–78, 1794, 1805–9, 1819, 1823–24, 1834–35.

[43] Cyril of Scythopolis, *Vita Sabae*, Ch. 73, ed. Schwartz, p. 177.

[44] *Vita S. Theodori Chorensis*, Ch. 19, ed. Ch. Loparev, *De Theodoro monacho hegumenoque Chorensi* (St. Petersburg, 1903); cf. *Patria Konstantinoupoleos* 3.184 (p. 273) and Janin, *Géographie*, Vol 3, pp. 546–47 for an alternate version of the origin of this foundation.

of a blank check for the erection of a *martyrion*.[45] After purchasing a suitable site, Mare sent a message to officials of the palace asking for craftsmen and supplies. These were dispatched forthwith, along with men to supervise the work, and Mare's building plans were realized in a matter of days, at least according to our source, John of Ephesus.

PRIVATE FOUNDATIONS

The age of Justinian, thanks to Procopius' *De aedificiis* and the magnificent surviving monuments, appears to us preeminently as an era of imperial foundations, despite the emperor's interest in the regulation of private institutions. Yet appearances are surely deceiving. Though private foundations suffered a temporary eclipse in relative importance for the first time since the fourth century, it is doubtful whether there was a diminution in actual numbers. Indeed, the most important personalities of the era took first rank as private founders of churches, monasteries, and philanthropic institutions.[46] Justinian's general Belisarius built a church and a *xenodocheion* outside Rome, and there was a private church on his estate in the suburbs of Chalcedon. Peter the Patrician, Justinian's ambassador to the Ostrogothic court in the late 530s, turned his residence in Constantinople into a *gerokomeion* (old age home). Flavius Bassus, praetorian prefect in 547, founded a church of his own in Constantinople. Pharasmanes, *epi tou koitionos* (chamberlain) of the emperor, reportedly founded the famous monastery of St. Mamas in this reign. Under Justin II (565–578), the renowned general Narses erected a large foundation in Constantinople which included a *gerokomeion*, a *xenon* (hostel), and a church. A number of lesser imperial officials and provincial magnates joined their more famous contemporaries in the erection of private foundations.[47] Taken together, these rival even the

---

[45] John of Ephesus, *Lives*, PO 18 (Paris, 1924), Thirty-Sixth History: Life of Mare the Solitary, p. 438.

[46] Belisarius: *Liber Pontificalis*, ed. Louis Duchesne, 2nd ed. (Paris, 1955), 296; Peter the Patrician: *Patria Konstantinoupoleos* 3.97 (p. 249); cf. Janin, *Géographie*, Vol. 3, p. 568; Flavius Bassus: *Patria* 3.50 (p. 235); cf. Janin, Vol. 3, p. 66; Pharasmanes: *Patria* 3.185 (p. 274) cf. Janin, Vol. 3, p. 314; Narses: *Patria* 3.94 (p. 249); cf. Janin, Vol. 3, pp. 555–56, 560.

[47] E.g., Sylvanos, *Dux Arabiae*, who erected a *martyrion* at Anasartha in Syria in honor of his daughter Chasidat, known from the inscription edited by L. Jalabert and René Mouterde, *Inscriptions grecques et latines de la Syrie*, Vol. 2 (Paris, 1939), No. 297; the *magistros* Bassus, from an inscription of a church at Imma, also in Jalabert and Mouterde, Vol. 2, No. 625; the family of the *illustris* Zosimus, the ex-prefect John, and the *comites* Peter and Anastasius, who founded a monastery at Scythopolis in Palestine late in Justinian's reign, known from inscriptions edited by G. M. Fitzgerald, *A Sixth Century Monastery at Beth-Shan (Scythopolis)* (Philadelphia, 1939), No. 1, pp. 13–14.

considerable total of imperial religious foundations recorded by Procopius and others.

FINANCIAL SUPPORT OF PRIVATE RELIGIOUS FOUNDATIONS

After a benefactor had successfully carried out the construction of his religious foundation, the provision of some sort of financial support to enable the institution to carry on its intended functions was naturally a matter of the greatest importance. In the fifth century the endowment of a private religious institution was a matter left to the discretion of the individual benefactor. Justinian's own investigations led him to the conclusion that conscientious private benefactors ordinarily made provision for the support of a predetermined number of clerics.[48] Apparently not all benefactors were as farsighted, since Justinian complained later that many rushed headlong into the construction of churches for the sake of the honor involved, neglecting, however, to make any provision for operating expenses.[49] Such negligence meant that services would have to cease eventually, and the foundation would be abandoned.

Reluctantly Justinian issued a law in 535 that obliges the local public church to provide *sitesis* (maintenance) for the clergy in private churches whose founders had neglected to do this themselves.[50] This must have placed a heavy burden on the cathedral church of the patriarchate of Constantinople, an institution that already had difficult financial problems of its own. A few years later, in 538, Justinian judged that the time had come to deal with the matter of endowments for private churches. He issued a law that required that each founder make provision in advance for the costs of lighting, for conducting services, for the support of the attending clergy, and for the maintenance of the building itself.[51]

Justinian did not presume to specify what sort of support a benefactor should provide for his foundation, but only that some provision be made for the four necessities he listed. There is in fact little uniformity on this matter to be observed in the surviving sources. Some institutions enjoyed formal landed endowments. The fathers of the Council of Chalcedon, in linking a prohibition against alienation of monastic property with the general ban on secularization, seem to have had in mind the landed endowments of some institutions of their own day.[52] In addition, there is

[48] *NJ* 3 (535), preface, lines 11–19.
[49] *NJ* 67 (538), preface, lines 16–23.
[50] *NJ* 6.8 (535), lines 4–13.
[51] *NJ* 67.2 (538), lines 5–11.
[52] *C. Chalc.*, c. 24 (R&P 2.271).

abundant evidence in Justinian's legislation, in inscriptions, and in other sources that churches and other religious institutions could own landed property.[53] Yet the bulk of Justinian's extensive legislation severely restricting the sale and leasing of ecclesiastical property clearly deals with the lands of public churches, especially those of the cathedral church of Constantinople. These *ekklesiastika choria* usually had peasant cultivators attached. When Anastasius bought up some *choria* belonging to the church of Amida in order to obtain land on which to found the city of Dara, he freed the peasant cultivators and gave them their own plots of land.[54] Subsequently Anastasius provided a new endowment or *ousia* for the cathedral church of Dara.

Properties donated by the emperor originated in the *domus divina*, the private property of the ruler earmarked for the expenses of the palace.[55] The *domus* included properties located throughout the empire, but many were concentrated in Cappadocia, for which Justinian issued a special law in 536 regulating the relationship of the administrators of these estates and the other government officials in the province.[56] Empress Theodora had her own *domus*, from which she, too, made donations of property to ecclesiastical institutions.

Some private foundations in the sixth century received their support from annuities, derived from income of properties earmarked for these disbursements. In a law of 530 Justinian ruled that these *presbia annalia*, as they were called, could not be commuted into a lump-sum payment by the benefactor or his family, but had to be maintained indefinitely, preferably through the hypothecation (mortgaging) of some specific piece of property.[57] The revenue derived from such a hypothecation was known as *prosodon* (income). Although explicit testimonies to the nature of the financial support of private churches are scarce in this period, it appears that some benefactors preferred to supply their foundations with *prosodon* or annuities so that the properties that provided these revenues would remain under their control.[58]

[53] *CJ* 1.2.17.2 (491–518); *CJ* 1.2.22 (530); *NJ* 7.1 (535); *NJ* 40 (535); *NJ* 42.3.2 (536); Procopius, *Historia Arcana* 11–19; Henri Grégoire, *Recueil des inscriptions grecques chrétiennes d'Asie mineure*, Vol. 1 (Paris, 1922), No. 2, an ex-voto inscription of peasants who cultivated lands of a church of St. Tryphon at Alexandria Troas; also No. 314, discussed below in note 105; Franz Cumont, "Nouvelles inscriptions du Pont," *REG* 15 (1902), 311–35, No. 23, at p. 321; Jean Lassus, *Sanctuaires chrétienes de Syrie* (Paris, 1947), 251, from Qabr Hiram (A.D. 575).

[54] Zacharia of Mitylene, *Syriac Chronicle* 7.6, trans. Hamilton and Brooks, pp. 165, 167.

[55] *CJ* 7.37.3 (531).

[56] *NJ* 30 (536): for the *domus divina* in general, see Rudolf His, *Die Domänen der römischen Kaiserzeit* (Leipzig, 1896), 28–33, 75–82, and Nicolas Svoronos, "Histoire des institutions de l'empire byzantin," *Annuaire de l'Ecole Pratique des Hautes Etudes* (*IVe section*) (1975–76), 455–76, esp. 467–74.

[57] *CJ* 7.37.3 (531).

[58] See the evidence from Byzantine Egypt, discussed below in Chapter 3.

Justinian's willingness to accept the substitution of the income of a specific property for an annual cash payment and his declaration that the property of a benefactor would in any case stand as attachable surety for annuities indicate his preference for formal property endowments as a superior means of supporting religious institutions. Nevertheless, the emperor himself acted more like a private benefactor toward his own imperial foundations by granting a *prosodon* instead of land in most cases. Procopius records such bequests to the *xenon* of Sampson in Constantinople, the nunnery of the Metanoia in the suburbs, the church of the Theotokos in Antioch, and to the church of the Theotokos built in Jerusalem at the request of St. Sabas.[59] Moreover, Justinian chose to support Sabas' *nosokomeion* in Jerusalem with a "pure and unending *prosodon*" of 1,850 *nomismata* annually.[60] Justin II also showed this preference for funding through a *prosodon*.[61]

Just as Flavius Valila had done, most benefactors made separate provision for the maintenance of clergy. Another of Justinian's laws, dating to 537, illuminates the manner in which a founder and his descendants made this provision.[62] The law states that the clergy were entitled to their *choregia* (salaries), but if they fled their posts, they would lose all rights to reclaim their compensation in the future. Yet the founder's family was not to take advantage of the absence of clerics to suspend the customary payments altogether, since that would mean a cessation of services in the church. The local bishop or (in the capital) the patriarch could step in and install new clerics to replace those who had run away from their posts. The benefactors had to provide as usual for these new appointees, but they were not obligated to pay the former appointees as well if the latter tried to return to their posts. If the benefactors attempted to cut off the customary *choregia*, the emperor ordered that a certain piece of their property was to be set aside for the *res privata*, the "ministry of imperial lands," which would assure the continuance of payments.[63]

Evidently, then, private benefactors ordinarily supported the clergy of their private churches through the payment of salaries rather than endowing their churches with specific properties which the clergy could have used to derive an income (that is, as clerical benefices).[64] This is hardly surprising, given the reluctance of private benefactors at this time to grant lands to support other institutional costs of operation. Justinian did not want to interfere with existing arrangements, but he realized that

---

[59] Procopius, *De aedificiis* 1.2.16; 1.9.10; 2.10.24; 5.6.26.
[60] Cyril of Scythopolis, *Vita Sabae*, Ch. 73, ed. Schwartz, p. 117.
[61] Theophanes, *Chronographia* a.m. 6058, ed. De Boor, p. 242.
[62] *NJ* 57 (537).
[63] For the *res privata*, see Jones, *LRE*, 412–27.
[64] On the absence of separate landed benefices for the clergy of the public churches of the Byzantine Empire, see Herman, "Bénéfices," col. 706.

if the family of the original benefactor decided to cut off support for the clergy of their private church, the only practical way to reverse this was the imposition of a third party to assure payments in perpetuity. Justinian's remedy amounted to a confiscation of private property by the state to achieve this end, a drastic measure to be sure, but one that may have been intended to approximate the effect of ordinary, voluntary reservation of the income from these properties for this purpose.

Despite the presumption of Justinian's law, even direct beneficiaries of imperial financial support were not exempt from the possibility of having their stipends cut off. A letter of Cassiodorus, praetorian prefect of Italy (533–537) in the service of the Ostrogoths, reports that certain *munera* (dedications) granted by imperial constitutions to churches in Bruttium and Lucania had been diverted illegally by government officials from their stated purpose of supporting the clergy officiating in these churches.[65] On another occasion, Emperor Anastasius cut off salaries that the monks of the monastery of Dalmatus in Constantinople had been accustomed to receive from the treasury as a means of exerting pressure on them in a war of nerves with his patriarch, Macedonius II (495–507).[66]

Like private and imperial institutions, public churches also provided salaries for their clergy, and the proliferation of these appointees led to severe strains on the financial resources of these institutions. Justinian asserted that the success of the clergy in converting members of the heterodox sects had required an increase in the number of clerics in the orthodox churches that was significantly beyond the numbers originally provided for by their founders.[67] Apparently the increase in the number of worshipers was not reflected in a parallel increase in voluntary offerings sufficient to support the additional clergy.

The common complaint, in both the capital and in Antioch, was not that the clergy was receiving less as their number increased, but rather that the cathedral churches themselves were running into debt in order to pay their salaries.[68] This indicates that the clergy of the public churches received a fixed salary rather than a share of whatever revenues each church had at its disposal. The problem was most acute for the cathedral church of Constantinople as the provider of last resort for private foundations of the capital that had exhausted their endowments or had never had one in the first place.[69] Not surprisingly, the financial offi-

[65] Cassiodorus, *Variae* 12.13, ed. Th. Mommsen, *MGH, AA* 12 (Berlin, 1894).

[66] Zacharia of Mitylene, *Syriac Chronicle* 7.8, trans. Hamilton and Brooks, p. 171.

[67] *NJ* 3.1 (535), p. 20, line 38–p. 21, line 3.

[68] So Jones, "Church Finance," based on *NJ* 3, preface, p. 18, line 31–p. 19, line 8, and Severus of Antioch, *Epistola* Sect. 1, No. 8, trans. Brooks.

[69] Exhausted endowments: *NJ* 3.2.1 (535), cf. preface, lines 23–32; no endowments: *NJ* 6.8 (536), lines 4–13.

cials of this church were famous for their resourcefulness. There is even a record of this church lending a certain Eusebius, its *keimeliarchos* (custodian of sacred vessels), to the church of the Holy Sepulcher in Jerusalem in 535 to apply his expertise to improve that church's financial position.[70]

Justinian, however, was not impressed by many of the expedients employed. He rejected the idea that the public churches should seek to purchase more property to bolster their income from endowment. He was appalled at such short-term expedients as the mortgaging and liquidation of property in order to raise cash for salaries. He decided instead, in 535, to impose an upper limit on the number of clergy in all churches (whatever the origins of their foundation) that were currently receiving financial assistance from the capital's cathedral church.[71] These limits were probably in excess of the number of positions provided for by the original founders but, by the emperor's candid admission, optimistically lower than the existing inflated numbers. Justinian expected that reduction by attrition would solve the problem, but the need of Emperor Heraclius (610–641) to resort to renewed legislation in the early seventh century shows that this was a vain hope.

For those private churches that had managed to avoid bankruptcy and had therefore stayed independent of the cathedral church, Justinian required only that they not exceed the established number of clerical positions set down by their founders.[72] Most of these private foundations lacked the great financial resources and ingenious management that enabled the cathedral church—for a time—to increase its staff without reducing salaries.

Little is known about the distribution of *choregia* at this time. Justinian's law on the maintenance of clergy in private churches suggests that benefactors supported them with payments in cash and in kind.[73] The ecclesiastical historian Evagrius recorded an anecdote about Thomas, a monk of Coele-Syria in the time of Ephraem, patriarch of Antioch (526–545).[74] According to the report, Thomas was physically assaulted by Anastasius, the *oikonomos* of the cathedral church, to whom he had reported for the reception of the annual *choregia* for his monastery. This suggests that, for the dependencies of public institutions at any rate, the financial officials of the churches paid the *choregia* annually in a lump

---

[70] NJ 40 (535).

[71] NJ 3 (535) preface, p. 20.

[72] NJ 3.2.1, lines 21–31.

[73] NJ 57.1 (537).

[74] Evagrius Scholasticus, *Historia Ecclesiastica* 4.32, ed. J. Bidez and L. Parmentier (London, 1898). For an example of the payment of an annual salary in an eleventh-century Byzantine monastery, see the *typikon* of Gregory Pakourianos, as discussed below in Chapter 8.

sum to representatives of the subordinate foundations. Such was also the practice of many private benefactors at a later time in Byzantine history.

Some sources also speak of *analomata* (cash allowances), which seem to connote more circumstantial disbursements than the legally mandated payments of *choregia*. John of Ephesus praised Empress Theodora's generosity in providing *analomata* to Theodosius, the exiled patriarch of Alexandria, to John of Hephaestopolis, and to other Monophysite refugees.[75] John also wrote more vaguely of two archimandrites from Amida and Sophanene, who traveled to Constantinople "for the sake of the needs of their convents."[76] Zachariah of Mitylene noted that Juvenal, patriarch of Jerusalem (422–458), magnanimously offered *analomata* to a disgruntled monk who had assaulted him, provided he left the country.[77]

Empress Theodora's efforts to win the esteeem of Mare the Solitary by offering him a gift of a hundred pounds of gold heighten the dramatic effect of another of John of Ephesus' monastic biographies.[78] Theodora's *sakkelarios* (treasurer) brought out the money in a sealed bag, but Mare, to the consternation of onlookers in the palace, hurled it aside with a curse. Theodora persisted in her attempt to make Mare her financial dependent, and sent her chamberlains to entreat him to relent and accept the money. Mare refused, but the sight of so many senators and other high officials visiting the ascetic later on in his countryside retreat convinced some robbers that he was in fact the regular beneficiary of imperial largess. The robbers set upon Mare in the hope of despoiling him of his supposed wealth, but John's hero easily subdued them all. The story itself may give some indication of how imperial subsidies were disbursed.

Even more so than with his requirement that benefactors provide for clerical salaries, Justinian's insistence on a similar provision for building repair and maintenance indicates his keen anticipation of the likely future problems of private foundations. Emperor Anastasius had already recognized the importance of building maintenance and renewal, for he included such needs among the few legally acceptable grounds for the alienation of church property.[79] Justinian himself concentrated much of his ecclesiastical building program around the replacement of older

[75] John of Ephesus, *Lives*, PO 18 (Paris, 1924), Twenty-Fifth History: Life of John of Hephaestopolis, p. 53; Forty-Seventh History: Of the Refugees in Constantinople, pp. 676–83.

[76] John of Ephesus, *Lives*, PO 18 (Paris, 1924), Forty-Second History: Lives of Mari, Sergius, and Daniel, p. 657.

[77] Zachariah of Mitylene, *Syriac Chronicle* 3.8, trans. Hamilton and Brooks, p. 55.

[78] John of Ephesus, *Lives*, PO 18 (Paris, 1924), Thirty-Sixth History: Life of Mare the Solitary, pp. 636–37.

[79] *CJ* 1.2.17.1 (491–518).

churches that had fallen into disrepair or had been destroyed by the Nika riot of 532.[80]

The emperor did not stop at requiring future benefactors to make some provision for maintenance but also dealt with the problem of existing private churches that were suffering in default of such a provision. He noted in a law of 538 the existence of numerous churches in Constantinople and in the provinces that were in danger of collapse or simply deserved rebuilding on a larger and handsomer scale.[81] He urged private benefactors of lesser means to imitate his example and rebuild these churches with the permission of the local bishop or the patriarch. Such a benefactor would be entitled to call himself *ktistes* (founder) of the church he restored but would not have to meet the customary expenditures (*dapanemata*) for the operation of the church. Justinian expected that those who had previously provided this financial support (that is, the founder's family or the holder of legal title to the church) would continue to do so. Thus for the first time an emperor sanctioned the restoration and beautification of existing ecclesiastical institutions while reserving to the founders' families the ultimate rights of ownership. A similar arrangement reappears in the late tenth century as the granting of monasteries and philanthropic institutions in *charistike*, for the same purposes of building maintenance, enlargement, and beautification.

RIGHTS OF PRIVATE BENEFACTORS

Justinian's legislation naturally was more concerned with fixing the obligations rather than confirming the rights of private benefactors toward their foundations. Nevertheless, the founders of religious institutions continued to exercise certain traditional rights in their foundations throughout this period of heavy regulation. Foremost among these rights of the lay founder and his descendants was the nomination of candidates for the clerical positions in the churches they erected and supported financially. In two laws of 537 and 546 Justinian recognized this right to *proballein* (in Latin, *designare*) clergy.[82] In the first law Justinian emphasized that the right of nomination did not imply that a patron should expect automatic acceptance and ordination of his candidates. On the contrary, the emperor ordered that the local bishop could appoint others if he found the patron's nominees unsuitable. This was part of the emperor's program of actively involving the local hierarchy in the selection

---

[80] John Malalas, *Chronographia* 18, ed. L. Dindorf, *CSHB* (Bonn, 1831), pp. 474–75; Procopius, *De aedificiis* 1.4.10.

[81] *NJ* 67.2 (538), lines 15–28; cf. Procopius, *De aedificiis* 1.4.10.

[82] *NJ* 57.2 (437) and *NJ* 123.18 (546); see also Zhishman, *Stifterrecht*, 50–54.

of clergy for estate churches. The second law recognized the same rights for the founder's heirs. In both laws Justinian tied the exercise of this right to the provision of financial support for the clerics so nominated. Justinian was not awarding any new privileges with these two laws, but only recognizing and limiting the established practice of lay nominations of clergy that probably dates back to the later Roman Empire, if not earlier.[83]

The emperor imposed fewer restrictions on founders' rights in philanthropic institutions. As early as 530 the emperor had recognized the right of a benefactor to propose (*epistanai*) individuals as administrators of these foundations.[84] As in the case of private churches, the custom was surely older than its legal recognition, since a law of 528 forbids simony in the case of a philanthropic administrator chosen through patronage (*dia prostasias*).[85] In contrast to his regulations on churches, Justinian did not give the local bishops an explicit right to reject these administrators and impose others of their own choice. Thus the lay right of nomination to the administration of a philanthropic institution appears to have been tantamount to appointment. Justinian did allow the bishops to supervise the administrations of these officials, but only in extreme cases could they expel the benefactor's appointees.[86]

Private benefactors who enjoyed a parallel right to the nomination of an abbot most commonly exercised it only on the occasion of the installation of the first appointee at the time of foundation.[87] Thereafter, either the current abbot nominated his own successor, or the choice was thrown open to the community at large in a special election after the death of the incumbent. Patrons intervened only in unusual circumstances, as when it was necessary to depose an abbot of doubtful orthodoxy.

Accordingly, Justinian's legislation on abbatial elections assumes a choice made by the community itself without reference to the founder's wishes. His first law of 530 makes such choices subject to the approval

[83] Such rights are implicitly recognized by John Chrysostom, *Homilium XVIII* (PG 60, col. 147, lines 17–24); *CJ* 1.3.16 (409) appears to assume the existence of such rights; *C. Chalc.*, c. 2 (451) (R&P 2.217) might have them in mind by including laymen among the intermediaries in simoniacal ordinations.
[84] *CJ* 1.3.45.3 (530).
[85] *CJ* 1.3.41.22 (528).
[86] *CJ* 1.3.45.3 (530); cf. *NJ* 131.10 (545).
[87] John of Ephesus, *Lives*, PO 19 (1926), Fifty-Fourth History: Life of Caesaria the Patrician, pp. 190–91, is instructive: the patrician Caesaria founded a nunnery, ca. 541, declining to assume the leadership herself, but choosing another woman to serve as archimandritess. The Fifty-Eighth History: History of the Convent of John Urtaya, p. 208, suggests the use of personal testaments to convey the monastery of Mar John Urtaya at Amida from one abbot to another.

of the local bishop, a requirement that even the fathers of Chalcedon had not imposed.[88] A second law of 535 actually turns the choice over to the discretion of the local bishop, though the emperor's final enactment on the subject in 546 limits the bishop to ordination of the candidate of the community's choice.[89]

Literary sources also depict imperial, ecclesiastical, and private founders exercising their rights of nomination. Evagrius, speaking of the early career of Gregory, patriarch of Antioch, notes his appointment as abbot of the monastery of St. Catherine on Mount Sinai by Justin II.[90] This emperor surely inherited his rights with respect to St. Catherine's from his predecessor Justinian, who founded it in the 550s. Zachariah of Mitylene informs us that Thomas, bishop of Amida, appointed and consecrated the priest Eutychian as bishop of the church of Dara which Thomas himself had built at the orders of Emperor Anastasius.[91] Similarly, Nicholas, archbishop of Myra, appointed his teenaged nephew as abbot in the prelate's newly founded monastery of Hagios Sion.[92] Nor is an example of a private foundation lacking. According to Cyril of Sythopolis' life of St. Abraamios, a certain John, an official of the imperial treasury under Anastasius, founded a monastery next to his ancestral graveyard in his hometown of Krateia in the province of Honoria, and he appointed Abraamios as the first abbot.[93] Plato, bishop of Krateia, happened to be John's brother, and he obligingly consecrated Abraamios as priest and abbot.

A benefactor's nominee to a private church or monastery received ordination from the bishop as confirmation of his appointment, while nominees to the leadership of private philanthropic institutions received a "commission of administration" (empisteutheisa tes dioikeseos) from the benefactor himself.[94] Justinian strictly forbade a layman to exact a fee for this commission, but he encouraged the nominee to offer part of his personal property to the institution that he was to administer. Justinian's avowed principle in these matters was to prohibit payments to individu-

---

[88] CJ 1.3.46 (530).

[89] NJ 5.9 (535); NJ 123.34 (546).

[90] Evagrius Scholasticus, Historia Ecclesiastica 5.6.

[91] Zachariah of Mitylene, Syriac Chronicle 7.6, trans. Hamilton and Brooks, p. 167.

[92] Vita Nicolai Sionitae Ch. 7, ed. Anrich, pp. 7–8.

[93] Cyril of Scythopolis, Vita Abraamii, ed. Eduard Schwartz, Kyrillos von Skythopolis (Leipzig, 1939), 244.

[94] NJ 123.16.1 (546); for philanthropic institutions in the Byzantine Empire, see Demetrios J. Constantelos, Byzantine Philanthropy and Social Welfare (New Brunswick, N.J., 1968); H. R. Hagemann, Die Stellung der Piae Causae nach justinianischem Rechte (Basel, 1953), and "Die rechtliche Stellung der christlichen Wohltätigkeitanstalten in der östlichen Reichshälfte," RIDA 3 (1956), 265–83; Timothy Miller, The Birth of the Hospital in the Byzantine Empire (Baltimore, 1985).

als but not to churches and other ecclesiastical institutions. He also encouraged nominees for ordination to make similar donations to their appointed churches.

Justinian realized that clerical appointments achieved through patronage were the principal cause for the growth in the numbers of the clergy in the cathedral church of Constantinople.[95] He also warned against comparable dangers in the case of privately founded churches now dependent upon the cathedral church.[96] Private benefactors, who ultimately had to foot the bill for any increase in staff, had a strong incentive not to exercise their rights of patronage capriciously and thereby endanger the survival of their foundations. Justinian attempted to create a similar restraining mechanism for the public churches by holding the patriarchs and their *oikonomoi* personally responsible for ordinations in excess of his prescribed limits. Those who allowed such appointments had to make good the loss to the church out of their own property, just as they would have done as private benefactors.[97]

Other traditional rights were of less interest to the imperial legislator and find mention in the sources only in passing. These included the founder's right of burial in his church, commemoration of his memory in services after death, and rental of ecclesiastical property to his family on favorable terms.[98] What was potentially the most important right of all to founders—the ability to profit financially from the administration of their religious foundations—can only be inferred from the sixth-century sources.

Although he condemned the alienation of property set aside for ecclesiastical institutions in the strongest terms, Justinian did not attempt to legislate on profiteering from such foundations by the founders. To be sure, his predecessor Anastasius had issued a law that forbade bishops and their clergy to collect *aparchai* (first fruits) or *prosphorai* (offerings) under compulsion, and this measure presumably forbade private patrons from collecting obligatory fees from the parishoners of their churches as well.[99] Indeed, the readiness of some benefactors to cut off financial sup-

---

[95] *NJ* 3.4 (535), p. 21, lines 21–27.

[96] *NJ* 6.8 (535), lines 4–13.

[97] *NJ* 3.2.1 (535), lines 31–39.

[98] For burial in private foundations, see Zachariah of Mitylene, *Syriac Chronicle* 8.5, trans. Hamilton and Brooks, p. 209; Fitzgerald, *Beth-Shan*, Nos. 2, 4, 5; for commemorative services, see *CJ* 1.3.45 (530); cf. Fitzgerald, No. 2; for rental of ecclesiastical property, see *CJ* 1.2.24 (530) in connection with the discussion below in Chapter 3 of such rentals at Aphrodito in Egypt.

[99] *CJ* 1.3.38 (491–518); cf. Herman, "Bénéfices," col. 713; for the attribution of this law to Anastasius, see Jones, *LRE*, 895; for other tithes in Byzantium, see H. F. Schmid, "Byzantinisches Zehntwesen," *JÖBG* 6 (1957), 45–110. Note that John Chrysostom had urged that the estate owner himself should donate *aparchai* to his church in *Homilium XVIII* (*PG* 60, col. 147, lines 17–24).

port when offered a reasonable pretext such as the flight of the attending clergy, despite the resulting termination of services, suggests that the revenues received from churches did not always make up for the costs of operation.

Moreover, the properties of churches and other ecclesiastical institutions continued to be liable to state taxes in this period.[100] Private churches that had endowments and other sources of income under the control or management of private individuals were no exception to this rule. Justinian described the need to raise cash to pay taxes as one of the few justifications he would accept for the alienation of ecclesiastical property, showing thereby how important he considered the fulfillment of this obligation.[101]

Justinian did not, however, like to see the treasury seizing lands belonging to churches in default of taxes, much less the actual churches themselves. His law of 537 directed that the churches should instead sell those properties for which they could not afford the taxes to private individuals, who would then assume the tax obligations toward the treasury. As a general policy, then, Justinian tried to get the treasury out of the business of owning churches and their properties. In keeping with this view, he also revised old laws that had provided for confiscated private churches to go to the treasury, and changed the recipient to the local public church.[102]

It would be a mistake, however, to make too pessimistic an assessment of the prospects for financial returns on the investments benefactors could hope to realize from their foundations. According to a law of 529, property donated to any religious institution by a member of the senatorial class was immune from taxation as a capital gain.[103] A law of 528 exempts benefactors from the necessity of making a public record of their donations if the declared value was 500 *solidi* or less, raising the limit for exemption thereby from the 200 *solidi* established by an earlier law.[104] Conceivably, benefactors could exploit these laws to change the

---

[100] Grégoire, *Recueil*, Vol. 1, No. 314 (A.D. 527), an important inscription preserving a rescript of Justinian ordering that the oratory of St. John at Lagbe in Pamphylia should be immune from damages to its landed property "since . . . it is fitting to preserve our taxpayers (*syntelestai*) unmolested"; see also the evidence from Byzantine Egypt discussed below in Chapter 3.

[101] *NJ* 46 (547).

[102] *CJ* 1.5.3, which amended *CTh* 16.5.30 (402), and *NJ* 131.14.1–2 (545), which amends *CJ* 1.5.10 (466–472?). Note also that *NJ* 7.11 (535) makes the local public church the recipient of confiscated monasteries; *CTh* 16.5.57.2 (415) was ahead of its time in making the local orthodox church the recipient of other confiscated churches.

[103] *CJ* 1.2.22 (529).

[104] *CJ* 1.2.19 (528); cf. *Institutes* 2.7.2 for the old limit of 200 *solidi* for donations *inter vivos*; *CTh* 8.12.1 (316?) made the original provision for registry of gifts in writing before a magistrate.

legal status or ownership of their property, and perhaps to avoid taxes in the process.

Moreover, there are indications that the return on endowment enjoyed by churches in this era need not have been contemptible. A stray reference in John Lydus' *De magistratibus* mentions a certain private benefactor, Eliamus, who had endowed a church near Pessinus in Galatia with twenty pounds of gold (1440 *solidi*) for the support of the attending clergy, and that this sum yielded an income (*prosodon*) of 80 *solidi*, which is a 5.5 percent annual return on the principal.[105] Lydus further informs us that his patron Phocas, praetorian prefect of the East in 532, "made haste to take the church into his friendship," at what result to the clergy we are left to speculate.

A second example concerns the endowment of the church of the Holy Sepulcher in Jerusalem, which, after benefiting from the investment counsel provided by the *keimeliarchos* Eusebius, yielded a return in 535 of 30 pounds of gold on 380, or almost eight percent.[106] Justinian, at any rate, thought this such an exceptional rate of return (the principal, he observed, could be recovered in less than thirteen years!) that he was willing to grant a special exemption from his laws prohibiting the alienation of ecclesiastical property in order to see it maintained.

Perhaps the most telling example of the value of a founder's rights comes from Justinian's own behavior. The emperor was as jealous as any private benefactor of his rights over imperial foundations. The bishop of Tralles coveted a monastery that John of Ephesus had built in the 540s with imperial funds. According to John, the emperor angrily denounced the attempted usurpation, saying, "What you want is to seize upon a monastery that belongs to me, and which was built with my knowledge and at my command." [107] In this instance, then, the emperor acted more in the character of a private founder than as the staunch partisan of episcopal rights so familiar to us from his regulatory legislation.

---

[105] John Lydus, *De magistratibus* 3.74, ed. R. Wuensch (Leipzig, 1903).
[106] *NJ* 40 (535).
[107] John of Ephesus, *Historia Ecclesiastica*, Ch. 36, ed. E. W. Brooks, *CSCO*, *Scriptores Syri*, Series 3, Vol. 3 (Louvain, 1936).

CHAPTER THREE

Private Religious Foundations in Egypt from the Evidence of the Papyri

THE evidence afforded by Egyptian Greek and Coptic papyrus documents of the fifth through the eighth centuries provides a vivid picture of a lay society profoundly shaped by Christian institutions from the largest cities to the smallest villages.[1] This society created, nurtured, directed, and exploited its religious foundations unself-consciously as integral parts of its social and economic order.[2] Here, enthusiastic patrons made a reality out of John Chrysostom's vision of the widespread dissemination of churches located on large private landholdings.[3]

The business documents and personal correspondence left behind by this society enable us to glimpse the inner workings of private religious foundations, to catch its sponsors in candid moments as they pursued their affairs unaware of the eyes of posterity, to determine how closely everyday practices corresponded to the mighty dictates of emperors and church councils. The vividness of the documents frequently is matched

---

[1] There are two useful inventories of ecclesiastical institutions in Egypt in this period, but both are somewhat out of date because of the papyri that have appeared since their publication: Paola Barison, "Ricerche sui monasteri dell'Egitto bizantino ed arabo secondo i documenti dei papiri greci," *Aegyptus* 18 (1938), 29–148, and Luciana Antonini, "Le chiese cristiane nell'Egitto dal IV al IX secolo secondo i documenti dei papiri greci," *Aegyptus* 20 (1940), 129–208.

[2] See the outstanding work of Ewa Wipszycka, *Les ressources et les activités économiques des églises en Egypte du IVe au VIIIe siècle* (Brussels, 1972).

[3] Fundamental for the existence of private religious foundations in Egypt is Artur Steinwenter, "Die Rechtsstellung der Kirchen und Klöster nach den Papyri," ZS 50, *Kanonistische Abteilung* 19 (1930), 1–50, an indispensable work, but still only an outline of the available materials, and his "Aus dem kirchlichen Vermögensrechte der Papyri," ZSR 75, *k.a.* 44 (1958), 1–34; Ewa Wipszycka, *Ressources*, 78–83, also has valuable observations on private churches, and at 175–89, provides a very useful general bibliography on the church in Byzantine Egypt. See also her "L'Eglise dans la chôra égyptienne et les artisans," *Aegyptus* 48 (1968), 130–38, and Roger Rémondon, "L'Eglise dans la société égyptienne à l'époque byzantine," *Chronique d'Egypte* 48 (1973), 254–77. For the private estates of Byzantine Egypt, see Jean Gascou, "Les grands domaines, la cité et l'état en Egypte byzantine," *T&M* 9 (1985), 1–90, with the older studies by E. R. Hardy, *The Large Estates of Byzantine Egypt* (New York, 1931) and A. C. Johnson and L. C. West, *Byzantine Egypt: Economic Studies* (Princeton, 1949) on the private estates of Byzantine Egypt.

by their frustrating inexplicability. While the absence of any attempt to influence or mislead is welcome, our sources naturally enough make no attempt to explain the idiosyncracies of their own intimately familiar world. Some knowledge of the general organizational principles of these private religious foundations, happily provided by Justinian's contemporary regulatory legislation, is helpful in dealing with this difficulty. Frequently, however, the papyrus evidence fails to confirm and clarify, but instead indicates the bewildering complexity of particular features of organization overlooked by the law in its broad prescriptions.

Within the Roman Empire, Egypt itself led an idiosyncratic existence, and so it is always possible that developments observed there in the papyri may have been different from those elsewhere. The lack of a comparable body of evidence from another province to serve as a control on the Egyptian papyri aggravates the problem. Yet nearly all of the phenomena of private religious foundations in Egypt, including various aspects of their construction, management, support, and exploitation, have parallels elsewhere in other eras of Byzantine history. Even the terminology standard in other ages finds expression in Egypt at an early date.[4] It seems reasonable, therefore, to assert an identity of the outlines and basic nature of private religious foundations in Egypt with those found elsewhere, although the particulars, the modus operandi, and the scale of benefactions may have been different.

Developments after the Arab conquest of Egypt had a great deal of continuity with those in the era of Byzantine rule. Even some of the new features, like the part-ownership of private churches, reappeared later elsewhere in the Byzantine world. Since evidence from the Byzantine Empire itself is scarce in the seventh and eighth centuries, Coptic sources have a real utility along with the Greek, especially to document developments and institutions that had their origins in Byzantine times and continued unchanged under Arab rule.

FOUNDERS OF RELIGIOUS INSTITUTIONS IN EGYPT

In Egypt, as in other areas of the empire, the emperors, the ecclesiastical hierarchy, and private patrons shared responsibility for the foundation of religious institutions. Imperial foundations, however, were relatively rare in Egypt. Several emperors founded important churches in Alexandria in the fourth and early fifth centuries. Two were named (colloquially at least) after their founders, Emperors Theodosius I and Arcadius.[5] A

---

[4] Steinwenter, "Rechtsstellung," 42–50, argues convincingly for the continuity of developments in Byzantine Egypt and subsequent ages in Byzantine Egypt; see also the comment of Herman, "Ricerche," 340.

[5] Antonini, "Chiese," 161, No. 2 and 163, No. 18.

converted pagan temple known as the Caesareum or the Kyriakon was one of the earliest of the imperial foundations. One of the charges brought by the great bishop Athanasius' enemies was that he permitted a service in this church in 355 before its official dedication by Constantius II, who had paid the expenses for its construction.[6] In reply to his critics, Athanasius noted the unusual circumstances that had led him to sanction emergency use of the church, and he stressed that he did not infringe the emperor's prerogatives by celebrating its formal dedication. Custom indeed prohibited him from doing so without the permission of the emperor as the founder of the church. Justinian, despite his reputation as a great imperial benefactor of religious foundations, apparently was not important as a founder in Egypt.[7] Quite possibly the fact that Egypt remained firmly Monophysite in sympathies during his reign dissuaded him from granting such lavish benefactions as he bestowed on neighboring Palestine.

The patriarchs of Alexandria were also active in erecting churches, but mainly in Alexandria. We lack details of the role they or their bishops surely must have played in the construction of the public parochial churches of Egypt.[8] Papyri show that these *katholikai ekklesiai* did exist in considerable number in the town of Aphrodito in the mid-sixth century. There were also public churches at Oxyrhynchus, Hermopolis, and Apollinopolis.

As the founders of churches and monasteries, laymen were also involved in a most fundamental way at the beginning of the existence of many ecclesiastical institutions. To cite just a few examples, Apollos, the *hypodektes* (estate treasurer) of Count Ammonios, an important landowner of Aphrodito in the early sixth century, founded a monastery of the Christ-bearing Apostles there near the end of his life. Apollos chose to become the institution's first abbot.[9] In the cases of the monasteries of St. Phoibammon and St. Epiphanios at Thebes, there existed a custom of handing down the directorship from one *proestos* (prior) to another by means of a personal testament.[10] In a series of wills, a succession of priors bequeathed the monasteries along with all their interior furnishings and attached lands. In part, the testamentary transmission was a device for

---

[6] Athanasius, *Apologia ad Constantium* 14–18 (*PG* 25, cols. 612–20).

[7] Cf. Procopius, *De aedificiis* 6.1.

[8] For public churches in Egypt, see H. Leclercq, "Alexandrie," *DACL* 1.1, cols. 1107–12, *P. Cairo Masp.* 3.67283 (Aphrodito), *P. Oxy.* 16.1900 (A.D. 528) and *P. Oxy.* 16.1967 (427) (Oxyrhynchus), *P. Lond.* 1.78 (ca. 610) (Hermopolis), *P. Grenf.* 2.95 (6th c.) (Apollinopolis).

[9] See J. Maspero's introduction to *P. Cairo Masp.* 1.67096 (573–74).

[10] See Steinwenter, "Rechtsstellung," 12–16 and "Byzantinische Mönchstestamente," *Aegyptus* 12 (1932), 55–64; Martin Krause, "Die Testamente der Äbte des Phoibammon-Klösters in Theben," *MDAI, Cairo* 25 (1969), 57–67; Ch. Bachatly, *Le monastère de Phoebammon dans le Thébaide* (Cairo, 1981).

the *proestos* to determine his successor, but these documents demonstrate the peculiarly personal conception of the ownership of "independent" (that is, privately funded and administered) monasteries which characterized Byzantine Egypt.

The use of a testament did open up the possibility that a future *proestos* might allow the monastery to slip into the hands of lay relatives just like any other part of his private property. Justinian, of course, had legislated extensively in support of declarations in canon law enjoining a rigid separation between an ecclesiastical official's private property, over which he had full powers of testamentary disposition, and his *phrontis* (care) of church property, which he could neither bequeath nor alienate in ordinary circumstances.[11] By the time of the monastic testaments of the mid-seventh century, the authors were aware of the dangers inherent in their use of these documents. Therefore it is not surprising to find repeated admonitions to the new *proestos* not to alienate the monastery to his relatives but to bestow it in turn upon a "God-fearing monk" of his own choice.[12] As the legislation of Justinian and the church fathers shows, the confusion of personal and ecclesiastical property made such alienations to laymen possible even in the case of public churches of the empire. With private foundations the danger was even greater, as Justinian's law against secularization of monasteries (with special reference to Egypt) makes clear.[13]

Occasionally, individuals in religious life founded their own monasteries and philanthropic institutions. The monk Psaios, for example, was allowed in 573/4 to build his own *xenodocheion* on the lands of Apollos' private monastery at Aphrodito.[14] It is more unusual to find civil magistrates involved in the work of erecting an *apanteterion* (a hostel for pilgrims similar to a *xenodocheion*) at Kom Ombo at an uncertain date in the sixth or seventh century.[15]

In those few cases where there is evidence, professional contractors, the *oikodomoi*, oversaw the actual labor of construction.[16] At Aphrodito, Count Ammonios employed an *oikodomos* named Jeremias who,

---

[11] C. Ant., c. 24–25 (ca. 326) R&P 3.166–70; Canones Apostolorum, c. 40 (ca. A.D. 400) R&P 2.55–56; CJ 1.3.41.14 (528), NJ 7.10 (535), NJ 131.13 (545), NJ 123.19 (546).

[12] KRU 75 (ca. 650) Djême, trans. Walter C. Till, "Erbrechtliche Untersuchungen auf Grund der koptischen Urkunden," SOAW, Vol. 229, Pt. 2 (Vienna, 1954), 199.

[13] NJ 7.11 (535).

[14] P. Cairo Masp. 1.67096 (573–74) Aphrodito.

[15] H. R. Hall, Coptic and Greek Texts of the Christian Period in the British Museum (London, 1905), pl. 2.

[16] P. Cairo Masp. 2.67138F2r.26, 67139F3r.27, F6r.13 (527–31) Aphrodito; P. Oxy. 16.2041 (6th or 7th c.), P. Oxy. 18.2197.11, 185 (6th c.). Gregory of Nyssa, Epistola 25 (PG 46.3, cols. 1093–1100) provides an example of the ecclesiastical employment of oikodomoi outside Egypt.

like ecclesiastical beneficiaries of the estate treasury, received a fixed annual salary in wheat. Jeremias' receipt of a standard salary suggests that he was retained by the count for construction projects including the churches and monasteries associated with his estate at Aphrodito. At Oxyrhynchus, the estate managers of the famous Apion family routinely provided bricks for the needs of their churches. One document from Oxyrhynchus (probably from the archives of the Apion family) provides a detailed listing of stones allotted for the construction of a church dedicated to St. Philoxenus.

In another papyrus of uncertain date and provenance, a count promises to provide a bishop with the requirements for the erection of an *episkopeion* (episcopal residence) in preference to undertaking the construction himself.[17] The nature of the structure doubtless accounts for this arrangement. Ordinarily, the founder retained for himself the rights of ownership over his benefaction. Here, however, the author speaks unambiguously of the foundation as the property of the bishop.

As noted above, Justinian was so concerned with the failure of heirs to carry out testamentary bequests for the construction of ecclesiastical institutions that he set time limitations for construction and named the bishop of the locality as overseer for all foundations.[18] In a Coptic document of the seventh century two individuals pledge themselves to a bishop for the completion of a church by a specified month, perhaps illustrating the principle of Justinian's law in operation.[19] Unfortunately it is not possible to determine if the individuals mentioned were the founders themselves or simply *oikodomoi*, who might have been under contract to build a church for the bishop.

LAY OVERLORDS AND OVERSEERS

As one might expect, there were many highly placed lay administrative officials in Egyptian private religious foundations. The founder of a monastery could always strengthen his position of authority by becoming a monk himself and personally directing the life of the ascetic community.[20] Other founders held honorary positions as heads of their monasteries without serving as community directors. This it seems was the role

[17] *P. Basel* 19, as corrected by Stylianos Kapsomenakis, *Voruntersuchungen zu einer Grammatik der Papyri der nachchristlichen Zeit* (Munich, 1938), 97–99; for *episkopeia*, see *C. Nicaen. II*, c. 13 (787) R&P 2.612.

[18] *CJ* 1.3.45 (530), as amended by *NJ* 131.10 (545).

[19] *BKU* 69 (ca. 600) Djême, trans. W. C. Till, "Die koptischen Rechtsurkunden aus Theben," *SOAW*, Vol. 244, Pt. 3 (Vienna, 1964), 18.

[20] E.g., Apollos in *P. Cairo Masp.* 1.67096 and the *stratelates* Theodore in *CPR* 4.34.3a.

of Count Kaisarios, commemorated as *ktistes* (founder) in the lintel inscription of the famous White Monastery of Shenute.[21]

Whether or not the founder took over the daily administration of his monastery, the mere fact of lay foundation served to inhibit the genuine independence of his institution for several generations. Apollos, the founder and *proestos* of the monastery of the Christ-bearing Apostles in Aphrodito, designated his son, the layman Dioscoros, as the *phrontistes* (guardian) and *kourator* (protector) of this institution after his death.[22] These titles were standard designations for the overlords of ecclesiastical institutions. In this particular case, a layman became the overlord of a monastery by reason of his blood relationship to the founder. Evidently even the entrance of a founder into religious life did not always result in the exclusion of lay influence in the institution's management in subsequent generations.

A few precious documents illustrate the roles of these lay overlords and overseers, though not all of these specify the precise offices they held. A document of shortly before 538 from Aphrodito shows the monks of the monastery of Apa Agenios addesssing Apollos, the *protokometes* (head townsman) of Aphrodito, asking for his aid as the agent of their "common master" Count Ammonios in the recovery of money owed them by one of the count's tenants.[23] The monks asked Apollos "to take care of" (*phrontizein*) themselves and their property. Their abbot had already written to the count asking that he send someone to deal with the problem. The abbot informs Apollos in this letter that he would shortly be receiving written instructions from the count on this matter. Another papyrus confirms that this monastery was under the administrative control of Count Ammonios.[24] Apparently he actually administered the institution through his subordinate Apollos, who was the author of this second document, a rent receipt. As the count's agent, Apollos seems to have had full control over the management of the monastery's property, since in neither of these documents do the institution's own officers handle its financial affairs.

In an undated document of the sixth or early seventh century, the director of a *nosokomeion* refers a question of the ownership of certain *epoikia* (farmsteads) to a Count Sen[..]itos, asking whether these properties, which made up a part of the institution's endowment (*moira*) and

---

[21] *SB* (ca. 400–430) Deir-el–Abaid; see Gustave Lefebvre, *DACL* 4.1, cols. 471–73, for background and dating.

[22] *P. Cairo Masp.* 1.67096 (573–74) Aphrodito.

[23] *P. Cairo Masp.* 1.67062 (before 538) Aphrodito; Steinwenter, "Rechtsstellung," 25, n. 1, supplies the name of the monastery.

[24] *PSI* 8.933 (538) Aphrodito.

which the author understood to be earmarked for the payment of taxes, had in fact been alienated by his master, the *chartoularios*, or by their common master, the *illustris*.[25] This institution evidently had three ranking administrators, a hierarchy analogous to that of Apa Agenios in Aphrodito. The *illustris* must have held a position comparable to that of Count Ammonios. The *chartoularios*, the "keeper of archives," was perhaps his local representative who fulfilled a role like that of Apollos. The author of the letter probably held the title of *nosokomos* in his capacity as director of the foundation. The author of this document and the author of its parallel from Aphrodito ran the daily operations of their religious houses but did not have final control over financial affairs, which the lay administrators evidently retained for themselves.

In another important yet enigmatic document of the sixth century, the author, Abba Andreas, reports on an inspection of the administration of the monasteries of Aphrodito undertaken by a certain Count Johannes.[26] The monks of one of these monasteries had brought charges of fiscal misadministration against their *proestos*. The count, judging from this letter, seems to have regarded his inspection duties as an irksome and time-consuming diversion from more important duties. He probably was an official of the same rank as Count Ammonios, a distant overseer who was accustomed to delegating his administrative responsibilities to subordinates.

Documentary evidence from Hermopolis in the mid-seventh century shows that even a cathedral church could come under lay direction as in the cases of the private institutions discussed above.[27] Like them, the Hermopolite church also had a triple level of administrators. At the top was the *dux* Senouthios, the *phrontistes* of the church. Next came Abba Menas, archdeacon and *dioiketes*. Finally, there was Joseph, "priest of St. Merkourios" (perhaps the patron saint of the cathedral church), who handled routine financial affairs for the church.

Another document of this cathedral church from the middle of the seventh century accords the title of *phrontistes* to the *illustris* Joannikios, who was apparently a successor or predecessor of Senouthios.[28] Thus the highest official of the church evidently was ordinarily a layman who was a high governmental official. Senouthios, as *dux* of the Thebaid, was not

[25] P. Amh. 8.154; cf. discussion by H. Leclercq, "Hôpitaux," DACL 6.2, col. 2761.

[26] P. Fouad 1.87 (6th c.) Aphrodito, with Jean Gascou, "P. Fouad 87: Les monastères pachômiens et l'état byzantin," BIFAO 76 (1976), 157–84.

[27] Stud. Pal. 3.271B (ca. 650) Hermopolis, reedited by Ewa Wipszycka, "Les factions du cirque et les biens ecclésiastiques dans un papyrus égyptien," Byzantion 39 (1969), 180–98, at 185.

[28] P. Berl. Inv. 11814 (ca. 650) Hermopolis, ed. Wipszycka, "Les factions du cirque," 180–81.

resident in the town of Hermopolis, so he had to delegate his administrative responsibilities to others.[29] The letter of complaint from the monks of Apa Agenios demonstrates that the overlord of an institution might still receive remonstrances on occasion and issue directives to subordinates, even if most problems and business transactions (as at Hermopolis) were settled locally. Unfortunately there is no indication whether the *phrontistai* of the cathedral church of Hermopolis held their position ex-officio as local magistrates or as the result of some long-standing family relationship with the church. Possibly the unusual situation of a lay protectorate over a cathedral church grew out of the troubled times of the Persian occupation of Egypt (618–628) or of the Arab Conquest.

In post-Byzantine times some monasteries were successful in eliminating lay *phrontistai*, or so it would seem from a series of documents in which the abbots themselves appear as the *phrontistai* of their respective institutions.[30] In light of this, it seems ironic that in 771/2 a certain Lord Psmo, "great *archon*," became *pronoetes* and *phrontistes* of the famous monastery of St. Phoibamon in Thebes,[31] for until that time that institution had been remarkably successful in preserving its autonomy.

The papyri also mention officials called *pronoetai* (overseers). Some of these (like the Lord Psmo mentioned above) appear scarcely distinguishable from *phrontistai* and *kouratores*, while others were clearly subordinate lay officials in the service of the churches and monasteries under clerical supervision.[32] *Pronoetai* of the latter sort in the service of the church probably had duties similar to those of their counterparts in the service of lay landlords. It was common for lower-ranking officials called *misthioi* to assist the *pronoetes* of an institution with his collection of rents and taxes and the keeping of accurate accounts.[33] Institutions with extensive or widely scattered estates employed several *pronoetai*, each of whom had a particular district under his charge. Sometimes, as at Hermopolis, there was a further specialization of the officials for separate collection of revenues in cash and in grain.[34]

An important letter from the chancellery of Archbishop Theophilus of

---

[29] Wipszycka, "Les factions du cirque," 186.

[30] *CPR* 2.163 (7th c.), with a deacon as abbot and *phrontistes*; *CPR* 4.34, a priest as abbot and *phrontistes*; *CPR* 4.117 (7th c.), a deacon as *phrontistes*; *P. Copt. Ryl.* 164, an abbot and *phrontistes*.

[31] *KRU* 104 (771–72) Djême, trans. W. C. Till, "Rechtsurkunden," 188.

[32] For the two types of *pronoetai*, see Steinwenter, "Vermögensrechte," 29.

[33] *P. Lond.* 5.1782 (7th c.) Hermopolis, executed by the *misthios* Theodosios for Senouthios, *pronoetes meridos ton chrysikon Hermopoleos*, probably identical with the Dux Senouthios of *Stud. Pal.* 3.271B who was *phrontistes* of the cathedral church at Hermopolis.

[34] See the discussion of F. G. Kenyon, ed., *Greek Papyri in the British Museum, Catalogue with Texts* (London, 1893), Vol. 5, p. 240, n. 1.

Alexandria (385–412) illustrates the employment of *pronoetai* by diocesan officials.[35] The author, Aurelius Timotheos, *pronooumenos* (chief *pronoetes*) of the *katholike ekklesia* of Alexandria, addressed this letter of complaint to the *riparioi* (constables) of Arsinoe. The offending *pronoetai*, Serapion and Timoros, were in charge of the church's estates in the village of Boubastos in the nome of Arsinoe. They had ignored a first and a second summons to come into the city and render their accounts.[36] Timotheos' letter invokes the services of the *riparioi* as police officers to compel the defiant *pronoetai* to render the missing accounts. Although technically subordinate, lay *pronoetai* evidently were not always obedient employees.

There were also lay officials known as *dioiketai* in ecclesiastical service. The title *dioiketes* has a generic rather than a specific meaning. Justinian considered both *oikonomoi*, the financial stewards of the churches, and the directors of philanthropic institutions to be *dioiketai*.[37] Although the fathers of the Council of Chalcedon evidently presumed that the *oikonomoi* would be clerics, some of those in private institutions in Egypt were laymen, such as Justos, the *lamprotatos* (most brilliant) *oikonomos* of a church of St. Theodore in Arsinoe in the sixth century.[38] In this instance his honorific identifies him as a layman; clerics usually bore the corresponding honorific *eulabestatos* (most pious). The double role of a certain Menas, who was both a notary of the Apion household and *oikonomos* of a *nosokomeion*, makes it possible that he, too, was a layman. Other ambiguous cases also exist that are difficult to decide one way or the other.[39]

Occasionally individuals appear in the sources performing managerial tasks similar to those usually undertaken by a clerical *oikonomos*. A lay official named Pynote represented the community of the clergy of St. Phoibammon in Aphrodito as estate manager by collecting the rent from an emphyteutic lease held by an unnamed lay official sometime in the sixth century.[40] Similarly, the *protokometes* of Aphrodito represented a local church in another rent receipt dated 511.[41]

At times laymen appear in more specific roles in the administration of monasteries and philanthropic institutions. A certain Flavios Artemido-

---

[35] *SB* 6.9527 (385–412) Arsinoe.

[36] See *P. Oxy.* 16.1894 (573) Oxyrhynchus, for the letter of appointment given by Makarios, *pronoetes* of a church at Oxyrhynchus, to Pambechios, *misthios* for the *kome* of Sarapion Chaeremonis.

[37] *CJ* 1.3.45.1b (530).

[38] *Stud. Pal.* 3.164 (6th c.) Arsinoe; cf. *C. Chalc.*, c. 26 (451).

[39] *P. Oxy.* 16.1898 (587), 16.2039.15 (6th c.) Oxyrhynchus, *P. Cairo Masp.* 3.67299 (7th c.) Arsinoe.

[40] *P. Ross. Georg.* 3.43 (6th c.) Aphrodito.

[41] *P. Cairo Masp.* 1.67101 (511) Aphrodito.

ros was *epitropos* (trustee) of the monastery of Apa Sourous in Aphrodito in the mid-sixth century.[42] Since it was this same Artemidoros who, in his capacity as *singoularis* (a tax official), received a donation of barley from Count Ammonios on behalf of this monastery in 528, he may well have been the count's manager of this institution.[43] Aeion, *epitropos* of a *xenodocheion* in the Apion village of Spania, provides a contemporary parallel from Oxyrhynchus to the role of Artemidoros at Apa Sourous.[44] In a document of the sixth or seventh century the *singoularis* Johannes holds the same official position as Artemidoros concurrently with his tenure as *epimeletes* (manager) of an *apanteterion* at Kom Ombo.[45] He too seems to have been subordinate to lay overlords.

In a remarkable document dated 570, Flavius Phoibammon, chief physician of Arsinoe, deeds his *xenon* to his brother John.[46] He describes his responsibility toward the *xenon* rather floridly as a "holy *dioikesis, epimeleia*, and *pronoia*," anticipating thereby some of the terminology of the administration of religious institutions current later in Byzantine history. Since Phoibammon expected that his brother would manage the institution as well as provide for its support, it is clear that this is a private ecclesiastical institution.

The lower ranks of the administration of Egyptian ecclesiastical institutions also included laymen in positions of responsibility. At Hermopolis, for instance, there were officials called *apaitetai* who were responsible for the collection of taxes from church lands.[47] They may have been attached to the staffs of the *pronoetai* or *phrontistai*.[48] Some lay *notarioi* (notaries) also appear in ecclesiastical service. Their status varied greatly. Menas, the notary who was also the *oikonomos* of a *nosokomeion* at Oxyrhynchus, has been mentioned already. Another Menas, who served the cathedral church at Hermopolis, was both *notarios* and *apaitetes*.[49] A certain Paphnutios, regularly a notary for the Apion family, also served as notary for documents issued from their church of St. Thecla and Menas' *nosokomeion*.[50] Some *misthioi*, "assistants" of the *pronoetai*, also appear as lay employees of religious foundations.[51]

---

[42] *P. Cairo Masp.* 2.67133 (530 or 545) Aphrodito; cf. *P. Lond.* 5.1704 (527 or 542) Aphrodito, also isssued by Artemidoros, probably from this same monastery of Apa Sourous.

[43] *P. Cairo Masp.* 2.67139F6v3; cf. *P. Cairo Masp.* 1.67088 (551?), in which Artemidoros represents Aphrodito as *desponikos dioiketes*; for information on titulature, see Germaine Rouillard, *L'administration civile de l'Egypte byzantine* (Paris, 1928).

[44] *P. Oxy.* 16.2058.131 (6th c.) Oxyrhynchus.

[45] H. R. Hall, *Coptic and Greek Texts*, 2, pl. 2 (6th–7th c.) Kom Ombo.

[46] *P. Cairo Masp.* 2.67151.182–95 (570) Arsinoe.

[47] *P. Lond.* 3.1060, 5.1782; *P. Berl. Inv.* 11814.

[48] As in *P. Berl. Inv.* 11814.

[49] *P. Lond.* 5.1783 (7th c.) Hermopolis.

[50] *P. Oxy.* 16.1898 and 1993 (587) Oxyrhynchus.

[51] *P. Oxy.* 16.1894 (573) Oxyrhynchus, *P. Lond.* 5.1782 (7th c.) Hermopolis.

The brotherhoods of the *philoponoi* appear in Coptic documents of the sixth century and in post-Byzantine times. The laymen who formed these associations were responsible for the administration of the properties of certain monasteries.[52] They promised obedience to the religious leaders of these monasteries and were thus subordinate to clerical supervision.[53] The chief *philoponos* sometimes held the rank of *oikonomos* in the monastery that employed him.[54] In a document of the eighth century, the *philoponion* of a monastery of Apa Theodore at Hermopolis receives recognition as a distinct corporate entity, represented by its *oikonomos*.[55]

CLERICS AND MONKS IN LAY SOCIETY

There was a significant presence of clerics and monks in lay society paralleling the lay penetration of ecclesiastical institutions.[56] Some of these clerics were in the service of the great property owners, even though the Council of Chalcedon had specifically condemned clerics who undertook to manage the estates of laymen. In fact, an Oxyrhynchus papyrus of 583 preserves the contract of a deacon who was a *pronoetes* and *hypodektes* for the Apion family.[57] Several other examples exist of sixth-century clerics involved in the management of the estates of this great landowning family.[58]

Monks also appear in the service of laymen at this time. The house of Apion, for example, ordered the archimandrite of the monastery of the Homoousion to provide six hundred loaves of bread to the people of Tarouthinos, an Apion village.[59] The monks of St. Andreas, an Apion private monastery, offered a variety of products for other dependents of the family.[60] Another Oxyrhynchus document shows a monk receiving wages from two secular officials, but unfortunately there is no clue as to the duties he was performing.[61]

Even more than monks, the secular clergy were dependent economi-

[52] For the *philoponoi*, see W. E. Crum, *BM Copt.* 1013, n. 4 for literary references; also Ewa Wipszycka, *Ressources*, 150, and "Les confréries dans la vie religieuse de l'Egypte chrétienne," *Proceedings of the Twelfth International Congress of Papyrology* (Toronto, 1970), 511–25.

[53] *CPR* 4.196 (7th c.).

[54] *BM Copt.* 1046 (7th c. or later); *KTM* 1 (8th c.) Hermopolis.

[55] *KTM* 1 (8th c.) Hermopolis; cf. *CPR* 4.195.

[56] See Wipszycka, *Ressources*, 154–73.

[57] *P. Oxy.* 1.136 (583) Oxyrhynchus; cf. *P. Oxy.* 16.1894, in which a layman becomes a *misthios* in church service under a lay *pronoetes*.

[58] *BGU* 1.305 (556) Oxyrhynchus in which a deacon serves as a rental agent of the Apion household; *PSI* 1.81 (6th c.) Oxyrhynchus, a deacon as an Apion *enoikologos*; *P. Oxy.* 27.2480 (565–66) Oxyrhynchus, a payment of 180 *diplai* of wine to a deacon for undisclosed services.

[59] *P. Oxy.* 16.1952 (6th c.) Oxyrhynchus.

[60] *P. Oxy.* 1.146 (555), 1.147 (556), 1.148 (556), 16.1911.147–50 (557).

[61] *P. Oxy.* 6.994 (499) Oxyrhynchus.

cally upon lay property owners. To all appearances, rural clerics earned their livings in the fields, just as ordinary parishioners did. The disposition of benefactors to subsidize monasteries more heavily than churches may reflect the notion that monks were thought to need greater freedom from heavy labor than the ordinary clergy, who certainly faced a harder lot.[62] Both at Oxyrhynchus and elsewhere in Egypt, the evidence for the dependence of ordinary clergy upon lay landlords for their livings is strong indeed.[63] Since the peasant clerics paid rents to the Apion family in excess of the family's own donations to their village churches, it appears likely that the clerics' land grants constituted their principal means of support.[64]

Although it is not impossible that large landowners only gradually obtained control of what had once been public churches staffed with clerics chosen by the local bishops, the involvement of Count Ammonios and the Apions in the construction of churches makes it more likely that these institutions were from their origins private churches with assigned dependent clerics. After the erection of such a church, the landlord doubtless exercised his prerogative to nominate local peasants for ordination by the local bishop in accordance with his rights under Justinian's laws.

Under the circumstances, it is reasonable to question how much freedom clerics in service at estate churches were able to maintain. An Oxyrhynchus document of 581, in which a priest pledges his hereditary lands as security for a loan from an official of the Apion estate, shows that there were still some independent landowning clerics even in the late sixth century.[65] Yet it is also true that a default on his loan could easily have put this priest in a position similar to that of most other clerics of the Apion house.[66] A document of the sixth century, in which a priest and an *oikonomos* are listed among the inmates of a private prison belonging to the Apion family, illustrates just how tenuous the independence of these clerics was at Oxyrhynchus.[67] Clerics elsewhere did not fare appreciably better.[68] A series of imperial laws condemning private prisons, including a law of Zeno's with specific reference to Egypt, pro-

---

[62] See Chart 1, "Apion Estate Donations," Part 2: Size of Ordinary Wheat Donations.

[63] For a list, see Wipszycka, *Ressources*, 163, n. 1; see also Chart 2: "Peasant Clerics at Oxyrhynchus."

[64] See Wipszycka, *Ressources*, 37; cf. Chart 2, for the comparison of these donations to their rents.

[65] *P. Oxy.* 16.1892 (581), esp. lines 6–36.

[66] *P. Princ.* 2.87 (612) Oxyrhynchus, lines 8–20; *P. Oxy.* 1.136.14 establishes that Great Tarouthinos was an Apion possession.

[67] *P. Oxy.* 16.2056.14, 16 (6th c.) Oxyrhynchus; for private prisons, see Olivia Robinson, "Private Prisons," *RIDA* 15 (1968), 389–98.

[68] *P. Antin.* 3.189 (6th–7th c.) Antinoopolis.

vides evidence of official concern about the problem.[69] On the other hand, the appearance of clerics as representatives of peasant communes in various legal transactions indicates a continued degree of personal independence.[70] Naturally enough, clerical employment in positions of managerial responsibility on the great estates must have brought some prestige and security, if not complete personal independence, to the fortunate clerics involved.

FOUNDERS' RIGHTS

Like the determination of the social status of clerics, the information about founders' rights to be gleaned from the papyrological sources is implicit rather than explicit. Through observation of the landowning patrons in their business transactions with ecclesiastical institutions, it is often possible to deduce their rights from their actions. Generally speaking, patrons had economic rights that included the power to sell, bequeath, or donate some institutions and the authority to manage and exploit the properties assigned to others. In the former they evidently had the usual rights of nomination of clerics, though details are lacking.

It is the evidence of the private disposal of churches from one unrelated layman to another that proves the existence of private religious foundations in Byzantine Egypt. A sixth-century papyrus from Hermopolis stands as testimony to the sale or lease of a property in which a private church was only one (and apparently not the most important) constituent part.[71] An Aphrodito document of the same century is a contract of sale between two laymen, Hermauos and Isaak, which likewise includes a private church among the assets of the property transferred.[72]

Despite (or perhaps because of) Justinian's condemnation of the Egyptians for the secularization of monasteries, there exists no evidence in the papyri of this abuse.[73] One papyrus of 512 records the case of the orthodox monk Eulogios who sold his monastery to the Meletian priest Pous.[74] This act was in violation of imperial legislation against the transfer of ecclesiastical foundations to religious sectaries, but it is likely that this "monastery" was no more than an individual cell. Perhaps the practice of founders retaining control of the administration and exploitation

---

[69] CTh 9.11.1 (388); CJ 9.5.1 (486); CJ 9.5.2 (529).

[70] P. Cairo Masp. 3.67283 (c. 548) Aphrodito; KRU 105; KTE 7 (8th c.) Ashmunen.

[71] P. Princ. 3.180 (6th c.) Hermopolis.

[72] P. Cairo Masp. 1.67097 (early 6th c.) Aphrodito.

[73] NJ 7.11 (535); P. Oxy. 16.1890 (508), despite the misleading comments of its editors, is not a case of private monastery ownership or secularization. See Roger Rémondon, "L'Eglise," 273.

[74] SB 1.5174 (512) Arcadia in the Faiyum; cf. SB 1.5175 (513). The stereotypical formula suggests that this was a common practice; see Steinwenter, "Rechtsstellung," 5–6.

of their monasteries' lands through rental agreements or other devices
(for which see the discussion below) reduced the incentive for their successors to suppress these institutions and seize their assets.

In comparison to outright lay ownership of the foundations, those in-
stances where laymen merely rented lands from various ecclesiastical institutions might seem to have been no more than mild abridgments of
their autonomy. At Aphrodito, however, it is necessary to view the rental
of church lands by laymen against the background of lay control and
administration of the institutions themselves. Count Ammonios is already familiar as the overlord of the monastery of Apa Agenios. So is
Apollos, the count's *hypodektes* in the period 527–529. By 531 he had
become *protokometes* of Aphrodito as well.[75] Before the end of the decade, Apollos became involved in the administration of Apa Agenios, as
two papyrus documents, one firmly dated to 538 and another somewhat
earier, testify.[76] The latter of the two Apa Agenios papyri titles him "Apa
Apollos," an honorary designation meaning "father" (the equivalent of
the Latin *abba*) in Coptic. Since this title is nearly always reserved for
monks or clerics, it appears that Apollos had founded his monastery of
the Christ-bearing Apostles in the interval between the two documents.[77]
This indicates that Apollos did not give up his management of the property of Apa Agenios when he became head of his own monastery. He was
in the seemingly ambiguous position of continuing as the subordinate of
the count with respect to Apa Agenios while serving as the abbot of his
own monastery with full rights of ownership and testamentary disposition.

Both Apollos and his brother Besarion rented land from another ecclesiastical institution, the Kaine Ekklesia (New Church) of Aphrodito.[78]
The tract of land in question was the kleros Ierados, which Apollos held
as tenant for six years, probably from 521 to 526. Apparently Apollos
took over the lease of this land from his brother Besarion, who seems to
have held it as a tenant in 518. In that year Besarion decided to sublease
the tract for cultivation by two local peasants, whom he obliged to share
the crops equally with him. If another document refers to this same tract
of land, it would appear that Besarion decided to exploit the tract directly in 519 with the help of a colleague, Victor. It is interesting to find
the rental of a certain tract of church property remaining within a single

---

[75] *P. Cairo Masp.* 67301.5 (531) Aphrodito.

[76] *P. Cairo Masp.* 1.67062 (before 538) Aphrodito, and *PSI* 8.933 (538) Aphrodito.

[77] For Apollos' role as founder of this monastery, see *P. Cairo Masp.* 1.67096 (573–74)
Aphrodito; for the honorific *Apa*, see Gustave Lefebvre, *DACL* 1.2, cols. 2494–2500.

[78] *P. Lond.* 5.1694 (518), 5.1705 (519), *PSI* 8.936 (521), 8.937 (521), and *P. Cairo
Masp.* 3.67307 (524) with emendations by Gertrude Malz, "The Papyri of Dioscoros,"
Studi in onore di Aristide Calderini e Roberto Paribeni (Milan, 1957), 345–56. For this
church, see *P. Cairo Masp.* 3.67283, p. 20, line 9, and Antonini, "Chiese," 191.

family. This is, moreover, a rare case in which it is possible to trace a nearly continuous tenancy of ecclesiastical land by such a family, even though it is unlikely that this was an unusual practice in Byzantine Egypt.

The poet Dioscoros, the son of Apollos who subsequently became *phrontistes* and *kourator* in his father's monastery, apparently did not rent the kleros Ierados himself.[79] By a law of 530 Justinian placed a twenty-year limit on ordinary rentals of church lands and a three-generation limit on lands held by emphyteutic lease.[80] It is possible that at the time of his father's death in 542 Dioscoros found himself disqualified by these provisions.

Flavios Artemidoros, another familar notable of Aphrodito, held positions both as the *epitropos* of the monastery of Apa Sourous and as a *singoularis* (a tax collector) for Count Ammonios' estate. The count's disbursement to him in the latter capacity on behalf of the monastery may have been intended to meet the institution's tax obligations.[81] The monks of Apa Agenios had urged Apollos to consider employing part of the money owed them for this purpose too.

A year after Apollos' death, his son Dioscoros appears in a rent receipt granted by Artemidoros as a tenant of land belonging to the Apa Sourous monastery.[82] The substantial rent of ninety-two *artabai* (one *artabe* equals three Roman *modii* or ¾ English bushel) of wheat suggests that a considerable tract of lease land was involved here. Although it cannot be proved that this rental arose out of a traditional leaseholding agreement, here once again we have a notably close intertwining of the administrative responsibilities and financial interests of the officials of the estate.

The pattern of interrelated ownership and leaseholding as well as a tolerant attitude toward laymen and clerics who pursued mixed careers in state service, private estate administration, and the management of ecclesiastical institutions is especially clear from this evidence at Aphrodito. It is just such a social setting, in which the conception of what constituted an "ecclesiastical" or "secular" responsibility was so ambiguous, that encouraged the development of private churches and monasteries.

The presence of estate officials like Apollos and Artemidoros at

---

[79] For Dioscoros, see Malz, "Dioscoros," 345–47; Jean Maspero, "Un dernier poète grec d'Egypte: Dioscore, fils d'Apollôs," *REG* 24 (1911), 426–81; Leslie MacCoull, "The Coptic Archive of Dioscorus of Aphrodito," *Chronique d'Egypte* 56 (1981), 185–93.

[80] *CJ* 1.2.24.4–5 (530), confirmed by *NJ* 7.3.1 (535); for the emphyteutic lease, see Howard Comfort, "Emphyteusis among the Papyri," *Aegyptus* 17 (1937), 3–24.

[81] *P. Cairo Masp.* 1.67088 (551), where he appears as *desponikos dioiketes tes komes Aphrodites,* and 2.67139F6v.3 (528); cf. *P. Cairo Masp.* 1.67062 (before 538).

[82] *P. Cairo Masp.* 2.67133 (543) Aphrodito; cf. *P. Cairo Masp.* 1.67087 (543), in which Dioscoros prosecutes the "son of Mousaios" for damage inflicted on another tract of land that he held from the monastery of Apa Sourous.

Aphrodito and Menas at Oxyrhynchus in high administrative posts in estate-supported monasteries almost certainly was the result of the exercise of lay rights of nomination of clerical personnel. Yet there is little direct testimony on the operation of these traditional rights of patrons in Egypt. An important but badly damaged document of 334 from Hathor shows a priest, Aurelios Pageos, arranging with the *proestotes* of a monastery to allow his brother Gerontios to assume Pageos' duties temporarily during his expected absence at a synod in Caesarea.[83] The agreement entitled Gerontios to oversee, administer, and act as financial steward for the monastery, as well as to appoint *oikonomoi*, provided that he did not attempt any innovations from established practices. Although not himself a layman, Pageos clearly held some position analogous to the lay *phrontistai* and *kouratores* discussed above. One of these, Count Johannes, did not hesitate to call to account and depose a *proestos* who had brought his monastery to financial ruin.[84] It seems reasonable, then, to assume that lay patrons, like Pageos and Gerontios, also made use of their powers of nomination and appointment in accordance with Justinian's legislation.

There is more explicit testimony on these rights from Coptic sources of the seventh and eighth centuries.[85] A letter from a suffragan to his superior bishop, for example, protests against the latter's reluctance to accept a priest ordained by the former.[86] The suffragan bishop declares the priest in question innocent of any taint of simony, emphasizing that the priest's nominators had moved him to bestow ordination rather than any illegal payment by the nominee himself. The suffragan's letter treats private nomination simply as a step in the usual process by which an individual became a priest.

A series of ostraca contains the sureties of candidates proposed to a bishop for clerical ordination or promotion.[87] This was a procedure required by Coptic canon law. The sureties were often clerics themselves, sometimes related to the candidates. Parish priests coopted colleagues this way in the early seventh century.[88] In one particularly relevant case, however, the sureties were laymen, and the church in question may well have been a private one, since it bore the name of a village rather than

---

[83] *P. Lond.* 1913 (334) Herakleopolis, ed. H. Idris Bell, *Jews and Christians in Egypt* (London, 1924), particularly lines 13–14; cf. Steinwenter, "Rechtsstellung," 21, with references.

[84] *P. Fouad* 1.87.

[85] See Artur Steinwenter, "Die Ordinationsbitten koptischer Kleriker," *Aegyptus* 11 (1931), 29–34.

[86] *VC* 39.

[87] *Ps–Basil* 47, trans. Wilhelm Riedel, *Die Kirchenrechtsquellen des Patriarchats Alexandrien* (Leipzig, 1900), 261.

[88] As in *CO* 36.

of a saint.[89] Perhaps the right to propose candidates and the obligation to stand surety for them were regarded together as an integral part of the nomination process.

FINANCIAL SUPPORT OF PRIVATE RELIGIOUS FOUNDATIONS

The papyri provide much more evidence than the legislation of Justinian for the financing of private foundations in Egypt, but the terminology familiar from the legal sources (for example, *sitesis*, *dapane*, and *choregia*) is almost entirely absent. Instead, we meet with six different types of financial support.[90] First, there are regular grants of cash to institutions, *collegia* of clergy or monks, or even on occasion to individuals, perhaps as representatives of *collegia*. These donations resemble the *presbia ton annalion*, the annual legacies or "annuities" regulated by Justinian in several laws.[91] Although the usual beneficiaries of *presbia* were a testator's relatives, ecclesiastical institutions and colleges of clergy were also eligible to receive them. Second, we find at Aphrodito disbursements in wheat earmarked as *ekphoria* from the benefactor Ammonios' properties. These will be discussed in detail below. Third, both at Aphrodito and at Oxyrhynchus there are records of other commodities supplied in kind, including barley, wine, and vinegar. Fourth, there are special cash donations on holidays, for feasts, or for special memorial services. Fifth, we occasionally find cash disbursements for specific purposes, for example, the payment of taxes and the purchase of bricks and firewood. Sixth, the so-called *prosphora* donations, perhaps the most common grants of all, are found throughout Egypt wherever documentary evidence is preserved.

The evidence from the papyri reveals, therefore, a variety and complexity in the forms of lay support for churches and other ecclesiastical institutions at which the legislation of Justinian only hints. A complicating consideration is that some of what appear at first to be charitable disbursements may have been payments for goods or services provided by the institutions as part of existing economic relationships between

---

[89] CO 31.

[90] Unspecialized, periodic donations: *P. Cairo Masp.* 2.67139F4r.7–8 (to religious institutions), 39F4r.9 (to a *sustema* or *collegium*), 38F1r.4 (to an individual); *prosphora* donations: see the detailed discusssion below, with examples in notes; disbursements from *ekphoria*: *P. Cairo Masp.* 2.67138F2r, 38F3r.27, 34, 39F4r; disbursements for specific purposes: *P. Cairo Masp.* 2.67139F6v.15 (for taxes), 39F5r.19 (for vegetables), 39F5r.20 (for bricks), 39F5r.23 (for bricks), 38F1v.8 (for firewood); commodities supplied in kind: *P. Oxy.* 16.1910–12, 18.2195 (wheat), *PSI* 8.953 (wine and vinegar), *P. Oxy.* 18.2197.11, 185 (bricks); *Stud. Pal.* 3.299 and *P. Cairo Masp.* 2.67139F6v.3 (barley); holiday, festal, and memorial donations: *P. Cairo Masp.* 2.67139F3r,25, 67141F5r.22–24, 28–29, *P. Oxy.* 16.1945.

[91] *CJ* 6.48.1.15–16, 26 (528–29); *CJ* 1.3.45.9–15 (530); cf. *CJ* 1.2.25 (530).

landowners and their religious foundations. It is, for example, not always possible to determine if a laconic entry in an estate register means "Give X amount of money to Y so he can buy Z for his institution," or "Give X amount of money to Y in exchange for commodity Z sold to us." The *prosphora* and memorial donations often were treated more like payments than grants since they were offered in exchange for some sort of memorial service in accordance with the expressed intentions of the donor. These nevertheless constituted important sources of financial support for the beneficiary institutions. Moreover, there was wide variation in the means of support employed by benefactors in different places. The natures of their respective household economies may have accounted for the preference of the Apion family for distributions in kind, while at Aphrodito under Count Ammonios cash allowances were more common.

PROSPHORA DONATIONS

Prosphora donations deserve special consideration. It is possible to distinguish two forms of these donations, *prosphora inter vivos* and *mortis causa*.[92] The former occurred through the generosity of living benefactors, and had affinity with other unspecialized forms of financial support for private ecclesiastical institutions. Some of these donations may actually have been contractual fulfillments of earlier testamentary benefactions that come under the designation of *prosphora mortis causa*. Benefactors provided grants of this latter sort from a deceased Christian's estate in expectation of prayers or memorial masses for his or her soul.[93]

Benefactors usually tendered *inter vivos* donations in the form of commodities.[94] In the case of a large donation, such as the 150 *artabai* of wheat that a certain Count Eudaimon provided as *prosphora* for an unnamed institution at Oxyrhynchus in 481, the grant may have been a credit given the foundation with the count's baker, which it could draw upon as needed in the form of baked bread.[95] The entries in Apion estate registers noting the provision of so many *artabai* of wheat or *diplai* of wine for a given indiction year "according to the orders of Our Master" seem to tally all the vouchers of this sort provided to each beneficiary

---

[92] For *prosphora*, see G. W. H. Lampe, *A Patristic Greek Lexicon* (Oxford, 1961), 1184, and Wipszycka, *Ressources*, 64–71; for the distinction between *inter vivos* and *mortis causa*, see *CJ* 1.2.14.1 (470); see also Richard Kay, "Benedict, Justinian, and Donations 'Mortis Causa' in the 'Regula Magistri'," *RB* 90 (1980), 169–93.

[93] See particularly Leopold Wenger, "Eine Schenkung auf den Todesfall," *ZSR* 32, *Romanistische Abteilung* (1911), 325–37, esp. 331–32, a commentary on *P. Mon.* 8.

[94] *P. Oxy.* 10.1322 (413), 16.1949 (481), *Ps-Ath.* 64, and *PSI* 8.953 (567–68).

[95] *P. Oxy.* 16.1949 (481).

institution.[96] Yet an Oxyrhynchus document of 587 shows that estate managers sometimes preferred other arrangements.[97] The stewards of the Apion household in this case delivered 371 *artabai* of wheat all at once to a *nosokomeion*, for which the institution's *oikonomos*, our acquaintance the notary Menas, gave a receipt.[98] Perhaps the philanthropic institutions, with their large resident populations, had their own baking facilities (as monasteries often did), or sold what they could not use on the open market.[99]

The size of the *prosphora* donations also varied considerably. At Oxyrhynchus, for instance, the Apion family provided the *nosokomeion* of Abba Elias with a *prosphora* grant of 371 *artabai* of wheat, while another institution received only 4 *artabai*.[100] Even the grant to a particular institution might vary greatly from year to year. Count Ammonios, for example, provided the monastery of Apa Patemos in Aphrodito with grants of 45, 6, and 13 *artabai* of wheat respectively for three consecutive indiction years.[101]

The requirements of bread and wine for the liturgy doubtless determined the specific form assumed by *prosphora* donations *inter vivos*.[102] Yet it seems clear that the *prosphora* represented more than a simple provision of these eucharistic elements in many cases. Philanthropic institutions and monasteries nearly always received donations larger than those of churches, and in general only they received more than purely nominal amounts each year. This suggests that the *prosphora* was also used to support the nutritional needs of the staffs of these institutions.

Some *prosphora* donations *inter vivos* may have represented a voluntary tithe on agricultural produce levied upon each seasonal harvest. This would account for annual variations. Perhaps John Chrysostom had something similar in mind when he urged private church founders to provide *apomoirai* (portions) and *aparchai* (first fruits) as "dowries" for their foundations. Coptic canon law agreed with John Chrysostom in viewing donations of *prosphora* as the natural accompaniment to the erection of a new church by a benefactor.[103] Complaints that arose from cases in which benefactors were reluctant to meet their traditional obligations in this respect prove that in post-Byzantine times the *prosphora*

[96] As *PSI* 8.953 (567–68) Oxyrhynchus, lines 30, 31, and 82–83.
[97] *P. Oxy.* 16.1898 (587).
[98] *P. Oxy.* 16.1898 (587).
[99] *P. Oxy.* 16.1890 (508) Oxyrhynchus, and *KRU* 106 (735) Djême.
[100] See Chart 1, "Apion Estate Donations," Part 2, "Size of Wheat Donations."
[101] *P. Cairo Masp.* 2.67139F4r.8 (7th ind.), 67138F2r.31 (8th ind.), 67139F6r.12 (9th ind.).
[102] So Wipszycka, *Ressources*, 66–67.
[103] Ps-Ath. 87 (Coptic Version), ed. Wilhelm Riedel, *The Canons of Athanasius of Alexandria* (London, 1904) (for the date and attribution of these canons, see Wipszycka, *Ressources*, 14–17), in which *prosphora* is employed to mean "offerings."

donations remained voluntary and thus subject to arbitrary suspension.[104] Moreover, Emperor Anastasius had associated *prosphorai* and *aparchai* in his law banning the compulsory collection of these offerings by the church. It seems then that the landlords themselves might have to provide the *prosphorai* that they could not compel their tenant cultivators to pay to the churches.

Attestation in the sources for *prosphora* donations *mortis causa* is relatively late (from A.D. 567), but still within the period when there is extensive documentation for *inter vivos* donations.[105] Most of our information comes naturally enough from last wills and testaments. There was a close connection between *prosphora* donations of this sort and the undertaking of funeral services for the deceased.[106] Indeed, some sort of provision for an offering for prayers for the soul of the deceased seems to have been a common practice, especially among the Coptic Christian population.[107]

The exact form of the services expected of the ecclesiastical institution in exchange for the *prosphora* donation must remain conjectural. A list of offerings to the monastery of the church of St. Sergius in Nessana in the early seventh century includes *prosphora* donations, with strokes appended after some entries, seeming to indicate the performance of memorial masses.[108] Other documents refer to memorial days connected with *prosphora* donations.[109] Several testaments speak of a *prosphora* obligation contracted for a specified number of months or years.[110] Perhaps the size or the value of the donation determined the number of years that the recipient monastery would continue to offer the customary services for the soul of the deceased on his or her memorial days.[111] Flavius Phoibammon, the physician of Antinoe, made testamentary provision for a *prosphora* donation and stipulated that the recipient monastery should accord him the exceptional honor of receiving his body for burial within its walls.[112]

[104] H. R. Hall, *Coptic and Greek Texts*, pl. 63, no. 3.

[105] Earliest *mortis causa* donations: P. Cairo Masp. 1.67003 and 3.67312 (ca. 567); latest *inter vivos* donations: P. Oxy. 16.1898, 1993 (587).

[106] See Eberhard F. Bruck, *Totenteil und Seelgerat im griechischen Recht* (Munich, 1926), esp. 302–17; also P. Lond. 1.78 (ca. 610) line 57, P. Mon. 8, and Ps-Basil 31.

[107] KRU 68 (729 or 744) Djême and VC 5 (620) Edfou.

[108] P. Ness. 2.79 (early 7th c.) Nessana, lines 25–43, with editor's comments, p. 229.

[109] P. Lond. 1.78 (ca. 610), lines 57–59; P. Cairo Masp. 2.67151 (570) Arsinoe, lines 163–68; KRU 77 (634) Djême. According to Ps-Basil, the custom of keeping memorial days for the dead dated back to Const. Apost. 8.42, ed. F. X. Funk (Paderborn, 1905).

[110] KRU 66/76 (ca. 700), 70 (750) Djême.

[111] Note P. Bal. 2.306 (8th c.) Deir el-Bala'izah, which is probably a list of persons entitled to memorial masses, perhaps a *katalogos ton makarion* as mentioned in P. Cairo Masp. 2.67151.

[112] P. Cairo Masp. 2.67151 (570) Arsinoe, lines 164–65. In later Byzantine times this was a special right reserved for the founder of an institution.

In 733 there was an unusual case of the alienation of a *prosphora* bequest, the proceeds of which a Theban abbot used for "the table of the poor" and the requirements of his monastery for assuring "the health [of the soul] of blessed Peschate."[113] These uses may indicate the usual employment of *prosphora* income. A Theban donor of 735 urged the sale of the property that constituted his *prosphora* donation, with the proceeds to be used for charity and the expenses of the monastery.[114]

Apparently only monasteries were recipients of *prosphora* donations *mortis causa*, but this may be due to accidents of preservation.[115] The actual donations might consist of landed property, wine or other commodities, or cash raised from the liquidation of movable property and real estate.[116] Once made, the donation became a permanent, inalienable part of the monastery's estate, its *diakonia*.[117]

The varied nature of what was offered as *prosphora* must have made conversions to liquid assets necessary from time to time. Thoughtful donors provided ahead of time for the liquidation of such properties.[118] Estate executors exercised a vague intermediary role between the deceased donor's estate and the *diakonia* of the monastery in this connection.[119] A certain Plein, said to have donated all of his land to a monastery as a soul offering, is mentioned in a document of the eighth century.[120] Nevertheless, in the very same document his surviving children renounce their rights to this land, which Plein actually had conveyed to them rather than the monastery at his death. Perhaps in this and similar cases the recipient monastery leased back to the donor's family by emphyteusis in exchange for rental income the lands that made up the *prosphora* donation.

Other documents which show a delay of varying length between the time of initial donation and that of final occupation by the recipient monastery give additional evidence that the intermediary's role sometimes extended beyond that of a testamentary executor to that of a tenant on

---

[113] *KRU* 13 (733) Djême.

[114] *KRU* 106 (735) Djême.

[115] Wipszycka, *Ressources*, 75, notes that pious Egyptians much preferred monasteries to churches for the performance of memorial mass services, or at least so it would seem on the basis of surviving evidence.

[116] *P. Cairo Masp.* 2.67151 (570), 3.67312 (567), and *KRU* 70 (750).

[117] *P. Cairo Masp.* 1.67003, lines 15–22, 2.67151, lines 121–23.

[118] In *KRU* 69 (729 or 744) a woman ordains that her husband should sell her share in a house and its attached property to her brother, then give the proceeds to a monastery as her *prosphora*. *KRU* 13 (733) is a unique example of the alienation of a *prosphora* bequest by a recipient monastery, but the varied nature of what might be given, e.g., the household furnishings, must have made conversion to more useful assets necessary from time to time.

[119] E.g., the husband of the author of *KRU* 69. *CPR* 4.178 (6th c.) and *ST* 56 are both addressed to intermediaries, with instructions to hand over the property of the donors after their decease to designated monasteries as *prosphora*.

[120] H. R. Hall, *Coptic Texts*, pl. 66, no. 2.

the donated land.[121] In a Coptic papyrus of 703 a monk tells of his near fatal illness which occasioned a *prosphora* donation to his home monastery. When his son nursed him back to health, the monks of the community declared, "Your son has snatched you away from your illness; it is right, then, that he should minister your *prosphora*." The monk then declares in this document: ". . . as it was agreed, they gave me everything that I had given them, to the last coin. I have given it to my son, so that he will give it for me." Another Coptic papyrus of the first third of the eighth century records the *prosphora* bequest of a certain Johanna to the *oikonomos* of a monastery which was only carried out much later by her son George. Documents of this sort indicate that there was something compensatory, or at least honorific, about the administration of a *prosphora* bequest that made the executor's role quite desirable for a relative of the deceased.

In the absence of financial accounts for the monasteries of Byzantine and Coptic Egypt, it is very difficult to estimate the importance of *prosphora* donations as a source of income for religious institutions. Perhaps it is significant that *proestos* Jacob of the Phoibammon monastery in Thebes mentioned in his will of A.D. 695 that the administration of *prosphora* was one of his principal responsibilities.[122] In the Byzantine Empire, from the late ninth century, commemorative offerings similar to *prosphora* donations *mortis causa* did play an important part in the support of monasteries and philanthropic institutions as well as small village churches.[123]

TAX OBLIGATIONS AND FINANCIAL DIFFICULTIES

The fact that ecclesiastical institutions and their properties were not routinely tax-exempt in the Byzantine Empire set the stage for a continuing series of disagreements between church and state authorities. The Egyptian sources give ample testimony to this state of affairs. A sixth-century document of unknown provenance shows the director of a monastery in the midst of negotiations with a *dux* for an extension of a deadline for a tax payment.[124] Other documents show that fiscally troubled monasteries borrowed money to pay their taxes from the tax collectors themselves,

---

[121] *CLT* 2 (703), *KRU* 18 (700–733) Djême, and the noteworthy *P. Cairo Masp.* 1.67003 (before 522?), esp. at lines 15–22, a letter of complaint by some monks to Flavios Marianos, *dux* of the Thebaid, concerning a *prosphora* dedication belonging to the *diakonia* of their monastery but contested by a certain Ezechiel.

[122] *KRU* 65 (ca. 695) Djême, lines 4–5.

[123] See the discussion below in Chapter 6.

[124] *SB* 6.9607 (6th c.) provenance unknown.

pledging their future revenues as security.[125] Under Arab rule, some institutions also borrowed from wealthy members of their own communities in order to meet their tax obigations.[126] Since many tax collectors in that era were clerics themselves, financially pressed institutions had some flexibility in meeting their obligations to the government.[127] Individual clerics sometimes had to sell their own lands when the revenues they obtained from them no longer sufficed even to pay the tax obligations.[128] Institutions also unburdened themselves of lands for this reason, in accordance with Justinian's special provision in his law on the alienation of church property.[129]

In Byzantine times the sources speak chiefly of taxes on church lands rather than on the churches themselves.[130] These lands were also subject to general imposts, such as the *embole*, destined for the distributions of wheat in the great cities of Alexandria and Constantinople.[131] In Aphrodito in the sixth century clerics paid a head tax just like other villagers, suggesting that clerical immunity from *capitatio* was now a thing of the past.[132] From Byzantine times into the period of Arab rule some churches in Aphrodito and Hermopolis also paid a unit tax in gold.[133]

Local imperial officials were zealous in exacting tax obligations, real or imagined. Thirteen clerics and a monk joined their fellow villagers of Aphrodito sometime before 548 in protesting to Theodora, consort of Justinian, against the unjust tax exactions of the local ruler, the pagarch of Antaeopolis.[134] In another protest, the monks of the monastery of Psinepolis complained to an unnamed ecclesiastical dignitary that Menas, another pagarch of Antaeopolis, had demanded public taxes (*demosia*)

---

[125] *P. Bad.* 6.173 (ca. 600) provenance unknown; *P. Bal.* 2.102, cf. 103 and 125. Kahle's introduction to his edition of *P. Bal.*, Vol. 1, pp. 41–42, provides a useful discussion of the taxation of Christian churches and monasteries in Egypt in post-Byzantine times.

[126] E.g., *P. Bal.* 2.293.

[127] *P. Bal.* 2.133, 136, 145, 290.

[128] *P. Cairo Masp.* 1.67088 (551?) Aphrodito, with editor's comments.

[129] *P. Michael.* 41 (539 or 554) Aphrodito, with editor's comments at pp. 79–80, shows a monastery that gave away its share in a property in order to avoid taxes; cf. *P. Cairo Masp.* 1.67117 (524) Aphrodito, which is a record of registration of the new owners of a property that had once belonged to a monastery; Justinian's law is *NJ* 46 (547).

[130] *P. Lond.* 3.1060, 3.1070A-D, 5.1782 (7th c.) Hermopolis, as discussed above in the text in connection with lay *pronoetai* in the service of the cathedral church of Hermopolis.

[131] *SB* 6.9144 (589) Aphrodito; *P. Cairo Masp.* 2.67138F1r.10, 15, cf. 1.67030; discussed by R. Rémondon, "Le monastère alexandrin de la Métanoia était-il bénéficiaire du fisc ou à son service?" in *Studi E. Volterra*, Vol. 5 (Milan, 1971), 769–81, and by Gascou, "Monastères pachômiens," 178–83.

[132] *P. Cairo Masp.* 3.67288 (early 6th c.) Aphrodito, col. 2, line 19; col. 3, line 16; col. 4, lines 24 and 34; col. 6, line l. The gradual disappearance of clerical immunity from *capitatio* is discussed above in Chapter 1.

[133] *P. Cairo Masp.* 3.67288 (early 6th c.) Aphrodito, col. 6, lines 1 and 5; *BM Copt.* 1100, Hermopolis.

[134] *P. Cairo Masp.* 3.67283 (ca. 548) p. 2, lines 1–10; p. 3, lines 21–22.

from lands traditionally exempt.[135] Menas did not shrink from using armed force to exact the disputed dues. The monks capitulated and paid three installments of the taxes. For a time the pagarch took over the administration of the monastery's property. The document unfortunately is quite damaged, making it impossible to understand the details of the dispute, but the dire consequences of misunderstandings with the authorities in disputes over taxes are clear enough. Perhaps defaults on tax obligations are one reason why some ecclesiastical institutions came under the curatorship of government officials.[136]

The Arsinoe physician Flavius Phoibammon arranged for his heirs to assume the tax obligations for the land he gave to the monastery of St. Jeremias as his *prosphora* donation.[137] Likewise, Count Ammonios appears to have paid the *demosia* for a church of St. Romanus in Aphrodito.[138] Later, Coptic canon law would insist on this sort of arrangement as a precondition for accepting any bequest of property.[139] While these arrangements must have helped to insure the institutions against disputes with officials such as that which faced the monks of Psinepolis, they inevitably required a continued interest of the heirs in their internal affairs as the price of continued payments on their behalf.

The church of Apollinopolis fulfilled a special obligation sometime in the sixth century by quartering troops. A papyrus receipt records this unusual government imposition on a cathedral church.[140] Under Arab rule, special exactions increased. Monasteries in some localities stood under obligation to provide expense money for local governors.[141] As early as the late fourth century, the officials of the *katholike ekklesia* of Alexandria had depended upon government officials to bring their own disobedient *pronoetai* to account.[142] Again, the situation worsened in later centuries, and certain monasteries were under the protection of Coptic Christian officials.[143] Doubtless the uncertain attitude of the Muslim authorities did much to foster this reliance on friendly local officials who were coreligionists.

It appears that private patrons heeded Justinian's prescriptions for the support of religious foundations. With the exception of tax obligations,

---

[135] *P. Cairo Masp.* 1.67021 (before 567) Aphrodito(?).

[136] E.g., Count Johannes in *P. Fouad.* 1.87 and Count Ammonios in *PSI* 8.933 and elsewhere (both of the sixth century); the *dux* and *phrontistes* Senouthios in *Stud. Pal.* 3.271B (7th c.); Lord Psmo, *archon* and *phrontistes* in *KRU* 104 (8th c.).

[137] *P. Cairo Masp.* 2.67151 (570) Antinoe.

[138] *P. Cairo Masp.* 2.67139F6v.15; cf. 39F6r.2 and 67138F1r.4.

[139] *Ps–Basil* 86.

[140] *P. Grenf.* 2.95 (6th c.) Apollinopolis.

[141] *P. Bal.* 2.294, line 1, 2.301, line 11.

[142] *SB* 6.9527 (385–412) Arsinoe.

[143] *VC* 8 (698 or 728) Djême; cf. *VC* 9, apparently a version of 8, and *KRU* 104 (771–72) Djême.

the sources are almost silent about Egyptian ecclesiastical institutions, especially private foundations, in serious financial difficulty.[144]

The public churches, being more dependent on the voluntary offerings of their parishioners, did face difficult times under Muslim rule.[145] Coptic canon law expected that churches would expend their whole income for eucharistic offerings, maintenance of clergy, illumination of the building, and charity for the poor.[146] There was, however, no provision for building maintenance, despite Justinian's requirement that founders see to this need. Coptic canon law simply obliged the bishop to ensure that churches did not fall into serious disrepair. The tendency of Islamic law to discourage or prohibit the rebuilding of Christian churches doubtless exacerbated the problem.

Coptic canon law directed churches with insufficient incomes to seek assistance from their bishops, but recommended recourse to a "rich man" if their prelates were unable to help.[147] Concurrent legislation against clerics who frequented the "houses of the rich" seems to indicate a movement of clergy into private service accompanying the commendation of churches to these powerful patrons.[148] Similar problems troubled the ecclesiastical hierarchy in Byzantium from the early seventh century until the formal recognition of the status of clergy in private service in the late ninth century.

PRIVATE RELIGIOUS FOUNDATIONS IN OXYRHYNCHUS

The papyri from Aphrodito and Oxyrhynchus supply the most fully detailed picture of the operation of private religious foundations in specific localities. The list of ecclesiastical institutions that the Apion family supported in Oxyrhynchus by itself documents a veritable ecclesiastical empire, including forty-seven churches, eleven monasteries, two *martyria*, and four philanthropic institutions.[149] The extent of the philanthropy of the Apion household has no parallel anywhere else in the Egyptian sources, even in Aphrodito, where the benefactions of Count Ammonios appear quite impressive. This said, it must be noted that many of the

---

[144] *P. Fouad.* 1.87 (6th c.), esp. lines 21–24, with Gascou, "Monastères pachômiens," 163–77.

[145] On the revenues of the public churches in post-Byzantine times, see *Ps-Ath.* 61, 63, 65.

[146] *Ps-Ath.* 65.

[147] *Ps-Ath.* 23.

[148] *Ps-Ath.* 24, cf. 22.

[149] For Christian institutions at Oxyrhynchus, see G. Modena, "Il Cristianesimo ad Ossirinco secondo i papiri," *BSAA* 9 (1937), 254–69; G. Pfeilschifter, "Oxyrhynchus: Seine Kirchen und Klöster," *Festgabe Alois Knöpfler gewidemet* (Freiburg, 1917), 248–64; P. Barison, "Ricerche," 75–83; L. Antonini, "Chiese," 172–83; and Chart 1, "Apion Estate Donations," Part 1, "Recipient Institutions."

Apion household's donations were nonetheless quite small. As far as wheat distributions were concerned, for example, only seven institutions received more than 10 *artabai*, while thirty-four received this amount or less.[150] It is not likely that the less fortunate institutions were able to subsist on such small annual disbursements of grain.[151] Yet the needs of a small church, with a single priest and perhaps a deacon attending, were actually more modest than one might imagine. An austere monk, for example, might subsist on a year's rations of 12 artabai of wheat.[152] Moreover, it was not necessary to maintain the clergy of estate churches at leisure. A landlord would ordinarily expect these clerics to provide most of their own support from working rented lands.

The possibility cannot be excluded that some of these churches were merely lay-assisted rather than true private churches and were able to count on supplementary revenues from other neighboring property owners or their own parishioners. It is also possible that their clergy had the benefit of some less readily apparent financial support, such as tenure of rental property at reduced rates.[153] Since the Apion estate registers do not provide any clues to the relative quality of the lands held by each tenant, it is impossible to test this hypothesis. Yet even if it could be established that the Apion family did not provide any special assistance to support the clergy of these churches, the evident restrictions on their personal liberty would suffice to indicate that the churches in which they served are unlikely to have been any more independent of this great landowning household.[154]

It is important in this regard not to confuse material prosperity with personal freedom. In the late sixth century the priest Paulos, a tenant of the Apion *epoikion* of Papsau, paid the estate managers over 76 *artabai* of wheat and somewhat less than 4 *nomismata* (*solidi*) in cash as the annual rent for his landholding.[155] The rent alone indicates that his holding was more than adequate to support him in comfort. Incidentally, the Apion household itself donated only 4 *artabai* of wheat and 1/2 *nomisma* to the church of Papsau where Paulos probably served.[156] Perhaps then a preferential rate on rents for clerics was not really necessary, provided that their landlords supplied them with sufficiently large properties from which they could support themselves. Once the estate managers had made this provision, they needed only to concern themselves with the

---

[150] See Chart 1, "Apion Estate Donations," Part 2, "Size of Wheat Donations."
[151] So Wipszycka, *Ressources*, 81.
[152] Jones, *LRE*, 792.
[153] Wipszycka, *Ressources*, 81–82.
[154] See especially *P. Oxy.* 16.2056.14, 16 (6th c.).
[155] *P. Oxy.* 16.1912.35 (584 or 599).
[156] *P. Oxy.* 16.1912.116.

liturgical (that is, eucharistic) requirements of the churches themselves. The 4 *artabai* of wheat and the 20 *diplai* of wine attested by another Apion estate document might well have sufficed for the celebration of the liturgy during each indiction year.[157]

Justinian, by contrast, seems to have envisioned that the clergy of private churches would receive a salary (either in cash or in kind) from their patrons. Yet the emperor may have legislated with an urban setting in mind where the possibility that a priest could make a living from the land was foreclosed.[158] The Apion household's arrangements for supporting clerics in the countryside seem to preserve the spirit, if not the letter, of the emperor's legislation. Moreover, the provision of bricks to clergy and churches by the estate managers might represent, at least in part, a fulfillment of Justinian's injunction to patrons to provide for building maintenance.

Although in the fiscal registers of the household the churches supported by the family take on the names of the estates in which they were located, it is reasonably certain that they bore the usual patronal titles in honor of the saints, the Blessed Virgin, or the archangels. In a document of 612 a peasant of the estate of Great Tarouthinos acknowledges a loan from the doorkeeper of the church of St. Theodore.[159] Since this was an Apion possession, it is probable that the Ekklesia Tarouthinos of the fiscal registers was this same St. Theodore's.[160] The fiscal managers' habit of referring to recipient churches by estate names increases the likelihood that these institutions were owned by the Apion family. By contrast, the registers usually do identify monasteries by their proper names, and always do so for philanthropic institutions.[161] This in turn would seem to indicate that they enjoyed greater autonomy than the estate churches.

A good number of the churches in Oxyrhynchus are identifiable by their proper names, thanks to a calendar of station churches dating to 536/7.[162] This is a list of the churches at which the bishop celebrated the liturgy on the major feasts of the year. The presence of St. Theodore's in this document is noteworthy.[163] Apparently diocesan officials did not treat Apion private churches as off limits and outside their spiritual jurisdiction, which is not surprising in view of Justinian's legislation on the subject. The appearance of other Apion churches in this calendar dem-

---

[157] *PSI* 8.953.8 (567) Oxyrhynchus.

[158] See especially *NJ* 57 (537).

[159] *P. Princ.* 2.87 (612) Oxyrhynchus.

[160] According to *P. Oxy.* 1.135.13–14, Great Tarouthinos was an Apion possession; for the *ekklesia* of this estate, see *P. Oxy.* 16.1911.72 (577).

[161] See Chart 1, "Apion Estate Donations."

[162] *P. Oxy.* 11.1357 (536–37) with the valuable commentary by the editors.

[163] *P. Oxy.* 11.1357.65; cf. line 63.

onstrates that they played a full and active part in the liturgical life of the greater Christian community in Oxyrhynchus.[164]

A curious Oxyrhynchite papyrus document of the sixth century provides an unusual insight into the means and life-style of one member of the rural clergy. He was a priest and a village elder of the Apion estate of Spania. In this document's account of furnishings stolen from his house appear a supply of grain, hammers, knives, and kitchen equipment; priestly vestments and small patens; household furnishings such as a reclining couch, a mattress, and a carpet.[165] Since the plunderers did not neglect to take the iron fittings of the doors, it is safe to assume that nothing of any value has been omitted from the list. The picture of this priest's possessions shows that he was surprisingly comfortable for his modest position as a village cleric. He had on hand an amazing 240 *artabai* of wheat, and the net value of his household furnishings alone was 86 *nomismata*. Perhaps it was his prosperity that made him a tempting target for the robbery in the first place. One hundred and twelve of his fellow villagers (including six other priests, a deacon, and the *epitropos* of a *xenodocheion*) had to compensate him for his losses. Aside from the testimony to this priest's personal fortune, the document incidentally provides an idea of the complement of clergy assigned to the religious institutions of an Apion village.

Of all these institutions, the monastery of St. Andreas in Oxyrhynchus provides the best picture of the implications of lay control over a religious foundation by this famous family. The dimensions of the support that various members of the Apion household afforded this monastery alone suffice to provide grounds for suspecting that this was a private religious institution. For example, the monastery received a customary donation each year of 1,000 *artabai* of wheat.[166] This grant, the largest for any estate supported institution in Byzantine Egypt, came at the specific written orders of Flavius Apion II, head of the household and consul in 539. In addition, the monastery received 12 *artabai* on "the day of the great man," probably the birthday of Apion himself. His son Strategios II also gave another 100 *artabai* of wheat out of his own resources. The

---

[164]St. Philoxenos (lines 24–27, 38, 58, 64) may also be an Apion church (cf. *Stud. Pal.* 10.35, line 11) if this document is actually from the Apion archives; likewise for St. Euphemia, mentioned both in the list of station churches (lines 41, 51) and in *Stud. Pal.* 10.35, line 6; much more certain is St. Serenos (lines 4, 28, 29, 53), attested as an Apion *martyrion* in *P. Oxy.* 16.1912.92. Although churches of St. Phoibammon and of the archangel Michael appear both in the list of station churches and in Apion estate documents (see Chart 1), the names are much too common to permit certain identification (cf. *BM Copt.* 1100, which shows there were three churches of the archangel Michael at Hermopolis).

[165]*P. Oxy.* 16.2058 (6th c.) Oxyrhynchus.

[166]*P. Oxy.* 16.1911.147–51.

household then paid the *chartoularios* John to transport the total of 1,112 *artabai* to the monastery.[167]

In return, the monastery supplied a number of free products to other dependents of the Apion estate. In 566 its *proestos* gave four reed mats to Justos, "water-pourer of the landlord's bath of the Great House," for the use of two doorkeepers.[168] At about the same time, the monks provided a cord of rope for the water bucket in the baptistry of St. Mary's, apparently an Apion private church.[169] A third contemporary document shows the monastery arranging for the transportation of hay from the landlord's loft to the monastery's stable.[170] All of these documents testify to the close relationship that existed between the monastery and the routine operations of the Apion estate.

There is little information on how closely the Apion family supervised the management of the ecclesiastical institutions on their properties. The double role of Menas, both an estate notary and the *oikonomos* of the *nosokomeion* of Abba Elias, suggests that the family insisted on tight control of these foundations.[171] That the family could order a monastery to provide bread for the tenants of one of their estates confirms the inference.[172]

There is a need for additional study of the estate registers to determine the size of clerical holdings and the amounts of rent owed, especially as compared to holdings and rents of tenants who were not clergy. Although the nature of the evidence makes it difficult to answer many questions, it may yet be possible to make further determinations about the status of the clergy in Oxyrhynchus and the means of their support by the Apion family.

PRIVATE RELIGIOUS FOUNDATIONS IN APHRODITO

Papyri from the town of Aphrodito provide another detailed picture of the financing of private religious foundations in Byzantine Egypt in the sixth century.[173] Once again, the most useful evidence comes from estate

[167] P. Oxy. 16.1911.152–3.

[168] P. Oxy. 1.148 (= Stud. Pal. 3.282) (556) Oxyrhynchus.

[169] P. Oxy. 1.147 (= Stud. Pal. 3.281) (556) Oxyrhynchus; this is perhaps the same church as the St. Mary's mentioned in P. Oxy. 18.2197.11 as the recipient of bricks from the Apion household (cf. St. Mary's as a station church in P. Oxy. 11.1357, lines 30–32, 45, 68).

[170] P. Oxy. 1.146 (= Stud. Pal. 3.280) (555) Oxyrhynchus.

[171] P. Oxy. 16.1898 (587).

[172] P. Oxy. 16.1952 (6th c.) Oxyrhynchus.

[173] For Aphrodito, see H. Idris Bell, "An Egyptian Village in the Age of Justinian," JHS 64 (1944), 21–36.

registers. Count Ammonios, one of the principal landowners in Aphrodito at this time, had these detailed estate registers kept for his files by
his agents, and the accounts for the indiction years seven through nine
(that is, A.D. 529–531) are fairly complete.[174] Later, these accounts came
into the hands of Dioscoros, son of the Apollos who had served as one
of Ammonios' estate managers. A more fortunate preservation of evidence for the determination of the nature and extent of private support
of religious foundations can hardly be imagined. Through these registers,
with the aid of some additional letters and receipts, it is possible to view
the complete package of private financial aids to ecclesiastical institutions in a way that is impossible again until the advent of the monastic
typika (foundation charters) of eleventh-century Byzantium.[175]

That private religious foundations existed in Aphrodito is certain,
thanks to the sixth-century papyrus mentioned above, which records a
contract between two laymen that includes a private church among the
assets of the property transferred. Such explicit testimony generally is
unavailable in other cases, and so it is necessary to examine the surviving
records to identify likely private institutions. A listing of all of the cash
and in-kind transactions between Ammonios and various clerics and religious institutions reveals the following patterns which suggest the existence of private ownership of these foundations: the receipt by certain
religious institutions of regular disbursements of significant size and of
uniform nature; the receipt of smaller packages of different forms of aid,
including disbursements in cash and in such commodities as wheat, barley, oil, wine, wool, and vestments; the receipt of salaries or land grants
by an institution's clerics (an indication that the institution itself belonged to the provider of these benefits); finally, a record of rent payments by clerics to Ammonios as their common landlord.

Ammonios' disbursements of wheat from the *ekphoria* (produce) of
his properties to the *oros* (monastery) of Aphrodito were his largest to
any ecclesiastical institution and merit special attention.[176] Jean Maspero, the editor of the Ammonios registers, interpreted these disbursements as rent payments made by the count for lands leased from this
monastery.[177] This interpretation of *ekphoria* as agricultural dues certainly would be legitimate in another context, for other documents from

[174] P. *Cairo Masp.* 2.67138 and 67139 (527–531) Aphrodito.

[175] See Chart 3: "Count Ammonios' Subventions to Ecclesiastical Institutions in Aphrodito."

[176] P. *Cairo Masp.* 2.67139F3v.1 (7th ind.), 38F2r.1 (8th ind.), 38F3r.18 (9th ind.). See
Chart 3 for details. For *oros* as monastery, see H. Cadell and R. Rémondon, "Sens et
emplois de *To Oros* dans les documents papyrologiques," REG 80 (1967), 343–49.

[177] P. *Cairo Masp.* 2.67138, p. 29.

Aphrodito employ this word in the sense of a rent payment.[178] The registers, however, are quite unequivocal and consistent in designating the lands from which the revenues were derived as those of the count, not of the monastery.[179] The receipt of this wheat, then, is clearly no proof that the *oros* was an independent, landowning institution. Instead, it appears that this monastery was at least partially dependent upon the count as a generous benefactor for its financial support.

Now in each of the three indiction years for which the estate registers show this payment to the *oros*, there was a variable grouping of seven or eight peasants who contributed all or part of their rents for the composition of the count's payments from his *ekphoria* to the monastery.[180] Since some of these same peasants appear in the registers for other indiction years as Ammonios' tenants without any concurrent obligations to the monastery, it would seem that they were primarily his dependents. Such is obviously the case for those peasants who paid rent (*phoros*) to the count, but who never contributed to the *ekphoria* payments. Therefore, the monastery appears to have relied upon the count to provide a work force for the cultivation of the lands he designated for the support of this institution.

Apa Agenios, an undoubtedly private monastery of Ammonios in Aphrodito, also had properties assigned for its support and likewise depended upon the count (called *despotes*) and his officials to administer them and assure continuance of rent payments.[181] Extant rent receipts issued to private individuals by public churches carefully underline the fact of the temporal nature of tenancy and the retention of the rights of ownership by the institutions themselves.[182] Private institutions like Apa Agenios, however, were beholden to the lay patrons who administered the properties set aside for their support.

Changes in the composition of the peasant work force as well as variations in the rents of individual peasants indicate that Count Ammonios made annual changes in his scheme of exploitation for the properties intended for the support of the *oros* of Aphrodito. A sublease agreement between Besarion, uncle of Dioscoros, and two peasants to work land rented by the former from the Kaine Ekklesia of Aphrodito (presumably a public church) demonstrates how the primary exploiters of ecclesiasti-

---

[178] *PSI* 8.936 (521), *P. Cairo Masp.* 1.67021 (before 567) verso, line 5, 2.67133 (543), 3.67289 (ca. 550) Aphrodito; cf. P. *Lond.* 5.1784, 1785 (ca. 650) Hermopolis and *P. Flor.* 3.289 (6th c.) Antaeopolis.

[179] *P. Cairo Masp.* 2.67138F2r.1, 67139F4v.9, 39F4v.1.

[180] See detailed figures in Chart 7: "*Ekphoria* from the Properties of Count Ammonios given to the *Diakonia* of the *Oros* of Aphrodito."

[181] *P. Cairo Masp.* 1.67062 (before 538) Aphrodito.

[182] E.g., *P. Flor.* 3.289 (6th c.).

cal lands enlisted peasants on a yearly basis for this purpose,[183] and perhaps Ammonios followed a similar procedure in arranging for the cultivation of his own properties. The *oros* of Aphrodito was likely as powerless as the monastery of Apa Agenios to compel the forwarding of rents from peasants engaged in this way. Yet perhaps this monastery, too, was aware of which peasants would be obligated to contribute their rents for its support.

Ammonios' disbursements to the *oros* of Hagios Apa Patemous also merit attention.[184] His registers distinguish two types of payments: an ordinary, non-specific one and a *prosphora* donation, both in *artabai* of wheat. While the ordinary payments hardly varied at all over three years, the *prosphora* held to no recognizable pattern, sometimes greatly exceeding, sometimes falling below the level of the former payment. It is most likely that custom fixed the non-specific payments, much like those made from the *ekphoria* of Ammonios' property to the *oros* of Aphrodito.

Another institution, the *oros* Psinabla, also appears as a beneficiary of the count's philanthropy, and may have been dependent upon him in a way comparable to the *oros* of Aphrodito.[185] Like that institution, the *oros* Psinabla received a large payment that the count raised by an assessment on a group of three peasant cultivators. One of these peasants, a certain Pekusios, also incurred a concurrent liability to the *oros* of Aphrodito.[186] The second peasant, Psachos, appears elsewhere as a regular tenant with obligations to Ammonios.[187] The remaining peasant is otherwise unknown. Although there is a record of this disbursement only for the seventh indiction year, this institution had received an allowance for oil in an earlier year, so some sort of ongoing relationship with the count seems indicated.[188]

The package of payments to the monastery of Apa Agenios naturally is of special interest, since that indisputably was a private religious foundation. Here too the recorded disbursements do not span the entire period covered by the registers, but come exclusively from the seventh indiction. They include a donation of 100 *artabai* of wheat (matching the donation to the *oros* Psinabla) and three supplementary grants for

---

[183] P. *Lond.* 5.1694 (518) Aphrodito.

[184] See Chart 3 for references. The amounts are as follows:

Indiction Year	Ordinary Donations	*Prosphora*
7th ind.	21a wheat	45a wheat
8th ind.	20a wheat	6a wheat
9th ind.	20a wheat	13a wheat

[185] See Chart 3 for references.

[186] 5 *artabai* of wheat to the *oros* Psinabla (P. *Cairo Masp.* 2.67139F3r.7); 26 *artabai* of wheat to the *oros* of Aphrodito (39F3v.7).

[187] P. *Cairo Masp.* 2.67139F3r.12, cf. 5.

[188] P. *Cairo Masp.* 2.67139F5r.10.

church holidays which total 70 *artabai*.[189] Although there is no mention of a group of contributing peasants, one must have existed for the support of this institution too, at least to make up the 100 *artabai*. At one time, this group included the *georgos* whose falling into arrears on his rent occasioned this monastery's complaint to Apollos. The list of disbursements to this monastery shows how limited the number and quantity of payments might be, even in the case of a fully proprietary institution.

If it was necessary for benefactors to assign real property for a monastery's financial support, they preferred to keep the land and its cultivators under their own control. Perhaps this was a natural consequence of the general agricultural labor shortage at this time. Without an independent base of financial support, religious foundations were in effect subordinated to the direction of their founding families. At the minimum, founders would not allow the exploitation rights of real property assigned for the support of a religious institution to escape their control.

It remains to determine how Ammonios maintained economic control of the lands that supported his private monasteries. That the count rented back the properties originally donated by himself or an ancestor and turned them over for exploitation by his own peasants is one possible explanation. If this was the case, perhaps the count retained rights of usufruct as a condition of the original donation, as did some administrators of *prosphora* donations elsewhere. On the other hand, it is possible that the count never formally donated properties to his monasteries at all, but simply designated certain of his own lands for their support.

Close examination of the dues owed by the peasants provides some evidence for resolving the problem. Among those peasants who in any given year had a liability to the *oros* of Aphrodito, there were always some who concurrently paid other dues to the count.[190] In some years these latter dues actually exceeded those paid in support of the monastery. In addition to these obligations, the count in his capacity as autoprageiac landlord also collected the *chrysika*, the government head tax, and in some cases also the *embole*, a tax in kind to provide the wherewithal for the grain dole in Alexandria and Constantinople. Ordinarily, a cash payment of about 19 *keratia* (with 22 *keratia* constituting the lightweight Alexandrian *solidus*) sufficed to pay a peasant's obligation for the *chrysika*. In exceptional cases the count's fiscal agents would have to devote at least part of a peasant's in-kind rent payments toward an unusually high *chrysika* obligation.

It was such a case that prompted a detailed accounting of the peasant

---

[189] See Chart 3 for references.
[190] See the asterisked entries for peasants in Chart 7; cf. Chart 8: "Payments of *Phoros* to Count Ammonios by his Tenants."

woman Tsenvictora's obligations for the eighth indiction year: 93½ *artabai* of wheat, 25½ *artabai* of barley, and 20 *keratia* in cash.[191] Ordinarily, the count kept all of the barley and one *keration* as his personal share of her dues, as he did, for example, in the ninth indiction. He also kept whatever was left of the wheat, after deductions for the *embole* and the support of the *oros* of Aphrodito. These deductions evidently had first claim on the wheat dues. The count's share was clearly a remainder, sometimes a very insignificant one, as in the eighth indiction, when Tsenvictora's high *chrysika* obligation created a need for a third deduction which reduced his share to a single *artabe*.

It is possible to reconstruct a table illustrating the obligations in wheat of all the peasants who were liable for the support of the *oros* of Aphrodito.[192] Much of the information must remain incomplete and conjectural, since the detailed accounting provided for Tsenvictora is not available for the other peasants. Happily, however, her case is readily employable as a model. Just as Tsenvictora did, some of these peasants (for example, Aganton, Bessourous, Henoch Pankam, and Phoibammon) enjoyed relatively stable rents. The shares of their rents claimed by the *oros* of Aphrodito and by the count (the latter being recorded in the register's *logos phorou*, or "accounts receivable," headings) were inversely related. The respective shares claimed by these two accounts from each peasant varied considerably from year to year, but together they add up to a fairly constant sum, equivalent to the balance of the peasant's dues in wheat after taxes and miscellaneous deductions. This pattern is particularly striking in the case of Agnaton, who consistently paid the largest rents of all the count's tenants, suggesting that he and the others enjoyed the benefit of some sort of rent control over the term of their leases.

The monastery's share of the dues from the group of seven or eight peasants assigned for its support each year also remained relatively constant at slightly more than 400 *artabai*, although the institution's shares of the dues of individual peasants varied considerably. Why, then, did the allocations of each peasant's rent in wheat vary each year, when both the dues of most peasants and the total amount of support supplied to the monastery remained nearly constant?

The answer hinges on determining precisely what the payments registered in the count's *logos phorou* represent. Some peasants in certain indiction years owed nothing to the monastery, but did pay the usual taxes and *phoros* to the count.[193] Some of these peasants had once owed rent for the support of the monastery, or were to come under such an obligation in a subsequent indiction year.[194] The payments of *phoros* by this group clearly were for lands rented from the count that had nothing to do with the financial support of the monastery. Yet among those seven or eight peasants who did form the annual group of cultivators liable for the suppport of the monastery, some also paid *phoros* to the count concurrently.[195] What, then, was the reason for incurring this obligation to the count?

The payments of these individuals to the *logos phorou* might have constituted the count's shares of peasant rents over and above the amounts pledged for the support of the monastery. The count would have taken care to see that the combined rents from all his tenants on these lands exceeded the sum that he himself engaged to pay annually to the monastery. The yearly variations in the *logos phorou* would have been the result of changes in the count's scheme for the exploitation of these properties. The departure of tenants on fixed rents, their replacement by others at higher rents, and the breakup or consolidation of old leaseholdings into tracts of different size might all have played a part in annual reorganizations of these estates.

Alternately, the differing allocations of rents paid by these individuals who had concurrent obligations to the count and the monastery may indicate that they held tenancies of more than one tract apiece. Perhaps custom or a contractual agreement fixed both a peasant's rental obligation and the size of his leasehold, but just what particular tracts would make up this grant could vary from year to year. A peasant might have held two or more tracts with differing obligations vis-à-vis the count and the monastery, not to mention the possibility of variations in taxes payable to the imperial authorities. Thus in a year when the monastery's share of a peasant's dues appears to rise at the expense of the count's *phoros*, perhaps what was actually happening was that this time the cultivator held more of those lands set aside for the support of the monastery than he had done in the previous indiction. The yearly variation in the allocation of peasant rents would then reflect the relative sizes of the tracts of those cultivators who rented both types of lands.[196]

External factors evidently had some impact on the size of the *phoros*. For some reason (tax evasion? slack enforcement?), Tsenvictora did not

[193] Cf. Charts 7 and 8.
[194] E.g., Henoch, son of Cholos, Henoch Pankam, and Joseph the Herdsmen in the eighth indiction.
[195] See the asterisked entries in Chart 7.
[196] E.g., the variable allocation of Agnaton's fixed obligations as shown in Chart 4.

pay for the *embole* in her dues for the seventh indiction, and the wheat that would have been used to meet this obligation accrued to the *logos phorou*.[197] In the next year, however, she was liable not only for the *embole* but also an increased *chrysika* obligation. These claims reduced the count's share of her rent to almost nothing. Perhaps that prompted a major readjustment in the lands she cultivated in the ninth indiction, reflected in the new allocation of her rent between the count and the monastery.[198]

Since the estate registers are concerned only with rents, not the leasing of the landed property from which this income was derived, it is impossible to say with certainty what underlay the variations in allocations of the dues of Ammonios' peasants. There is even an outside chance that the allocation was no more than a bookkeeping device of the count's estate managers, that is, a means of noting from whose rent payments they assembled the customary donations of wheat sent to the monastery. The figures, then, would have had no actual relationship to the patterns of land tenure in Aphrodito. This, however, runs against the evidence of the monastery of Apa Agenios' knowledge of the identity of its cultivators and the amount each owed, though it is possibe that arrangements might have differed in the case of the *oros* of Aphrodito.

Whatever the explanation for this phenomenon, it is likely that the lands supporting the monastery were, at most, hypothecated or "mortgaged" to the maintenance of that institution. Since Justinian was in the process of restricting the tenure of emphyteutic leases granted by religious institutions to laymen,[199] hypothecation of personal property would have offered a satisfactory way for benefactors to provide secure financial support while also maintaining indefinitely their economic control over the income-producing properties themselves.

It remains to determine the relative importance of the rents set aside (by whatever deice) for the support of the *oros* of Aphrodito in comparison to the other rental income of the count recorded in the registers. The relatively small yield of the latter supports other indications that Ammonios owned more lucrative (or less encumbered) properties elsewhere in the towns of Antinoe, Antaeopolis, and Peto.[200] Yet, at least for his Aphrodito properties, the records for the period covered by the registers appear to be complete for the important wheat accounts.[201]

[197] See Chart 5.
[198] See Chart 6.
[199] See *CJ* 1.2.24.4–5 (530).
[200] See Chart 9: "Count Ammonios' Employment of Revenues in Wheat"; cf. *P. Cairo Masp.* 2.67138F1r.1–8, F1v.1–6 (evidently traces of an earlier usage of this codex) and the various partially integrated entries for Peto, e.g., 2.67138F2v.8–20, F3r.27–33, etc.
[201] The same cannot be said for the cash and barley accounts, which are in a much worse state of preservation.

The interpretation of the figures provided by the registers is affected somewhat by the meaning attributed to the payments to the *logos phorou*. If these are understood only as rental profits, then they must be reckoned along with the rents due to the monastery itself as constituent parts of the value (as expressed in rental income) of the property set aside for its support. Otherwise, all payments recorded under the *logos phorou* must have derived from lands of the count that were free of this special charge.[202]

Regardless of the way the *phoros* payments are understood, in every year the rents from the lands assigned for the support of the monastery exceeded those from the count's other lands, and usually by a very significant amount. Assuming that the figures in the registers are at least representative for this locality, and that the lands assigned to support the monastery were not tariffed at higher rents than other properties (that is, that these rents give fair indications of the relative sizes of the properties on which they were paid), certain conclusions are possible.

First, the registers confirm existing evidence that the foundation and maintenance of a large private monastery (the 400 *artabai* provided annually to the *oros* would have fed thirty to forty monks) was a very expensive undertaking.[203] Such a foundation must have been beyond the resources of all but the wealthiest private benefactors, and even they would have had to pledge or hypothecate the best part of their landed property simply to meet operating expenses. Apparently this was because, unlike peasant clerics who might be practically self-supporting on their leaseholds, sixth-century monks were not expected to earn their livings from the land either at Aphrodito or at Oxyrhynchus. Monks, therefore, must have required a considerable income from a landed endowment or a large annual gift to allow them sufficient time to carry out their spiritual responsibilities. The puzzling picture of the reluctant heirs of a testamentary benefactor in need of legal compulsion to complete a promised foundation, which is portrayed in Justinian's contemporary legislation, becomes entirely understandable.

Second, it is readily appreciable why the founder would insist on some device for retaining rights of economic exploitation of "consecrated" lands if he did choose to donate these to a monastery, for it would have been an extraordinary act of generosity for someone to construct and endow a completely independent monastery with ample lands and cultivators of its own. It is no wonder, then, that many monasteries were organized as proprietary institutions thanks to these economic realities.

---

[202] This is assumed in the construction of Chart 9. The former possibility would yield higher percentages of wheat revenues devoted to the support of the *oros*.

[203] Based on the calculation of Jones, *LRE*, 792, that 10 to 13½ *artabai* of wheat could maintain a man for a year.

Third, it is clear that even some undoubtedly private institutions like
the monastery of Apa Agenios might well leave little trace of the financial
support they must have received from their benefactors, even when (as
in this instance) we are fortunate to possess fairly extensive fiscal records.

CHURCHES IN COPTIC EGYPT

Churches, of course, were much less expensive to build and operate. At
Thebes (Coptic Djême) in the eighth century it is common to find
churches under the direction of their clerical founders.[204] Yet given the
traditional interest of private landowners in the ownership of churches,
perhaps it was inevitable that the passage of time would bring about an
erosion of the autonomy of these institutions. The natural desire of mar-
ried clerics to provide for their children, whether or not these offspring
chose to take orders, often led the clergy to deed their churches to them
as their most substantial economic asset.[205] It is not unusual, therefore,
to find daughters or granddaughters of clerics as the possessors of a part
or the whole of a church in this century.[206] The exclusion of women from
legal succession, when it occurred, was a matter of choice, not of principle.[207]

The post-Byzantine Coptic sources also provide the first example of a
division of inherited rights of ownership in private churches. This was a
natural enough development, given the prevailing conceptions of these
institutions as economic assets.[208] By the third generation of owners, individual shares could be as small as one-fifteenth.[209] Even more so than
entire private churches, these church shares came to be considered as
mere ancillary parts of private estates.[210] Yet in cases where a church had
a substantial landed endowment or other economic perquisites, even a
mere share of its worth might be of considerable value.[211]

The owner of a share of a church enjoyed the right of disposal over it,
but since he or she held only a part ownership of the whole institution,

[204] KRU 66/76 (before 749) and 70 (750).
[205] See KRU 70, lines 26–32, trans. W. C. Till, "Erbrechtliche Untersuchungen," p. 186.
[206] Susanna, granddaughter of Elisaios, archdeacon of the monastery of Apa Patemute
(cf. ST 115) in KRU 66/76; Tbasbes, daughter of Apa Victor in KRU 70.
[207] KRU 66, lines 30–31; KRU 76, lines 28–31; the testatrix herself was a woman.
[208] KRU 18 (700–733), 66/76, 70; cf. the discussion below, Chapter 6, of late Byzantine
parallels.
[209] In KRU 66/76, Susanna's three sons Hemai, Schenute, and Stephanos divided her one-
fifth share in a church. For a valuable commentary on this document, see Ludwig Stern,
"Zwei koptische Urkunden aus Theben," Zeitschrift für Ägyptische Sprache und Alter-
thumskunde 1 (1884) 140–60; Steinwenter's comments, "Rechtsstellung," 16–19, and
"Vermögensrechte," 17 are also important.
[210] Cf. KRU 70.
[211] KRU 76, lines 26–27; cf. KRU 66, line 29, and Steinwenter, "Rechtsstellung," 17.

the church itself stood in no danger of secularization.[212] Even an eighth-century monastery did not hesitate to alienate an estate it had inherited from a layman which included a share in a church.[213] In another case, the daughter of a cleric converted her share, inherited from her father, into a *prosphora* donation to another local monastery.[214]

One alternative to a division of rights of ownership by the heirs of a founder was for the family to install one of their number as prior or as *oikonomos* of the institution.[215] This would facilitate hereditary succession to the office and family control of the foundation's resources. In such a case, the other members of the family considered that they had a right to object to alienations of property undertaken without their consent. The owner of a private church might also elect to award simple visitation rights (on major feast days) to one of his heirs in lieu of a share of ownership.[216]

In these respects, Coptic religious foundations anticipated or paralleled similar developments in the contemporary Byzantine Empire, to which this study now turns.

[212] *KRU* 18, lines 38–42.

[213] *KRU* 18, in which the priest Joannes sells the property with annexed church share that his monastery had received from a layman Georgios (or more likely, his wife Johanna after his death). The recipient was a cleric, Apa Victor. Note the comments of Steinwenter, "Rechtsstellung," 18, on this document.

[214] *KRU* 70, lines 38–39.

[215] *KRU* 18, lines 43–55.

[216] *KRU* 76, lines 28–31; cf. *Ps-Ath*. 44 (Coptic version).

Apion Estate Donations to Ecclesiastical Institutions in Oxyrhynchus (Sixth Century A.D.)

Abbreviations

Units of Measure
a = *artabe*, a measure of grain, about 3/4 of an English bushel
ch = *choinix*, a measure of grain, about an English quart
d = *dipla*, a double measure of wine, vinegar, etc.
k = *keration*, 1/22 of a *solidus* or *nomisma*
n = *nomisma*, the standard gold coin, the *solidus* of Constantine

Institutions
e. = *ekklesia*, a church
k. = *koinobion*, a coenobitical monastery
m. = *monasterion*, a monastery
mr.= *martyrion*, a martyr's shrine
n. = *nosokomeion*, a hospital
x. = *xenodocheion*, a hostel or guest house

Part One: Recipient Institutions

Citation / Institution	Grants	Bookkeeper's Note/Estate Reference
P. Oxy. 7.1053 (5th ind./587 or 602?)		
.23 e. Abba Hierakionos	3n	
P. Oxy. 16.1898 (6th ind./587)		
.25 n. Abba Elias	371a	as *prosphora*
P. Oxy. 16.1910 (11th ind./593?)		
.3 e. Limeniados	9a wheat	*kata to ethos*
.3 e. Herakleias	6a wheat	*kata to ethos*

.4 x. Leonidou	64a wheat	*kata to ethos*
.4 mr. (Leonidou)	20a wheat	*kata to ethos*

P. Oxy. 16.1911 (5th ind./557)

.72 e. Apelle	4a wheat	.82 (an *epoikion*)
	1/2n less 1/2k	
.72 e. Tarouthinou	1/2n less 1/2k	.93 (a *ktema*)
.73 e. Trigeou	4a wheat	.160 (a *ktema*)
	1/2n less 1/2k	
.73 e. Anta	1/2n less 1/2k	
.74 e. ....ou	4a wheat	.116? (Loukiou)
	1/2n less 1/2k	
.74 e. Kissonou	1/2n less 1/2k	.82 (an *epoikion*)
.75 e. Kotuleeiou	4a wheat	.91 (a *ktema*)
	1/2n	
.75 e. Tarousebt	1/2n less 1/2k	.31 (an *epoikion*)
.92 mr. Hagiou Serenou	3 1/2a wheat	*en ktemati Tarouthinou*
.94 " " "	2n	*kata durean*
.147 m. Abba Andreou	1000a wheat	*kata to ethos*
.149 " " "	12a wheat	"for the day of the great man"
.150 " " "	100a wheat	*kata keleusin tou despotou*

P. Oxy. 16.2912 (2nd ind./584 or 599?) (all *kata to ethos*)

.116 e. Papsau	4a wheat, 1/2n	.18 (an *epoikion*)
.116 e. Piaa	3a wheat, 1/2n	.31 (as part of Papsau)
.116 e. Kleonos	3a wheat, 1/2n	.53 (an *epoikion*)
.117 e. Theou	3a wheat, 1/2n	.33 (an *epoikion*)
.117 e. Hagios Appheu	3 1/2a wheat, 4n	
.117 e. Thyesobtheos A'	3a wheat, _n	.146 (a *ktema*)
.117 e. Thyesobtheos B'	3a wheat, _	.146 (a *ktema*)
.118 e. Chenetorios	4a wheat, 1/2n	.43 (an *epoikion*)
.118 e. Samakionos	4a wheat, 1/2n	.82 (an *epoikion*)
.118 e. Oualenos	4a wheat, 1/2n	.66 (an *epoikion?*)
.119 e. Hagios Michaelios	4a wheat, 3n	
.119 e. (Petne?)	2 1/2a wheat, 4n	(cf. .98, a *kome*)

P. Oxy. 16.1913 (lst-3rd ind./553-555)

.8 k. Abba Apollos	133 1/3a wheat	*ek keleusis tou despotou*
.58 m. Pruchtheos	20a wheat	

.58 m. Bekru	20a wheat	

P. Oxy. 16.1993 (587)

.20 e. Hagias Theklas	4a wheat	as *prosphora*

P. Oxy. 16.2024 (11th ind./593?)

.6 e. Nesos Leukadiou	16a wheat	*hyper megales ousias*
.6 " " "	6a wheat	*hyper dikaiou Diogenous*
.7 e. Purgou	8 1/2a wheat	
.21 e. Nesos Leukadiou	32 1/2a wheat	(total of the preceding)

P. Oxy. 18.2195 (10th ind./576) (all *kata to ethos* except .187)

.86 e. Euangeliou	6a wheat 1/2n less 1/2k	(cf. 1916.28)
.86 e. Tillionos	4a wheat 1/2n less 1/2k	.1 (an *epoikion*)
.87 e. Erotos	6a wheat 1/2n less 1/2k	
.87 e. Nekontheos	2a wheat 2n less 1 1/2k	.20 (an *epoikion*)
.88 e. Arorures	3 1/2a, 8 ch wheat	
.88 e. Archangelos Michael	3 1/2a, 8 ch wheat	
.187 e. Nekontheos	3a wheat 1n less 4k	.20 (an *epoikion*)

P. Oxy. 18.2196 (5th ind./586?)

.10 e. Matreu	150 *litrai* of bread 17d of wine 50 (or 150?) *folleis* of meats(?) 6 1/4 *xestai* of oil	

P. Oxy. 18.2197 (6th c.)

.11 e. Hagia Maria	unspecified number of bricks	

P. Oxy. 19.2243A (9th ind./590) (all *kata to ethos*)

.76 e. Trigou	6a wheat 1n less 1k	.83 (an *epoikion*)
.76 e. Notinou	4a wheat _1/4n less _1/4k	
.77 e. Polemonos	6a wheat 1n less 1k	
.77 e. Archangelos Michael	2a wheat 1/4n less 1/4k	
.78 e. Pesta	1/4n less 1/4k	.20 (an *epoikion*)
.78 e. Heraklea	4a wheat	

P. Oxy. 27.2480 (14th ind./565)

.44 x. Abba Apionos	80d vinegar	*logos eusebeias kata to ethos*
.46 k. Abba Herme	13d vinegar	*logos eusebeias kata to ethos*
.119 m. Orous	6d vinegar	
.120 k. Abba Pamoun	50d vinegar	
.282/89 e.____	12d (vinegar)	
.283/90 e.____	12d	
.284/91 e.____	12d	
.285/92 e.____	4d	
.299 ————. Hagios Iou[stos?]	—(d)	
.300 m.____	—	
.303	20d	
.304	6d	
.305	52d	
.306	16d	
.307 x.____	—	

PSI 1.89 (9th ind./6th c.)

.1 k. Hagios Abba Herme	25a wheat as *prosphora* *kata to ethos*

PSI 8.953 (1st ind./567)

.8 e. Papsau	20d wine
.9 k. Abba Sarmatou	100d vinegar[1]
.10 (e.) Hagios Serenos	20d wine
.11 e. Abba Hierakionos	16d wine
.12 m. Pela	360d wine, 60d vinegar[1]
.30 e._____s	120d wine[2]
.31 e. Hagia Euphemia	52d wine[2]
.82 e. Johannes ton Evange- listes	72d wine[2]

[1] For the fifteenth indiction.
[2] As *prosphora, kata keleusin tou despotou.*

Part Two: Size of Wheat Donations

<table>
<tr><td colspan="2"><u>Ordinary Donations</u></td><td colspan="2"><u>Prosphora Donations</u></td></tr>
<tr><td>2a</td><td>two institutions</td><td>4a</td><td>e. Hagios Thekla</td></tr>
<tr><td>2 1/2a</td><td>one institution</td><td>25a</td><td>k. Hagios Abba Herme</td></tr>
<tr><td></td><td></td><td>371a</td><td>n. Abba Elias</td></tr>
<tr><td>3a</td><td>six institutions</td><td></td><td></td></tr>
<tr><td>3 1/2a</td><td>two institutions</td><td></td><td></td></tr>
<tr><td>3 1/2a, 8ch</td><td>two institutions</td><td></td><td></td></tr>
<tr><td>4a</td><td>thirteen institutions</td><td></td><td></td></tr>
<tr><td>6a</td><td>six institutions</td><td></td><td></td></tr>
<tr><td>8 1/4 a</td><td>one institution</td><td></td><td></td></tr>
<tr><td>9a</td><td>one institution</td><td></td><td></td></tr>
<tr><td>16a</td><td>one institution</td><td></td><td></td></tr>
<tr><td>20a</td><td>three institutions</td><td></td><td></td></tr>
<tr><td>64a</td><td>one, x. Leonidou</td><td></td><td></td></tr>
<tr><td>133 1/3 a</td><td>one, k. Abba Apollo</td><td></td><td></td></tr>
<tr><td>1112a</td><td>one, m. Abba Andreou</td><td></td><td></td></tr>
</table>

CHART TWO

Peasant Clerics in Oxyrhynchus

<u>Citation/Name</u>   <u>Location of Leasehold</u>
P. Oxy. 16.1911 (577)

Citation/Name	Location of Leasehold
.125 Phoibammon, deacon	*ktema tou Loukiou*
.125 Pamouthios, deacon	" " "
.131 Phoibammon Isak, deacon	" " "
.133 Phoibammon Jakob, deacon	" " "
.203 Joannes, priest	*epoikion tou Kotuleeiou*
(cf. .75 ekklesia tou Kotuleeiou)	

P. Oxy. 16.1912 (584 or 599?)

Citation/Name	Location of Leasehold
.20 Joseph, priest	*epoikion tou Papsau*
.22 Phoibammon, priest	" " "
.35 Paulos, priest	" " "
.36 _____, priest	" " "
(cf. .116 ekklesia tou Papsau)	
.47 Apa Horos	*apo Thuesobtheos*
(cf. .117 ekklesia tou Thuesobtheos)	
.56 Apollos, priest	*epoikion tou Chenetorios*
(cf. .118 ekklesia tou Chenetorios)	
.74 Anouthios, priest	*epoikion tou ———u* ·

P. Oxy. 16.1917 (6th c.)

.5 Herakleianos Apa Siriou	*phrontis tou Ibionos*
.5 Aphunchios, deacon	" " "
.12 Tittos, priest	
.11 Tittos, monk	" " "
.19 Pamoun, priest and *oikonomos* of Hagios Apa Tittos	" " "
.23 Joannes, priest	" " "
.25 Georgios, priest and *oikonomos* of Hagios Apa Pamouthios	" " "
.29 Apuotes, priest	" " "
.36 Menas, priest	" " "
.78 Pamouthis, priest	*epoikion tou Ostrakinou*
.116 Phoibammon, priest	*epoikion tou Sassou Katou*

P. Oxy. 16.2019 (6th c.)

.13 Apa Horos, priest	
.18 (same?)	*epoikion tou Terutheos*

P. Oxy. 16.2036 (late 5th c.)

.3 [Joan]nes, priest	*epoikion tou Tbe[ke]*
.32 Apa ⟨Pa⟩noute, priest	*epoikion tou Nikeros*

P. Oxy. 16.2037 (late 6th c.)

.19 Pambechios, priest	
.23 (same?)	*mechane tes Patase*
.34 Phoibammon, deacon	*mechane tes Kelechou*

P. Oxy. 16.2038 (late 6th or 7th c.)

.3-4 Origenes, priest	*epoikion tou Orth[oniou]*
.19 Pek{s}usis, deacon	" " "

P. Oxy. 16.2056 (5th c.) List of Prisoners

.14 Agathos, *oikonomos*	*epoikion tou Terutheos*
.16 Pekusios, priest	" " "

P. Oxy. 18.2195 (576)

.4 Petros, priest	*epoikion tou Tillonos*
.12 Elias Petrou, priest (cf. .86 ekklesia tou Tillonos)	" " "

.62, 64 Maximos Pekusios, priest   *epoikion tou Erotos*
   (cf. .87 ekklesia tou Erotos)
.135 Apa Horos, priest   *epoikion tou Euangeliou*
   (cf. .86 ekklesia tou Evangeliou)
.168 Kollouthos, priest   *epoikion tou Nekontheos*
.169-70 Phoibammon, priest   "   "   "
.181 Abona, priest   "   "   "
.183 Pinoute, lector   "   "   "

P. Oxy. 18.2197 (6th c.) Bricks

.77 Zachia, priest
.137 Psesios. *oikonomos*
.140 Phib Isaak, *oikonomos*
.141 Joseph, priest
.162 Apa Hor, *georgos* and priest
.193 Joannes, priest and *georgos*
.208 Phoibammon, priest

P. Oxy. 19.2243A (590)

.15 Joannes, priest   *epoikion tou Amatenes*
.22 Joannes, priest   *ktema Pesta*
   (cf. .78 ekklesia Pesta)
.23 tos, priest   *ktema Herakla*
   (cf. .78 ekklesia Herakla)

PSI 3.179 (602?)

.13 Aurelius Onnophrios, priest   *epoikion Apelle*
   (cf. *P. Oxy.* 16.1911.72 ekklesia Apelle)

CHART THREE

Count Ammonios' Subventions to Ecclesiastical Institutions in Aphrodito (from *P. Cairo Masp.* 2.67138–39)

<u>Source Abbreviations:</u> examples
   38F2v.8 = *P. Cairo Masp.* 2.67138, Folio Two, verso, line eight
   39F6r.2 = *P. Cairo Masp.* 2.67139, Folio Six, recto, line two

a = *artabe*   k = *keration*   n = *nomisma*

5th ind. = A.D. 527   7th ind. = A.D. 529   9th ind. = A.D. 531
6th ind. = A.D. 528   8th ind. = A.D. 530

Arrangement is by order of appearance in the registers

Ekklesia tou Romanou (for which see *P. Cairo Masp.* 3.67283, p. 2, line 10)
38F1r.4 *Logos tou Chrysikou*, 5th ind., 2n less 2 k
39F6r.2 *Logos tou Apollou tou hypodektou*, 1n less 3 k
39F6v.15 *Logos* of the 6th ind., for *demosia*, 4 + n less 4 + k

Oros (monastery) of Aphrodito (cf. *P. Fouad* 1.87)
38F1r.10 *Logos tes Tsenvictoras*, 8th ind., 72a wheat
38F1r.15   "   "   " 9th ind., 21a wheat
38F2r.1 *Logos ton ekphorion ton ktematon tou komitos*, 8th ind., 403a wheat
38F3r.18 *Logos tes diakonias tes Aphrodites*, 9th ind., 400 3/4a wheat
39F3v.1 *Logos tou sitou dothenton eis ten diakonian tou hagios Oros tes Aphrodites*, 7th ind., 413a wheat
39F4r.3 (Duplicate entry of the preceeding)
39F4v.9 *Logos tes krithes ton ktematon tou komitos*, 7th ind., 8a barley
39F5r.9 *Logos ton analomaton*, 5th ind., from the *ekphoria* of the 6th ind., to
Apa Isakios of the *diakonia* for oil, 3n less 6k (cf. 39F5v.4)
39F5v.19 *Logos ton analomaton*, 7th ind., to Apa Isakios in the *diakonia* for
vegetables, 3n less 6k
39F6r.9 *Logos tou komitos*, 9th ind., 400 3/4a wheat Convent(?) of Loukanos
38F2r.27 *Logos tou sitou*, 8th ind., to Chairemon, son(?) of Loukanos, 9a
wheat
39F4r.9 *Logos ton ekphorion ton ktematon tou komitos*, 7th ind. to the daughters of Loukanos, nuns, 16a wheat
39F6r.10 *Logos tou komitos*, 9th ind., to the daughters of Loukanos, 20a
wheat

Oros of Hagios Apa Patemous
38F2r.31 *Logos tou sitou*, 8th ind., to Apollos the baker, on behalf of the *prosphora* of Apa Patemous, 6a wheat (cf. *P. Oxy.* 16.1949)
38F2r.25 *Logos tou sitou*, 8th ind., to Hagios Patemous, 20a wheat
39F3r.19 Given to the baker Apollos on behalf of Apa Patemous, 4a wheat
39F4r.8 *Logos ton ekphorion ton ktematon tou komitos*, 7th ind., to the *oros*
of Hagios Apa Patemous, 21a wheat
39F4r.6 Same, but as *prosphora*, 45a wheat
39F6r.11 *Logos tou komitou*, 9th ind., 20a wheat
39F6r.12 Same, but as *prosphora*, 13a wheat

Monastery of Peto
38F2v.8 *Logos ton demosion tou komitos*, 8th ind., various sums, apparently
paid in installments
38F2v.19 Same, but for 9th ind., one installment payment
39F2v.14 *Logos tes emboles tou komitou*, 7th ind., 22a wheat

Oros of Psinabla
39F3r.1 *Logos tou sitou*, 7th ind., through Apa Pheib, monk, 100a wheat (cf.
39F4r.4)
39F4r.4 *Logos ton ekphorion ton ktematon tou komitos*, 7th ind. (duplicate
entry of the preceeding)
39F5r.10 *Logos ton analomaton*, 5th ind., from the *ekphoria* of the 6th ind., to
Apollos, *hypodektes*, on behalf of Apa Pheib for oil, 3n less 6k

Monastery of Apa Agenios (for which see *PSI* 8.933)
39F3r.21 Given to Apa Agenios, 100a wheat
39F3r.25 To Apa Agenios, for Easter, 15a wheat
39F3r.25 To Apa Agenios, for another holiday, 15a wheat
39F4r.7 *Logos ton ekphorion ton ktematon tou komitos*, 7th ind. (duplicate entry of the preceeding)
39F4r.13 *Logos tes hagias charas*, 40a wheat

Monastery(?) of Apa Endios
39F5r.23 *Logos ton analomaton*, 6th ind., from the cash of the 7th ind., to Apa Endios, through Senouthos, for vestments of the monks, 1n less 4k

Monastery of Apa Sourous (for which see *P. Cairo Masp.* 2.67133)
39F6v.2 *Logos Menas*, to Artemidoros, *singoularis*, on behalf of barley (for/ of?) Apa Sourous, for the 6th ind., 2n less 4k

Miscellaneous
38F1v.8 *Logos tou Apollou tou hypodektou*, to the priest of Ama Maria (a church at Aphrodito, for which see *P. Cairo Masp.* 3.67283, p. 2, line 6), for firewood 2n
39F6r.14 *Logos tou komitos*, 9th ind., to the monks of Antinoe, 6a wheat
39F6r.2 *Logos tou Apollou tou hypodektou*, on behalf of the oil of the priest Hermios, 2n less 3 k.
39F6v.13 *Logos* of the 6th ind., to the daughters of David, for the *demosia*, 2n less 7k (cf. 39F4r.9)
39F6v.14 Same, but through Solomon, 1/3n less 1/4k

CHART FOUR

Wheat Obligations of Peasants under Obligation to the *Oros* of Aphrodito

Peasant/ Ind. Yr.	Total Dues in Wheat	*Embole*	Misc. Deductions	Balance Owed	*Oros'* Share	*Logos Phorou*
Agnaton						
7th ind.	(285a)	50 2/3a[1]	NR	(235a)	152a	83a
8th ind.	(283a)	50 2/3a[1]	NR	(235a)	193a	42a
9th ind.	(285a)	50a[1]	NR	(235a)	218a	17a
Bessourous						
7th ind.	(15 1/2a)	NR	NR	(15 1/2a)	---	15 1/2 a
8th ind.	(15a)	NR	NR	(15a)	7a	8a
9th ind.	(15 1/2a)	NR	8a[2]	(7 1/2a)	---	7 1/2a

Peasant/ Ind. Yr.	Total Dues in Wheat	Embole	Misc. Deductions	Balance Owed	Oros' Share	Logos Phorou
Henoch, son of Cholos						
7th ind.	(35a)[2]	NR	NR	(35a)[2]	30a	(5a)[2]
8th ind.	(44 1/6a)	16 2/3a	NR		---	27 1/2a
9th ind.	(52 1/3a)	17 1/3a	NR	(35a)	---	35a
Henoch Pankam						
8th ind.	(62a)	20a	NR	(42a)	---	42a
9th ind.	(61a)	NR	NR	(61a)	61a	NR
Heraklios, son of Valantios						
7th ind.	(71 2/3a)	24 2/3a	NR	(47a)	42a	5a
8th ind.	(73 2/3a)	(24 2/3a)[4]	NR	(51a)	43a	8a
9th ind.	(72a)	(20a)[4]	NR	(52a)	51a	1a
Joannes, son of Promaous						
7th ind.	(40a)	NR	NR	(40a)	40a	NR
8th ind.	(40a)	NR	NR	(40a)	40a	NR
9th ind.	(25a)	NR	NR	(25a)	22a	3a
Joseph the Herdsman						
9th ind.	(19a)	NR	NR	(19a)	19a	NR
Pekusios						
7th ind.	(77a)	NR	5a[5]	(72a)	26a	46a
8th ind.	(25a)	NR	NR	(25a)	25a	NR
9th ind.	(26a)	NR	NR	(26a)	---	26a
Phoibammon, son of Karpos						
7th ind.	(40a)	20a	NR	(20a)	20a	NR
8th ind.	(43a)	20a	NR	(23a)	23a	NR
9th ind.	(43 1/2a)	20a	NR	(23 1/2a)	7 1/2a	16a
Tsenvictora						
7th ind.	(94a)	NR	NR	(94a)	72a	22a
8th ind.	93 2/3a	16 2/3a	4a[6]	(73a)	72a	1a
9th ind.	93a	20a	NR	(73a)	21a	52a
Victor Pathalme						
7th ind.	(31a)	NR	NR	(31a)	31a	NR

[1] *Modii* in the text converted here to *artabai*.
[2] Wheat paid in exchange for seed.
[3] See 38F3r.41.
[4] Includes 18 2/3a in the 8th ind. and 20a in the 9th ind. paid by Heraklios' co-contributor, Talous.
[5] Wheat paid to the *oros* of Psinabla.
[6] Wheat paid to meet *chrysika* obligation.
NR = No recorded entry

CHART FIVE

Disposition of Tsenvictora's Wheat Obligations

	7th ind.	8th ind.	9th ind.
Embole	NR	16 2/3a	20a
Oros of Aphrodito	72a	72a	21a
Chrysika	NR	4a	NR
Logos Phorou	22a	1a	52a
Total Obligations	94a	93 2/3a	93a

Source: 38F1r.9-15

CHART SIX

Tsenvictora's Account

	7th ind.	8th ind.	9th ind.
Obligations:			
Wheat	(94 1/2a)	93 1/2a	93 1/2a
Barley	17 1/2a	25 1/2a	25 1/2a
Cash	22k	1n less 2k (= 20k)	20k
Deductions:			
Embole	NR	16 2/3a wheat	20a wheat
Oros	72a	72a wheat	21a wheat
Chrysika	NR	2 1/4k less 3 k (=47k) Paid by: 1) Cash, 1n less 2k (=20k) 2) Barley, 25 1/2a (worth 23k) 3) Wheat, 4a (worth 4k)	1n less 3k (19k)
Logos Phorou	22 1/2a wheat	1a wheat	52a wheat 25 1/2a barley 1k cash

Note: The Alexandrian *nomisma* was made up of 22 *keratia* (instead of the standard 24), and is so reckoned here.

CHART SEVEN

Ekphoria from Properties of Count Ammonios Given to the *Diakonia* of the *Oros* of Aphrodito

Tenant	7th ind.	8th ind.	9th ind.
Agnaton	152a*	193a*	218 3/4a*
Bessourous	*	7a*	*
Heraklios, son of Valantios	42a	43a*	51a*
Henoch, son of Cholos	30a*	*	*
Henoch Pankam		*	61 1/2a
Joannes, son of Promaous	40a	40a	22a*
Joseph the Herdsman		*	19a
Pekusios	26a*	25a	
Phoibammon, son of Karpos	20a	23a	7 1/2a*
Tsenvictora	72a*	72a*	21a*
Victor Pathalme	31a		
TOTALS	413a	403a	400 3/4a
No. of Contributors	8	7	7

*Tenant also had a liability to Count Ammonios for *phoros* in this year.

CHART EIGHT

Payments of *Phoros* to Count Ammonios by His Tenants

Tenant	7th ind.	8th ind.	9th ind.
Agnaton, *georgos*	83a	42a	17a
Bessourous	15 1/2a	8a	7 1/2a
Cholos the Potter	NR	4a	4a
Henoch, son of Cholos	(5a)	27 1/2a	35a
Henoch Pankam	NR	42a	NR
Heraklios, son of Valantios	5a	8a	1a
Joannes, son of Promaous	NR	NR	3a
Kephalaios	15a	NR	NR
Kollouthos Psim	NR	NR	21 1/2a
Papnouthes	NR	NR	1a
Pekusios	46 1/2a	NR	26 1/2a
Pheib Psenthaesi	NR	18 1/2a	22 1/2a
Phoibammon, son of Karpos	NR	NR	16a
Phoibammon Thakore	26 1/2a	25 1/2a	22 1/2a
Psachos	1 1/2a	NR	NR
Psaios, the priest's son	44 1/2a	NR	NR

Talous	NR	NR	5 1/2a
"Those from Peto"	NR	106a	NR
Topos Pathakore	NR	NR	12 1/2a
Tsenvictora	22 1/2a	(1a)	52a
Victor the Herdsman	NR	60a	NR
Victor, priest, and Stephen	NR	(2a)	2a
TOTALS	266 1/2a	344 1/2a	249 1/2a

NR = No recorded entry

CHART NINE

Count Ammonios' Employment of Revenues in Wheat[1]

	7th ind.	8th ind.	9th ind.
Donations to the *Oros*	413a	403a	400 3/4a
Phoros Revenues	266 1/2a	344 1/2a	249 1/2a
Total Disposable Revenue	679 1/2a	747 1/2a	650 1/4a
Percentage of Revenue devoted to the *Oros*	60.7%	53.9%	61.6%

[1] Excludes payments for taxes such as *embole.*

CHAPTER FOUR

Private Religious Foundations in Byzantium, 565–1025

THE HISTORIAN of the internal development of the Byzantine church must contend with a scarcity of evidence after leaving the well-documented sixth century. The poorly documented interval that lasts down to the eleventh century nevertheless was an era of considerable importance for the history of the empire's private religious foundations because private benefactors were successful in undermining and finally in overthrowing Justinian's regulatory system.

CHALLENGES TO JUSTINIAN'S LEGISLATION

Fortunately hagiography provides some important insights into private foundations and the public churches in this obscure era. The life of St. Theodore of Sykeon, bishop of Anastasiopolis in the late sixth century, is particularly instructive.[1] As a youth, Theodore served in a rural church dedicated to St. George and managed to eke out a living from the offerings of parishioners. It appears, therefore, that *eukteria* without provision for clerical maintenance continued to exist despite Justinian's legislation on the subject. When Theodore founded his own monastery, he took advantage of his acquaintance with Emperor Maurice (582–602) to ask for a small gift to help his institution with its work of providing for the nourishment of the local poor. Maurice responded generously with an annual gift of 600 *modii* of wheat (the equivalent of 200 Egyptian *artabai*), an imperial *presbion annalion* of the sort mentioned in Justinian's legislation.[2]

Only when Theodore became bishop of Anastasiopolis was he freed from the necessity to depend on local charity or imperial philanthropy.

[1] *Vita S. Theodori Syceotae* Ch. 15, ed. A.-J. Festugière, "Vie de Théodore de Sykéôn," *Subsidia hagiographica* 48 (1970), with Frank Trombley, "Monastic Foundations in Sixth-Century Anatolia and Their Role in the Social and Economic Life of the Countryside," *GOTR* 30 (1985), 45–59, esp. 45–51.
[2] *Vita*, Ch. 54.

He received a fixed salary of 365 *solidi* a year, derived from the landed endowments of the cathedral church.[3] This episcopal church, like those of Byzantine Egypt, relied upon local magnates to manage its properties and handle relations with the peasants of the *choria* which made up its endowment. Theodore's biographer deemed his investigation and deposition of one such manager (who bore the title of *protektor*) a noteworthy example of the bishop's intolerance for injustice. Yet even the pious Theodore intervened here only in the face of an armed rebellion of the peasants from one of the church's estates.

Later on, Theodore decided to resign his episcopal see and retire to the calmer life of an abbot. He remained in touch with the imperial court, and sometime after 595 he visited Constantinople where he obtained important privileges for his monasteries.[4] Maurice designated these institutions as places of asylum from imperial officials. More important, he exempted them from the usual subordination to the local bishop, Theodore's successor at Anastasiopolis, and placed them instead directly under Cyriacus (595–606), the patriarch of Constantinople.[5]

We are not told about the motivation behind Theodore's attempt to secure these privileges, but it is not unreasonable to suppose that some sort of difficulty had arisen between the founder and the new bishop of Anastasiopolis. In any case, the exemption from local episcopal control helped to set a precedent for a new category of monasteries located outside the capital but directly dependent upon the patriarch of Constantinople. This exemption was clearly opposed to the canon of the Council of Chalcedon that had ordered the subordination of all monasteries to the local bishops and also to the Justinianic legislation enacted to enforce it. Maurice's concession, therefore, marks a fundamental change of attitude.

Theodore himself had followed ordinary canonical procedure when he founded his first monastery by sending his nominee for the hegoumenate to the local bishop for approval and ordination.[6] Exemptions like that accorded Theodore would serve to remove one of Justinian's most important checks on the powers of private benefactors since the patriarch could hardly hope to exercise the same strict scrutiny as the local prelates. This was the first important step in the dismantling of Justinian's regulatory system.

The troubled times of the seventh century saw a further undermining

---

[3] *Vita*, Ch. 78; cf. Justinian's annuity of the same amount awarded to an elderly widow in Procopius, *Historia arcana* 29.25.

[4] *Vita*, Ch. 82, esp. lines 12–18.

[5] See Grégoire, *Recueil*, Vol. 1, No. 225, a patriarchal *stauropegion* issued to a church of St. Michael at Hieronda in Caria by Patriarch Cyriacus (595–606).

[6] *Vita*, Ch. 41.

of Justinian's regulations. This process occurred very slowly, and several novels of Emperor Heraclius (610–641) illustrate his attempts to shore up the old system with some allowances for changed circumstances.[7] In 612 Patriarch Sergius I (610–638) appealed to Heraclius for a law to set new goals for regulating the size of the complements of clergy in the cathedral church of Hagia Sophia and its dependencies.[8] The figures that Justinian had set in his novel of 535 had proven to be unrealizably low, and the old problem of maintaining the financial well-being of the great church in the face of increasing salary obligations persisted. Sergius also hoped the emperor would grant him more flexibility in order to reward wealthy candidates with ordination as a return for substantial free-will donations to the church. There seemed to be no reason to deny these generous benefactors appointments simply because there were no existing vacancies under the current quota system.

Heraclius complied with Sergius' requests and substantially increased Justinian's quotas for most categories of clergy. He also brought the church of the Theotokos at Blachernai (founded by Empress Pulcheria) under the quota system for the first time. Moreover, the emperor gave the patriarch discretionary authority to promote wealthy benefactors outside of the ordinary quota system by setting a new quota for "supernumerary" appointments.

This new arrangement failed to satisfy many prospective benefactors who feared challenges to their tenure of *ekklesiastika offikia* or disliked the necessary publicity associated with admission under the special quota. These considerations also concerned benefactors who wanted to secure places in the cathedral clergy for others. No one wished to appear to be buying his way to special exemption from the ordinary quota for clerical appointments. So the church simply lost the important donations of property that it had come to depend upon from these sources. Heraclius felt constrained, therefore, to issue another law in 619 which permitted the patriarch greater flexibility and less publicity in determining who should be admitted to the staff of the cathedral church and its dependencies.[9]

A mass of rural clergy in search of better livings was one of the factors behind the insistent pressure for appointments in public churches. Justinian, of course, already had attempted to deal with the problems caused

[7] See I. Konidaris, "Die Novellen des Kaisers Herakleios," in *Fontes Minores*, Vol. 5, ed. Dieter Simon (Frankfurt, 1982), pp. 33–106.

[8] Heraclius, *De numero clericorum magnae ecclesiae* (612), ed. Konidaris, "Die Novellen," 62–72, with commentary, 94–100 = Franz Dölger, *Regesten der Kaiserurkunden des oströmischen Reiches von 565–1453* (Munich-Berlin, 1925–65), No. 165; cf. Herman, "Niederklerus," 382–83.

[9] Heraclius, *De numero clericorum magnae ecclesiae* (619), ed. Konidaris, 80–84 = Dölger, *Regesten* No. 175.

when clerics abandoned their original appointments. The Persian occupations of Anatolia in 616 and 626 could only have increased the pressures for clerical appointments in the cathedral and other churches in the capital. Some enterprising clerics succeeded in gaining more than one of these appointments. Since not only the emperor and the patriarch but also a multitude of private patrons had rights of nomination to their respective churches located in close proximity to one another, there were ample opportunities for pluralism.

Even in the public churches, the authorities were unable to prevent appointments to clerical positions secured through bribes or the patronage of influential individuals. Private patrons had fewer scruples, and on occasion hired migratory clerics whose very ordinations were questionable. In the case of the public churches, the principal concern of the authorities was the strain that the extra salaries (*diaria*) put on the financial resources of the cathedral church. In the case of private churches, wherein finances were the business of their patrons, the authorities were still concerned that clerics would not be able to perform their duties adequately with more than one assignment.

Clearly this problem could not be dealt with adequately simply by imposing admission quotas. So Heraclius issued a law in 617 that enacted financial penalties for patrons who received, appointed, or transferred clergy without the approval of the patriarch.[10] He strictly forbade pluralism, and he sought to enforce this prohibition by providing that pluralists would lose all of their positions along with their *diaria* for a period of three years.

Although private patrons had been obliged by Justinian to submit their candidates for ordination to the patriarch or the local bishop for his approval, Heraclius' law banning pluralism suggests that either this was not done or that the procedure had been reduced to a meaningless formality. The law reasserted the Justinianic principle and also closed a major loophole in the earlier legislation, for patrons were now explicitly prohibited to employ previously ordained clergy from the countryside in their city churches.

Sources remain scarce for the balance of the seventh century, but the canons of the Synod in Trullo, which met in 692, illustrate the continued pressures on the regulatory system of Justinian.[11] For instance, the synod deemed it necessary to renew the old canon of the Council of Chalcedon that banned the secularization of monasteries and the alienation of their

---

[10] Heraclius, *De clericis Constantinopolim venientibus sine jussu patriarchae non recipiendis* (617), ed. Konidaris, 72–78, with commentary, 100–102 = Dölger, *Regesten* No. 212.

[11] See V. Laurent, "L'oeuvre canonique du concile in Trullo (691–692)," *REB* 23 (1965), 7–41.

properties.[12] This reenactment carried an additional clause condemning anyone who gave out monasteries to laymen. The reference of the clause is obscure, and its correct interpretation was a matter of controversy even among Byzantine canonists. Perhaps the practice that the synod condemned was an extension to monasteries of Justinian's program of granting out churches for the purposes of repair and beautification, or a completely new program not otherwise attested which anticipated the features of the late tenth-century *charistike*.

The fathers of the synod also reaffirmed Justinian's restrictions on liturgies conducted in private dwellings.[13] They did not absolutely forbid the celebration of the holy liturgy in private chapels, but they did obligate the officiating clergy to obtain episcopal approval for the service beforehand. In another canon, the synod reserved baptisms for the public churches.[14] As was customary, these canons set penalties for disobedient clergy to assure enforcement, but now a sanction of excommunication against recalcitrant laymen appears as well.

PATTERNS OF PATRONAGE IN THE ERA AFTER JUSTINIAN

As might be expected, the pace of private construction of churches and monasteries slowed considerably, beginning with the difficult times that the empire endured toward the close of the sixth century. High officials of the court remained the most important benefactors in Constantinople.[15] The patrician Narses opened a church, a *gerokomeion* (old age home), and a *xenon* there in 571. The patrician Smaragdus, an exarch of Ravenna, erected another philanthropic institution in Constantinople in the reign of Tiberius II (578–582). Emperor Maurice's *parakoimomenos* Stephen erected a *xenon* and a *gerokomeion* in the capital during his tenure of office.

Justinian's successors Justin II (565–578), Tiberius II (578–582), and Maurice erected new imperial foundations and repaired some older ones.[16] Patriarch Cyriacus (595–606) erected a rare patriarchal foundation, a church dedicated to the Theotokos.[17] The troubled reigns of Pho-

---

[12] C. Trull., c. 49 (R&P 2.423–24).

[13] C. Trull., c. 31 (R&P 2.371); cf. Herman, "Niederklerus," 407.

[14] C. Trull., c. 59 (R&P 2.438–39).

[15] Theophanes, *Chronographia* a.m. 9063 (ed. De Boor, p. 243); *Patria Konstantinoupoleos* 3.62 (p. 238), 3.94 (p. 249), 3.197 (p. 277); cf. Janin, *Géographie*, Vol. 3, pp. 555, 560.

[16] Theophanes, *Chronographia* a.m. 6062 (ed. De Boor, p. 243), a.m. 6073 (p. 251); *Patria Konstantinoupoleos* 3.23, 32, 35, 36, 46, 47, 123, 147, 164 (pp. 220, 227, 229, 234–35, 255, 263, 267); cf. Janin, *Géographie*, Vol. 3, pp. 142, 229, 237, 337–38, 483, 567.

[17] Theophanes, *Chronographia* a.m. 6090 (ed. De Boor, p. 277); cf. Janin, *Géographie*, Vol. 3, pp. 174–75.

cas (602–610) and Heraclius, however, allowed no scope for expensive new foundations at a time when the very existence of the empire was at stake. Only a great loan of the treasures of the public churches of Constantinople arranged by Patriarch Sergius provided Heraclius with the money he needed to field armies for the long war of national salvation against the Avars and the Persians.[18]

A few new foundations occurred in the reigns of Heraclius' successors.[19] Heraclius' grandson Severus converted his own house into a *gerokomeion* in the reign of Constans II (641–668). Severus' wife, Anna, built a church next to her husband's *gerokomeion*. The patrician Karpianos built a church dedicated to the Theotokos in the reign of Constantine IV (668–685). Of course these were only modest contributions to the ecclesiastical landscape of the empire when compared to the impressive legacy of Justinian and his associates in the sixth century.

In this era, just as earlier in Byzantine Egypt, there was no sharp delimitation between secular and religious life. The patrons of this age were often prominent participants in the political and military affairs of the empire. Some, as Apollos of Aphrodito had done, chose to withdraw from secular life in order to lead their own foundations as *hegoumenoi*. Other patrons took this step only under the cloud of imperial disfavor or political disgrace. Some of these reluctant abbots, given a favorable change in the political climate, might even reconsider their retirement and return to active secular careers.

Philippicus, Emperor Maurice's brother-in-law, led the Byzantine army against the Persians from 584 to 589.[20] In 594, the same year that Maurice appointed him Count of the Excubitors, he founded a private monastery dedicated to the Theotokos at Chrysopolis opposite Constantinople on the Asiatic shore of the Bosphorus. When Phocas overthrew Maurice in 602, Philippicus prudently withdrew to his monastery, where he took clerical orders. As it turned out, Philippicus lived to see Heraclius' successful revolt against Phocas. The new emperor freed Philippicus from his involuntary seclusion and reappointed him in 612 as a general. Yet Philippicus did not live long enough to renew his military career, but died shortly after his recommissioning and was buried at Chrysopolis. After his death, his monastery became an imperial institution.

Theodotus, the abbot of a monastery at Stenon in suburban Constan-

---

[18] Nicephorus, *Breviarium*, ed. K. De Boor, *Nicephori archiepiscopi Constantinopolitani opuscula historica* (Leipzig, 1880), p. 15; Theophanes, *Chronographia* a.m. 6113 (ed. De Boor, pp. 302–303); Kedrenos, *Compendium historiarum*, ed. I. Bekker, CSHB (Bonn, 1838–39), 1.714.

[19] *Patria Konstantinoupoleos* 3.49 (p. 235), 3.53 (p. 236), 3.108 (p. 251); cf. Janin, *Géographie*, Vol. 3, p. 187, 556.

[20] Theophanes, *Chronographia* a.m. 6076–80 (ed. De Boor, pp. 254–262), 6086 (p. 272), 6098 (p. 293); Nicephorus, *Breviarium* (ed. De Boor, p. 7).

tinople, also left his foundation in order to accept an offer from Emperor Justinian II (685–695, 705–711) to serve as his *logothetes tou genikou* (chief financial minister).[21] His audacity and cruelty quickly made him one of the most hated ministers of Justinian II. He perished in the bloodletting after Leontius' successful coup d'etat in 695. Gregory, a native of Cappadocia, began his career as a *kleisurarchos* (commander of a mountain fortress).[22] He later became *hegoumenos* of the monastery of Florus in Constantinople, an old private foundation. He was a friend of Emperor Leontius (695–698), whose rise to the throne he foretold.

In contrast to these private patrons, the patriarchs of Constantinople after the death of Justinian I were nearly all careerists in the public church system who had advanced through the ranks of the patriarchal bureaucracy or had served as directors of the public philanthropic institutions.[23] This began to change toward the end of the seventh century. Two patriarchs of Justinian II, Paul III (688–694), a layman and imperial *asekretis* (personal secretary), and Cyrus (705–712), an abbot of a monastery at Amastre who helped the emperor recover his throne, were selected from outside the ordinary avenues of promotion, as was Germanus I (715–730), who had been bishop of Cyzicus before his elevation.

As the life of Theodore of Sykeon demonstrates, private foundations differed from public churches in their means of financial support. Private benefactors still preferred to support their foundations with revenues from hypothecated personal property.[24] The rich Cypriot landowner and merchant Philentolos used hypothecated incomes to support his *nosokomeion* founded near Constantia in the second quarter of the seventh century, as did Andrew, archbishop of Crete (ca. 712–740), when he funded a new *xenon* in his diocese out of his personal resources. Even Emperor Justin II, like his predecessor Justinian, preferred the use of hypothecated revenues to formal landed endowments.[25]

Another emperor, Justinian II, was a notable benefactor of the basilica of St. Demetrius, the cathedral church of the archbishop of Thessalonica. A fragmentary inscription dated to 688 records his grant of tax-free salt

[21] Theophanes, *Chronographia* a.m. 6186 (ed. De Boor, p. 367); Nicephorus, *Breviarium* (ed. De Boor, pp. 37, 39).

[22] Theophanes, *Chronographia* a.m. 6187 (p. 368); Nicephorus, *Breviarium* (p. 38).

[23] For the backgrounds of the patriarchs of Constantinople in this period, see Ephraem, *De patriarchis*, ed. I. Bekker, CSHB (Bonn, 1840), lines 9780–85, 9801–9905. According to Louis Bréhier, *Le monde byzantin*, Vol. 2 (Paris, 1948), 483, forty-five of the forty-seven patriarchs after this period were monks, providing a striking contrast in backgrounds.

[24] F. Halkin, "La vision de Kaioumos et le sort éternel de Philentolos Olympiou," AB 63 (1945), 56–64, esp. 62; Nicetas the Patrician, *Vita S. Andreae*, ed. A. Papadopoulos-Kerameus, *Analekta Hierosolymitikes Stachylogias*, Vol. 5 (St. Petersburg, l898), 169–79, esp. 176, lines 16–26.

[25] Theophanes, *Chronographia* a.m. 6058 (ed. De Boor, p. 242).

flats to this church for the *diaria* of the officiating clergy and the illumination of the building.[26] His use of land grants to support a public church was traditional, but the tax-free status of this particular imperial donation appears to be an important innovation.[27] This was a break from the legal principle of the fourth century that ecclesiastical properties should always bear the burden of government taxes even if clerics were granted personal immunities.

FATE OF PRIVATE RELIGIOUS FOUNDATIONS IN THE FIRST AGE OF ICONOCLASM (726–787)

Contrary to what one might expect, Emperor Leo III (717–741) and his campaign against the employment of icons in Byzantine churches did not have an immediately adverse effect on the empire's private religious foundations.[28] As the Arians, Montanists, and other sectarian dissidents had done before them, the iconodules found refuge in private foundations after Leo III announced the government's new policy in 730. The case of Patriarch Germanus I (715–730), who opposed iconoclasm, is instructive. After Leo had him deposed, Germanus simply retired to the Chora monastery on his family estate of Platanion outside Constantinople.[29] The parents of Stephen the Younger, also conscientious iconodules, likewise departed with their son from the capital at this time and settled across the Bosphorus at Chalcedon. They decided to place the young Stephen in the venerable monastery of St. Auxentius, a private foundation of the late fifth century. Here Stephen rose through the ranks of minor offices to achieve the hegoumenate in the reign of Leo III's son and successor Constantine V (741–775).

The existence of numerous private religious foundations under managements independent of the ecclesiastical hierarchy certainly made it difficult for iconoclasm to gain quick and universal acceptance. Perhaps Leo III was misled into believing that he had won an easy victory over his opponents, for, during the first iconoclast emperor's reign, a short

[26] A. A. Vasiliev, "An Edict of the Emperor Justinian II," *Speculum* 18 (1943), 1–13; Henri Grégoire, "Un édit de l'empereur Justinien II, daté de septembre 688," *Byzantion* 17 (1944–45), 119–124a.

[27] See George Ostrogorsky, "Pour l'histoire de l'immunité à Byzance," *Byzantion* 28 (1958), 165–254, esp. 178.

[28] For the course of Iconoclasm under Leo III, see Stephen Gero, *Byzantine Iconoclasm during the Reign of Leo III*, CSCO Vol. 346, *Subsidia*, Vol. 41 (Louvain, 1973), and Dietrich Stein, *Der Beginn des byzantinischen Bilderstreites und seine Entwicklung bis in die 40er Jahre des 8. Jahrhunderts* (Munich, 1980).

[29] Theophanes, *Chronographia* a.m. 6221 (ed. De Boor, p. 409); *Vita S. Michaelis Syncelli*, ed. Th. Schmitt, "Kahrié-Djami," *IRAIK* 11 (1906), 227–94, esp. 251; Stephanus Diaconus, *Vita S. Stephani junioris* (PG 100, cols. 1069–1186, esp. 1088AB); cf. Janin, *Géographie*, Vol. 2, pp. 44–45 and Vol. 3, p. 533.

distancing from Constantinople was all that was necessary for the icon-odules to obtain freedom for their religious practices.

Constantine V's more determined enforcement of iconoclasm revealed the extent of popular opposition as well as the location of its strong-holds.[30] He easily won the assent of the bishops assembled at the Council of Hiereia (754) for his condemnation of the icons. With support from the hierarchy of the church assured, the resistance of the private foun-dations was all the more apparent. The imperial government became aware that the private monastic communities formed the backbone of opposition to iconoclasm.

Since the ecclesiastical hierarchy lacked any effective control over these institutions, the government had to undertake a systematic visitation of each foundation to compel adherence to the iconoclastic doctrine of Hiereia. Stephen the Younger's hagiographic life preserves the instruc-tions Constantine V gave to the patrician Kallistos on the occasion of his visit to the monastery of St. Auxentius: "When you come upon Mount Auxentius . . . persuade the individual of the name of Stephen who re-sides there . . . to subscribe to the synod [of Hiereia], saying, 'In friend-ship to you, our pious and orthodox emperors Constantine [V] and Leo [IV], moved by the piety of your life, order you to subscribe to the defi-nition (*horos*) of our orthodox synod.' Give palm branches and figs to him, and other things that are fitting for the support (*trophe*) of an as-cetic." [31]

At this point, far from being motivated by a passionate hatred of mo-nasticism, Constantine V appears here offering symbolic gifts promising imperial maintenance for monks who were willing to accept icono-clasm.[32] Indeed, his contemporary Patriarch Constantine II (754–766) had been a monk and bishop of Pisidian Sylaeum before his elevation, and the prelate continued to wear monastic habit till nearly the end of his patriarchate.[33] Some monks, including Sergios, a member of Stephen's own community, followed the patriarch's example and accepted icono-clasm.[34] Those who could not had to flee the hitherto safe areas outside Constantinople on either side of the Bosphorus and the Propontis for more distant refuges.

[30] For the course of Iconoclasm under Constantine V, see Stephen Gero, *Byzantine Icon-oclasm during the Reign of Constantine V*, CSCO, Vol. 384, *Subsidia*, Vol. 52 (Louvain, 1977); E. J. Martin, *A History of the Iconoclastic Controversy* (London, 1930); Alfred Lom-bard, *Constantin V, empereur des Romains* (Paris, 1902); Kathryn Ringrose, "Monks and Society in Iconoclastic Byzantium," *Byzantine Studies* 6 (1979), 130–51 (an important study of the problem from the perspective of social history).

[31] Stephanus Diaconus, *Vita* (PG 100, col. 1124A).

[32] Cf. the contrary opinion of Gero, *Constantine V*, 249.

[33] For Patriarch Constantine II, see Theophanes, *Chronographia* a.m. 6245 (ed. De Boor, p. 427), and Ephrem, *De patriarchis* (CSHB, lines 9915–30).

[34] Stephanus Diaconus, *Vita* (PG 100, cols. 1125B; cf 1120B).

The resistance and flight of these monks aggravated the traditional tensions between the ecclesiastical hierarchy and the private foundations. Stephen the Younger, the leader of the monastic opposition, gave advice on where persecuted monastic communities could flee for safety.[35] He established contacts with lay opponents of the emperor, including some of the most important military governors.[36] Constantine V turned bitterly against his monastic opponents and supported the ecclesiastical authorities in their attempts to reduce the foundations to their proper state of canonical submission. He got the populace of Constantinople to promise that they would not accept communion from monks, a concession that reserved the sacrament for the public churches.[37] The bishops and the metropolitans gave the emperor's iconoclastic policy wholehearted support.

Eventually Constantine V had to resort to more drastic measures to crush the resistance of the private foundations. As Justinian had done with earlier sectaries, Constantine V employed fiscal sanctions against his opponents. The monastery of St. Auxentius had tax liabilities to the government. Kallistos enlisted the services of Aulikalamos, chief tax collector for the district of Nicomedia, to bring suit against Stephen.[38] Later the government confiscated the foundation. Constantine V then ordered the monastery destroyed and the community dispersed.

The emperor had Stephen brought to trial in 763 at the monastery of Philippicus at Chrysopolis.[39] Theodosios, metropolitan of Ephesus, and Constantine, archbishop of Nicomedia, represented the ecclesiastical hierarchy at the trial, while Kallistos and other officials presented the government's case against Stephen. Constantine, who was Stephen's nominal ecclesiastical superior, displayed the hatred of the hierarchy for the leaders of the stubbornly independent private foundations. Theodosios and Kallistos had to break off a physical assault that the archbishop made on Stephen. Since Stephen refused to assent to Hiereia, the court sent him into exile. Sometime later, Constantine V himself ordered him imprisoned at Phiale. Finally a mob, with the emperor's acquiescence, lynched the iconodule leader in Constantinople on November 28, 765.[40]

Stephen's death marked a turning point in the emperor's policy. Patriarch Constantine II put aside his monastic habit. On August 21, 766, Constantine V staged a theatrical humiliation of some monks in the hip-

---

[35] Vita, cols. 1113C, 1117CD.

[36] Theophanes, Chronographia a.m. 6259 (ed. De Boor, p. 443); cf. Lombard, Constantin V, 146, and Martin, Iconoclastic Controversy, 61.

[37] Stephanus Diaconus, Vita (PG 100, col. 1112B); cf. Lombard, Constantin V, 150.

[38] Vita, col. 1125C.

[39] Vita, col. 1140B; cf. 1141B.

[40] Theophanes, Chronographia a.m. 6257 (ed. De Boor, p. 436); Nicephorus, Breviarium (ed. De Boor, p. 72); Stephanus Diaconus, Vita (PG 100, col. 1177BC).

podrome in Constantinople. Four days later he uncovered a conspiracy against the throne which included nineteen high imperial officials.[41] Perhaps the emperor's treatment of Stephen and the confiscation of the monastery of St. Auxentius alarmed these officials, who may well have owned private foundations of their own that had not yet been affected by iconoclasm. Constantine V executed the ringleaders and exiled the rest.

Shortly thereafter an informant implicated Patriarch Constantine II in the conspiracy. The patriarch may also have been horrified at the new anti-monastic bent of the emperor's policy.[42] A monk himself for most of his life, Constantine II declined to participate in the trial of Stephen the Younger. The emperor deposed and exiled the patriarch for the time being. In October 767 he brought him back to the capital for execution.

The emperor chose an individual of an entirely different background as Constantine's successor. He was Nicetas I (766–780), who had spent his whole career in the bureaucracy of the public church system.[43] He was *archon* of the patriarchal monasteries at the time of his elevation on November 16, 766.[44] The new patriarch must have been quite familiar with the problematic relationship of the great monastic foundations to the authorities of the patriarchate. Now he was to preside over the church during the most severe challenge ever launched against the existence of private foundations in the Byzantine Empire.

Once he had secured Nicetas' election as patriarch, Constantine V turned his attention to crushing his opponents and enforcing iconoclasm throughout the empire. He announced his opposition to monastic vocations, appointed new iconoclastic *strategoi* (military governors) for the provinces, and secularized or destroyed some of the oldest private monasteries in Constantinople (767/68).[45] The emperor's governors, particularly Michael Lachonodrakon, *strategos* of the Thrakesion theme, followed his example zealously. Theophanes reports that in 771/72 this governor sold all the monasteries in his jurisdiction and liquidated their

[41] Theophanes, *Chronographia* a.m. 6257 (ed. De Boor, pp. 437–39); Nicephorus, *Breviarium* (ed. De Boor, p. 74).

[42] So Lombard, *Constantin V*, 148; Martin, *Iconoclastic Controversy*, 66; and Gero, *Constantine V*, 133; cf. Constantine II's abandonment of monastic habit under pressure from the emperor: Theophanes, *Chronographia* a.m. 6257 (ed. De Boor, p. 437); his refusal to participate in the trial of Stephen the Younger: Stephanus Diaconus, *Vita* (*PG* 100, col. 1140B).

[43] For Nicetas I, see Franz Fischer, *De patriarcharum Constantinopolitanorum catalogis* (Leipzig, 1884), 290; Ephrem, *De patriarchis* (*CSHB*, lines 9931–37); Nicephorus Callistus, *Enarratio de episcopis Byzantii* (*PG* 147, cols. 449–68, at 460); Gero, *Constantine V*, 137, n. 102.

[44] For this office, see Jean Darrouzès, *Recherches sur les offikia de l'église byzantine* (Paris, 1970), 312–13.

[45] Theophanes, *Chronographia* a.m. 6259 (ed. De Boor, pp. 442–43); cf. Gero, *Constantine V*, 138–39.

interior furnishings and means of support.[46] A renegade abbot, Leo Kou-
loukes, carried out the confiscations and sent the proceeds to the emperor.

The iconoclastic sympathizers who purchased these former monasteries retained possession of them until the Second Council of Nicaea commanded their restitution in 787.[47] While Constantine V certainly intended to crush opposition to his religious policy, it is also possible that
he intended to punish lay patrons who had proven disloyal and to reward
faithful followers who henceforth represented the imperial government
in the provinces.[48]

Patriarch Nicetas took advantage of the emperor's anti-monastic zeal
to strengthen the public church system. He permitted imperial governors
to use the nomination rights of dispossessed iconodules to promote clerics sympathetic to iconoclasm. The Second Council of Nicaea later challenged the legitimacy of these appointments.[49] He encouraged the foundation of new churches, perhaps to replace private monastic chapels that
perished in the secularizations. The Nicaean fathers criticized these foundations since the public church authorities had consecrated them without
relics in deference to the emperor's opinions.[50]

In 768 Nicetas initiated a program of restoring *katholikai ekklesiai*
that had collapsed over the course of time.[51] After Constantine V's death
in 775, Nicetas even permitted the revival of monastic foundations. Theophanes records that the new emperor, Leo IV (775–780), actually favored abbots as his nominees for vacant metropolitan sees.[52] Nicetas was
evidently a capable and conscientious patriarch, a staunch defender of
the interests of the public churches and undeserving of the blackened
reputation accorded him by the iconodules at the Council of Nicaea.

Leo IV and Patriarch Nicetas already had the support of the ecclesiastical hierarchy, and they had now sponsored a revival of loyal iconoclastic monasteries. The emperor felt confident enough in this loyalty to
impose monastic tonsure as a penalty upon some iconodule courtiers
whose sympathies became known after the elevation of Paul IV (780–784)
to the patriarchate.[53] By contrast, tonsure certainly would not have been
a feasible punishment for iconodules as recently as Constantine V's reign.

---

[46] Theophanes, *Chronographia* a.m. 6263 (ed. De Boor, pp. 445–46).

[47] *C. Nicaen. II*, c. 13 (R&P 2.612).

[48] Note the sale of monasteries reported by Nicephorus, *Antirrheticus adversus Constan-
tinum Copronymum* (PG 100, cols. 205–534, at 439D), the circumstances of the liquidation of monasteries in the Thracesian theme as described by Theophanes, *Chronographia*
a.m. 6259 (ed. De Boor, pp. 442–43), and the reference in the preceeding note.

[49] *C. Nicaen. II*, c. 3 (R&P 2.564).

[50] *C. Nicaen. II*, c. 7 (R&P 2.580); cf. Nicephorus, *Antirrheticus* (PG 100. col. 344).

[51] Nicephorus, *Breviarium* (ed. De Boor, p. 76).

[52] Theophanes, *Chronographia* a.m. 6268 (ed. De Boor, p. 449).

[53] Theophanes, *Chronographia* a.m. 6272 (ed. De Boor, p. 453).

REVIVAL OF PRIVATE RELIGIOUS FOUNDATIONS

Leo IV's premature death in 780 led to the rise of his wife, Irene, to imperial power as regent for their son Constantine VI (780–797). This proved crucial to the victory of the iconodules over the iconoclasts. The monasteries developed by Leo IV and Nicetas might well have remained loyal to iconoclasm and subordinate to the ecclesiastical hierarchy, if Irene had not gained the throne and reconstituted the church on an entirely different basis.

The career of Theophanes the Confessor, which bridged the reigns of Leo IV and Irene, is particularly relevant. This important figure, whose chronicle is our principal account of the first age of iconoclasm, began his career in the service of Leo IV. The emperor sponsored a marriage for Theophanes with the daughter of a convinced iconoclast. Theophanes treated his bride cooly as a fleshly distraction from his secret monastic vocation. He further aroused the ire of his father-in-law by liquidating his spouse's dowry for charitable purposes. The vociferous protest of his father-in-law to Leo IV remains a stunning denunciation of the ideals cherished by pious Byzantine philanthropists.[54]

Theophanes had to await the deaths of Leo IV and his irate father-in-law before he could put his unfortunate spouse away and found the monasteries he had long desired. These were Polychronion at Sigriana and another on the island of Kalonymos located on a family estate.[55] He was only one of a number of private benefactors who took part in the revival of ecclesiastical foundations under iconodule auspices. Empress Irene herself, her patriarch Tarasius (784–806), and such important figures as Plato of Sakkoudion and his nephew Theodore the Studite owned newly founded private monasteries.[56] Usually these patrons erected their foundations on patrimonial suburban estates (*proasteia*), as Rufinus had done many centuries earlier.

Irene was also active in the construction of new imperial churches and monasteries in Constantinople and its vicinity.[57] One of these, a monas-

---

[54] *Vita S. Theophanis*, Ch. 8 (*PG* 115, cols. 16–17), with discussion by J. B. Bury, *History of the Later Roman Empire from Arcadius to Irene* (London, 1889), Vol. 2, p. 524.

[55] *Vita S. Theophanis*, Ch. 12 (*PG* 115, col. 22), and C. Van de Vorst, "Une panégyrique de de S. Théophane le Chronographe par S. Théodore Studite," *AB* 31 (1912), Ch. 6, pp. 21–22.

[56] For these foundations, see Theophanes, *Chronographia* a.m. 6295 (ed. De Boor, p. 478), Ignatius Diaconus, *Vita Tarasii*, ed. I. A. Heikel, *Acta societatis scientiarum Fennicae* 17 (Helsinki, 1891), 390–439, esp. 404, 421; *Patria Konstantinoupoleos* 3.160 (p. 266), Michael the Monk, *Vita S. Theodori* Ch. 6 (*PG* 109, col. 121C), and Janin, *Géographie*, Vol. 2, pp. 68, 177–81; Vol. 3, pp. 481–82. For St. Theodore, see Charles Frazee, "St. Theodore of Studios and Ninth Century Monasticism in Constantinople," *Studia Monastica* 23 (1981), 27–58.

[57] *Patria Konstantinoupoleos* 3.17 (p. 219), 3.77 (p. 243), 3.85 (p. 246), 3.154 (p. 265); cf. 3.9 (p. 216).

tery on the island of Prinkipo, became her place of exile after her deposition in 802. This institution became a favored place for settling retired empresses and princesses whose continued residence in Constantinople would have caused embarrassment to the government.

In the supportive environment of Irene's reign, the patrician Michael was able to employ all of his possessions for the establishment of a new monastery in Constantinople dedicated to the Theotokos of Psicha. He was even able to obtain Irene's permission for St. John the Psichaite and one of his brothers to transfer out of the imperial monastery of Pege to serve as *hegoumenos* and *oikonomos*, respectively, of his own foundation.[58]

Tarasius, imperial *protasekretis* (chief personal secretary) before his elevation to the patriarchate in 784, was an important private benefactor in his own right. While still a layman, he founded a private monastery on his patrimonial estate at Stenon outside Constantinople.[59] As patriarch, he was consistently receptive to the needs and interests of private foundations. He relied upon the *hegoumenoi* of iconodule monasteries for support and furthered the careers of their protégés. His own monastery at Stenon provided a training ground for two of his own protégés, Theophylact and Michael, whom he advanced to the bishoprics of Nicomedia and Synadon respectively.[60]

Thanks to Irene, the iconodule representatives of the private foundations had achieved what no other group of proscribed sectarians had done since the "orthodox" opponents of the Arians triumphed at the Council of Constantinople in 381: they had emerged from hiding and persecution to assume control of the public church system. Tarasius, a magnate and private benefactor promoted from the ranks of the laity to the highest office of the church, personally symbolized the victory of the private foundations.

Although Tarasius came from an entirely different background from the ecclesiastical careerist Nicetas, he nevertheless continued the strengthening of the public church system begun by his predecessor. Tarasius' protégé Theophylact began his career as his assistant during his term as *protasekretis*. When Tarasius became patriarch in 784, Theophylact helped direct the monastery at Stenon with the assistance of Michael

---

[58] *Vita S. Joannis Psichaiae*, ed. I. Van den Ven, "La vie grecque de S. Jean le Psichaite, confesseur sous le règne de Léon l'Arménien (813–820)," *Le Museon* n.s. 3 (1902), 97–125, esp. Ch. 5, at 110–11.

[59] E.g., Peter of Atroa, protégé of *hegoumenos* Paul: see V. Laurent, "La vie merveilleuse de Saint Pierre d'Atroa," *Subsidia Hagiographica* 29 (1956), Ch. 6, pp. 81–85; also Nicetas, protégé of Nicephorus of Medikion: see Janin, *Géographie*, Vol. 2, p. 166; and of course Theodore of Studium, protégé of Plato of Sakkoudion.

[60] See Albert Vogt, "S. Théophylacte de Nicomédie," *AB* 50 (1932), 67–82, with his edition of the *Vita* at 71–82.

of Synadon. Later he worked on the restoration of deteriorating *katho-likai ekklesiai*, a project that Tarasius inherited from Nicetas. When Tarasius appointed Theophylact metropolitan of Nicomedia, the new bishop busied himself with the erection of new parochial churches and a diocesan *nosokomeion*. Theophylact's friend Michael had already become bishop of Synadon by the time the Council of Nicaea convened in 787. Although he received his training (as Theophylact had done) in a private foundation, he was active in erecting churches, monasteries, and philanthropic institutions in his diocese.[61]

SECOND COUNCIL OF NICAEA

The careers of Tarasius' protégés illustrate the irony that the representatives of the private foundations could not help but become involved in activities that aided the rival public churches once they assumed responsible positions in the ecclesiastical hierarchy. Nevertheless, one of the principal tasks of the Second Council of Nicaea, assembled under Tarasius' presidency to restore the place of the holy icons in the Byzantine church, was to redress the damage done to private foundations by Constantine V's anti-monastic policies.[62]

The process of rebuilding destroyed monasteries and founding new ones was already well under way even before 787. The *hegoumenoi* of the monasteries of Dios, Kallistratos, and Floros, three of the institutions that Constantine V had destroyed or secularized in 767/68, were among the participants at the council.[63] Unfortunately, pious zeal outstripped the available capital in many cases, and the council had to revive Justinian's warning to clerics, monks and laymen not to attempt construction without adequate resources for completion.[64]

It was a more difficult matter to attempt to recover monasteries and episcopal palaces (probably those of iconodule bishops) from the beneficiaries of Constantine V's secularizations. It was a source of embarrassment to the council that not only laymen but even monks and clerics were in possession of former monasteries and *episkopeia*.[65] In reaction to this state of affairs, the council ordered that henceforth the bishops

---

[61] His *Vita* remains unpublished, but K. Doukakis, *Megas Synaxaristes*, Vol. 9, 2nd ed. (Athens, 1963), 224, provides a summary; cf. the comments of Vogt, "S. Théophylacte," 73, n. 2.

[62] *C. Nicaen. II*, c. 13 (R&P 2.612); cf. c. 12 (R&P 592–93).

[63] Gregory of the monastery of Callistratus, Antonius of the monastery of Dios, and Eustratius of the monastery of Maximus, all mentioned in *C. Nicaen. II, Acta* (ed. Mansi, Vol. 13, col. 152ACD). For these institutions, see Janin, *Géographie*, Vol. 3, pp. 98, 275–76, 323.

[64] *C. Nicaen. II*, c. 17 (R&P 2.625)

[65] *C. Nicaen. II*, c. 13 (R&P 2.612).

and abbots should not lease out even profitless tracts of land to state officials.[66] The administrators of the churches and monasteries were to reserve these lands for rental by lay or clerical peasants, an example of preferential class discrimination which anticipated the imperial agrarian legislation of the tenth century. The council also cautioned these administrators that they should be on guard for unscrupulous magnates who might use clerics and husbandmen as fronts in order to secure these lands illegally.

The clerical administrators of the great foundations were often the social equals of the local landed magnates. They were not immune from the temptation to detach the properties of these institutions for their own enrichment or that of their relatives. The council severely condemned this evil practice and declared that the *autourgion*, the landed endowment of a church or monastery, should always remain intact and inalienable. The strong pressures for alienation of these lands, probably stimulated by the iconoclastic secularizations, anticipate the donations of entire institutions to influential laymen which were to occur in subsequent centuries.

It is unclear whether the council permitted foundations to grant out individual properties for management by lay curators as public churches had customarily done. The council certainly did take a hostile view of clerics termed *meizoteroi* who held managerial *kouratoreia* (curatorship) of secular estates.[67] Perhaps the council attempted to draw a strict distinction between secular and ecclesiastical estates by prohibiting clerical management of the former and lay management of the latter. Indeed, it seems that the choice of the word *autourgion*, which literally means "self-worked farm," implies internal management by the institution that owned this land.

The old problem of migratory clerics who left their assigned churches for better paying ones or migrated to Constantinople to serve laymen in their private *eukteria* continued to plague the church. The Council of Nicaea issued another disapproving canon against these clerics which proved to be as ineffectual as the earlier condemnations of Justinian and Heraclius. Apparently there was little the authorities could do to curb the flow of this economically motivated migration of clergy.

Even Byzantium's saints abandoned miserably paid or unendowed clerical positions for better opportunities elsewhere. The life of St. John the Psichaite provides a good example of this.[68] John's father was a priest named Leo who abandoned a church in a Galatian village sometime in the 770s or 780s in order to provide better support for his family. Leo had hoped that his children would not follow his wretched profession

---

[66] C. Nicaen. II, c. 12 (R&P 2.592–93).
[67] C. Nicaen. II, c. 10 (R&P 2.587–88).
[68] Vita S. Joannis Psichaiae, Ch. 2–3 (ed. Van den Ven, pp. 104–5, 106–7, 108).

but would find promising careers in secular life when they came of age. Yet, as it turned out, all were inspired to adopt monastic vocations. Leo reluctantly gave his blessing to their plans and decided to take monastic vows himself. He put his wife and daughter in a local Bithynian monastery and departed with his three sons for Constantinople. There they all became monks in the imperial monastery of the Theotokos surnamed Pege (the Source) (ca. 784). After Leo's death, Patriarch Tarasius himself ordained John as a deacon. This was the beginning of an illustrious career accomplished in spite of the canonical regulations that would have made John's rise to prominence impossible had his father been scrupulous enough to obey them.

The council's canon issued against migratory clerics demonstrates that even the iconodule magnates who now controlled the church could not ignore one of the most persistent problems stemming from the existence of privately directed and funded religious institutions. Yet it was often in Tarasius' interests to promote individuals like John the Psichaite, especially since the episcopal hierarchy had many iconoclastic sympathizers in its ranks as lately as 786.[69]

The drain of clerical manpower to the capital had serious consequences for both rural and urban churches. The fathers of the Council of Nicaea acknowledged that pluralism was rampant everywhere.[70] They stuffily reminded urban pluralists that there were plenty of canonically approved secular occupations available in Constantinople if a single clerical post could not provide for an incumbent's needs. The shortage of clergy in the countryside may have played some part in the closing of churches by bishops, a practice that the present council condemned.[71] Apparently little had changed since Heraclius had addressed the problem of pluralism a hundred and fifty years earlier. This time the ecclesiastical hierarchy decided to concentrate on eradicating urban pluralism while tolerating it in the countryside, where there was a serious shortage of clerical manpower.

IMPERIAL POLICY AND PRIVATE RELIGIOUS
FOUNDATIONS (802–813)

Irene's partiality toward religious benefactors was extended at great cost to the imperial treasury. Perhaps it is significant that Nicephorus I (802–811), her successor who came to power after a successful coup d'etat, had been her *logothetes tou genikou*, the chief of imperial finances. Un-

---

[69] Theophanes, *Chronographia* a.m. 6278 (ed. De Boor, p. 461).
[70] C. *Nicaen. II*, c. 15 (R&P 2.620)
[71] C. *Nicaen. II*, c. 4 (R&P 2.566–67).

willing as he was to continue her policies, Nicephorus I aroused the ire of the great benefactors, and Theophanes, their spokesman and principal source for his reign, criticized the emperor severely.

The revolt in 803 of Vardanes, *strategos* of the Anatolic theme and owner of an important private monastery on the island of Prote, made Nicephorus I aware of the opposition to his rule amongst the great magnates and their monastic supporters.[72] He would not allow the patrician Niketas, *strategos* of Sicily under Irene, to leave court in order to embrace monastic life.[73] When Tarasius died in 806, the emperor passed over Theodore the Studite and supported another layman, his *protasekretis* Nicephorus, as the new patriarch.[74] Ecclesiastical bitterness culminated in 808 when several bishops, monks, and three high officials of Hagia Sophia were implicated in the revolt of the patrician Arsaver.[75]

Not surprisingly, Nicephorus I treated the church harshly in his laws of 810, which introduced considerable changes in the levying of taxation in the Byzantine Empire.[76] Of all these laws, which Theophanes designated the "ten wickednesses," the fifth was the most injurious to ecclesiastical interests. This provision obligated the peasants of philanthropic institutions, churches, and imperial monasteries to pay the *kapnika* (hearth taxes) to the government.[77] Moreover, Nicephorus made the liability for payment retroactive to the first year of his reign.

The lay dependents of these religious institutions did not ordinarily enjoy immunity from taxation. Who had originally exempted these peasants from the *kapnika*? Irene, with her reputation as a friend to religious foundations and private benefactors, is the most likely possibility.[78] It is hard to believe that Constantine V would have enacted a measure of this sort, although the exemption might have been part of his son Leo IV's program of encouraging iconoclastic monasteries. It is possible that Nicephorus I himself may have made the concession early in his reign, but the emergence of monasteries with landed endowments during the reign of Irene accords best with a grant made by her to encourage them. Be that as it may, Nicephorus I now discovered (as Theodosius I and his successors had done with respect to Constantine's program of clerical

[72] Theophanes, *Chronographia* a.m. 6295 (ed. De Boor, pp. 478–80); for this foundation, see Janin, *Géographie*, Vol. 2, 70–72.

[73] *Synaxarium*, ed. D. Papachryssanthou, "Un confesseur du second iconoclasme: La vie du Patrice Nicétas (+ 836)," *T&M* 3 (1968), 309–51, esp. Ch. 1, 325.

[74] Theophanes, *Chronographia* a.m. 6298 (ed. De Boor, p. 481); for Nicephorus I, see P. J. Alexander, *The Patriarch Nicephorus of Constantinople* (Oxford, 1958).

[75] Theophanes, *Chronographia* a.m. 6300 (ed. De Boor, pp. 483–84).

[76] Dölger, *Regesten* Nos. 372–79.

[77] Theophanes, *Chronographia* a.m. 6302 (ed. De Boor, pp. 486–87).

[78] George Ostrogorsky, *History of the Byzantine State* (New Brunswick, N.J., 1969), 188. For another view, see Paul Speck, *Kaiser Konstantin VI.*, Vol. 1 (Munich, 1978), 383, with n. 392.

tax exemptions) that the costs in lost revenue due to this immunity were simply too heavy for the government to accept.

Theophanes says that Nicephorus I also took into imperial curatorship the better part of the properties of these religious foundations.[79] This meant that the government took over the management of their landed endowments. Nicephorus I also doubled the property taxes paid by many religious institutions and their peasants in order to increase the government's share of revenue from those lands not under state management.

Although the increased taxation seemed to Theophanes to be an outrageous burden for such benefactors as himself to bear, a conscientious government could not have acted otherwise. During the reign of Irene, private benefactors began to abandon the old practice of supporting their religious foundations with hypothecated revenues in favor of formal landed endowments. The favorable tax rates and the exemption from *kapnika* served to encourage benefactors to make generous bequests of their personal property.

As has been noted, the patrician Michael donated all of his personal property to his new monastery of the Theotokos of Psicha. Eustathios and Niketas, the sons of St. Philaret the Merciful (d. 792), granted their *proasteia* to the family monastery of St. George the Praepositus in Paphlagonia.[80] This institution was probably among those founded by Philaret's widow, Theosebe, after his death. The practice of granting landed endowments to private foundations became more and more common during the first half of the ninth century. Therefore, the imperial government simply could not allow the properties that made up these endowments to escape taxation.

Nicephorus I resorted in the following year to even more drastic measures to exploit the wealth of the empire's religious institutions for the benefit of the government.[81] He ordered the quartering of military officers in monasteries and *episkopeia* and placed the resources of these institutions at the disposal of the boarders. He carried out secularizations of consecrated vessels. His *logothetes tou genikou*, the patrician Niketas, drew up a new tax register for the churches and monasteries and demanded eight years' back taxes from the magnates' households.

After Nicephorus I's death, Michael I (811–813) chose to follow a different policy toward the empire's religious institutions.[82] He gave large

[79] Theophanes, *Chronographia* a.m. 6302; cf. 6303 (ed. De Boor, pp. 486–87, 489).

[80] Nicetas of Amnia, *Vita S. Philareti eleemosynarii*, ed. M. H. Fourmy and M. Leroy, "La vie de S. Philarète," *Byzantion* 9 (1934), 85–170, esp. 155, 157, 165–67.

[81] Theophanes, *Chronographia* a.m. 6303 (ed. De Boor, p. 489); cf. Dölger, *Regesten* Nos. 370, 380.

[82] For Michael I's policy, see Theophanes, *Chronographia* a.m. 6304, 6305 (ed. De Boor, pp. 493–94, 500).

cash gifts to the patriarch and the clergy of the public churches. He visited the monastery of Tarasius and donated a valuable silver votive offering in honor of the deceased patriarch. According to Theophanes, in a
matter of days Michael I's generosity wiped out the evil effects of Nicephorus I's financial economies. The new emperor did retain his predecessor's program of imperial curatorship of ecclesiastical properties. The
sources also speak of his awards of imperial monasteries to court favorites. Michael I not only permitted the patrician Niketas to undertake the
monastic career denied to him by Nicephorus I; he also put the monastery at Chrysonike (near the Golden Gate in Constantinople) at his disposal.[83] Niketas, confident of his tenure of this institution, followed contemporary practice and donated a *proasteion* to it. The emperor also
induced Theophano, the wife of Stauracius, son of the late emperor Nicephorus I, to go into retirement by offering her a grant of the imperial
monastery of Hebraika in Constantinople.[84]

PRIVATE RELIGIOUS FOUNDATIONS IN THE SECOND AGE OF ICONOCLASM (813–842)

Leo the Armenian, *strategos* of the Anatolikon theme, deposed Michael I in July 813. Michael fled with his family to the church of the
Theotokos tou Pharou (probably founded by Constantine V) and accepted monastic tonsure. As the new emperor, Leo V (813–820) ordered
the emasculation of Michael's two sons and sent them with their father
to the imperial monastery on Prote (recently confiscated from Vardanes
by Nicephorus I).[85] Michael's wife, Prokopia, retired to her own private
monastery in Constantinople.[86] One of Michael's sons, Niketas, later became patriarch under his monastic name, Ignatius (847–858, 867–877).
He was an important private benefactor in his own right who erected
several new religious foundations before his elevation to the patriarchate.[87]

Leo V resolved to revive the iconoclastic religious policy favored by
his militarily successful predecessors Leo III and Constantine V. He had
Patriarch Nicephorus deposed and replaced him with the layman Theodotus Melissenus (815–821). A synod under the new patriarch's presi-

---

[83] *Synaxarium* Ch. 2 (ed. Papachryssanthou, p. 325).

[84] Theophanes, *Chronographia* a.m. 6304 (ed. De Boor, p. 494).

[85] Theophanes, *Chronographia* a.m. 6305 (ed. De Boor, p. 502); Theophanes Continuatus, *Chronographia* (*CSHB* 40–41).

[86] *Patria Konstantinoupoleos* 3.153 (p. 264); for this foundation, see Janin, *Géographie*,
Vol. 3, pp. 442–43.

[87] For details, see Janin, *Géographie*, Vol. 2, pp. 42, 63, 65, 67, 133, 135, 173.

dency condemned the Second Council of Nicaea and reaffirmed the authority of the iconoclastic Council of Hiereia (754).[88] The new iconoclastic emperor followed the lead of Nicephorus I and Michael I by maintaining the imperial government's role in the management of ecclesiastical institutions and properties. A recently discovered inscription of 813 preserves the epitaph of Sisinnios, a *basilikos kourator* (imperial curator) of Tzurulon, seat of a bishopric in Thrace near Adrianople.[89] This imperial official, who was probably one of those who administered the ecclesiastical properties in imperial *kouratoreia*, records the restoration of a monastery of the Theotokos as his proudest accomplishment. This is an interesting testimony to an otherwise unattested activity of imperial curators.

Leo V made full use of his powers of patronage and the resources of financial assistance to reward his followers and punish his iconodule opponents. Iconoclastic bishops and the priests of the public churches received *annona*, a subsidy in kind, from the imperial treasury.[90] Before their iconodule sympathies were known, Leo V lodged Michael the Synkellos and the Graptoi brothers at the Chora monastery, and provided for their needs out of its resources.[91] He deprived the patrician Niketas, a faithful iconodule, of his tenure of the imperial monastery of Chrysonike.[92] Niketas had to seek refuge in the *proasteion* that he had earlier donated to this monastery. In similar fashion, the iconodule monks of the Chora monastery fled to Kastoreon, an outlying property owned by that institution.[93] Thus the endowment properties of these two insitutions enabled some iconodules to defy the government and preserve their traditional religious observances.

The emperors of this era, Leo V, Michael II (820–829), and Theophilus (829–842), relied chiefly upon the hierarchy of the public churches for support. Yet many *hegoumenoi* also supported the government's policy in the second age of iconoclasm. Theodore the Studite, one of the leaders of the iconodule opposition until his death in 826, despaired over the iconoclastic sympathies of the monastery of Philippicus at Chrysopolis.[94] Iconoclastic abbots of monasteries in the Isaurian Decapolis de-

---

[88] P. J. Alexander, "The Iconoclastic Council of St. Sophia (815) and Its Definition (*Horos*)," *DOP* 7 (1953), 35–66.

[89] Ihor Ševčenko, "Inscription Commemorating Sisinnios, 'Curator' of Tzurulon (A.D. 813)," *Byzantion* 35 (1965), 564–74.

[90] Gloss on Ignatius Diaconus, *Vita Nicephori* (*PG* 100, col. 81), reported by Herman, "Bénéfices," col. 714.

[91] *Vita S. Michaelis Syncelli* (ed. Schmitt, p. 234); cf. Janin, *Géographie*, Vol. 3, p. 548.

[92] *Synaxarium* Ch. 2 (ed. Papachryssanthou, p. 325).

[93] *Vita S. Michaelis Syncelli* (ed. Schmitt, p. 254).

[94] Theodore of Studium, *Epistolae* Nos. 41, 79, ed. J. Cozza-Luzi, *Nova patrum bibliotheca*, Vol. 8 (Rome, 1871), 34, 67.

fended the government's policy against iconodule bishops.[95] Thanks to these exceptions, the government's struggle to gain acceptance of iconoclasm in the early ninth century was more than a straightforward contest between the ecclesiastical hierarchy and the private foundations, as it had been in the time of Constantine V.

Like Constantine V, Theophilus relied upon a visitation of private foundations (begun in 829) to obtain from them recognition of the authority of his patriarch, Antonius I (821–834), and, by extension, his iconoclastic policy.[96] The patrician Niketas had to leave his current refuge for a more distant *proasteion*. The iconoclastic hierarchy continued to press Niketas to recognize their authority. Finally he was able to purchase an uncompleted church of St. Michael at Katesia, which he completed and employed as his residence until shortly before his death in 836.[97]

Theophilus continued the policy of his predecessors with respect to granting imperial foundations to favored courtiers for their personal exploitation.[98] Leo the Philosopher received the church of the Forty Martyrs in Mese (built by Tiberius II and Maurice) from the emperor as a reward for offering public instruction. Theophilus also awarded the Philippicus monastery at Chrysopolis to his son-in-law Caesar Alexios Mousele in order to facilitate his retirement into monastic life. When Alexios founded his own private monastery of Ta Anthemiou at Chrysopolis, the monastery of Philippicus evidently returned to direct imperial control, since it later became the burial site for Theophilus' son Michael III (842–867). The church of the Forty Martyrs also remained an imperial institution after Leo the Philosopher became metropolitan of Thessalonica. Like the subsequent *charistikarioi* of the eleventh century, the incumbents of these grants held the status of temporary possessors of the foundations, with a right to the exploitation of their revenues. The arrangements did not alter the constitutional status of these institutions since the emperor retained the ultimate rights of ownership.

Theophilus and his wife, Theodora, themselves played important roles as benefactors. The emperor, acting on a personal appeal by the residents of a nunnery in Constantinople founded by the wife of Constantine VI, restored their structurally unsound building in 840 and converted it into

---

[95] Francis Dvornik, *La vie de Saint Grégoire le Décapolite et les slaves macédoniens au IXe siècle* (Paris, 1926), Ch. 3, 48; cf. Hélène Ahrweiler, "The Geography of the Iconoclast World," in *Iconoclasm*, ed. A. Bryer and J. Herrin (Birmingham, 1977), 21–27, esp. 27.

[96] *Synaxarium* Ch. 4 (ed. Papachryssanthou, p. 327).

[97] *Vita S. Nicetae Patricii* Ch. 14 (ed. Papachryssanthou, "La vie du Nicétas," p. 337).

[98] John Skylitzes, *Synopsis historiarum*, ed. J. Thurn, (Berlin-New York, 1973), p. 103, lines 45–48; Theophanes Continuatus, *Chronographia* 3.18 (CSHB 108–109); Leo Grammaticus, *Chronographia*, ed. I. Bekker, CSHB (Bonn, 1842), p. 686; cf. Janin, *Géographie*, Vol. 2, pp. 17–18; Vol. 3, pp. 483–84 and Herman, "Ricerche," 349.

a *xenon*.[99] He employed both hypothecated revenues and a formal landed endowment to assure financial support. His wife relied entirely upon landed property to support the monastery that she erected in Constantinople in honor of St. Panteleimon. Theophilus' command to the disgraced courtier Martiniakos that he should take monastic vows and convert his house into a monastery gives further proof of the emperor's benevolence toward private foundations that were loyal to iconoclasm.[100]

LEGISLATION OF THE COUNCIL OF CONSTANTINOPLE (861)

Theophilus proved to be the last of the iconoclastic emperors, however. During the reign of his son and successor Michael III (842–867) the iconodules recovered their losses. In 861 a council was held in Constantinople to confirm the election of Photius (858–867) and the deposition of Ignatius (847–858) as patriarch.[101] Several of the canons issued by this council provide the next opportunity to view internal developments in the Byzantine church. From the evidence provided, it is clear that lay patrons were continuing to strengthen their control over individual clerics and monks. The fathers of the council had to condemn once again those clerics who conducted liturgies in the chapels of private dwellings without episcopal permission. According to the canon, these churches were breeding grounds for "discord, anarchy and scandal," consequences of their virtual independence from episcopal supervision.[102]

The divided allegiance of the monastic hierarchy in the second age of iconoclasm had brought about similar disturbances in monastic life. Michael the Synkellos, upon his appointment by Patriarch Methodius (843–847) as *hegoumenos* of the Chora monastery, recalled its refugee monks from the church of St. Tryphon at Kastoreon.[103] Other iconodule monks preferred to stay in the homes of sympathetic laymen where they had found safety at the onset of persecution by the authorities.[104] The Council of Constantinople now commanded them to return to their original assignments, though it did permit local bishops to regularize appointments

[99] Pseudo-Symeon, *Chronographia* Ch. 26, ed. I. Bekker, *CSHB* (Bonn, 1838) pp. 645–46; *Patria Konstantinoupoleos* 3.155 (p. 265); Janin, *Géographie*, Vol. 3, pp. 558–59.

[100] Leo Grammaticus, *Chronographia* (*CSHB* 635); *Patria Konstantinoupoleos* 3.98 (p. 249); Janin, *Géographie*, Vol. 3, p. 340.

[101] For this council, see Theodore Balsamon, *Commentaria ad C. Const. I et II* (R&P 2.648) and Francis Dvornik, *The Photian Schism: History and Legend* (Cambridge, 1948), 77.

[102] *C. Const. I et II*, c. 12 (R&P 2.687–88).

[103] *Vita S. Michaelis Syncelli* (ed. Schmitt, p. 254).

[104] *C. Const. I et II*, c. 4 (R&P 2.658–59).

of some monks to private residences for the "salvation of the inhabitants."

The council hoped to check the growth of clerical and monastic communities in private residences where the local hierarchy could not hope to exercise effective supervision. The legislation, however, hardly had any chance of success since the council apparently was unwilling to ban the participation of clerics in the ecclesiastical service of the laity for fear of angering these important providers of lay philanthropic assistance. Moreover, clerics of the mid-ninth century, like their predecessors in previous centuries, continued to take positions in the management of lay households and estates. The present council added its condemnation of this practice to those of earlier councils, apparently with a similar lack of success in suppressing it.[105]

It is to the credit of this council that it did not simply decry long-standing abuses. The participants also enacted the first important regulations of private foundations since Heraclius' novels in the early seventh century. These were necessary because a steady erosion of Justinian's original regulations over the previous three centuries had resulted in a situation in which private benefactors had virtually unlimited powers of disposition over their foundations.

Despite civil and canon law, a determined benefactor might now simply dispense with the requirement for episcopal approval before undertaking construction. The council noted that some patrons bestowed the name of monastery on part of their personal property, but would treat it no differently after its dedication than any other part of their estates. Even such inappropriate activities as innkeeping might become associated with it. The founder might name himself as the *hegoumenos*, or in any event would be sure to reserve for himself the right to make the appointment. He would ignore the local bishop's customary right to approve and consecrate the *hegoumenos*. In some cases the properties dedicated for the support of the monastery might even be sold, in flagrant violation of canon law.

Evidently benefactors had recovered the nearly unlimited powers that their ancestors had enjoyed before Justinian's regulatory legislation was drawn up. The council recognized the mortal danger and acted to prevent the ecclesiastical foundations of the empire from slipping into complete dependence upon their private patrons. The council fathers turned to renewed and reinforced legislation as an immediate remedy.[106] They

---

[105] C. Const. I et II, c. 11 (R&P 2.686).

[106] C. Const. I et II, c. 1 (R&P 2.648–49); for an example of a *brevion* of an Egyptian *martyrion*, see P. Bad. 4.54 (5th c.), with Julius Kurth, "Ein Stück Klosterinventar auf einem byzantinischen Papyrus," *BNJ* 1 (1920), 142–47.

restored the local bishop to his former role as the overseer of construction and the approver of appointments to the hegoumenate. Moreover, they reinforced the old legislation with a new and momentous measure to secure some autonomy for privately founded monasteries and to protect their means of financial support.

The council started by restating the basic principles of Zeno's original law on private foundations. The really novel element was a requirement for a specific record of properties for each foundation. Specifically, it ordered that each founder should draw up a *brevion* (inventory) of the properties assigned for the support of his monastery and deposit it in the archives of the local bishop. Of course the practice of providing landed endowments for private religious foundations had become popular as early as the eighth century, but the council's requirement of an inventory gave a strong impetus to this practice which soon became nearly universal. This change in the means of endowment ultimately permitted private monasteries to enjoy more autonomy from their patrons and to approach the independence of the public churches, which had always enjoyed incomes from their own properties.

The council also paid attention to another problem that had occupied Justinian and was once again becoming critical. This was the matter of the repair and restoration of the older private religious foundations of the empire.[107] Conditions throughout much of the empire in the early ninth century were still very unsettled. The frontiers were still not secure, and armed conflict with the Arabs and Bulgars frequent. These conditions undoubtedly played an important part in the disruption of many religious foundations. Proud families of benefactors may have seen to the proper maintenance of some of these old foundations, but certainly many others faced gradual deterioration and eventual collapse as their founding families died out or turned their interests elsewhere.

Some well-meaning bishops of the ninth century were concerned about the plight of these troubled foundations and intervened to provide assistance. They appropriated whatever incomes these foundations still possessed and even added diocesan funds to accomplish some restorations. Some overzealous bishops pursued these projects so far that the economic well-being of their dioceses became endangered. The fathers of the council decided that the risks were too great, and prohibited the use of diocesan funds for any future restoration projects. Henceforth, if a bishop were to undertake the restoration of a non-episcopal monastery in violation of the canon, that institution would become diocesan property. This fateful decision postponed the problem of arranging for the

---

[107] C. Const. I et II, c. 7 (R&P 2.673–74); cf. NJ 67.2 (538).

restoration of deteriorating monasteries for another century. In the interim, concerned clerics could only resort to ingenious circumventions of the council's legislation.

PRIVATE RELIGIOUS FOUNDATIONS DURING THE REIGN OF BASIL I (867–886)

The extant civil (as opposed to ecclesiastical) legislation practically ceases after the *Ekloga* of Leo III. The *Epanagoge*, Basil I's brief introduction to the major recodification of Byzantine law he was planning, provides the most testimony from these sources since the novels of Heraclius.[108] Photius, whose second patriarchate (878–886) occurred in the latter half of Basil I's reign, played an important part in the authorship of the *Epanagoge*'s chapters on religious affairs.[109] These chapters, like the *Epanagoge* as a whole, contain many simple recapitulations of Justinian's fundamental regulations, but also some original material which provides some valuable information at a time of considerable importance for the development of the Byzantine church.

The persistent problems of the institutional church are still very much in evidence in the *Epanagoge*. Many of these problems stemmed from the idiosyncratic organization of private religious foundations in Byzantium and the consequences of their uneasy coexistence with the public churches of the empire. It is not surprising, then, to see yet another complaint about liturgies sponsored by laymen without episcopal consent, demonstrating that this concern of the recent Council of Constantinople was still current.[110]

The private patrons of the empire now had what amounted to their own corps of clergy recruited largely from migrants from the countryside. For all practical purposes, these clerics were independent of the ordinary diocesan authorities. The clergy of a private church were not beholden to the local bishop for their appointments. They might even have received their ordinations from prelates in other localities. Even in the matter of financial support, these clerics depended upon their patrons rather than their nominal ecclesiastical superiors.

A corps of imperial clergy also existed by the late ninth century.[111] These clerics staffed such imperial foundations as Basil I's Nea Basilika

---

[108] *Epanagoge Basilii Leonis et Alexandri*, ed. K. E. Zachariä von Lingenthal, *Collectio librorum juris Graeco-Romani ineditorum* (Leipzig, 1852), 60–217, esp. 67–68, 77–88.

[109] Cf. Ostrogorsky, *HBS*, 240–41.

[110] *Epanagoge* 9.18.

[111] Theophanes Continuatus, *Chronographia* (*CSHB* 325–31); Leo Grammaticus, *Chronographia* (*CSHB* 265, 294); Constantine Pophyrogenitus, *De cerimoniis aulae byzantinae*, ed. J. Reiske, *CSHB* (Bonn, 1829–40), Ch. 49, 693; Janin, *Géographie*, Vol. 3, pp. 361–64; Herman, "Niederklerus," 379–81.

(dedicated 881). The emperor, as the lay benefactor par excellence, made the appointments to these positions himself and provided the necessary financial support. A chief priest with the title of *protopapas* headed the college of the imperial clergy. The emperor might choose to reserve some of the positions for honorary appointments. For example, Leo VI allowed Theodore Santabarenos to draw a stipend from the Nea Basilika as an appointee of this sort. The existence of independent clergy serving in the private chapels of magnates in the reign of Basil I's successor Leo VI indicates that arrangements for private institutions were similar to those of imperial foundations, though naturally on a smaller scale. The conspicuous example of the independence of the imperial clergy doubtless made it difficult for the ecclesiastical hierarchy to insist that private patrons subordinate their own clerics to the local bishops.

The *Epanagoge* also contains another condemnation of clerics and monks who entered private service as managers of estates and households.[112] Among the prohibited occupations was now also service as a government tax collector. It was easy enough for the authorities to condemn the means chosen by many patrons to allow their clerics to earn a living. Nevertheless, unless the government or the ecclesiastical hierarchy was willing to provide alternative sources of income (apparently a prohibitively costly idea), these condemnations were going to continue to fall on deaf ears.[113]

Indeed, the *Epanagoge* indicates that the clerics of the late ninth century were as willing as their counterparts of the late eighth century to desert poorly paid positions in their original churches for better paying ones elsewhere.[114] The clergy showed little inclination to follow the exhortation of the Second Council of Nicaea to stay in their original positions and seek out "honorable" secular employments as supplements to their incomes.[115] The coexistence of separately organized public and private churches continued to encourage and facilitate a stream of uncanonical transfers to the more remunerative positions.

Which churches were the usual beneficiaries of these transfers? As a general answer, the newer (and therefore, mainly private) foundations probably offered more dependable stipends, and urban churches (public or private) ordinarily compensated their appointees better than rural ones.[116] Perhaps some older yet well-endowed and maintained institu-

---

[112] *Epanagoge* 9.3.
[113] See Herman, "Professioni vietate," 23–44.
[114] *Epanagoge* 9.6.
[115] *C. Nicaen. II*, c. 15 (R&P 2.620).
[116] Note the attractiveness of clerical appointments in the private chapels of the magnates and the inability of poorer proprietors to maintain clerics in their churches during the reign of Leo VI (886–912), as evidenced below in connection with my discussion of this emperor's novels on ecclesiastical affairs. See also *Epanagoge* 9.6.

tions continued to attract candidates for appointment. Most older institutions, however, suffered from the vicissitudes of time and, as already seen, lacked even the funds to manage essential repairs without outside assistance.

Quite aside from these traditional problems posed by the existence of independently directed private foundations, the public churches faced unique problems of their own. Their endowments were made up preponderantly of agricultural estates along with some urban properties.[117] Civil and canon law practically prohibited sale of these properties and imposed severe limits on the options for their development and exploitation. The result was a persistent shortage of liquid capital which would also plague private foundations by the middle of the next century. The *Epanagoge* notes that the public churches lacked enough capital to restore the buildings they had inherited in order to make them fit for profitable rental.[118] Some institutions did not even have sufficient cash to pay their taxes to the state. In this case, the *Epanagoge* follows Justinian's example and allows an exception to the ban on alienation of property to meet the obligation.[119] As a rule, the government preferred that the public churches should resort to rentals and emphyteutic leases of their endowed properties to meet pressing needs for cash.[120] The *Epanagoge* limits these rentals to the traditional thirty years. The restrictions on alienations and the regulations of leases also applied to private churches.

The *Epanagoge* shows that the government encouraged the cathedral church of Constantinople and its dependencies to grant out its properties to the emperor, the state treasury, cities, or other ecclesiastical institutions on two-year emphyteutic leases.[121] This indicates the survival of Nicephorus I's program of imperial curatorship of ecclesiastical properties. If the public churches employed these leases extensively, the program would have worked to the disadvantage of the landed magnates who had previously been responsible for the management of many of these properties.

Basil I followed in the tradition of his great predecessor Justinian by undertaking a considerable program of ecclesiastical construction in Constantinople.[122] The Nea Basilika, which he began in 876 and completed in 881, was only the most outstanding example of his labors. A severe earthquake in 870, which destroyed or severely damaged many

---

[117] *Epanagoge* 10.3–4.
[118] *Epanagoge* 10.4.
[119] *Epanagoge* 10.7; cf. *NJ* 46 (537).
[120] *Epanagoge* 10.2–3; cf. *NJ* 123.6 (546).
[121] *Epanagoge* 10.5.
[122] Skylitzes, *Synopsis historiarum* (ed. Thurn, pp. 161–65); *Patria Konstantinoupoleos* 3.29a (p. 225), 3.86 (p. 246), 3.162 (p. 267), 3.182 (p. 272), 3.186 (p. 274); cf. Janin, *Géographie*, Vol. 3, pp. 361–64, and Herman, "Niederklerus," 385.

old churches (some dating back to the days of Justinian), provided the initial stimulus. The emperor quite naturally concentrated on imperial churches and monasteries for which he, as ruler of the day, had a special responsibility. He also endowed Hagia Sophia with a special estate to assure an adequate supply of income for the illumination of the cathedral church.

Perhaps the most important act of Basil's reign with respect to private foundations was his recognition of the patriarch's right to bestow his *stauropegion* (charter of foundation) on churches outside the diocesan boundaries of Constantinople.[123] Patriarchal "stauropegial" foundations had existed since the time of Maurice's concession to Theodore of Sykeon, but henceforth they would become increasingly important as the means by which private benefactors escaped the supervisory and regulatory powers of the local bishops.

In sum, the ecclesiastical policy of Basil I contained a number of promising initiatives such as the new regulations of leases and rentals of ecclesiastical property, the rebuilding of damaged churches, and the recognition of patriarchal *stauropegia*. These did not, however, attack the root causes of the profound disorders in the internal organization of the Byzantine church. Strong-willed patrons and inexorable economic forces combined with the basic weakness of the public church system to undermine existing legislation designed to protect their interests. The prelates of the empire had never acquiesced in this development, and Basil I's government lent its support to the hierarchy, as the *Epanagoge* demonstrates.

LEO VI'S REVERSAL OF POLICY: CONCESSIONS TO THE MAGNATES

Suddenly, at the end of the ninth century, Basil I's son and successor Leo VI (886–912) withdrew the official government support that the institutional church had hitherto enjoyed in this struggle. The new law code, known as the *Basilika*, and the novels that Leo published during his reign amply demonstrate the extent of the government's change of policy. Now it is a well-known fact that Leo's *Basilika* is not an original work of great value as a historical source, but rather a translation and recodification of Justinian's law code.[124] In most cases, Leo's lawyers simply rearranged earlier legal materials in more logical and convenient categories. Justinian's novels, when they chose to employ them, appear in a new order, but with the texts unchanged for the most part. Naturally it is of great inter-

---

[123] *Epanagoge* 3.10 (p. 68).
[124] Ostrogorsky, *HBS*, 244.

est to observe the fate of Justinian's regulation of private religious foundations in this rearrangement and reediting.

Zeno's fundamental law on private foundations does appear in the *Basilika*, but only in a short, mutilated form that deprives it of its significance.[125] Leo's lawyers omitted Justinian's law regulating the sale, exchange, and donation of monasteries. They retained his law on runaway clerics, but omitted all the rest of the important provisions of his legislation from the period 537–538. The series of laws in which Justinian summarized his earlier legislation (those iussued 545–546) fared better, but Leo's novels would soon gut the stricter provisions.[126]

Even more than the revisions to the *Basilika*, Leo VI's novels on the sacramental capacities of chapels in private dwellings unmistakably illustrate his disposition to favor the great lay benefactors of the empire.[127] These novels from the patriarchate of Stephen I (886–893) announce a clear shift of policy with respect to these institutions which earlier emperors and councils had restricted severely. Moreover, Leo's elaborate justifications indicate that he was well aware of the controversial nature of the changes he was instituting.

In the preface to the first of these novels, Leo VI acknowledges Justinian's intention (although he does not refer to him by name) to permit chapels in private dwellings only when the patrons employed clergy from the public churches: "It seemed better to those of ancient times that religious services and assemblies in private dwellings ought to be conducted only by the priests belonging to the public churches (*katholikai ekklesiai*), but others, who were assigned to a private dwelling and happened to be living in a private condition of life, were not to conduct a liturgy or any other religious service." [128]

Leo VI correctly attributes the restriction to the fear that diocesan officials could not ensure the orthodoxy of household clergy stationed permanently in these chapels. The emperor brushes this concern aside, even though as recently as 861 the fathers of the Council of Constantinople had denounced these churches as breeding grounds for all sorts of evils. According to Leo VI, Justinian's restriction simply denied domestic liturgies to orthodox property owners who were too scrupulous to employ a cleric of dubious credentials and theological convictions:[129]

---

[125] Compare *CJ* 1.2.15 to *B* 5.1.7, ed. H. J. Scheltema and H. Van der Wal, *Basilicorum libri LX* (Groningen, 1953-).

[126] *NJ* 123.16 = *B* 3.1.29–31; *NJ* 123.17 = *B* 3.1.32; *NJ* 123.18 = *B* 3.1.33; *NJ* 131.7 = *B* 5.3.8; *NJ* 131.8 = *B* 5.3.9.

[127] Leo VI, *Novellae* 4, 14, 15, ed. P. Noailles and A. Dain, *Les novelles de Leon VI le Sage* (Paris, 1944); see also George Ostrogorsky, "Observations on the Aristocracy in Byzantium," *DOP* 25 (1971), 3–32, esp. 4.

[128] *Novella* 4 (ed. Noailles and Dain, p. 23, lines 1–5).

[129] *Novella* 4 (p. 23, lines 9–24).

The aim which those setting this safeguard had in mind, namely, that they could take forethought by this means for the safeguarding of the piety of the faith, is worthy of praise and approbation. Yet, contrary to their expectations, it does not appear that the safeguard provided by the law for this purpose has achieved and maintained its aim. On the contrary, the law appears opposed to the pious property owners and to zeal for the divine liturgy. The unholy priest, chosen unknowingly, might thereby impart, at some time or another, his own impious pollution to someone else. . . . For who is so complacent and indifferent about personal opinion as to call upon a priest whom he does not know to officiate, choosing him in ignorance of his religious observance and personal conduct? On the contrary, the cherishers of apostasy and those who officiate impiously will not wish to have dealings with those who are not their associates in impiety. Therefore, the law does not actually safeguard [the faith] in the way that it was intended to do.

Actually, private patrons had defied Justinian's law at least since the time of Heraclius. In arguing their cause, however, Leo VI fails to provide an explanation for the unwillingness of patrons to rely upon diocesan clergy for the celebration of domestic liturgies as Justinian had directed.

In order to draw attention away from the special interests for which he drew up this legislation, Leo VI maintains that Justinian's restriction affected the poor people of the empire as well as the rich patrons of private chapels: "Moreover, it is an obstacle to a great advantage for the orthodox. Although by divine grace oratories (*eukterioi oikoi*) have been erected to God in nearly every dwelling, not only of the eminent but also of the more lowly, the salaries (*choregiai*) and maintenance (*therapeia*) of priests cannot be assured by all in an equal manner. Those who lack resources for the private acquisition of priests very often remain without a share in the divine mysteries, and the holy sanctuaries are deprived of the sacraments that ought to be celebrated in them." [130] In the course of his argument, Leo VI testifies to the broad dissemination in his day of private religious foundations as well as to how essential they had become for servicing the religious needs of the lower classes. He makes a particular point of decrying the lapses that the inability of the poorly endowed churches to hire clerics caused in the celebration of endowed masses for the dead. [131]

The emperor's remedy for the plight of both rich and poor benefactors was to decree that household priests, as well as those of the public

[130] *Novella* 4 (p. 23, line 24—p. 25, line 6).
[131] *Novella* 4 (p. 25, lines 7–10).

churches, should have permission to offer mass in private chapels, subject only to the approval of the patrons themselves. This law meant that the diocesan authorities had to recognize and regularize the status of all the household clergy, a measure that surely would have horrified the conscientious Photius, had he still been patriarch at this time.[132]

This in itself was a severe blow to diocesan discipline, as well as to the prestige of the public clergy and their churches. Leo VI made matters worse in a second law that overturned canon law and permitted household clerics to perform baptisms in private chapels.[133] Since the patrons' chapels now had expanded sacramental capacities, the magnates no longer had any reason to patronize the public churches or to respect the authority of the local hierarchy.

Despite the emperor's pretensions to the contrary, the ecclesiastical hierarchy no longer obliged the patrons of private chapels to resort to regular diocesan clergy each time they needed a priest for a liturgy. Canons of the Second Council of Nicaea and the more recent Council of Constantinople demonstrate that these chapels had had their own resident clerical staffs for at least a hundred years before Leo VI's laws.[134] The Second Council of Nicaea had even allowed lay patrons to receive migratory priests if these clerics obtained the permission of their former bishop and the patriarch. The Council of Constantinople, for its part, also acknowledged the existence of household clerics, whom the hierarchy expected to control by reserving the choice of appointees for themselves.

These were liberal and realistic provisions. The councils had gone as far as conscientious ecclesiastics could toward accommodating the wishes of private patrons without a complete breakdown of diocesan discipline and loss of control over appointments. That they were not sufficient for the special interests behind Leo VI's legislation indicates the determination of these patrons to make no concesssion to episcopal choice and supervision of their clerics.

It is not at all clear how Justinian's legislation was responsible for the plight of the poor (and presumably rural) benefactors who could not afford to maintain their own clergy, nor how Leo's new law would help them. Justinian did not prevent the private churches of the countryside from having their own standing clergy, though he did insist that they should be subordinate to the local bishops. These churches were full participants in the liturgical lives of their communities (as the papyrological evidence from Byzantine Egypt demonstrates), and were quite different in function, if not in ownership, from the private chapels located in the personal residences of the magnates. Leo VI simply misinterpreted Jus-

---

[132] For Photius' opinions, see *C. Const. I et II*, c. 12 (R&P 2.687–88) and *Epanagoge* 9.6 (p. 81).

[133] Leo VI, *Novella* 15 (ed. Noailles and Dain, pp. 59–61).

[134] *C. Nicaen. II*, c. 10 (R&P 2.587); *C. Const. I et II*, c. 12 (R&P 2.687–88).

tinian's law and unfairly blamed it for the financial difficulties of rural churches in his own day.

Perhaps some rural communal churches relied upon clergy hired from local *katholikai ekklesiai* on a part-time basis in order to economize, but Justinian's law certainly did not forbid them to have their own resident clergy. Occasional employment would at least help account for Leo VI's confounding of rural private churches with the private (and primarily urban) chapels of the magnates. Ironically, it was the attraction of these chapels, with their generally well compensated positions, that made it difficult for many rural churches, public and private, to retain their clergy.[135] Leo VI, by regularizing the status of the household clergy and removing the last suspicions of illegality from the magnates' private chapels, could only have worsened the relative position of rural churches.

The emperor's concessions to the magnates could only have aggravated the existing tensions between the public church system and private religious foundations. Yet even Leo VI could not overlook the problem of private individuals who undertook to erect new ecclesiastical foundations without sufficient funds to complete the work. The emperor's contribution to alleviating the problem was a modest one. He set a standard for the minimum size for a monastic foundation, specifically a building of proportions large enough for at least three monks.[136] Especially since he passed up the opportunity to set minimum levels for endowments, Leo VI may actually have done more harm than good by permitting the proliferation of extremely small monastic foundations. The problem of arranging for the support of these tiny monasteries would become critical in another sixty years, until Basil II offered a better solution.

The reign of Leo VI, then, marks a crucial turning point in the history of the relationship between public and private religious foundations in Byzantium. For at least the next two centuries, the ecclesiastical hierarchy was left to fight a losing battle as it tried to retain some semblance of unity and of its own authority over all the religious foundations of the empire.

THE TRIUMPH OF PRIVATE BENEFACTORS

The triumph of the private benefactors over the public church authorities had a great impact on other aspects of the ecclesiastical life of Byzantium.[137] By the tenth century the great processions that had characterized

---

[135] Cf. Heraclius, *De clericis*, ed. Konidaris, p. 74; *C. Nicaen. II*, c. 10; *C. Const. I et II*, c. 12 (R&P 2.687–88); *Epanagoge* 9.6 (p. 81).

[136] Leo VI, *Novella* 14 (ed. Noailles and Dain, pp. 55–58), with B. Granić, "Das Klosterwesen in der Novellengesetzgebung Kaiser Leons des Weisen," *BZ* 31 (1931), 61–69.

[137] Thomas Mathews, "'Private' Liturgy in Byzantine Architecture: Toward a Reappraisal," *Cahiers archéologiques* 30 (1982), 125–38; Gordana Babić, *Les chapelles an-*

the early Byzantine liturgy had been curtailed. A new style of ecclesiastical architecture was developed to suit the medieval liturgy, and churches became smaller than even the reduced populations of the times would have seemed to require. Even major churches such as that of the Theotokos erected in 907 by Constantine Lips, *drungarios* (admiral) of the fleet under Leo VI, displayed characteristic architectural features of private foundations such as mortuary chapels and other diminutive chapels for the celebration of private liturgies.[138] This is not to suggest that all these changes occurred any more suddenly than the triumph of the private benefactors themselves, for the erosion of the Justinianic system of regulation had begun even in the sixth century. Yet from the tenth century, private benefactors clearly held the upper hand in their struggle with the public authorities of the church, and their impress on ecclesiastical life is all the more evident.

Despite these developments, the public authorities continued to play an important part in the administration of some religious foundations. We know from the *De administrando imperio* of Constantine VII that in the Peloponnesus, in the reign of Romanus Lecapenus (919–944), there were no less than six categories of monasteries: imperial, patriarchal, archiepiscopal, metropolitan, episcopal, and independent (that is, private) monasteries. [139] All of these had to supply horses for the imperial cavalry.

The possession of a separate landed endowment came to be one mark of institutional autonomy for a religious foundation. In the early tenth century, the cathedral church of Hagia Sophia and its dependencies continued to enjoy revenues derived from large estates worked by peasant cultivators.[140] Yet it was the emperor who provided the *rogai* (salaries) of the clergy of the cathedral church, in his capacity as the patron of Hagia Sophia. That Patriarch Nicholas Mysticus (901–907, 911–925) had to request an official of the treasury to resume payment of these salaries after an arbitrary suspension indicates the dependence of the public churches on their ultimate patron and benefactor.[141]

This was an age when certain resourceful abbots led their monasteries to positions of considerable affluence and economic power. We hear of

---

nexes des églises byzantines (Paris, 1969), esp. 47–58.

[138] Mathews, "'Private' Liturgy," 127–31; for Constantine Lips and his foundation, see *Patria Konstantinoupoleos* 3.35 (p. 289) and Theophanes Continuatus, *Chronographia* (CSHB 371), with Janin, *Géographie*, Vol. 3, pp. 307–10.

[139] Constantine Porphyrogenitus, *De administrando imperio*, Ch. 52, ed. R. J. H. Jenkins and G. Moravcsik (Budapest, 1949).

[140] Nicholas I Mysticus, *Epistolae* Nos. 164 (915–918) and 165 (914–918), ed. R. J. H. Jenkins and L. G. Westerink, *Nicholas I Patriarch of Constantinople: Letters* (Washington, D.C., 1973).

[141] Nicholas I, *Epistola* No. 72 (914–918).

their purchases of communal lands and their encouragement of individual gifts and testaments in their favor.[142] Since at least the late eighth
century, it was common practice for prospective monks to donate part
or all of their property to a monastery upon entrance.[143] This also
strengthened monastic endowments considerably. Ultimately these activities helped to upset the delicate balance of property ownership in the
countryside. A favored monastery might even use its influence to obtain
stratiotika ktemata (soldiers' landholdings) in violation of the laws and
the intended purposes of these properties.[144] Emperor Romanus Lecapenus had to take drastic action in his famous novel of 934.[145] He included *hegoumenoi*, philanthropic administrators, archbishops, metropolitans, and other ecclesiastical officials along with lay magnates in the
list of individuals forbidden to obtain the property of peasants under any
circumstances. He did not abolish the traditional donations of monastic
postulants, but he did direct that a prospective monk should sell his land
to another peasant and then give the proceeds to the monastery that he
wished to join. Romanus' successor Constantine VII confirmed these restrictions in a law of his own dated to 947.[146]

As it happened, Romanus Lecapenus' behavior as a magnate and private benefactor was at odds with his public stance as the protector of the
independent peasantry against expansionary ecclesiastical institutions.
He allowed the imperial monastery of Lakape, located at the emperor's
birthplace, to acquire *stratiotika ktemata* in Armenia by a special exemption from the provisions of his own law on property acquisition.[147]
Nicephorus Phocas (963–969) subsequently ordered the monastery to
return these properties to their original possessors.

Under Romanus Lecapenus, the conservative spirit of Nicephorus I
and Basil I prevailed over the prodigality of Irene with respect to special
immunities for churches and their properties, clergies, and dependents.
Some monasteries did enjoy tax immunities for their properties, but apparently this occurred through special exemption. Most ecclesiastical in-

---

[142] Romanus Lecapenus, *Novella de potentibus ab acquisitione praediorum arcendis*
(934), Ch. 1 (*JGR* 3.245–47) = Dölger, *Regesten* No. 628.

[143] Romanus Lecapenus, *Novella de potentibus*, Ch. 8 (*JGR* 3.251); Justinian permitted
this practice in *NJ* 123.16.2; over two centuries later, *C. Nicaen. II*, c. 19 (R&P 2.630–31)
accepted *apotagai* (entrance gifts) as an ordinary requirement for prospective monks; Herman, "Armut," 439–50, provides a detailed treatment of these compulsory "gifts."

[144] E.g., the Monastery of Lakape mentioned by Nicephorus Phocas, *Novella de fundis
militum Armenicorum* (963–969), Ch. 1 (*JGR* 3.290.18–25) = Dölger, *Regesten* No. 720;
cf. commentary by Peter Charanis, "Monastic Properties and the State in the Byzantine
Empire," *DOP* 4 (1948), 53–118, at 59–60, n. 18a.

[145] Romanus Lecapenus, *Novella de potentibus* (934) (*JGR* 3.241–52), with commentary
by Ostrogorsky, *HBS*, 274–76.

[146] Constantine VII Porphyrogenitus, *Novella de potentibus praedia pauperum acquiren-
tibus* (947) (*JGR* 3.252–56), esp. Ch. 2 = (Dölger, *Regesten* No. 656).

[147] See above, note 144.

stitutions continued to pay taxes in the tenth century.[148] The acute need
for manpower during the dark days of the Bulgarian War (913–927) even
caused the government to reconsider its traditional policy of allowing
clerics immunity from *angareia* (compulsory labor services). Patriarch
Nicholas Mysticus complained of officials who allowed the impressment
of clerics and monks into military service despite all precedent to the
contrary.[149] Under the circumstances, the patriarch's attempt to extend
this traditional immunity to the non-clerical, agricultural dependents living on ecclesiastical properties presumably failed, despite his bold assertion that this too was a privilege granted by the earliest of the Christian
emperors.

The cathedral church of Hagia Sophia was particularly vulnerable to
confiscations of its resources in times of emergency since so many of its
properties had originally been imperial donations or were now under
government management.[150] Nicholas Mysticus had to plead with one
government official to fulfill his duty to forward wheat due the cathedral
church from a rural *chorion* that had been obliged to supply it for conversion into eucharistic bread. The church could demand greater ac-
countability from its stewards (*kouratores*) of internally managed estates. It is uncertain whether these officials were laymen or clerics. It
appears that it was a lay *kourator* who resigned his position as manager
of the church's estates at Strongylizon in northern Greece because of a
dispute with the *oikonomos* of the cathedral church.[151] Nicholas Mysticus hoped to persuade him to reconsider, and he wrote the *strategos* of
the theme of Strymon requesting that he assist the *kourator*'s efforts to
prevent illegal alienations of church property.

The early tenth-century sources have little to say about the endowments and the management of private churches. Gross abuses perpe-
trated by the more unscrupulous patrons still occurred as in the mid-
ninth century. Nicholas Mysticus confessed his inability to do much to
prevent individuals from plundering churches and dissolving monasteries
in the diocese of Patras in Greece.[152] The patriarch did not specifically
identify these individuals, but their conduct is similar to that of patrons
condemned by the Council of Constantinople in 861.

That same council had prevented bishops from spending diocesan
funds to restore non-diocesan monasteries. Fifty years later Nicholas
Mysticus granted the *pronoia* (oversight) of a monastery of this sort in

[148] Cf. Constantine VII Porphyrogenitus, *De administrando imperio* Ch. 52; for exemptions, see Nicholas Mysticus, *Epistola* No. 73 (n.d.).
[149] Nicholas Mysticus, *Epistolae* No. 37 and 150 (915–918?), cf. 164 (915); Basil I's
confirmation of this exemption in *Epanagoge* 9.16.
[150] *Epistola* No. 165 (914–918), cf. 59 (914–918?) and *Epanagoge* 10.5.
[151] *Epistolae* Nos. 35–36 (914–918).
[152] *Epistolae* Nos. 35 and 123 (914–918).

epidosis (the technical term for the concession of an ecclesiastical institution from one ecclesiastical authority to another) to Bishop Andrew of Patras.[153] The monastery in question had apparently suffered from bad management under its previous administrator. The patriarch, then, appears to have been determined to take an active role in the restoration of mismanaged institutions in spite of the existing canonical prohibition.

Acting in this same spirit, Bishop Andrew of Patras expelled a monk named Gregory from a monastery that he had been governing by virtue of his kinship to the founder.[154] Andrew replaced him with a non-relative whom he deemed better qualified to look after the monastery's interests. Gregory, apparently stunned by this affront to his patron's rights, took his protest directly to the patriarch. Nicholas Mysticus then had to resolve the conflicting claims of personal property rights and the good religious order of the monastery. He ruled that if Gregory had committed no wrong, there was no justification for depriving him of the hegoumenate. If, on the other hand, Gregory was obviously unsuitable, Andrew was to provide him with a *paramythia*, a monetary allowance derived from ecclesiastical revenues. The bishop of Patras, in the latter case, would have been buying out Gregory's rights of patronage in the monastery.

On another occasion, the son of a patron became embroiled in a conflict with the current abbot of a monastery founded by his father.[155] The young man sought to reside in the monastery, receive maintenance, and obtain instruction in religious life. When the abbot rebuffed him, he took a complaint about the abbot's alleged lack of piety to the patriarch with a request for relief. Nicholas Mysticus found some confirmation of the bad report on the abbot and promised to investigate the matter further. He permitted the young man to become a novice, but left the election of a new abbot, if one was needed, to the brethren of the monastic community. He reserved for himself approval of the nominee. This monastery probably had a patriarchal *stauropegion* which would have given Nicholas Mysticus the authority to hear this case and make these dispositions. It is noteworthy that the patron's son retained a vested interest in the well-being of the institution, and obviously thought he was entitled to special consideration.

It was more common for patrons to exercise untrammeled rights of disposal over their institutions. An important legal case came before the court of Basil II (976–1025) a half century later; it illustrates the ease with which patrons in the era of Romanus Lecapenus could transfer

[153] *Epistola* No. 123 (914–918).
[154] *Epistola* No. 119 (914–918), lines 17–23.
[155] *Epistola* No. 105 (919–925), esp. lines 1–5.

ownership of a monastery.[156] A certain layman donated his house to a
monk who transformed it into the monastery of Piperatos (location unknown). The monk later gave it to the young Romanus Lecapenus before
his accession to the throne in 919. After he became emperor, Romanus
in turn gave it to the *protovestiarios* Marinos. The monastery then became the personal property of this courtier and his heirs. It would make
a reappearance in history when Patriarch Nicholas II Chrysoberges
(979–991) sought to claim patriarchal rights of overlordship in this monastery.

Even in the time of Romanus Lecapenus, the ecclesiastical hierarchy
was finding the maintenance of unrestricted private property rights in
religious institutions to be an irritating limitation of its powers and responsibilities. Romanus Lecapenus and Constantine VII also had good
reason to wish to curtail the power of the great benefactors and their
foundations in order to further the government's program of stabilizing
property ownership in the countryside. Yet for various reasons the natural alliance of the government and the ecclesiastical hierarchy against the
great magnates, broken since Leo VI, did not reform.

This was partly a result of the church's own uncertain attitude toward
private property rights. The painful experiences of the Bulgarian War,
when the government sequestered the revenues of Hagia Sophia and can-
celled clerical immunity from military service, contributed to distrust between the old allies. A wary hierarchy might have seen Romanus' restrictions in the expansion of private foundations as a threat to the public
church's common interest in the preservation of its endowed properties.
Even Nicholas Mysticus found it difficult on occasion to resolve the conflict between his desire for the well-being of all ecclesiastical institutions
and his respect for the private property rights of patrons.

The emperor was also not disposed to seize the moment and attempt
to resolve some of the longstanding difficulties between the interests of
the public churches and those of private foundations. Indeed, he remained a traditional private benefactor at heart. He had acted like any
other private patron in casually disposing of the monastery of Piperatos
as a reward for a faithful friend. He had granted the special exemption
from his own legislation for his monastery of Lakape. Moreover, he
weakened the reformist momentum established by Nicholas Mysticus by
appointing his young son Theophylact (933–956) as patriarch. The new
leader of the Byzantine church did not generally take his responsibilities
seriously, though he did restore at least one long decayed private monastery. Significant reforms had to await his successor Polyeuctus (956–
970) and the energetic Emperor Nicephorus Phocas.

---

[156] Eustathios Rhomaios, *Peira* 15.4 (*JGR* 1.43).

CHAPTER FIVE

The Crisis of Private Religious Foundations in Byzantium and Its Resolution

NICEPHORUS Phocas (963–969) was not afraid to disregard established traditions governing the roles of the emperor and the private benefactor in the Byzantine church. It was he, for instance, who took the unprecedented step (ca. 964) of reserving for himself the approval of all episcopal elections.[1] Like Romanus Lecapenus, Nicephorus Phocas was a private benefactor in his own right. He was a friend of St. Athanasios the Athonite. His gift of an imperial *solemnion* (dedicatory offering) of 244 *nomismata* made possible Athanasios' foundation of the monastery of Lavra on Mount Athos.[2] At Athanasios' suggestion, the emperor granted a constitutionally independent form of government for this monastery in his foundation charter (now lost, except for some brief excerpts).[3] This was an important change from the usual practice of both private and imperial benefactors, who ordinarily imposed a proprietary form of government on their foundations.

LEGISLATION OF NICEPHORUS PHOCAS

Like his predecessor Romanus I, Nicephorus Phocas was well aware of the insatiable appetite of the great ecclesiastical foundations for new acquisitions of property. He realized that this led to severe dislocations of the traditional pattern of property ownership, which in turn threatened

---

[1] Dölger, *Regesten* No. 703; Skylitzes, *Synopsis historiarum* (ed. Thurn, p. 285); Leo Diaconus, *Historia* 6.4, ed. C. B. Hase, *CSHB* (Bonn, 1828), 98–99; and Zonaras, *Epitome historiarum* 17.1, with my "The Crisis of Byzantine Ecclesiastical Foundations, 964–1025," *BF* 9 (1985), 255–74.

[2] Text not extant, but fragments preserved in the *Typikon* of St. Athanasios for the Lavra Monastery on Mount Athos, ed. Ph. Meyer, *Die Haupturkunden für die Geschichte der Athosklöster* (Leipzig, 1894), 102–22, with record of the *solemnion* at 115; cf. Dölger, *Regesten* No. 704

[3] Preserved in the *Typikon* of St. Athanasios (ed. Meyer, p. 107, lines 11–16) = Dölger, *Regesten* No. 704.

the military strength of the empire.[4] Unlike Romanus Lecapenus, Nice-phorus Phocas was prepared to subordinate his personal interests as a benefactor to the pressing need for reform of the empire's private religious foundations.

The emperor took upon himself the formidable task of reversing traditional patterns of private philanthropy dating back to late Roman times. He knew that personal vanity was an important element in the motivation of benefactors who were willing to devote the large sums necessary for the erection of the empire's private religious foundations.[5] Most benefactors, therefore, would prefer to found a church or monastery of their own rather than contribute toward the maintenance or repair of an existing foundation. That way the benefactor would gain for himself the prestigious title of *ktistes*, the "founder," acclaimed by John Chrysostom and Justinian in ages past. Because of this prevailing attitude, the empire came to possess over the centuries an ever increasing number of religious foundations. Nicephorus Phocas thought that there were now more in existence than could be justified:[6]

> In times gone by when such institutions were not sufficient, the establishment of them was praiseworthy and very useful; surely the good done by those who established them was more abiding, for they wished to provide food and care for the bodies of men in one case, and in the other, to pay attention to the conduct of the soul and the higher life. But when their number had increased greatly and has become disproportionate to the need, and people still turn to the founding of monasteries, how is it possible not to think that this good has not mixed with evil, that darnel has not been added to the wheat?

While the newer foundations often enjoyed material prosperity, each year many other institutions fell into serious financial trouble or physical decay for lack of capable management or sufficient funds for repairs:[7]

> This is indeed obvious to anyone, for at a time when there are thousands of other monasteries which have suffered by the lapse of time and need much help, we show no zeal in spending money for their rehabilitation, but turn our attention instead to the cre-

---

[4] Skylitzes, *Synopsis historiarum* (ed. Thurn, p. 274); Zonaras, *Epitome historiarum* 4.81.

[5] Nicephorus Phocas, *Novella de monasteriis* (964/5) (*JGR* 3.292–96) = Dölger, *Regesten* No. 699.

[6] *Novella de monasteriis* (964) (*JGR* 3.294.8–19), trans. Peter Charanis, "Monastic Properties and the State in the Byzantine Empire," *DOP* 4 (1948), 53–118, at 56–57, with minor revisions by the author.

[7] *Novella* (964) (*JGR* 3.294.25–34), trans. Charanis, "Monastic Properties," 57.

ation of new monasteries of our own. We do this in order that we may not only enjoy the name of having founded something new, but also because we desire that our foundation should be clearly in evidence and be apart by itself to the end that our name may appear throughout the world and be celebrated in accordance with the divine prophecy.

All previous attempts to deal with the problem of providing for the repair of dilapidated religious foundations, including the program of Justinian and the efforts of the bishops of the mid- ninth century, were no more than rescue operations. Now Nicephorus Phocas went to the root of the problem by banning practically all new foundations of monasteries and philanthropic institutions.

The emperor was pragmatic enough to realize that he could not completely halt the disposition of the laity to make pious donations. He did presume to think that he could channel these benefactions in new, more socially useful directions. Accordingly, he issued a law (964/5) in which he recommends that the wealthy should henceforth sell properties that they would otherwise have donated to new foundations and give the proceeds to the poor.[8] The law commands those benefactors who were not attracted to this sort of income redistributive charity to turn their attention to the ruined and dilapidated foundations that badly needed financial assistance for repairs and capital improvements.[9] These institutions then were to use the benefactors' money to acquire field hands and livestock in order to put their current properties to better use. The law strictly forbids benefactors to make direct grants of lands and buildings. In the emperor's opinion, these troubled institutions could not hope to maintain such gifts properly without adequate capital, much less operate them at maximum efficiency.[10]

Nicephorus Phocas made a special provision for those monasteries and philanthropic institutions that actually had shortages of endowed property due to careless administration and bad planning. He exempted these institutions from the laws of Romanus Lecapenus and Constantine VII, which effectively forbade religious foundations from purchasing peasant properties.[11] He proposed to provide the exemptions on a case-by-case basis. The emperor promised to investigate the need and confirm the necessary purchases for these institutions so that they could build up adequate endowments.

The situation portrayed by the law, in which many monasteries had

---

[8] *Novella* (964) (*JGR* 3.295.5–11).
[9] *Novella* (964) (*JGR* 3.295.12–18).
[10] *Novella* (964) (*JGR* 3.295.24–37).
[11] *Novella* (964) (*JGR* 3.295.37–296.7).

come to possess extensive properties yet were deficient in capital assets, recalls the plight of the public churches described by the *Epanagoge* during the reign of Basil I.[12] How did these monasteries lose their original patrons and become effectively independent, yet capital deficient, institutions? Religious foundations that were tightly bound economically and administratively to the estates of their patrons (as most were until the late eighth century) usually shared the fate of these estates.[13] This was nearly always true for private churches, since they never had the benefit of the institutional autonomy that private monasteries enjoyed at certain times in Byzantine history. Until the switch to formal landed endowments, private monasteries, like private churches, followed the rest of a patron's property when he bequeathed, donated, or sold it to a third party. Yet occasions evidently arose when there was no one to assume the traditional role of protector for a religious foundation.[14]

In some cases a responsible party, such as the ecclesiastical official whose predecessor had granted the original *stauropegion* for the foundation, might step in and arrange the administration on a new basis as a diocesan, metropolitan, or patriarchal institution.[15] Other foundations might be left to fend for themselves with whatever resources were at their disposal. Especially since the Council of Constantinople's decision to prevent bishops from restoring independent monasteries with diocesan funds, such cases were likely to become more common.

Possibly many patrons bound by the council's regulation requiring a formal list of consecrated properties had assigned only such lands as made their foundations financially viable, but withheld cultivators and livestock in order to ensure that they themselves would continue to exercise the management and exploitation of these properties. Private foundations operating under an arrangement of this sort might well have been left with plenty of land, but no means to exploit it, upon the demise of their patrons' families. It is also possible that these institutions once had both sufficient properties and the means to exploit them, but when they lost their powerful patrons' protection, they could not prevent the loss of their valuable cultivators and livestock to covetous neighboring land-

---

[12] *Epanagoge* 10.3–4.

[13] E.g., Eustathios Boilas' churches in the mid-eleventh century and Michael Attaliates' *ptochotropheion* in the late eleventh century, both discussed below in Chapter 6.

[14] E.g., the case of the Monastery of St. Zachary on the plain of Atroa at the foot of Bithynian Olympus, which was abandoned until restored by Peter of Atroa, ca. 800, according to his *Vita* (ed. Laurent, p. 89); cf. Janin, *Géographie*, Vol. 2, p. 151.

[15] As bishops and metropolitans did in the late tenth century, when the original peasant proprietors of small monasteries died without providing for the future administration of their foundations. See Basil II, *Peri ton dynaton* (996) Ch. 3 (*JGR* 3.313–14); cf. *C. Nicaen. II*, c. 4 (R&P 2.566–67) which condemned bishops who simply closed churches.

lords. Finally, it is possible that the monasteries (like the public churches mentioned in the *Epanagoge*) gradually found themselves the recipients of bequests of marginal lands and other dilapidated properties that drained away their capital resources without adding appreciably to income.

Whatever the real causes for their plight, the lot of these institutions must have been extremely difficult. Canon law prevented them from alienating existing property in order to raise capital. The imperial agrarian legislation of Romanus Lecapenus and Constantine VII practically forbade extensions of their endowments in order to secure increased revenues. Standing without patrons, they no longer enjoyed the usual financial benefits of private institutions in these relationships. The bishops were under strict orders not to provide assistance. The traditions of private philanthropy made it unlikely that any benefactors unrelated to the original patrons would come to their rescue either. Until Nicephorus Phocas' law, it must have seemed that these institutions were doomed to slow decay and ultimate dissolution.[16]

The emperor's diagnosis of the causes for the problems facing private religious foundations was certainly very perceptive. His remedy was drastic, and not a little presumptuous. Although he did not abolish private monasteries, his law did prevent the endowment of any more new foundations, with the exception of *kellia* (individual monastic cells) and *laurai* (collections of *kellia*). The ban was doubtless a shock to the institutional church and to private benefactors alike. Ultimately it became clear that it was not necessary to pay the drastic price of foregoing all new foundations in order to aid the existing monasteries and philanthropic organizations. The emperor's law was also flawed by his neglect to include a financial incentive for the restorer of a foundation to replace the rights and monetary compensations he would have obtained as the patron of a new institution. Soon a new program would be developed that would avoid these shortcomings of Nicephorus Phocas' legislation.

FATE OF NICEPHORUS PHOCAS' LEGISLATION

Nicephorus Phocas' successor John Tzimisces (969–976) most likely not only maintained his predecessor's law but even used it as a guide for his own philanthropic activities.[17] He matched his predecessor's generous donation to the Lavra monastery on Mount Athos with another imperial

---

[16] Anastasius' law, *CJ* 1.2.17, had allowed institutions to alienate property to raise funds for structural restorations, but the editors of the *Basilika* did not retain this law; it may have been repealed as early as Justinian's codification (so Jones, *LRE*, 897).

[17] See my "A Disputed Novel of Emperor Basil II," *GRBS* 23 (1983), 273–83.

solemnion of 244 *nomismata*.[18] He was especially concerned with the restoration of old ecclesiastical institutions. The historian John Skylitzes records his rebuilding of the monastery of Damideias in the Armeniac theme, and Leo the Deacon mentions his restoration and enlargement of the *nosokomeion* of Zoticus in Constantinople.[19] The emperor's greatest philanthropic endeavor was his rebuilding and beautification of the Church of Christ Chalke at Constantinople which Romanus Lecapenus had founded earlier in the century.[20] He also increased the number of stipends for the clergy in this church to allow an increase in manpower from twelve to fifty clerics, although he had to grant some new estates to the church to supply the additional financial support. Except in this last instance, John Tzimisces faithfully adhered to the spirit of the existing legislation on permitted forms of ecclesiastical philanthropy.

The same cannot be said about Basil the Parakoimomenos, regent for the young Basil II from 976 to 985. A man very much afflicted with the vainglory and desire for fame denounced by Nicephorus Phocas in his law, Basil erected a huge and costly new monastery dedicated to his patron saint, Basil the Great.[21] When Basil II took over the reins of government for himself, he made a stunning demonstration of his opinion of the validity of Nicephorus Phocas' law by ordering the demolition of this foundation.

Eventually, however, Basil II saw fit to change his mind on this issue. On April 4, 988, faced with a most serious revolt by Bardas Phokas and Bardas Skleros, he issued an extant novel that repeals the law of his predecessor and calls back into effect previous lenient legislation governing the erection and endowment of religious institutions.[22] In seeking an explanation for this sudden reversal of policy, the novel can be interpreted as a significant but costless concession to the landed magnates just then wavering in their loyalties to the crown. Alternatively, Basil II can be accepted at his word, as he points to the suspension of new religious foundations as the cause of divine displeasure, "an injustice not only to the churches and the philanthropic institutions, but to God himself."

Whatever his motives may have been, this was not to be the only occasion upon which Basil II would demonstrate his friendship to private benefactors. At about the same time, Patriarch Nicholas II Chrysoberges (980–992) attempted to assert control over the monastery of Piperatos

---

[18] Dölger, *Regesten* No. 744, text not extant, but mentioned in the *Typikon* of St. Athanasios (ed. Meyer, p. 114).

[19] Skylitzes, *Synopsis historiarum* (ed. Thurn, p. 285); Leo Diaconus, *Historia* 6.5 (*CSHB* 99).

[20] *Patria Konstantinoupoleos* 3.213 (p. 282).

[21] Michael Psellos, *Chronographia* 1.20, ed. Emile Renauld (Paris, 1926–28).

[22] Basil II, *Novella quae legem Nicephori de monasteriis tollit* (988) (*JGR* 3.303) = Dölger, *Regesten* No. 772.

(once owned by Romanus Lecapenus), perhaps on the basis of a patriarchal *stauropegion*.[23] When the dispute came to his court, the emperor upheld the private property rights of the owners of this monastery. The decision conforms well to Basil II's novel of 988, which called back into effect the weak provisions of the *Basilika* and Leo VI's novels as the basis for government regulation of private foundations.

Earlier patriarchs had taken over old private monasteries in order to rebuild them from ruins or to undertake restorations. Photius had taken over the monastery of the *magistros* Manuel (d. 838) for rebuilding.[24] Patriarch Theophylact followed Photius' example by restoring the monastery of Rufinus at Chrysopolis, one of the oldest private foundations. Since 861 and the decree of the Council of Constantinople, the patriarchs and the bishops had to find ways to circumvent the prohibition of the expenditure of diocesan funds for the restoration of private foundations. Among the ways to achieve this were the employment of the prelate's personal resources to meet the costs of renovation (in which case the monastery became his hereditary personal possession) and the transformation of the restored institution into a patriarchal or diocesan monastery. Thus the monastery of Manuel became Photius' private property, which passed after his death to his nephew Sergios, perhaps a relative of the future patriarch of that name. The monastery of Rufinus, on the other hand, became a patriarchal institution from the time of its restoration by Theophylact.[25]

Whatever Nicholas Chrysoberges plans were for the monastery of Piperatos, he evidently had not counted on opposition from its owners, who successfully established that their institution was *autodespoton* (independent) and had never been conceded to an ecclesiastical overlord. Basil II's unwillingness to allow Nicholas Chrysoberges to assume control over Piperatos undermined the patriarch's ability to gain clear title to old private foundations (as the Council of Constantinople required) before undertaking his own restorations.

Earlier emperors had not always been so scrupulously respectful of private property rights in ecclesiastical institutions. In 899 Leo VI was preparing to rebuild a monastery that he had confiscated from the disgraced courtier Leo Katokoilas in order to place it at the disposal of his spiritual director, Euthymius.[26] Euthymius, who would later serve as Leo

[23] Eustathios Rhomaios, *Peira* 15.4 (*JGR* 1.43).

[24] See Balsamon, *Comm. ad C. Const. I et II*, c. 7 (R&P 2.674–75).

[25] This monastery was Theophylact's burial site, according to Michael Glykas, *Annales*, ed. I. Bekker, *CSHB* (Bonn, 1836), p. 563; it became the residence of Patriarch Eustratius Garidas (1081–84) after his abdication, according to Theodore Skoutariotes, *Synopsis chronike*, MB 7, p. 182; cf. Janin, *Géographie*, Vol. 2, p. 39.

[26] *Vita Euthymii patriarchae CP*, ed. Patricia Karlin-Hayter (Brussels, 1970), 29; cf. Janin, *Géographie*, Vol. 2, p. 23, and Vol. 3, pp. 285–89.

VI's patriarch (907–912), was informed of the origins of this monastery by Katokoilas' relatives. Euthymius then insisted that Leo VI should recall Katokoilas from exile, pay him a just price for the monastery, and obtain clear title to the property before he would consider accepting the emperor's gift of this institution.

There is no testimony on what legal mechanism, if any, was employed to permit private benefactors to undertake the restoration of ruined ecclesiastical foundations in accordance with Nicephorus Phocas' law of 964. Did these benefactors actually receive deeds to these properties, as Euthymius had obliged Leo VI to do in 899? If transfers of ownership or rights of use over these institutions did occur, then the essential features of the *charistike* may have germinated as early as the reign of Nicephorus Phocas. On the other hand, it seems more likely that it took contemporaries some time to realize the need for a legal mechanism to respect the conflicting claims of private property rights and the critical need for institutional restorations. The Piperatos case, then, probably provided the stimulus for the development of the *charistike*, because henceforth it was no longer possible for the ecclesiastical hierarchy to take over an old institution without regard for the owner's property rights.

Nicholas Chrysoberges shared Nicephorus Phocas' concern for dilapidated and ruined monasteries. This patriarch (and possibly some of his immediate predecessors as well) subscribed to the policy of matching needy institutions with potential benefactors who possessed the necessary resources to undertake restorations. This is clear because it was Nicholas' policy that his successor Sisinnius II (996–998) reversed when he stopped donations of patriarchal monasteries to laymen (in *charistike*) and to other ecclesiastical authorities (in *epidosis*).[27]

The donation of monasteries in *epidosis* from one ecclesiastical authority to another dates back at least to the first patriarchate of Nicholas Mysticus (919–925).[28] It appears that the program was originally intended to assist institutions suffering from mismanagement. By the late tenth century, the ecclesiastical hierarchy was also employing *epidosis* to arrange internal transfers of monasteries to compensate for significant differences in the endowments of episcopal, archiepiscopal, and metropolitan sees. Diocesan monasteries had now become the principal means of financial support for the hierarchy of the public churches. In the tenth century the metropolitan sees had the best endowments of monasteries, perhaps because they were powerful and energetic enough to assert control over weak private foundations.[29] Under ecclesiastical *epidosis*, cer-

---

[27] Balsamon, *Comm. ad C. Nicaen. II*, c. 14 (R&P 2.613.30–614.5).

[28] Nicholas Mysticus, *Epistola* No. 105 (919–925).

[29] *Actes de Lavra*, Vol. 1, No. 8 (989), ed. Paul Lemerle (*Archives de l'Athos*, Vol. 5) (Paris, 1970).

tain metropolitans handed over some of these monasteries to their dependent bishoprics on a temporary basis to bolster their financial support. Nicholas Chrysoberges himself, in an extant document of 989, asserted his *pronoia* for the *sustasis* (support) and *diamone* (maintenance) of monasteries, which led him to concede a dilapidated monastery of the Theotokos of Gomatou at Erissos under *epidosis* to the Lavra monastery of St. Athanasios on Mount Athos.[30] *Epidosis*, then, was one among a number of precedents that paved the way for the *charistike*.

DEVELOPMENT OF THE *CHARISTIKE*

The *charistike* was a public program sponsored by the emperor and the ecclesiastical hierarchy for the private management of religious institutions.[31] The grant of a foundation in *charistike* did not disturb the ultimate rights of ownership over an ecclesiastical institution, but merely separated the rights of management and financial exploitation for a third party. All grants were temporary and limited to one, two, or (rarely) three lifetime tenancies. Thus the program was ideally suited as a vehicle to overcome the legal difficulties of arranging for the restoration of ruined ecclesiastical institutions.

Under this program, private individuals obtained the management of an ecclesiastical foundation by appealing to the emperor, who held the rights of ownership over imperial foundations, or to the office of the patriarch, metropolitan, or bishop that had originally issued a private foundation's *stauropegion*.[32] Successful petitioners were to offer plans for the restoration and beautification of their awards, but it was difficult to ensure that these *charistikarioi* carried them out. Some of the new bene-

[30] St. Lazaros of Mount Galesion's difficulties with the metropolitan of Ephesus in the mid-eleventh century provide a good example of this conflict. See the discussion below in Chapter 8.

[31] The principal source is the hostile John V of Antioch, *Oratio de disciplina monastica et de monasteriis laicis non tradendis*, ed. Paul Gautier, "Réquisitoire du patriarche Jean d'Antioche contre le charisticariat," *REB* 33 (1975), 77–132, esp. Ch. 10, lines 278–85). Modern work on the *charistike* includes: Herman, "Ricerche," 316–29, and "Charisticaires," *DDC*, Vol. 3 (Paris, 1942), cols. 611–17; Placide de Meester, *De monachico statu iuxta disciplinam byzantinam* (Vatican City, 1942), 101–8; J. Moutzourès, "Ta charistika kai eleuthera monasteria," *Theologia* 34 (1963), 536–69; 35 (1964), 87–123, 271–304; Jean Darrouzès, "Dossier sur le charisticariat," *Polychronion: Festschrift Franz Dölger* (Heidelberg, 1966), 150–65; Paul Lemerle, "Un aspect du rôle des monastères à Byzance: Les monastères donnés à des laics, les charisticaires," *Académie des Inscriptions et Belles-Lettres. Comptes rendus des séances de l'année 1967, janvier-mars* (Paris, 1967), 9–28; and Hélène Ahrweiler, "Charisticariat et autres formes d'attribution de fondations pieuses aux Xe-XIe siècles," *ZRVI* 10 (1967), 1–27, which provides the best constitutional analysis of the *charistike*.

[32] Alexius Studites, *Hypomnema A'* (1027) (R&P 5.21.15–23) = V. Grumel, *Les regestes des actes du patriarcat de Constantinople*, Vol. 1: *Les actes des patriarches* (Chalcedon, 1932–47), No. 833; for imperial donations, see below, note 36.

factors discharged their obligations satisfactorily, but as time passed on, the *charistikarioi* of baser motives predominated. Since the administration of the program was so decentralized, there was no way to assure uniformly meritorious *charistikarioi*, so favoritism and widespread abuse flourished.

The persistent petitions of influential laymen soon began to undermine the original purposes of the *charistike*. The turning point occurred when the authorities began to grant out well- endowed, financially stable institutions which did not require the restorations so urgently needed by other, less financially remunerative foundations.[33] A similar transformation in the use of *epidosis* had already occurred by the tenth century. It had always been more profitable for a patron to reap the financial rewards of administering a wealthy private monastery than to commit the capital and the property necessary to found a new monastery. Similarly, the rewards of administering a healthy monastery under the *charistike* far surpassed those of restoring a ruined one.

The diversity of motives behind the creation of the *charistike* contributed to the subversion of its original purposes. Patriarch Nicholas Chrysoberges' use of the *charistike* represented an attempt to make the improvement (*beltiosis*) and maintenance (*sustasis*) of existing ecclesiastical institutions financially attractive to private benefactors no longer bound by Nicephorus Phocas' restrictions on philanthropic donations.[34] Perhaps the patriarch hoped that the financial rewards possible under the *charistike* would serve to narrow the perceived benefits of erecting a new foundation and those of restoring an old one. Otherwise it would have been unrealistic for him to suppose that private individuals, gratified by the end of the ban on endowing new foundations, would continue to divert their personal resources for the rebuilding of older institutions.

Symeon the New Theologian, appointed by Nicholas Mysticus as *hegoumenos* of the old imperial monastery of St. Mamas in Constantinople, may have been one of these new benefactors. Symeon devoted himself to rebuilding this monastery after his installation as its director in 980.[35] Local inhabitants had been using part of the site as a cemetery. Symeon removed the obstructions and restored the entire facility. He also replaced the furnishings in the monastery's church, a building that dated back to the time of Justinian.

Although Basil II had diverted the patriarchate from its old methods

[33] John of Antioch, *De monasteriis* Ch. 9, lines 257–63.
[34] Patriarchal intentions are discernible from Alexius Studites, *Hypomnema A'* (R&P 5.20–24).
[35] Niketas Stethatos, *Vita Symeonis novi theologi*, ed. Irénée Hausherr, OC 12 (1928), Chs. 30, 34, pp. 40–42, 46.

of taking over independent ecclesiastical foundations, his role in the selection of the *charistike* as the preferred alternative is unclear. He himself
employed the *charistike* extensively to the end of his long reign.[36] In donating imperial monasteries under the program, he may simply have
been continuing the practice of such ninth-century emperors as Michael
I, Leo V, Theophilus, and Leo VI. It is unlikely, however, that he was
aware of Justinian's similar program for churches. Basil II's grants were
like Justinian's in that they were conditional upon the incumbent's undertaking restorations. The grants bore a closer resemblance, however,
to those of the ninth-century emperors, since Basil II disposed of them as
rewards for secular services to the state. In 999, for example, George
Trachaniotes, the *catapan* (governor) of Byzantine Italy, granted a monastery to a certain Christopher as a reward for his services to the imperial
cause against the Saracens. Christopher was to hold the monastery (evidently in *charistike*, although the word itself is not used) as a lifetime
grant, with the understanding that it would pass thereafter to his son,
the monk Theophilos. The two recipients were obliged to protect and
beautify the foundation. Trachaniotes, for his part, promised to write the
emperor requesting a chrysobull that would confirm the award.

Basil II's intentions for the *charistike*, then, appear to have been different from those of the church, even if he hoped that they could be reconciled with the tasks of institutional rebuilding and restoration. His subordinate Trachaniotes' use of the *charistike* as a personal reward shows
that the secular concerns of the imperial government influenced the program from its beginnings. For the moment, the different intentions har-
bored for the program did not appear incompatible. This was doubtless
because there had already been a long history of imperial and private
exploitation of religious institutions. The ability of a private patron to
extract a profit from the management (if admittedly not from the construction) of a proprietary religious institution was widely known and
accepted. Even the public churches had often depended upon powerful
laymen, either as nominal employees or as tenants on fixed leases, for
the management and exploitation of their properties. Moreover, the government itself had been involved in the curatorship of much ecclesiastical
property since the early ninth century. So the new development of the
charistike originated and flourished in the tolerant atmosphere of a society long accustomed to lay and government exploitation of ecclesiastical institutions and properties.

[36] Francisco Trinchera, *Syllabus graecarum membranarum* (Naples, 1865), No. 10 (999),
cf. Ahrweiler, "Charisticariat," 15, n. 82; Yahya ibn-Said, *Historia*, ed. I. Kratchkovsky
and A. A. Vasiliev *PO* 23 (1932), 445.

DISSENT OF PATRIARCH SISINNIUS II

Even at this early stage in the history of the *charistike*, there was a notable dissenter from the new policy for administration of ecclesiastical foundations. Basil II's third patriarch, Sisinnius II, proved to be a determined opponent of both the *charistike* and *epidosis*. He issued a decree that ordered the return of all patriarchal monasteries alienated by his predecessors, not only those entrusted to laymen through the *charistike*, but also those granted to other ecclesiastical authorities under *epidosis*.[37] The new patriarch was an extremely learned man renowned for his knowledge of medicine and law.[38] He based his objections to these programs upon a conservative interpretation of the forty-ninth canon of the Synod in Trullo, which he interpreted as a ban on all external exploitation of the properties of ecclesiastical institutions.[39] Sisinnius' action would make him a hero to the opponents of the *charistike* in the late eleventh century, but in his own day he was unable to prevent Basil II from continuing to grant out imperial monasteries under the program. Sisinnius' decision to condemn not only the *charistike* but also *epidosis*, which had benefited many in the ecclesiastical hierarchy, probably weakened his position within the church as well.

BASIL II'S LAW *PERI TON DYNATON* (996)

The strong-minded emperor was determined to promote his own policy in spite of Sisinnius' unwillingness to cooperate. Basil II's famous novel *Peri ton dynaton*, issued in January 996 before Sisinnius' elevation to the patriarchate, illustrates the emperor's own perception of the issues.[40] It is the most forceful law in the long series of enactments against the insatiable territorial ambitions of the magnates that goes back to the original law on property speculation issued by Romanus Lecapenus in 922. While the law's bearing on that problem has justly occupied scholarly attention, it remains important also for the problem of private religious foundations, specifically those of peasant communities.

Bound only by the lenient legislation of Leo VI, pious villagers often built churches on their own land in the ninth and tenth centuries. Individual villagers might be joined subsequently by fellow peasants who

[37] Grumel, *Regestes* No. 809; recorded by Balsamon, *Comm. ad C. Nicaen. II*, c. 13 (R&P 2.612).

[38] Joel, *Chronographia* (CSHB 60); see also my "Sisinnius II: A Reform Patriarch of the Reign of Basil II," *BSC* 9 (1983), 54–55.

[39] See above, note 27.

[40] Basil II, *Peri ton dynaton* (966) (*JGR* 3.306–18), esp. Ch. 3; = Dölger, *Regesten* No. 783.

would all embrace monastic life. A crisis of administration occurred when the original founders passed away. They had left their inheritances to the institutions, and, according to canon law, it was necessary to preserve the ecclesiastical character of these foundations. The local bishops intervened at this point, annexed the foundations as diocesan monasteries, and granted them out to wealthy magnates *kata dorean* (as a gift, that is, in *charistike*). As a result, the magnates continued to gain communal property in violation of the spirit of existing imperial legislation.[41] It appears, then, that the operation of the *charistike*, which Basil II himself would continue to promote over the objections of Sisinnius II, had created a loophole in the laws that forbade transfers of land from the peasants to the magnates.

The bishops had a motive besides personal greed and partiality toward the magnates for their actions. They really had to step in and prop up poorly endowed foundations in order to preserve their ecclesiastical character. The fateful decision of the Council of Constantinople forbade them to use diocesan funds for this purpose, and so the natural recourse was to employ the *charistike* as a means of obtaining lay financial assistance. Basil II ordered that the lay *charistikarioi* should lose their rights over these institutions and return them to the peasant villagers as communal *eukteria*. The bishops and metropolitans were to enjoy their traditional rights of commemoration in the liturgy (*anaphora*), approval of clerical nominations (*sphragis*), and correction of spiritual errors (*diorthosis*), but were not to receive anything else that might connote ownership of these institutions.[42]

Basil II wanted these monastic foundations to be considered as communal proprietary churches rather than as diocesan monasteries liable to being granted out under the *charistike*. This suggests that the old distinctions between churches and monasteries had blurred considerably, perhaps as a result of the atrophy of the public church system in the countryside. In any case, it was not at all unusual anymore for small monastic chapels to fulfill the functions of parish churches just as Basil II's law ordains in this instance.

The emperor's respect for private property rights in foundations in this law is thoroughly consistent with his repeal of Nicephorus Phocas' novel as well as his decision in the Piperatos case. He did allow some exceptions to his general rules for the treatment of communal churches. Those *eukteria* that were under imperial *pronoia*, and had received *solemnia* (dedicatory offerings) or *photapsiai* (allowances for the expense of illu-

---

[41] *Peri ton dynaton* (966) Ch. 3 (*JGR* 3.313.14–314.1).
[42] *Peri ton dynaton* (*JGR* 3.314.1–18).

mination) were to remain integral parts of the public church system, but Basil II would not permit the bishops and metropolitans to give them out to third parties under the *charistike*.[43]

Basil II also excepted from the restriction of his law individually or communally organized monasteries of a good size (a minimum of eight to ten monks) and with proper endowment. The ecclesiastical authorities could grant these institutions out to whomever they wished.[44] Foundations of this sort had to have an endowment sufficient to support their inhabitants since Basil II, unlike Nicephorus Phocas, was unwilling to grant waivers of the laws of Romanus Lecapenus and Constantine VII forbidding the acquisition of peasant properties by ecclesiastical institutions. The emperor also provided that the bishops and metropolitans should not try to evade the general principle of his law by suddenly increasing the number of monks at communal churches in order to qualify for the exemption allowed for larger institutions.

Basil II's third and last category of exemptions concerned large monasteries of ancient foundation.[45] He allowed the bishops and metropolitans to grant out these institutions regardless of the number of monks resident in them, even if they had become totally depopulated through the hierarchy's neglect. Most likely Basil II refers here to the numerous privately founded monasteries that had lost their original patrons over the centuries. It is notable that he placed no restrictions on the bishops with respect to granting these institutions out for repairs and renovations to *charistikarioi* and indeed seems to have censured the bishops for not giving them attention earlier.

State policy with respect to private foundations had begun to conflict with the government's struggle to reverse the patterns of land ownership in the Byzantine countryside. Therefore, Basil II's regulation of land ownership and private religious foundations in the same novel was more than fortuitous. His novel seeks to chart a careful course, allowing the bishops sufficient latitude to arrange for the restoration of needy institutions while insuring that these projects did not further disturb the imbalance of land tenure in favor of the wealthy benefactors.

Basil II's law, then, attempted to preserve the independence of small private churches in the face of the threat posed by the *charistike*. Other

---

[43] *Peri ton dynaton* (*JGR* 3.314.18–24); for imperial *solemnia*, see *Suda*, ed. Anna Adler, *Suidae Lexicon* (Leipzig, 1933–38), Pt. 4, p. 395, No. 768; the Marcian taxation treatise, ed. Franz Dölger, *Beiträge zur Geschichte der byzantinischen Finanzverwaltung besonders des 10. und 11. Jahrhunderts*, repr. ed. (Hildesheim, 1960), 117; the donation of Romanus Lecapenus to St. Panteleimon and those of Nicephorus Phocas and John Tzimisces to the Lavra monastery discussed elsewhere in this chapter.

[44] *Peri ton dynaton* (*JGR* 3.315.26–316.3).

[45] *Peri ton dynaton* (*JGR* 3.315.13–19).

sources confirm this picture of the continued existence of private churches.[46] The imperial jurist Eustathios Rhomaios, for example, had to judge a case (sometime before 1034) on the distribution of income derived from the private church of a village in the theme of Chaldia.[47] It seems that a number of individuals had come to join the original proprietors in the ownership of this church dedicated to St. Auxentios (which gave its name to the village). They all shared in the income from pious offerings made at the church. The jurist had to establish a scheme for allocating the church's income, apparently because the officiating priest had challenged the proprietors' present arrangements.

Eustathios made a distinction between votive offerings, which served as furnishings or decorations for the church, and all other forms of income. The former he reserved for the church itself. He divided the rest into four shares. The church received one share, while the lay holders of *pronomia* (privileges) obtained three shares to divide among themselves. The jurist also took care to preserve the independence of the *protopapas* (head priest) by stipulating that the owners could remove him from the financial administration of the church only for misappropriation of funds.

Eustathios Rhomaios' decision, recorded in his lawbook which was complied sometime after 1034, clearly reflects the legal thinking of Basil II's times. The jurist shared this emperor's approval of private property rights in ecclesiastical institutions. His neat distinction between the gifts and revenues necessary for the operation of St. Auxentios on the one hand and the surplus income that rightfully belonged to the proprietors on the other parallels the contemporary allocation of ecclesiastical revenues under the *charistike*. Indeed, insofar as the arrangements at St. Auxentios were representative of traditional practices in private churches, they demonstrate once again that Byzantine society accepted the compatibility of an owner's private profit with the proper functioning of an ecclesiastical institution.

RESOLUTION OF THE CONFLICT OVER THE *CHARISTIKE*

Despite this sentiment, Sisinnius II was able to stop patriarchal participation in the *charistike*. He could hardly prevent its employment by

[46] E.g., Christopher Phagoura's private oratory at Chrysopolis restored by Symeon the New Theologian (see below, Chapter 6), the Church of St. Auxentius in the theme of Chaldia (see Eustathios Rhomaios, *Peira* 15.8 [*JGR* 1.44]; and the Monastery of the *protovestiarius* Symeon on Bithynian Olympus (see Skylitzes, *Synopsis historiarum*, ed. Thurn, p. 396).

[47] Eustathios Rhomaios, *Peira* 15.8 (*JGR* 1.44); cf. Ahrweiler, "Charisticariat," 7; Herman, "Chiese private," 306–7. For the *Peira*, see H. J. Scheltema, "Byzantine Law," in *The Cambridge Medieval History*, Vol. 4 (2nd ed.), Pt. 2, pp. 55–77, at 71–72.

other authorities as long as the emperor, the metropolitans, and the bishops thought that it was possible to allow a lay administrator a personal
profit without endangering a religious foundation's original purposes.
Yet the emperor was soon to anger the ecclesiastical hierarchy with a
measure more clearly opposed to their interests. This was his law of
1002, which required wealthy property owners to assume the burden of
the defaulted taxes of their poorer neighbors.[48] This obligation, the *allelengyon*, had traditionally been vested collectively in the defaulters' fellow peasants in the fiscal commune. Sisinnius II's successor Sergius II
(999–1019) led a delegation of bishops and abbots in protesting to the
emperor against the severe burden that this shifting of the burden of
paying the *allelengyon* had placed on ecclesiastical institutions.[49] Basil II,
whose scorn of learned advice was proverbial, refused to change his mind
and cancel the legislation.

The emperor was concerned with obtaining the cooperation of the
church in the use of the *charistike*. His law on the *allelengyon*, issued at
a time when the patriarchate was declining to participate in this program, must have placed great pressure on all of the hierarchy for their
cooperation. It may well have been at this time that, faced with this burden of increased taxation, the leaders of the church began to grant out
even wealthy institutions in order to escape the new fiscal obligations
which they could not easily pay by themselves.[50]

The new patriarch, Sergius II, came from a family that was familiar
with the problems of deteriorating institutions and the benefits of cooperation with the emperor.[51] Long ago, Romanus Lecapenus had aided in
the restoration of his family's monastery of the *magistros* Manuel, inherited from Patriarch Photius. Another family religious foundation, the
church and monastery of St. Panteleimon in Constantinople, had also
been the beneficiary of imperial largess, for Romanus Lecapenus had
awarded it a *solemnion* to provide for the living expenses of its resident
monks. Perhaps this appreciation prompted him in 1016 to issue a decree

[48] Dölger, *Regesten* No. 793, recorded by Skylitzes, *Synopsis historiarum* (ed. Thurn, p.
347, lines 76–80).

[49] Despite Ostrogorsky, *HBS*, 307, Skylitzes says nothing about protests against this law
by lay magnates.

[50] According to *Epanagoge* 10.7, the public churches had difficulty meeting their tax
obligations in the late ninth century, even before they faced the additional burden imposed
by Basil II's law on the *allelengyon*.

[51] Theophanes Continuatus, *Chronographia* 4.50 (*CSHB* 433–34); Joel, *Chronographia*
(*CSHB* 60); Zonaras, *Epitome historiarum* 17.8; and Nikephoros Kallistos, *Enarratio de
episcopis Byzantii* (*PG* 147, col. 461). The identity of Sergius, nephew of Photius and
Patriarch Sergius II, asserted by the sources, seems impossible unless he is conceded a lon-
gevity of nearly a hundred years. For the monastery of Manuel, see Janin, *Géographie*, Vol.
3, pp. 320–22.

reversing his predecessor's opposition to the *charistike* and *epidosis*.[52] Sergius advanced an alternative explanation of the forty-ninth canon of Trullo, which he interpreted as prohibiting donations of monasteries only when secularization of the facility resulted. He ruled that the grants were canonical if the beneficiaries preserved the ecclesiastical character of the donated institutions.

By this time it must have been as difficult for contemporaries as it has been for historians today to determine the correct meaning of this Trullan canon. The patriarchate certainly had at its disposal ample canonical precedent with which to justify continued opposition to the *charistike*.[53] The decision to disregard this earlier legislation and to reinterpret the Trullan canon was a capitulation to contemporary pressures and the wishes of the emperor. Perhaps the patriarch hoped to trade cooperation in the *charistike* for a concession on the *allelengyon*. Basil II had promised to give the matter due consideration when he returned from the Bulgarian War. The patriarch took the occasion of the emperor's triumphal return to Constantinople in 1019 to press once again for its repeal.[54] Yet Basil II still turned a deaf ear to the request.

The patriarchate was actually hard pressed to defend the rights that it already possessed. In 998 Sisinnius II had allowed the metropolitan of distant Alania to collect a small amount of personal provisions from the patriarchal monastery of St. Epiphanios in Kerasos whenever he had to undertake the difficult journey to Constantinople.[55] Upon the metropolitan's death, his clergy sought to represent this concession to Basil II as a grant of full proprietary rights over this monastery. Sergius II feared that Basil II would accept this usurpation of a patriarchal monastery as a metropolitan institution. He managed to locate a copy of the original concession of Sisinnius II and issued a *hypomnema* (memorandum) in May 1024, which set the record straight.[56]

Ultimately, the patriarch was no more successful than Sisinnius II in cooperating with Basil II for the best interests of the church. If he had hoped to trade patriarchal participation in the *charistike* for repeal of the *allelengyon*, he miscalculated badly. Basil II never did repeal the *allelengyon*, and the resumption of patriarchal grants under the *charistike* re-

---

[52] Grumel, *Regestes* No. 821; reported by Balsamon, *Comm. ad C. Nicaen. II*, c. 13 (R&P 2.614.5–24).

[53] E.g., *C. Nicaen. II*, c. 12, 13 (R&P 2.592–93, 612), as well as *C. Chalc.*, c. 24 (R&P 2.271), which Balsamon himself cited in connection with Sisinnius II's original decree against the *charistike* and *epidosis*.

[54] Skylitzes, *Synopsis historiarum* (ed. Thurn, p. 365, lines 1–3).

[55] Sisinnius II, *Typikon* (998), ed. Gerhard Ficker, "Das Epiphanios-Kloster in Kerasus und der Metropolit Alaniens," *BNJ* 3 (1922), 92–104, at 93.

[56] Sergius II, *Hypomnema* (1024), ed. Ficker, "Epiphanios-Kloster," 94–95.

opened another category of institutions liable to abuse at the hands of unscrupulous laymen. It was not until 1027, safely after the death of Basil II, that Patriarch Alexius Studites (1025–43) was able to issue legislation designed to curb the abuses of the *charistike*. His condemnation of past practices indicates that the latter years of Basil II's reign had constituted a period of rampant abuses and reckless disregard for the original purposes of institutional rebuilding and restoration.

The temptation for the *charistikarioi* to exploit their temporally limited grants in wanton fashion was extremely strong. The authorities had probably hoped that these new benefactors would pattern their behavior on that of conscientious founding families, ut the newly assigned patrons lacked their piety and enlightened self-interest. The church already had many unhappy experiences with lay tenants who recklessly abused its rental properties.[57] Now, instead of individual properties, the institutions themselves and all their landed estates suffered blatant misuse and even secularization.[58] The seeming naïvety of the patriarchate may indicate only the intensity of the pressures brought to bear against it by the emperor and the laity interested in gaining access to the wealth of the church.

---

[57] For these problems, see *NJ* 7.3.2 (535), *NJ* 120.8 (544), and *P. Cairo Masp.* 1.67087.
[58] Alexius Studites, *Hypomnema A'* (R&P 5.21.23—22.1).

CHAPTER SIX

Private Religious Foundations in the Age of the *Charistike*

B Y THE end of the eleventh century, we are told that nearly all monasteries, large or small, ancient or modern, had come into the hands of the *charistikarioi*.[1] Reportedly the only exceptions were a few very recent foundations, whose patrons would naturally have wanted to direct them personally. Many of the institutions that the emperors and the ecclesiastical hierarchy let out in *charistike* originated as private foundations, although they had now become public responsibilities. Thus, while the development of the *charistike* is important chiefly for the history of the public churches of the empire, it also had an important bearing on the fate of the old private foundations. With its development, a new class of temporary beneficiaries replaced the traditional founding families. *Charistikarioi* were chiefly laymen, but some religious, especially monks, also played an important part in restoring ecclesiastical foundations out of their personal resources. Niketas Stethatos' life of Symeon the New Theologian provides an early example of this activity.[2] When Symeon had to leave the capital in 1012 after a dispute with a patriarchal official, the nobleman Christopher Phagoura gave him a ruined oratory of St. Marina located on his personal property at Chrysopolis. Symeon spent the next few years restoring it as part of a new monastic foundation. This is one small indication that the granting out of a religious institution in *charistike* occasionally might have led to the improvement of that institution's well-being. Indeed, it ought to be emphasized that the historical record of the *charistike* is derived chiefly from sources that differ only in the degree of hostility with which they view it. While it would be perverse to argue against the overwhelming evidence that the *charistike* was a flawed institution, exploited by many unscru-

---

[1] John of Antioch, *De monasteriis* Ch. 9, lines 267–75.
[2] Niketas Stethatos, *Vita* Ch. 100 (ed. Hausherr, p. 138): for Symeon, see A. Kazhdan, "Predvaritelnie zamechaniya o mirovozzrenii vizantiiskogo mistika x–xi vv. Simeona," *Byzantinoslavica* 28 (1967), 1–38; for this foundation, see Janin, *Géographie*, Vol. 2, p. 25, and Jean Darrouzès, "Le mouvement des fondations monastiques au XIe siècle," *T&M* 6 (1976), pp. 159–76, No. 11, p. 162.

pulous individuals, it should not be forgotten that nothing in the way of a defense for it survives from its promoters and beneficiaries. That the *charistike* seems to have operated in such a way as to transfer the administration of much property from the benefactor families of the pre-Basilian nobility to individuals of more modest wealth but rising political ambitions cannot but have earned it additional ill will from those aggrieved magnates who were to support its abolition at the end of the eleventh century.

REFORMS OF PATRIARCH ALEXIUS STUDITES (1025-43)

One of the early critics of the *charistike* was Alexius Studites, the last patriarch of Constantinople elected during the reign of Basil II. Not long after the emperor's death, he took action to curb abuses in the program. His first *hypomnema*, a document issued in synod in November 1027, restates the original purposes of the *charistike* for the maintenance (*diamone*), well-being (*euthenia*), and the enlargement (*platysmos*) of ecclesiastical foundations, and bemoans the scandalous misuse of the grants.[3] The patriarch proposed to remedy the abuses principally by setting up the office of his chancellor, the *chartophylax*, as the clearing-house for approval and registration of all grants of ecclesiastical institutions, regardless of the donor or the recipient. He hoped that henceforth the owners of these institutions would pay more attention to the character of the prospective recipients and require them to post security. He apparently reserved for himself the right to reject unsuitable grants or recipients, although it is not evident that either he or his successors made use of this authority.

To preserve the effectiveness of this mechanism for controlling who would receive the grants, Alexius had to forbid the original recipients to transfer their rights to other parties. The success of the patriarchate in enforcing this regulation ensured that the *charistikarioi* would never become the de facto owners of the institutions they managed. It was possible to include a secondary or tertiary beneficiary (usually, though not always, a relative of the original recipient) in the original letter of donation. Yet no one could expect henceforth to hold a perpetual, hereditary *charistike*.

Alexius Studites also forbade men to hold a *charistike* over a convent of nuns, or women to hold one over a monastery. A decision recorded in Eustathios Rhomaios' lawbook the *Peira* shows how this sort of situation could come about.[4] The patrician Panberios owed 62 *litrai* of gold to the

---

[3] Alexius Studites, *Hypomnema A'* (1027) (R&P 5.20–24); commentary by Grumel, *Regestes* No. 833, and Herman, "Ricerche," 320–21.

[4] Eustathios Rhomaios, *Peira* 15.16 (*JGR* 1.48); cf. Lemerle, "Charisticaires," 22.

protospatharia Maria, daughter of (Bardas?) Skleros, and was unable to repay the debt. Panberios held the *charistike* of the monastery of St. Mamas in Constantinople, and a court decision directed that he could acquit his debt by transferring the rights to administer this institution to Maria Sklerina. Perhaps this monastery was the institution of the same name which Symeon the New Theologian had worked to restore under Patriarch Nicholas Chrysoberges in the 980s.[5] Alexius Studites' decision of 1027 aimed to remove such cases as this from the jurisdiction of the imperial courts, and to prevent a woman from ever again holding the *charistike* of a monastery.

The patriarch was also concerned with the proper operation of *epidosis*. Metropolitan sees that had let out their dependent monasteries under this program to subordinate bishoprics were now seeking them back because the metropolitans were unable to meet their tax obligations to the state. Basil II's law imposing the payment of *allelengyon* upon ecclesiastical institutions was still in effect, and it probably played an important part in the financial difficulties of the metropolitan sees. Alexius Studites had not yet secured repeal of this law, so he supported the metropolitans by ordering the bishops to return these monasteries to their original overlords.

A few months later, in January 1028, Alexius Studites issued his second *hypomnema*, a document that supplements and strengthens his earlier legislation on the *charistike*.[6] Once again the patriarch decried the rapacity of evil *charistikarioi*, who appropriated the incomes of the institutions that they were supposed to protect and drove away the monks who resided in them. Alexius ordered that the metropolitans should expel such evildoers, by force if necessary. He also directed that litigation arising out of such cases be tried only in the court of the patriarchal synod, and denied the competence of secular courts to deal with countersuits brought by the *pronoetai* (that is, the *charistikarioi*) of these institutions. The patriarch obliged all *pronoetai* to render accounts for their ecclesiastical *diakoniai*, thereby subjecting the holders of *charistike* to the same constraints applicable to the administrators of individual tracts of ecclesiastical property.

Other provisions of the second *hypomnema* reveal the extent to which laymen had enlarged and consolidated their hold over the institutional church in the century that had passed since Leo VI's concessions to the magnates. One such provision condemns the local magnates who obtained by petition the rights of public churches (*katholikai ekklesiai*) for their own private foundations. By 1028 the ecclesiastical authorities were

[5] Janin, *Géographie*, Vol. 3, p. 327.
[6] Alexius Studites, *Hypomnema B'* (R&P 5.25–32); commentary by Grumel, *Regestes*, Vol. 1, No. 835.

in a very weak position to resist the aggrandizement of private churches, even those in private dwellings, because Leo VI had sanctioned these sites as places of regular worship and baptism. Alexius Studites hoped to restrict private institutions to a single service of the liturgy each feast day. As his means of enforcement, he relied upon the traditional sanction of deposition of the offending cleric.

As we have seen, the metropolitans depended upon the revenues of their monasteries to meet their tax obligations. Some of these monasteries had provisions in their charters of foundation which specified a certain *syneisphora* (contribution) which they were to pay to their metropolitans. Over the course of time, certain unspecified individuals (*charistikarioi?*) had diverted these payments to themselves. Alexius now ordered that they should return them to the metropolitans.

Certain metropolitans and bishops had actually endangered the financial stability of their sees by granting out their own monasteries to laymen under the *charistike*. Alexius ordered that these officials should select only the *idioperiorista* (self-determined, that is, independent, privately founded, non-diocesan) monasteries for future donations. He instructed the metropolitans and bishops to retain control over those institutions that served as their own residences (*episkopeia*), as well as those that provided essential financial support for the operation of their sees. The patriarch pronounced the annulment of all grants of monasteries that did not conform to these new regulations.

In a little over forty years since the *charistike* had begun during the reign of Basil II, the program had come to pose a grave danger to its ecclesiastical sponsors. If Alexius Studites had not taken such decisive action in 1028, it might have been only a matter of time before laymen controlled not only the church's institutions and properties, but its bishoprics as well.

Given the extent of lay control over the church, it is not surprising that the patriarch felt constrained to reaffirm the basic principle that individual clerics should be obedient to their superiors, the metropolitans. In this matter, too, Leo VI's concessions had aggravated long standing problems. Clerical insubordination before diocesan authorities had always been an undesirable accompaniment of the proliferation of private churches in Byzantium, and now that laymen controlled nearly all the monasteries as well, the evils multiplied.

It is easy, with the advantages of hindsight, to criticize Alexius Studites' response to the rampant abuses of the *charistike*.[7] He decided to attempt to reform the program rather than to abolish it entirely. Abolition of the

---

[7] E.g., Charanis, "Monastic Properties," 78, but cf. Herman, "Ricerche," 321 and "Charisticaires," col. 613.

charistike was probably not a feasible alternative to reform at the time he chose to take action, for Basil II's law on the *allelengyon* remained in effect until after the accession of Romanus III Argyrus (1028–34).[8] The already hard-pressed public churches surely could not have taken back all of the monasteries granted out to laymen because they could not hope to meet their tax obligations.

The prevalence of the *charistike* in the eleventh century did not mean the total eclipse of traditional private institutions. The literary sources continue to mention private institutions in a most incidental way, taking their existence for granted as commonplace in Byzantine society.[9] Skylitzes, for example, relates that the *protovestiarios* Symeon, a courtier of Constantine VIII (1025–28), fled to his private monastery on Mount Olympus in Bithynia when he fell out of favor with Michael IV (1034–41). In 1017 a court official, the *koubouklesios* Stephen, made a donation in *despoteia* of a monastery of the Theotokos (located near the famous Lavra monastery on Mount Athos) to his daughter, the nun Maria. In the 1040s a series of private foundations came into existence in Greece for which government officials served as benefactors. Some similar foundations on Cyprus in the 1090s parallel the earlier foundations in Greece. Moreover, the famous courtier and literary savant Michael Psellos mentions in passing several private hereditary monasteries in his extensive correspondence of the mid-eleventh century.[10] By themselves these incidental references might suffice to demonstrate the continued existence of traditional private foundations in the age of the *charistike*. There is also documentary evidence, however, which presents a more vivid view of these institutions than any other sources since the Egyptian papyri of the sixth century.

THE WILL OF EUSTATHIOS BOILAS (1059)

The most important of these documents is the will of the provincial magnate Eustathios Boilas (1059), which makes provisions for three

[8] Skylitzes, *Synopsis historiarum* (ed. Thurn, p. 375, lines 54–55); cf. Ostrogorsky, *HBS*, 322.

[9] Skylitzes, *Synopsis historiarum*, p. 396, lines 28–32; Darrouzès, "Fondations," pp. 166–68, Nos. 33–34, 42–45, 47; *Actes de Lavra*, Vol. 1, No. 22 (1017), ed. Lemerle.

[10] Monastery of Narsou, of which Psellos was ephor: Michael Psellos, *Epistola* 135, ed. K. A. Sathas, *MB* 5 (Paris, 1876); for this institution, see Paul Gautier, "Précisions historiques sur le monastère de *Ta Narsou*," *REB* 34 (1975), 101–10; Monastery of Morocharzanon, Psellos, *Epistola* 99 (ed. Sathas); Monastery of Patrikios, *Epistola* 138 (ed. Sathas); Monastery of the Vestarch of Melios, *Epistola* 81, ed. Eduard Kurtz and Franz Drexl, *Michaelis Pselli scripta minora*, Vol. 2 (Milan, 1941); for all these institutions, see Ahrweiler, "Charisticariat," 25–26.

churches that belonged to his family.[11] These were a church of the Theotokos that Boilas had built himself, a church of St. Barbara, which was
his family's traditional place of interment, and a church of St. Modestos
erected by Boilas' mother.[12] The first two institutions were located at the
center of Boilas' landed possessions in the theme of Iberia, annexed by
Basil II at the turn of the century. The church of St. Modestos was located
in Cappadocia, Boilas' old homeland before his migration to Iberia.

The provisions of Boilas' will for his private churches are old fashioned
and traditional. The will deeds properties for the support of the foundations, but it retains effective control of these lands for Boilas' heirs. So,
although early on the will bequeaths half of his property of Bouzina to
the church of the Theotokos in "complete and inalienable *despoteia*," it
subsequently states that his children and heirs were to be the lords and
masters of all his personal property, contingent on their fulfillment of his
wishes regarding the support of the clergy and provision for commemorative masses.[13] Boilas clearly intended that the Theotokos should have a
patrimonial rather than an independent administration. In a similar vein,
the will speaks of the furnishings of this church as consecrated offerings,
but allows Boilas' daughters rights of use (*chresis*) and ownership (*despoteia*) over them. Boilas restrained his descendants only from alienating
consecrated offerings without the consent of the priests. These arrangements seem little changed since the days of Justinian and the great landowner benefactors of Roman Egypt.

As a conscientious benefactor, Boilas tried to foresee the needs of his
churches. The half of the property of Bouzina that he earmarked for the
support of the church of the *Theotokos* was to provide 26 *nomismata*
annually for the *rogai* (salaries) of the attending clergy. One of these
clerics also received *annona* (wages in kind).[14] Boilas encouraged one
deacon to supplement his income from his skill as a calligrapher, but we
do not hear of non-ecclesiastical employments for the other clergy. Boilas
staffed his church in part with freedmen whom he encouraged to become
clerics.[15] The practice dates at least to the late fourth century and perhaps
was a common feature of the operation of private churches in Byzantium.[16] Boilas provided special legacies for four of these freedmen clerics

---

[11] Eustathios Boilas, *Diatyposis*, reedited by Paul Lemerle, *Cinq études sur le XIe siècle
byzantin* (Paris, 1977), 20–29, with commentary, 29–35; Speros Vryonis, Jr., "The Will of
a Provincial Magnate, Eustathius Boilas (1059)," *DOP* 11 (1957), 263–77, provides an
English translation and some valuable commentary.

[12] *Diatyposis*, lines 99–103: church of the Theotokos; lines 103–8: church of St. Barbara; lines 232–38: church of St. Modestos.

[13] *Diatyposis*, lines 99–103; cf. 117–19

[14] *Diatyposis*, lines 99–103, 215–19.

[15] *Diatyposis*, lines 201–2, 203–6, 210–12, 215–19; cf. 219–20.

[16] E.g., Polychronius, the freedman priest of the consul Caesarius, mentioned above in
Chapter 1.

in addition to their normal salaries. The will mentions only one cleric who received a grant of landed property.[17] Apparently the rest of the clergy lived adjacent to the church of the Theotokos as a monastic brotherhood.

Boilas' will maintains that he had spent 300 *nomismata* on the furnishings of the Theotokos.[18] The long list of sacrificial vessels, vestments, icons, and books shows that Boilas furnished his church generously, though the foundation of a private church was not always so expensive. He provided 12 *nomismata* annually for the costs of illuminating this church which, added to the clerical salaries, produces a figure of at least 38 *nomismata* for the annual cost of running the institution.[19] At least four or five clerics shared the 26 *nomismata* allotted for salaries, which varied according to the clerical rank of the individuals concerned.

Boilas therefore fulfilled three of the four traditional requirements of Justinian's law on the funding of private foundations, despite their omission by Leo VI from the text of the *Basilika*. The will does not make specific provision for structural maintenance, a significant omission in light of the contemporary record of ruined and dilapidated private foundations. Perhaps similar omissions by benefactors over the ages were crucial in bringing on the crisis of private foundations in the late tenth century that led to the innovation of the *charistike*.

Boilas had already laid to rest his mother, wife, and son in St. Barbara's. His will provides for his own burial there, too, and for funeral services and memorial masses.[20] He allowed 12 *nomismata* yearly for these memorial services. In addition to this specific endowment, Boilas granted St. Barbara's an annual income of 200 *modii* of wheat, 1,000 *litrai* of wine, and an unspecified amount of fresh fruit. These two separate grants recall the distinction between *prosphora* donations *mortis causa* and *inter vivos* found in Byzantine Egypt. As in the time of Leo VI, the revenues that churches received as a result of endowments for commemorative masses continued to be important for their financial wellbeing.

Apparently Boilas had not yet built the church of the Theotokos at the time of his relatives' deaths. Subsequently, he preferred to continue to use St. Barbara's as the common resting-place for his family. Since burial in a church was a special privilege usually limited to the founder's family, it is probable that St. Barbara's was a private church just like the church of the Theotokos, but with separate arrangements for its financial support. Boilas' will also sets up a cash endowment of 3 *nomismata* for his de-

---

[17] *Diatyposis*, lines 203–6; cf. 198, 219–21.
[18] *Diatyposis*, lines 117–19.
[19] *Diatyposis*, lines 99–103.
[20] *Diatyposis*, lines 103–8.

ceased mother's church of St. Modestos in Cappadocia.[21] He may also have made some arrangements for its future administration, but the damaged state of the text at this point frustrates a determination of his plans. Boilas may have been exceptional in showing such concern for a family foundation so far distant from the bulk of his property. It is easy to deduce from this example how many private foundations might have come to fend for themselves as independent institutions in the absence of such a conscientious benefactor.

Boilas's will, composed on the frontiers of the empire, shows scarcely any recognition of the dangers facing private ecclesiastical foundations in the mid-eleventh century. Other private benefactors showed a keener awareness of the perils of the *charistike* for the fiscal and spiritual health of their foundations. Astute founders who wished to preserve the independence of their benefactions and keep them out of the hands of *charistikarioi* realized that they could not leave them without protectors and expect them to retain independence for long. The problem was particularly vexing for a founder in religious life who did not have natural heirs or a family to look after the foundation after his death.

EVIDENCE FROM MONASTIC CARTULARIES

The survival of some eleventh-century monastic cartularies from Mount Athos and Byzantine Italy permits additional study of the construction, management, and transmission of private monasteries. Laymen of this era characteristically relied upon individual clerics, particularly monks, to take the initiative in the construction of new foundations. In turn, these clerics frequently employed other laymen to carry out the actual labor of erecting these institutions.[22] Clerical initiative, however, did not necessarily lead to clerical ownership of the foundations once they were completed.

An Italian document of 1061 makes this point clear.[23] A certain Calones, who was a *taxiarch* (military commander), had granted a small piece of land to a monk named Gerasimos, along with a charter granting him use of the land conditional upon his erection of a church and a monastery. The charter allowed Calones to expel Gerasimos if he did not fulfill the terms of the grant satisfactorily. Sometime after Calones' death,

[21] *Diatyposis*, lines 232–35.

[22] Trinchera, *SGM* No. 15 (1015); for monastic proprietors, see André Guillou, "La classe dei monachi-proprietari nell'Italia bizantina (sec. x–xi). Economia e diritto canonico," *Bulletino dell'Istituto Storico Italiano per il Medio Evo* 82 (1970), 159–72.

[23] Gertrude Robinson, "History and Cartulary of the Greek Monastery of St. Elias and St. Anastasius of Carbone, Part Two: Cartulary," OC 15 (1929), 118–275, Doc. No. 8 (1061).

his sons and heirs John and Nicholas did precisely that, replacing him with another monk named Hilarion. The troubled times of the Norman occupation of southern Italy made it impossible for Hilarion to fulfill the terms of the contract also, and he voluntarily turned over his administration to the brothers. Then the site reverted to wasteland in the absence of a capable developer. Finally, John succeeded in convincing the abbot of the monastery of St. Athanasios to take over the property with rights of "perpetual *despoteia*."

The monks Gerasimos and Hilarion held a responsibility similar to that of the laymen who received an ecclesiastical institution in *charistike* from the emperor or an ecclesiastical official. The *charistike*, however, was always associated with an institution already in existence, whereas the contract drawn up by Calones is a private document envisioning the creation of a new foundation as a condition of tenure. Perhaps there were similar written or verbal agreements between the proprietors of private churches and their chosen clergymen to provide some sort of financial support in exchange for the performance of liturgical services. It is noteworthy that in Calones' contract the proprietor was able to dismiss his clergyman without interference from the ecclesiastical hierarchy. Only after two failures to secure suitable clerics capable of fulfilling the terms of the contract under the traditional arrangements did Calones' heirs turn the church over to an independent monastery as an unconditional donation.

A document from Byzantine Italy shows a monk and his son granting a *castrum* (fortified settlement) in 1015 to the abbot of the monastery of St. Anania, once again on the condition that the recipient would erect a new church on the site.[24] Another document, of 996, shows the *protos* of the Athonite monasteries and the other *hegoumenoi* granting the ruined monastery of Monoxyletou in *despoteia* to Athanasios, abbot of the imperial monastery of Ta Melana with a view to its restoration.[25] Although a simple property transaction is concluded here according to long-established norms for the transmission of private ecclesiastical property, there is evidence of the strong contemporary concern with the restoration of ruined monasteries which was being pursued concurrently under the *charistike*.

In 1024 Tornikios Kontoleon, *strategos* of the theme of Hellas, arranged to purchase the monastery of Pithara, a small monastery on Mount Athos, from the monk George Charzana for the sum of 210 *nomismata*.[26] Tornikios planned to become a monk himself and was entitled by an extant bill of sale to transmit it to his chosen successor and his

[24] Trinchera, *SGM* No. 15 (1015).
[25] *Actes de Lavra*, Vol. 1, No. 12 (996), ed. Lemerle.
[26] *Actes de Lavra*, Vol. 1, No. 25 (1024), ed. Lemerle.

disciples, but not to sell it to outsiders. All of these documents incorporate the old principle of institutional subordination to the proprietor which was derived from the traditional practice of lay owners of religious institutions. This rule governed even those foundations erected by monasteries themselves until the idea of independent, self-governing monasteries became popular later in the eleventh century. Laymen also turned to the clergy to restore existing private foundations. In a document of 1053, Luke Tromarchos and his three brothers donate their hereditary private monastery of St. Andreas in Calabria to the abbot of the Holy Trinity monastery at Kava.[27] The family monastery had been deserted since the Norman invasions early in the century, and the lay owners apparently hoped that the abbot of Holy Trinity would have the necessary resources to attempt its restoration. The incident recalls the work Symeon the New Theologian did in restoring Christopher Phagoura's oratory of St. Marina at Chrysopolis.

An Athonite document dating from the second quarter of the eleventh century illustrates how a hereditary monastery might pass from one private owner to another.[28] The founder of an Athonite monastery, a monk named Theodosios, had sold a half-share in his institution to Theodore, uncle of the author of this document. Theodosios gave the other half to his disciple and successor Basil, who in turn dedicated it to the Theotokos (that is, to the monastery itself). By the date of the document, Michael, *proestos* of the Lavra monastery on Mount Athos, had gained control of this second share of the monastery of the late Theodosios. The *proestos* sought to make this latter institution a *metochion* (dependent monastery) of the Lavra monastery. The author of the document, a monk named Sabas, meanwhile had inherited the first share from his uncle Theodore. Sabas improved the property by establishing a residence, a church, and some vineyards, all at his own expense. When Sabas became old and infirm, he was no longer able to look after the property, so he decided to reunite his share with that held presently by the *proestos* Michael. Sabas received in exchange a promise from Michael that he would never alienate the property from the possessions of the Lavra monastery, and an assurance of lifetime support for himself and two of his disciples in Lavra. The founder Theodosios' arbitrary disposal of his monastery indicates how lay benefactors must have been free to divide ownership in their proprietary institutions among their heirs. We have already seen this development in connection with the Coptic churches of Egypt in the eighth century.

Another Italian document of 1041, the testament of a certain Basil-

[27] Trinchera, *SGM* No. 40 (1053).
[28] *Actes de Zographou*, ed. W. Regel, E. Kurtz, and B. Korbalev (*Actes de l'Athos*, Vol. 4), *VV Prilozhenie* 13 (1907), No. 2 (1023 or 1038).

Blasios of Armentum, portrays his role as the owner or administrator of several ecclesiastical institutions.[29] He willed two of these, a monastery of the Archistrategos (St. Michael) and another of the Theotokos, to his surviving brother Sergios. Sergios was to enjoy full proprietary rights over these institutions, including the capacity to dispose of them as he saw fit. Basil-Blasios' other brother, Blasios, had been a priest. The catapans, the Byzantine governors of southern Italy, had given him an estate, confirmed by imperial seals. It was apparently on this land that he built the oratory of Hagia Sophia. Blasios' sons and heirs were minors at his death, so their uncle Basil-Blasios administered the property for them. Since the bulk of Basil-Blasios' property was in the eparchy of Latinianum, while the oratory was near Bari on the Adriatic coast, he chose to administer his trusteeship through an ecclesiastical *oikonomos*, to whom he gave a written contract of responsibilities. Basil-Blasios paraphrased this document in his testament: "I gave all into his [the *oikonomos*'] hands, the furnishings of the church and all the [consecrated] vessels with the outlying properties. Nothing is to be changed with regard to such properties except with respect to their improvement (*eis beltiosin*). He shall maintain this tenure until the end of his life, and when he dies, there shall be no lack of someone to undertake this without my ordering it." [30] One *oikonomos*, a priest named Constantine, had already died, and the incumbent of 1041 was Chrysillos Christodoulos, a priest of Orvieto, whom Basil-Blasios confirmed in his tenure in the document under examination here.

This contract invites comparison with the charter of Calones the *taxiarch*. In both cases the subordinate officeholders were performing functions analogous to those of the *charistikarioi*, but their authority derived from purely private contracts. Calones' charter was a specialized variant of a landlord's agreement with a cleric for the performance of services in his proprietary church. Basil-Blasios' charter looks instead to standard trusteeship agreements for its model.[31] The *charistike*, as employed by the emperor and the ecclesiastical authorities, must have drawn upon contracts of both types for its format and terminology.[32]

In yet another Italian document, of 1049, the proprietress Gemma bequeaths a garden and some surrounding property as a "consecrated and personal share" of her church of St. Bartholomew.[33] Gemma designated the gift for the support of the clergy in this church. Her three nephews,

---

[29] "Carbone," No. 2 (1041).

[30] "Carbone," No. 2, lines 51–57, trans. Gertrude Robinson.

[31] See *NJ* 131.15; cf. Knecht, *Kirchenvermögensrecht*, 51–52.

[32] Compare the wording of Basil-Blasius' contract as quoted above with John of Antioch's paraphrase of a *charistikarios*' contract in *De monasteriis* Ch. 10, lines 278–85.

[33] "Carbone," No. 4 (1049), esp. lines 10–15.

as her legal heirs, retained ownership of the church itself. In such a case, the church's ownership of the garden was strictly a technical one, much like the church of the Theotokos' claim to half the income derived from Eustathios Boilas' property of Bouzina. Both Gemma's and Boilas' provisions seem to reflect the influence of the Council of Constantinople's injunction that founders should provide a formal list of "consecrated" property intended for the support of monastic foundations. Of course the council said nothing about the support of churches, and Byzantine canonists never required a formal landed endowment for those private foundations. If founders like Gemma and Boilas chose to do so anyway, this was a voluntary gesture, patterned on contemporary practice with private monastic foundations.

This important difference in the requirements for endowment meant that private churches would continue to have a very close economic and administrative relationship with their patrons' families, while privately founded monasteries would be better prepared to become independent institutions over the course of time. The fact that private monasteries had had specific endowments since the mid-ninth century also must have made them more attractive business propositions to prospective *charistikarioi*, and may explain why we rarely hear of churches being granted out in *charistike*.[34]

The tremendous respect for private property rights in ecclesiastical institutions characteristic of Byzantine society dictated special precautions whenever a transaction might appear to infringe those rights. A document of 1050 from Byzantine Italy illustrates this point.[35] The *hegoumenos* Theodore appointed a priest named Theophylact as his successor, deliberately passing over his own brother, Luke, for the directorship of his monastery. The document in question is Luke's formal renunciation of any rights to the succession. Luke claimed that his advanced age prevented him from assuming the hegoumenate for himself. He accepted a lifetime promise of maintenance from the monastery as compensation for his exclusion from the succession. This recalls Nicholas Mysticus' ruling that the founder's heir was entitled to compensation if it was necesary to exclude him from the administration of a family monastery.

Theodore's use of a will to transmit the hegoumenate of his monastery to his chosen successor was not unique. The spiritual directors of St. Basil's, another monastery of Byzantine Italy, also employed testaments during the eleventh century to bequeath both the hegoumenate and the institution itself to the candidates of their choice. One of these documents, the will of *hegoumenos* Cosmas naming Theodore and Niketas

---

[34] See John of Antioch, *De monasteriis* Ch. 8, lines 241–51, but for churches given in *charistike*, see below, note 54.

[35] Trinchera, *SGM* No. 37 (1050).

as his successors, still survives and dates to 1007.[36] These testaments recall the practice of the Coptic abbots of the Epiphanios and Phoibammon monasteries in seventh- and eighth-century Egypt. Like its predecessors, the more recent document demonstrates the prevalent conception of monasteries as a form of private property.

Late in the eleventh century, some private proprietors chose to surrender their old family foundations as free grants to independent monasteries. This is particularly noticeable in late Italo-Greek documents dating from the period after the demise of Byzantium's political control of Italy in 1071.[37] In one document of 1108, the proprietress Trotta declares that she has given up a monastery she erected herself as well as a church she restored because it was improper for a member of the laity to be an overlord of a monastery or to make use of ecclesiastical property.[38] Such sentiments could hardly have come from a Greek philanthropist of Byzantine times. The author's use of the Greek language and the traditional technical vocabulary do not obscure the influence of the Gregorian reform movement in respect to voluntary renunciation of proprietary rights in ecclesiastical institutions.

THE *PTOCHOTROPHEION* OF MICHAEL ATTALIATES

It is fortunate that the historian Michael Attaliates decided to dedicate the bulk of his modest personal resources to found a private *ptochotropheion* (almshouse), and that his detailed *typikon* (regulatory foundation document) of 1077 for this institution is preserved.[39] This document provides the most specific picture of a private ecclesiastical institution in the Byzantine Empire. Attaliates' foundation actually comprised two institutions, the *ptochotropheion* itself, which was located in Rhaidestos on the Sea of Marmara, and a monastery in Constantinople dedicated to Christ Panoiktirmos, the "all merciful." [40] Attaliates had to purchase the building that he was to turn into the *ptochotropheion*, but he had already inherited the properties he would consecrate for its support. He also ob-

---

[36] "Carbone," No. 1 (1007); cf. Guillou, "Monaci-proprietari," p. 161.

[37] Trinchera, *SGM* No.49 (1086); "Carbone," No. 17 (1108).

[38] "Carbone," No. 17 (1108), lines 21–25.

[39] Michael Attaliates, *Diataxis*, ed. Paul Gautier, *REB* 39 (1981), 5–143; important commentary by Lemerle, *Cinq études*, 67–112, which largely supersedes Waldemar Nissen, *Die Diataxis des Michael Attaliates von 1077: Ein Beitrag zur Geschichte des Klosterwesens im byzantinischen Reiche* (Jena, 1894). For Attaliates' views on the church, see A. Kazhdan, *Studies on Byzantine Literature of the Eleventh and Twelfth Centuries* (Cambridge, 1984), 73–77.

[40] On these institutions, see Lemerle, *Cinq études*, 77–79, as well as the imperial chrysobulls accorded Attaliates' foundation by Michael VII (1074) and by Nicephorus III (1079), ed. P. Gautier, *REB* 39 (1981), 100–23; for the Monastery of Christ Panoiktirmos, see Janin, *Géographie*, Vol. 3, pp. 526–27.

tained the monastery by purchase from a private individual, his sister-in-law Anastaso. He joined it administratively to the new *ptochotropheion*. Henceforth, the two institutions were to share a common administrator and draw on joint revenues as a single ecclesiastical foundation.

Attaliates' *typikon*, which he termed a *diataxis* or "testament," is very much concerned with the problem of maintaining the independence of the foundation in the face of the contemporary threat posed by the *charistike*. The *diataxis* strictly prohibits the foundation from ever falling under the authority of a *charistikarios* or any other overseer.[41] The historian viewed his foundation as an integral part of his personal property, which the *diataxis* bequeaths to his eldest son, Theodore.[42] The properties and revenues that Attaliates attached to his foundation constituted the better part of his fortune, though not the whole of it, judging from a few exceptions that he was careful to distinguish. He placed his son at the head of the foundation as *ptochotrophos* and hoped that the succession would follow from his direct line of heirs in succeeding generations. He took precautions to rule out any claims that collateral heirs might bring against the foundation and his direct heirs. He was prepared to allow one of their number to assume the directorship only if the direct line died out sometime in the future.

Theodore and the rest of Attaliates' line of direct heirs was to have the right of *kyriotes* (overlordship) over the *ptochotropheion*. By contrast, Attaliates limited any future director from the collateral line to the status of an ephor.[43] Only if both the direct and the collateral lines of his descendants should chance to die out was Attaliates prepared to allow the foundation to fend for itself as a truly independent and autonomous institution. Attaliates expressed complete confidence in his son Theodore as his chosen heir. He alone of the future directors of the foundation could not be deposed. Attaliates only forbade him to alienate the foundation to someone outside the family (for example, to a *charistikarios*) or to disregard his instructions as laid down in the *diataxis*.[44] The administration of the foundation would also bring material rewards to its lay directors, since Theodore and successors in the direct line were to receive two-thirds of the revenues left over after expenses and distributions mandated by the *diataxis* had been discharged.[45]

Attaliates, to his credit, foresaw the possibility that one of his descendants might prove to be an unworthy candidate for the directorship of the

[41] Michael Attaliates, *Diataxis*, ed. Gautier, lines 247–62, but cf. 398–423.

[42] *Diataxis*, ed. Gautier, lines 124–26, 280–91, 324–30; Lemerle, *Cinq études*, 80, 102–3.

[43] *Diataxis*, ed. Gautier, lines 398–423; Lemerle, *Cinq études*, 80–81.

[44] *Diataxis*, ed. Gautier, lines 826–40; Lemerle, *Cinq études*, 85.

[45] *Diataxis*, ed. Gautier, lines 602–18.

foundation.[46] The *diataxis*, therefore, establishes grounds for removal of an unsuitable director: embezzlement of funds intended for the operation of the facilities or the payment of salaries, failure to protect the foundation's properties, or neglect of structual maintenance. The founder did not intend that so drastic a step as the removal of one of his direct heirs from his patrimony should be undertaken lightly. The *diataxis* orders that accusers should provide three written warnings at three-month intervals for the benefit of an errant director. Attaliates was willing to allow even a female director to head the foundation if a suitable male candidate could not be found among his relatives to replace the unworthy heir. To mollify such a displaced director, Attaliates allowed him a small annual pension, equivalent to a monk's salary, as compensation for his loss of rights.

The *diataxis* does not make clear how or by whom such a challenge to incompetent or dishonest administration of the foundation would occur. It is likely that the tenure of heirs in family institutions such as this was almost unshakable. Contemporary indulgence of lay direction of ecclesiastical institutions and the foundation's status as private property would assure an heir's position practically beyond challenge. Yet this particular founder seems to have tried to curb the heir's authority somewhat by affirming the immunity of both the *hegoumenos* and the *oikonomos* from arbitrary dismissal.[47] Attaliates' descendants could not remove these officials except for an extremely serious offense such as a lapse into heresy, sexual misconduct, or the display of "contempt or arrogance" toward his heir. The inclusion of the last-named offense suggests that prudent administrators would still have to behave with great deference toward the real masters of the institution. Attaliates was less generous in according proprietor's rights to the heirs of his collateral lines. Such a director he allowed only 150 *modii* of barley and two monks' salaries as compensation.[48] He was, moreover, obliged by Attaliates to share the management of the foundation with the *hegoumenos* and the *oikonomos*.

Attaliates employed the *diataxis* to outline in great detail the expenditures of his foundation.[49] The support of the clergy in both the *ptochotropheion* and the monastery claimed a large share of the mandated disbursements. These clerics, who were all to take monastic vows, received both a *roga* (cash salary) and a *siteresion* (an allowance in grain), the same system of mixed compensation employed by Eustathios Boilas for

---

[46] *Diataxis*, ed. Gautier, lines 295–301, 903–20; Lemerle, *Cinq études*, 86.

[47] *Diataxis*, ed. Gautier, lines 669–76; cf. Lemerle, *Cinq études*, 84.

[48] *Diataxis*, ed. Gautier, lines 361–79; Lemerle, *Cinq études*, 80.

[49] See Lemerle, *Cinq études*, 82–83, 105–8 for details of the expenditures that Attaliates mandated for his foundation.

the clergy of his church of the Theotokos in Iberia. Attaliates recognized the burden that an unregulated increase of clergy would place on the limited resources of his foundation. Therefore, he strictly limited the number of clerical positions, though he was willing to permit an increase in the future if growth in the foundation's income should permit it.[50]

Liturgical expenses were another important component of the mandated disbursements of the *diataxis*. These included funds for holiday services and feasts, as well as for commemorative masses for the repose of the founder's soul. Since he made no specific provision for structural maintenance (even though its neglect was one of the grounds for deposing a director), Attaliates must have expected that his heirs would provide for this expense out of their personal resources. By showing some concern, Attaliates was more conscientious and farsighted than many of his predecessors and contemporaries.

A seemingly unique feature of the fiscal operation of Attaliates' foundation was his provision of subsidies from its revenues for other, needier institutions.[51] Four monasteries and three churches shared a small annual distribution of 13 *nomismata* under this program. One of the monasteries was the nunnery of St. Prokopios, where Attaliates was *charistikarios* in apparent violation of Alexius Studites' decree against a male serving as the director of a female institution. Attaliates had rebuilt this institution from ruins after a raid staged by the Turks. Another of the foundations aided under this program was a monastery of St. George, where Attaliates' son and successor was serving as *charistikarios*.

These cases demonstrate that an individual's participation in the *charistike* was not incompatible with the traditional endeavors of founding and directing private institutions. Indeed, in this case it was revenue from a private institution that made the family's *charistike* over the older foundations possible, since Attaliates notes that these monasteries had no incomes of their own. The churches that were beneficiaries under this program received smaller grants than the monasteries.[52] Perhaps these were either private churches on the estates of Attaliates or local *katholikai ekklesiai* of Rhaidestos. One of these, a church of St. Michael, appears once to have been the bishop's own church (that is, an *episkopeion*), which according to the legislation of Alexius Studites ought not to have been granted out under the *charistike*. A similar conversion to private administration may have occurred here, another result, perhaps, of the disorder caused by the Turkish invasions.

After the payment of all mandated expenses, the foundation itself en-

---

[50] *Diataxis*, ed. Gautier, lines 681–703; Lemerle, *Cinq études*, 84.

[51] *Diataxis*, ed. Gautier, lines 506–29; Lemerle, *Cinq études*, 83.

[52] The three churches received 1 *nomisma* each; two of the four monasteries received 2 *nomismata*, while two others received 3 each.

joyed a share in any surplus revenues.[53] Under Theodore and Attaliates' direct heirs, this was to be one-third of the total surplus. Under the administration of an heir from his collateral line, Attaliates envisioned a different scheme, setting aside an allowance (as mentioned above) for the ephor and dividing the balance between the foundation's treasury and charitable distributions to the poor. In the absence of any heir from the founder's family, the foundation would claim all surplus revenues.

Four *proasteia* in Thrace and the rental income from some properties in Constantinople (including a bakery, a perfumery, and two houses) formed the relatively modest financial base for the operations and disbursements of the foundation.[54] These incomes also helped to pay the salaries of the clergy in the church of St. George of the Cypresses, the family burial site.[55] This church was located in the southwestern sector of the capital and dated back to the late ninth century. Attaliates established a memorial endowment at this church for his own soul, those of his parents, and his late spouses. He bequeathed the building to his heirs as a proprietary possession.

Attaliates was scrupulous in ruling out certain sources of income allowed by other founders for their foundations. He would not countenance the exaction of entrance fees from prospective monks, particularly objecting to the *apotage*, a gift of property by the postulant.[56] The founders of the great independent monasteries in the twelfth century shared Attaliates' scruples in rejecting the *apotage*, but it is probable that earlier patrons of private institutions had found it a lucrative source of income. Attaliates did require a rather high tonsure fee of 10 *nomismata*, but that was earmarked for the expenses of the inaugural service and feast at the postulant's installation.[57]

The founder did permit two sources of outside income which he judged harmless. One was the foundation's provision of an annuity in kind, termed a *siteresion*, to a layman in exchange for the donation of a piece of landed property.[58] Another document of the mid-eleventh century, the legal treatise *Meditatio de nudis pactis*, speaks of an independent monastery that sold annuities of this sort to laymen.[59] In some cases

[53] *Diataxis*, ed. Gautier, lines 610–13, 621–24; Lemerle, *Cinq études*, 83.

[54] *Diataxis*, ed. Gautier, lines 424–54; Lemerle, *Cinq études*, 81.

[55] *Diataxis*, ed. Gautier, lines 448–54; Lemerle, *Cinq études*, 81; Janin, *Géographie*, Vol. 3, p. 75.

[56] *Diataxis*, ed. Gautier, lines 779–91; Lemerle, *Cinq études*, 84; C. *Nicaen.* II (787), c. 5 (R&P 2.572–573), cf. c. 19 (R&P 2.631).

[57] *Diataxis*, ed. Gautier, lines 709–17; Lemerle, *Cinq études*, 84.

[58] *Diataxis*, ed. Gautier, lines 782–84; Lemerle, *Cinq études*, 84.

[59] H. Monnier and G. Platon, "La *Meditatio de nudis pactis*," *Nouvelle revue historique de droit français et étranger* 37 (1913), 135–68, 311–36, 474–510, 624–53; 38 (1914–15), 285–342, 709–59, see especially Title 8 in 37 (1913), 334–36, with commentary in 38 (1914–15), 298–323; the whole now reprinted in H. Monnier, *Etudes de droit byzantin* (London, 1974).

the payment of *siteresion* may simply have been a way of providing a lifetime compensation for a layman whose property was desired by a religious foundation. Attaliates also permitted the foundation to solicit donations from the laity for the purpose of funding commemorative masses for the dead.[60] The practice goes back at least to the late sixth century and the *prosphora* donations of Byzantine Egypt.

In both fund-raising schemes, the lay contributors had no claims to the ownership of the beneficiary institutions, but simply held contractual agreements that they could enforce in court.[61] In the case of the *siteresion*, the laymen who had purchased shares in the monastery's distribution of grain were almost like bondholders in a corporation. Reform-minded clerics and lay patrons had traditionally relied upon annuities in the form of pensions to compensate legal heirs whom considerations of good religious order compelled them to displace from their inherited patrimonies. Perhaps the general sale of shares of *siteresia* to laymen unrelated to the founder's family grew out of that practice. Those laymen who had established endowments for the celebration of memorial masses also had a claim on the performance of services by the recipient institutions. This helps to explain why the suspension of services in a church or monastery was a serious matter, quite aside from the inconvenience this caused parishioners.

Attaliates also strove to maintain the independence of his foundation from the host of alleged "protectors" that abounded in the age of the *charistike*. At the very time when he was composing his *diataxis*, the *charistike* had come to encompass nearly all of the monasteries and philanthropic institutions of the empire. The abuses that had always plagued the *charistike* were approaching the point where conscientious clerics would shortly be speaking out against them and demanding reforms. Any benefactor who did not bind his foundation very closely to his personal estate might well fear the imposition of a "protector" over it after his death. Although a close family association might well stave off the imposition of a *charistike*, this alone could be no guarantee that a foundation would fare any better under an unscrupulous heir. Forced to choose between the uncertainties of allowing his foundation to fend for itself in these troubled times and linking it, for better or worse, to his descendants as their personal property, Attaliates chose the latter, more traditional option. He could not have foreseen that his beloved son Theodore would die without descendants a short time after his own death in 1085. The foundation then did become independent.[62] Its subsequent

---

[60] *Diataxis*, ed. Gautier, lines 785–86; Lemerle, *Cinq études*, 84.
[61] Just as the anonymous *protospatharios* attempted to do in the case recorded by the *Meditatio de nudis pactis*, Title 8.9 (ed. Monnier and Platon).
[62] Lemerle, *Cinq études*, 111–12.

fate is unknown. The outcome illustrates the limitations of the best planning that even a conscientious benefactor could devise for his foundation. In 1083, a scant six years after Michael Attaliates composed his *diataxis*, another Byzantine philanthropist, Gregory Pakourianos, drew up his own *typikon* which incorporated an independent and self-governing constitution for his foundation.[63] Pakourianos' rejection of the old proprietary form of organization chosen (albeit with reservations) by Attaliates was not simply fortuitous, since a vigorous reform movement against lay influence in the administration of ecclesiastical property had begun in the interim.

[63] A more detailed discussion of this document follows below in Chapter 8.

CHAPTER SEVEN

The Reform Movement against the *Charistike*

JOHN OF ANTIOCH

THE monasteries and philanthropic institutions that had suffered so much abuse at the hands of unscrupulous *charistikarioi* found their strongest champion in John V the Oxite, patriarch of Antioch from ca. 1089 to 1100.[1] He denounced the whole program of the *charistike* in a bold tract known as the *Oratio de monasteriis laicis non tradendis*.[2] This document presents a wealth of information on the controversial institution and indirectly sheds light on the operation of earlier private foundations as well.

From his vantage point in the early 1090s, John could not accurately discern the origins of the *charistike*, but his narrative is still of interest for its indication of the beliefs of contemporaries.[3] His tract singles out the iconoclastic Emperor Constantine V as the originator of the practice of disregarding the testaments of the founders and granting out monasteries and philanthropic institutions to laymen. Though this is simplistic, there is at least some factual basis for seeing this unpopular emperor as one of the forerunners of Basil II in initiating the *charistike*. According to John of Antioch, the use of the *charistike* lapsed after the triumph of the orthodox party in 842. Later an insidious revival occurred, sponsored by unnamed emperors and patriarchs under the pretext of aiding ruined and destroyed institutions. At first, the magnates obtained these institutions for the specific purposes of *philokalia* (restoration), *kalliergia* (embellishment), and *psychike ophelia* (spiritual benefit). Yet the passage of time brought human greed into play, and the magnates began to receive the *oikonomia* (administration) also of those foundations that

---

[1] For the career of this reformer, see V. Grumel, "Les patriarches grecs d'Antioche du nom de Jean (XIe et XIIe siècles)," *EO* 32 (1933), 279–99, esp. 286–98; and Paul Gautier, "Jean V l'Oxite, Patriarche d'Antioche: Notice biographique," *REB* 22 (1964), 128–57.

[2] Ed. Paul Gautier, "Réquisitoire," *REB* 33 (1975), 91–131, which replaces the old edition of *PG* 132, cols. 1117–49; commentary by Herman, "Ricerche," 322–23.

[3] John of Antioch, *De monasteriis* Chs. 8–9 (ed. Gautier, lines 241–77).

really did not require outside financial assistance. At this point the magnates' role as restorers gave way to that of administrators of the institutions and their endowed properties.

John of Antioch credited Patriarch Sisinnius II as the only cleric who would not tolerate the innovation of the *charistike*, even though the full extent of its evils was not yet evident in his day.[4] John's sketchy narrative skips up to his own day, when practically every monastery except the smallest and most recently founded had a "protector" under the *charistike*. His account of the development of the *charistike*, then, has some correspondence with actual events, but John was ignorant of, or else deliberately omitted, the detailed information that would be so helpful in clarifying the role of Basil II and his patriarchs. Even if John was actually better informed than he gives the appearance of being in this tract, it would have been a difficult task to condemn the *charistike* while sparing the memory of many otherwise conscientious emperors and patriarchs who had promoted it.

For his part, John rejected the use of the *charistike* even for its original benign purposes of reconstruction and renovation. He considered these professed aims to be no more than a cloak for horrible abuses, and openly doubted whether a single institution existed that had actually benefited from the *charistike*.[5] As a matter of fact, however, there were protectors who took seriously the interests of the institutions that they held in *charistike*. Michael Attaliates and Psellos can be cited among the apparently conscientious *charistikarioi*.[6] In the main, however, the evidence indicates that John's condemnation of the *charistikarioi* was well-deserved.

John scored a telling point by asking why well-endowed institutions with surplus revenues came to be given out in preference to those that needed rebuilding and had no incomes.[7] *Charistikarioi* defended this practice by asserting that by taking over their administrations, they relieved these rich institutions of their tax obligations. John dismissed this argument, claiming that the magnates had it in their power to alleviate the burden of taxation without the need for formal exemption (*exkousseia*).[8] Yet perhaps the magnates' defense once had validity in the days before the repeal of Basil II's law on the *allelengyon*.

The remainder of John of Antioch's tract is devoted to the condemnation of specific abuses of the *charistike*. To all appearances, the *charistikarioi* behaved as if they were actually owners in full title of the institu-

---

[4] *De monasteriis* Ch. 9, lines 264–67.
[5] *De monasteriis* Ch. 13, lines 357–61.
[6] On the "good *charistikarios*," see Herman, "Ricerche," 325.
[7] *De monasteriis* Ch. 13, lines 361–69.
[8] *De monasteriis* Ch. 13, lines 369–72.

tions they were supposed to protect and improve on a temporary basis. Technically, of course, they had received only a limited tenure of these foundations, with their rights (*dikaia*), privileges (*pronomia*), dependent properties, and other sources of income.[9] Although legally the *charistikarioi* did not enjoy rights of outright ownership, they had become the de facto overlords of these monasteries and philanthropic institutions. The new "benefactors" who undertook the administration of these institutions for conservation (*sustasis*) and maintenance (*diamone*) certainly exercised many of the rights ordinarily reserved for the founders and their families. Often the very same abuses that had characterized the administrations of some of the more unscrupulous private proprietors now reappeared under the *charistikarioi* who assumed their places.

The operation of the *charistike*, therefore, can provide some indication of the problems inherent in the administration of ordinary private foundations and the abuses to which they were liable. Like private founders, the *charistikarioi* enjoyed the right to make nominations or appointments to the clerical positions within their institutions. John of Antioch lamented their use of a written mandate (an *engraphon prostagma*) to order a *hegoumenos* to accept candidates for tonsure.[10] The more presumptuous *charistikarioi* ignored the *hegoumenos* altogether and simply informed their local agents of new appointees chosen by themselves. This reminds us of earlier difficulties encountered in attempts to reconcile patrons' rights to nominate clergy for their foundations with effective episcopal supervision.

Charistikarioi also availed themselves of the contemporary practice of enrolling laymen on the payrolls of the monasteries they held in *charistike*.[11] The practice appears to have been closely related to monasteries' sale of shares of *siteresia* to interested laymen. Ordinarily, the laymen enrolled under this program (*exomonitai*) resided outside the monastery, but in time some (*esomonitai*) came to take up residence within the institution also. Eventually the emperors and the patriarchs had also come to enjoy rights to place laymen in monasteries given out under the *charistike*. Perhaps such rights were reserved by these officials when they gave out institutions under their wardship to lay *charistikarioi*. Here, too, we see the exercise of an old privilege once enjoyed by private founders of religious institutions.

The *charistikarioi* of the large, well-endowed monasteries in the later stages of the *charistike* were receiving fully operational religious institutions run in accordance with the principles laid down in their founders' *typika*. Unlike those ruined or insolvent institutions whose plight might

[9] *De monasteriis* Ch. 10, lines 278–85.
[10] *De monasteriis* Ch. 14, lines 443–53.
[11] *De monasteriis* Ch. 14, lines 471–78.

excuse the imposition of a radically different form of administration, these monasteries could not easily accommodate changes in their governance without conflict with established practices. According to John of Antioch, these *charistikarioi* often took it upon themselves to redistribute the incomes of the institutions that they administered in order to assure themselves adequate financial compensation.[12] In extreme cases, they diverted all the income for their own purposes, cutting off monastic salaries, allowing the buildings to deteriorate, and suspending the celebration of endowed memorial masses.

Evidently some *charistikarioi* could not content themselves with the financial compensations traditionally reserved for the patron and his family. For them the operation of a religious foundation had become largely a business proposition. This was an important difference from the attitude of a traditional patron of a private foundation, for whom personal profit was only a subsidiary consideration, a socially condoned compensation for the real financial sacrifice necessary to create a monastery or philanthropic institution in the first place.

John of Antioch also complained that the appointment of a *charistikarios* had a pernicious effect on discipline within a religious institution.[13] The *hegoumenos* and his *oikonomos* lost control of the daily administration of the monastery, including the important oversight of finances. Traditional patrons presumably exercised some control over the property endowments granted to their institutions, but the *charistikarioi* abused their authority by cutting back or totally eliminating the funds that the monasteries needed to function properly. John maintains that perceptive monks realized who was really in control of their destinies, and turned their attention to pleasing the *charistikarios* rather than their *hegoumenos*.[14]

The mere presence of a higher authority tended to undermine religious discipline, since monks who thought they had been treated unfairly by their *hegoumenos* could appeal to the *charistikarios*. Two hostile parties often arose among the brothers in monasteries where the *hegoumenos* was bold enough to stand up to the *charistikarios*.[15] Since John contrasted this situation to the good order that he claimed prevailed when the monasteries stood under the regulations of their founders, it may be that founding families under the old system of private administration were less prone to exploit their positions of authority to the disadvantage of the *hegoumenoi*.

Unlike many of the founding families, who might reside near, retire to,

[12] *De monasteriis* Ch. 14, lines 414–25.
[13] *De monasteriis* Ch. 14, lines 425–28.
[14] *De monasteriis* Ch. 15, lines 483–94.
[15] *De monasteriis* Ch. 15, lines 495–512.

and be buried in their own monasteries, the *charistikarioi* often spent most of their time at court in Constantinople far away from their administrative responsibilities. Indeed, the holder of more than one *charistike* could hardly expect to administer each institution in person. Michael Psellos, who held the *charistike* in at least twelve institutions, is an example of one courtier whose administrative responsibilities perhaps outweighed his financial gains.[16] As an individual of some scruple, and with access to the court and government officials, Psellos was much in demand for service as a *charistikarios* of unattached monasteries seeking a powerful patron.[17] He had to turn down one monastery's offer (a reminder that a *charistike* was not always imposed involuntarily on an institution from above), and he transferred the burden of another *charistike* to someone else. Psellos knew a good business proposition when he saw one, however, and it is amusing to read a letter expresssing his indignation on an occasion when he failed to obtain a coveted *charistike*.[18]

A man of Psellos' prominence necessarily had to rely upon agents to supervise the administration of the many institutions he held in *charistike*. These agents were known as *pronoetai*, a traditional designation for property managers which can be traced back to Byzantine Egypt. One of Psellos' letters mentions a *pronoetes*, and in others we find him promoting various candidates for monastic appointments to his *pronoetai*.[19] In one of these, he deplores a *hegoumenos'* resistance to one of his nominees, thus confirming John of Antioch's complaints, but also demonstrating that a conscientious *hegoumenos* could make a stand for good religious order in defiance of a powerful *charistikarios*. Here again, it is likely that by their use of *pronoetai*, the *charistikarioi* adopted one of the features of the administrations of some of the traditional private patrons.

The distance of absentee *charistikarioi* from their charges must have diminished their understanding of the traditions and needs of their communities. Yet John of Antioch thought that *charistikarioi* of lesser means, who actually took up residence in their monasteries, happened to pose the greatest threat to monastic discipline.[20] Patriarch Alexius Studites had already attempted to ban the granting of a monastery to a protector of the sex oppposite to that of the resident community, but when a *charistikarios* took up residence with his whole family inside a monastery, the possibilities for sexual misconduct increased. The presence of numerous lay brethren as pensioners in the monasteries aggravated the problem. John asserted that in some cases the number of non-religious resident in

---

[16] On Psellos' role as a *charistikarios*, see Lemerle, "Charisticaires," 22.
[17] Psellos, *Epistolae* 149, 150 (ed. Sathas); cf. Herman, "Charisticaires," col. 615.
[18] Psellos, *Epistola* 178 (ed. Sathas).
[19] Psellos, *Epistolae* 95, 164, 205 (ed. Kurtz-Drexl).
[20] John of Antioch, *De monasteriis* Ch. 15, lines 516–27.

a monastery might come near to exceeding the monastic community it-self.[21]

Deprived of their ordinary sources of income, some monastic com-munities had to turn to the sordid alternative of innkeeping, for which their facilities were structurally, if not conceptually, well-suited.[22] Church councils had long ago legislated against lay patrons who used their mon-asteries for this purpose, and now the abuse returned under the *charisti-karioi*. The fiscal exactions of the *charistikarioi*, the residence of large numbers of laymen, and the need to find new sources of income might compound existing difficulties and drive some monasteries under the *charistike* to the ultimate indignity of complete secularization.[23]

Now it is very important to realize that John of Antioch was not minded to include the pious laity and their labors in founding and sup-porting private religious institutions in his condemnation of the *charis-tikarioi* and the *charistike*. Indeed, he commended, at least by inference, the good order that he claims prevailed in the times before his own, when traditional private foundations dominated the religious landscape of the empire.[24] No better proof of John's benevolence toward private religious institutions is forthcoming than the fact that he considered himself to be the legal owner of a private monastery outside his own patriarchate of Antioch. The institution was the monastery of Theotokos ton Hodegon in Constantinople, an imperial foundation that John Tzimisces granted in the tenth century to the patriarch of Antioch as his official residence in the capital.[25] After John's expulsion from Antioch by the Latin Prince Bohemund in 1099, he returned to Constantinople, resigned his patriar-chate, and retired to this monastery.[26] While serving as its director, John got involved in a serious quarrel with the monastic community. At the height of the difficulties, he fled the monastery in the middle of the night. In an extant document, John explains the circumstances that led him to this action, alleging that the monastery stood in his personal *despoteia*.[27]

It appears that John confused this institution's status as the monastery of the Antiochean patriarchate in Constantinople with the notion that it belonged to him as his personal property. Despite his misunderstanding, it seems clear that John himself had no straightforward objections to the idea of private ownership of religious institutions. The focus of John of

[21] *De monasteriis* Ch. 14, lines 472–74.
[22] *De monasteriis* Ch. 15, lines 510–12.
[23] *De monasteriis* Ch. 14, lines 477–78.
[24] *De monasteriis* Ch. 14, lines 414–25.
[25] For this monastery, see Janin, *Géographie*, Vol. 3, pp. 208–12; for its historical con-nection with the patriarchs of Antioch, see Gautier, "Jean V l'Oxite," 113 and 115, n. 13.
[26] For the chronology of these events, see Gautier, "Jean V l'Oxite," 132.
[27] John of Antioch, *Peri tes phuges* (ed. Gautier, "Jean V l'Oxite," 146–56, esp. 154, lines 12–17).

Antioch's objection to the *charistike* was not, then, the involvement of private individuals in the foundation, direction, or ownership of monasteries, but rather their exaction of personal profit from these activities.[28]

LEO OF CHALCEDON

Historians have long recognized the significance of John of Antioch's tract in stimulating the challenge that brought about the demise of the *charistike*,[29] but a fundamental rejection of the traditional acceptance of the derivation of private profits from the direction of religious institutions had already gained a considerable following in ecclesiastical circles by the time of its publication.[30] This reevaluation is traceable ultimately to Leo, metropolitan of Chalcedon in the 1080s, who advocated the protection of all ecclesiastical property from exploitation by laymen.[31] His initial opposition to governmental requisitions of *keimelia* (sacred vessels) and other treasures of the churches and monasteries of Constantinople obliged contemporaries to reexamine their permissive attitudes toward official use of ecclesiastical property and led them eventually to question other forms of lay exploitation of ecclesiastical institutions as well. Thus Leo can be considered the original stimulus for the growth of a mighty reform movement that ultimately transformed traditional attitudes on the proper role of the laity in the administration of ecclesiastical property.

Early in the reign of Alexius Comnenus (1081–1118), the empire faced a grave threat to its existence from the invading forces of the Norman

[28] See the subtitle of *De monasteriis* (ed. Gautier, p. 91).

[29] Herman, "Charisticaires," col. 614, and "Ricerche," 324; Lemerle, "Charisticaires," 18; Ahrweiler, "Charisticariat," 21.

[30] V. Tiftixoglu, "Gruppenbildungen innerhalb des konstantinopolitanischen Klerus während der Kommenenzeit," *BZ* 62 (1969), 25–72, and K. Th. Polyzoides, *Ho vasileus kai hoi laikoi eis to en genei dioiketikon ergon tes ekklesias epi Alexiou Komnenou (1081–1118)* (Thessalonica, 1979) provide general discussions of ecclesiastical politics during the reign of Alexius Comnenus.

[31] V. Grumel laid the foundations for the study of Leo of Chalcedon in "L'affaire de Léon de Chalcédoine: Le décret ou 'semeioma' d'Alexis Ier Comnène (1086)," *EO* 39 (1941–42), 333–41; "L'affaire de Léon de Chalcédoine: Le chrysobulle d'Alexis Ier sur les objets sacrés," *Etudes byzantines* 2 (1944), 126–33; and "Les documents athonites concernant l'affaire de Léon de Chalcédoine," in *Miscellanea Giovanni Mercati* (Vatican City, 1946), Vol. 3, pp. 116–35. P. Stephanou, "Le procès de Léon de Chalcédoine," *OCP* 9 (1943), 5–64, provides the most detailed account of Leo's career, but without the advantage of Grumel's redating (in his "Documents athonites") of several important documents. Paul Gautier, "Le synode des Blachernes (fin 1094): Etude prosopographique," *REB* 29 (1971), 213–84, offers some additional suggestions for the dating of important events in the controversy. Basile Skoulatos, *Les personnages byzantins de l'Alexiade* (Louvain, 1980), 172–75, provides a capsule biography of the reformer. Apostolos Glavinas, *He epi Alexiou Komnenou (1081–1118) peri hieron skeuon, keimelion kai hagion eikonon eris (1081–1095)* (Thessalonica, 1972), provides a useful narrative of the controversy.

prince Robert Guiscard.[32] At the time of Guiscard's capture of Dyrrachium in the fall of 1081, the Byzantine government found itself without the necessary financial resources to pay a badly demoralized army and to recruit new soldiers. The emperor sent an urgent appeal to his mother, Anna Dalassena, and his brother the *sebastokrator* Isaac,[33] who were governing the capital on his behalf, asking for whatever funds they could manage to raise on short notice. They decided upon expropriating valuable consecrated vessels and works of art in the capital's churches and melting them down in order to obtain gold and silver bullion.[34]

Alexius' regents searched diligently for some legal or canonical grounds to allow the confiscation. Apparently unaware of Heraclius' resort to the wealth of the city's churches in a similar hour of extreme peril for the state, they decided to justify their action on a provision of a novel of Justinian that permitted the sale of consecrated vessels to ransom prisoners of war.[35] The government could hardly claim that the terms of Justinian's law condoned a requisition of ecclesiastical property for the purpose of fielding an army, but the circumstances in which the state found itself must have seemed dire enough to justify a very broad interpretation. A considerable number of laymen were benefiting from ecclesiastical property at that very moment through the *charistike*, certainly for much less exalted purposes. Moreover, the emperor's uncle, Isaac I Comnenus (1057–59), had managed a generation earlier to carry out a much more extensive confiscation of ecclesiastical incomes without substantial opposition.[36]

This time the *sebastokrator* Isaac took the precaution of summoning the patriarchal synod under Eustratius Garidas (1081–84), and presented to it the government's case for the expropriation. The patriarch could be counted upon not to oppose the government's plans. He was a favorite of Anna Dalassena, who had engineered his elevation to office after she forced the abdication of his pious predecessor, Cosmas I (1075–

[32] Anna Comnena, *Alexiad* 4–6, ed. Bernard Leib (Paris, 1937–45); Ferdinand Chalandon, *Essai sur le règne d'Alexis Ier Comnène (1081–1118)* (Paris, 1900); Glavinas, *Eris*, 39–54; P. Stephanou, "Procès," 39–57.

[33] Glavinas, *Eris*, 54–64; for Isaac Comnenus, see Skoulatos, *Personnages*, 124–30, and D. Papachryssanthou, "La date de la mort du sébastocrator Isaac Comnène, frère d'Alexis Ier," *REB* 21 (1963), 250–55.

[34] Anna Comnena, *Alexiad* 5.2; Polyzoides, *Vasileus*, 58–69 and Gautier, "Blachernes," 213, with n. 1, explain the origins of the government's financial difficulties.

[35] The precedent (contra Gautier, "Blachernes," 213) was undoubtedly *NJ* 120.9–10 (544) (= *B* 5.2.11–12); see Leo of Chalcedon, *Epistole pros [Marian] ten Protovestiarisan*, ed. Alexandros Lauriotes, "Historikon zetema ekklesiastikon epi tes basileias Alexiou Komnenou," *EA* 20 (1900), 404–5, esp. 405A, lines 21–23 (see Grumel, "Documents athonites," 327–28 for the identity of the recipient of this letter).

[36] Michael Attaliates, *Historia*, ed. I. Bekker, *CSHB* (Bonn, 1853), pp. 60–62; Psellos, *Chronographia* 7.60, ed. E. Renauld (Paris, 1926–28); Zonaras, *Epitome historiarum* 18.5; critical discussion by Ahrweiler, "Charisticariat," 20–21.

1081).[37] A courageous patriarchal official named John Metaxas did step forward to challenge Isaac and object to his use of canonical precedent.[38] Notwithstanding his opposition, the *sebastokrator* succeeded in getting the synod's approval for the requisition.

Isaac apparently decided to make the requisitions in those institutions to which the patriarchate had undisputed title, limiting the seizures, therefore, to public institutions and studiously avoiding private foundations.[39] Two years later Alexius Comnenus could summon the *proestotes* of the capital's monasteries and prove, by careful checking of the *brevia* of their consecrated possessions, that the government had not touched the dedications of their benefactors.[40] Ordinarily, the pressing circumstances and Isaac's precautions, particularly his respect for private property, would have sufficed to ensure an uneventful requisition in a society long accustomed to routine lay exploitation of ecclesiastical resources.

It was the sight of the *sebastokrator*'s workmen prying the gold and silver ornaments off the doors of the church of the Theotokos ton Chalkoprateion that shocked Leo of Chalcedon and provided the impetus for the reform movement.[41] We know Leo best through the eyes of Alexius Comnenus' daughter, the princess and historian Anna Comnena. Although she was an enthusiastic partisan of her father, she could not suppress a certain grudging admiration for the redoubtable metropolitan of Chalcedon. "He was," she declares, "a free-speaking man who showed himself to be in spirit the true image of a bishop."[42] Anna criticizes his insufficient knowledge of canon law, and complains that his lack of training in formal logic made it difficult for him to express his ideas clearly. Yet Anna admits that he lived virtuously and had a reputation for absolute incorruptibility. From the moment of his first vehement protests to the *sebastokrator*, he became a persistent opponent of the government's use of ecclesiastical property.

Leo quickly gathered a party of supporters to his side. These followers, whom Anna Comnena dubs "the Chalcedonians," included some dis-

---

[37] For this patriarch, see Anna Comnena, *Alexiad* 3.2; Zonaras, *Epitome historiarum* 18.21; Michael Glykas, *Annales* (*CSHB* 600); Theodore Skoutariotes, *Synopsis chronike* (*MB* 7, p. 182); Skoulatos, *Personnages*, 87–89.

[38] Anna Comnena, *Alexiad* 5.2; cf. *Acta cuiusdam synodi Constantinopoli congregatae sub Alexio Comneno* (1094) (*PG* 127, col. 973D); with Gautier, "Blachernes," 275–76; Skoulatos, *Personnages*, 198–99.

[39] Including Theotokos ton Chalkoprateion, an imperial foundation from its origins in the mid-fifth century, and Hagios Aberkios, a church in the patriarchal palace (see Janin, *Géographie*, Vol. 3, p. 7), which Leo claimed had suffered losses in the requisitions (see I. Sakkélion, "Decrét d'Alexis Comnène portant déposition de Léon, Metropolitain de Chalcédoine," *BCH* 2 (1878), 102–28, at 118, line 15.

[40] Anna Comnena, *Alexiad* 6.3.

[41] *Alexiad* 5.2; see now also my "A Byzantine Ecclesiastical Reform Movement," *MH* n.s. 12 (1984), 1–16.

[42] *Alexiad*, 7.4; cf. 5.2.

senting members of the home synod such as Basil, the metropolitan of Euchaita, and some high government officials such as George Palaeologus, the emperor's confidant and one of his generals.[43] Leo's ecclesiastical supporters constituted for the moment only a minority in the synod, yet they vehemently denounced the supporters of the government as "the flatterers."

In the summer of 1082 Leo wrote directly to the emperor to urge a formal investigation of the requisitions that would examine the founder's *brevia* of the monasteries to determine precisely what losses had been sustained.[44] At the same time, he pressed the emperor for the deposition of Eustratius Garidas and the restoration of the former patriarch Cosmas.[45] The pressure that the Chalcedonians brought to bear against the government soon forced Alexius Comnenus to make concessions. In a chrysobull of August 5, 1082, he promised that neither he nor his successors would ever again resort to requisitions of ecclesiastical property.[46] He also pledged, as Heraclius had done, to repay all that the government had seized when the fortunes of the empire improved.

These concessions did not suffice to quiet the emperor's critics. During the winter of 1083–84 Alexius found it necessary to hold a meeting of the senate, the leaders of the armies, and dignitaries of the church to defend once again the government's resort to confiscation.[47] He hoped to put to rest the exaggerated rumors of the extent of the confiscation by acceding to Leo's demand and calling in the *brevia* of the monasteries for examination. He also took the occasion to announce specific plans for repayment to those institutions that the investigation proved to have suffered losses. He tried to make amends for the initial affront to Leo's sensibilities by allotting an annuity from the treasury as compensation for damages to Theotokos ton Chalkoprateion. These actions temporarily relieved the emperor of the brunt of hostile criticism which the Chalcedonians now directed against the patriarch.

Eustratius Garidas proved to be an easy target. All of our sources, even those hostile to the cause of Leo of Chalcedon, agree that Eustratius was unsuitable for his high office. The emperor, preoccupied with the Norman War, was annoyed that the patriarch could not keep the church in

[43] For the term, see Anna Comnena, *Alexiad* 5.2; for Basil of Euchaita, see Sakkélion, "Décret," 116, line 13; for George Palaeologus, see *Alexiad* 7.4 and Skoulatos, *Personnages*, 99–105.

[44] Leo of Chalcedon, *Epistole pros ton basilea Alexion ton Komnenon* (ed. Lauriotes, "Historikon Zetema," 403–404), with Glavinas, *Eris*, 65–67.

[45] Leo of Chalcedon, *Epistole*, 404, lines 12–17; cf. Grumel, "Documents athonites," 126.

[46] Alexius Comnenus, *Novella de sacris vasibus in publicum usum non convertendis* (1082) (*JGR* 3.355–358) = Dölger, *Regesten* No. 1085; Polyzoides, *Vasileus* 70–78; Glavinas, *Eris*, 73–78; for the dating of this novel, see Grumel, "Chrysobulle," 130–33.

[47] Anna Comnena, *Alexiad* 6.3, with Polyzoides, *Vasileus*, 78–81.

good order, but he resisted demands for Eustratius' deposition.[48] Leo of
Chalcedon now went directly to the emperor to accuse Eustratius of sacrilege in uncanonically alienating holy icons and other treasures of the
church during the recent requisitions.[49] The emperor must have realized
that the indictment of Eustratius was an indirect attack on his own government which had actually carried out the expropriation. Eustratius demanded a formal inquest in order to clear himself of the accusations. The
emperor consented and formed a commission that included the highest
officials of the patriarchate and Basil of Euchaita as a token member of
the opposition. Sometime in early 1084 this commission exonerated the
patriarch.[50]

Undeterred by this setback, Leo's followers continued to harass the
embattled patriarch. They finally drove Eustratius to abdication in July
1084.[51] Alexius Comnenus then permitted the election of Nicholas III
Grammaticus (1084–1111). He appears to have been a reformer, or at
least was soon to demonstrate his reformist sympathies.[52]

The reformers of the Chalcedonian party had forced Alexius to a series
of humiliating concessions and reversals of policy. The emperor might
then have thought that he had finally bought peace in the church, but at
this moment the Chalcedonians chose to escalate their demands. Both
Eustratius and his newly chosen successor had already begun a program
of reasserting control over ecclesiastical properties lost to laymen
through the *charistike*. This patriarchal reform, about which we will
have more to say shortly, was very much in the same spirit of hostility to
lay employment of consecrated property as the Chaledonians' own program. Leo, however, was still bent on avenging past wrongs, and refused
to celebrate the liturgy with the new patriarch in the cathedral church of
Hagia Sophia.[53]

Leo was not moved by personal hostility to the new patriarch, but
rather by the mention (*anaphora*) of Eustratius during the liturgy as a
past patriarch in good standing. Leo wanted a formal condemnation of
Eustratius, even though he had been cleared by the emperor's commission of the charge of sacrilege.[54] The new dispute arose during another
of the emperor's absences on campaign against the Normans. After Guis-

[48] Anna Comnena, *Alexiad* 5.8–9.
[49] Sakkélion, "Décret," 116, lines 1–7; Glavinas, *Eris*, 93–95; Grumel, "Semeioma,"
334.
[50] "Décret," 116, lines 14–20.
[51] Theodore Skoutariotes, *Synopsis chronike* (MB 7, p. 182), with Glavinas, *Eris*, 96–
98.
[52] For this patriarch, see Skoutariotes, *Synopsis chronike* (MB 7, p. 182), John Zonaras,
Epitome historiarum 18.21, and Skoulatos, *Personnages*, 253–56.
[53] Sakkélion, "Décret," 117, with Glavinas, *Eris*, 100–104.
[54] Grumel, "Semeioma," 336; Polyzoides, *Vasileus*, 81–84.

card's death on July 17, 1085, the emperor returned to learn of this new source of discord within the church. Exasperated by Leo's intransigence, he initiated legal proceedings against him on November 30, l085.[55]

Leo' shortcomings, so aptly noted by Anna Comnena, became evident when he found himself so suddenly obliged to defend his belligerent conduct. A pro-government pamphlet presents the emperor's case against Leo and notes the metropolitan's frequent changes of position during the legal proceedings.[56] Leo vacillated from a militant stand at one point, when he demanded the removal from the diptychs of the names of many former patriarchs, to abject surrender, when he agreed to reestablish communion with the patriarch on the eve of what was to be the concluding session of the inquest.[57] The hostile account bears out Anna Comnena's contention that Leo was no rhetorician or canonist. The government's case against Leo was actually rather weak, but Leo did not have at hand the appropriate canonical citations that might have greatly embarrassed the emperor. A scholiast on the government pamphlet who was well disposed to Leo notes with exasperation his hero's unpreparedness.[58] Leo was also unwilling to name the individuals who had witnessed the patriarch's participation in the requisitions, doubtless to protect his confidential informants.

By the day of the final session, in January 1086, Leo had recovered his courage and resolution. After detailing some technical reasons why he should not have to celebrate the liturgy with the patriarch, he stunned the assembly with a new, extreme statement of belief on the alienation of ecclesiastical property. He declared flatly that all alienations of consecrated property, regardless of the circumstances, were evident cases of impiety. The only permitted transformations, according to Leo, were from one sacred employment to another (thus apparently permitting the continued employment of *epidosis*, but clearly not the *charistike*).[59]

Leo had taken the critical step of broadening his specific condemnation of the government's expropriation into an inflexible principle, which would make impossible any sort of alienation of ecclesiastical property to laymen. Alexius, who was present, immediately realized the revolutionary nature of such a doctrine, and denounced it as having the appearance of piety, but the force of a denial of truth. How, he asked, could

[55] Sakkélion, "Décret," 119, with Glavinas, *Eris*, 104–8, Grumel, "Semeioma," 336, and Polyzoides, *Vasileus*, 84–90.
[56] *Semeioma epi te kathairesei tou Chalkedonos*, ed. Sakkélion, "Décret," 113–28; commentary by Grumel, "Semeioma," 334–38.
[57] Sakkélion, "Décret," 120; cf. Grumel, "Semeioma," 336.
[58] Sakkélion, "Décret," 123, n. 3, and 127, n. 2, where the scholiast cites C. *Const. I et II*, c. 10 (R&P 2.684–686); cf. Glavinas, *Eris*, 108–15.
[59] Sakkélion, "Décret," p. 123, line 23–p. 124, line 6, with general discussion by Glavinas, *Eris*, 117–26.

Leo implicitly condemn as impious all those Christians who, relying on
the principles of laws and canons, had violated his doctrine?

Alexius quickly secured the censure of Leo on the technical grounds of
insubordination: he had brought a complaint against Patriarch Eustratius directly to the emperor without first having recourse to an ecclesiastical tribunal, and he had refused to accept the imperial commission's
subsequent exoneration of the patriarch.[60] The synod, sitting as a court,
also confirmed the legality of the requisitions yet endorsed the emperor's
resolution not to resort to it again.

Leo refused to follow the synod's directive to reconcile himself with
the patriarch and the rest of the church. He also made some incautious
statements comparing the supporters of the requisitions to the iconoclasts. His enemies managed to trap him with a charge of heresy based
on his view that an insult to an icon was an affront not only to the image
of the saint but to the holy man himself.[61] This opinion, his opponents
charged, led to the error of according worship (*latreia*) to an icon rather
than merely the appropriate veneration or (*proskynesis*). The synod then
reassembled, probably in February or March 1086, and issued a tome of
deposition against Leo, adding the charge of heresy to the earlier one of
insubordination.[62]

Leo might well have faded from public attention had not the beginning
of the Patzinak (Petcheneg) invasions in 1086 forced the emperor, in spite
of all his promises, to a new requisition of ecclesiastical property. This
time the churches and monasteries suffered not only the loss of ornaments, icons, and sacred vessels, but also of landed property.[63] Leo and
his supporters benefited from a sudden rejuvenation of public support.
The government in turn moved quickly to secure another synodal condemnation, which this time meant Leo's banishment to remote Sozo-
polis.[64] At last it appeared that the government had rid itself of a persistent, insufferable opponent.

[60] Sakkélion, "Décret," 124–26; cf. Grumel, "Semeioma," 338–40.

[61] Anna Comnena, *Alexiad* 5.2; Leo of Chalcedon, *Epistole pros [Marian] ten Protovestiarisan* (ed. Lauriotes, "Historikon zetema," 404), with commentary by Grumel, "Documents athonites," 129; Niketas Choniates, *Synopsis ton dogmaton ton kinethenton*, ed. T.
L. F. Tafel, *Annae Comnenae supplementa historiam graecorum ecclesiasticam seculi XI et
XII spectanta* (Tubingen, 1832), 5–7; cf. Grumel, "Semeioma," 340–41.

[62] Anna Comnena, *Alexiad* 5.2, with P. Stephanou, "La Doctrine de Léon de Chalcédoine
et de ses adversaires sur les images," *OCP* 12 (1946), 177–99; for the date, see Grumel,
Regestes No. 941, but cf. Gautier, "Blachernes," 214, n. 9.

[63] For the second requisition, see Anna Comnena, *Alexiad* 5.2; M. Goudas, "Byzantiaka
engrapha tes Hieras Mones Vatopediou," *EEBS* 3 (1926), 113–34, Doc. No. 4, at 128–31;
Leo of Chalcedon, *Epistole pros ton basilea* (ed. Lauriotes, p. 403); cf. Gautier, "Blachernes," 214, Glavinas, *Eris*, 135–39, Grumel, "Chrysobulle," 133, and Stephanou,
"Procès," 26–27.

[64] Anna Comnena, *Alexiad* 5.2 (p. 159); Grumel, *Regestes* No. 955; cf. Gautier, "Blachernes," 215–16, with nn. 10–11, and Glavinas, *Eris*, 138–46.

It is impossible to discount the influence of Leo's spectacular defiance of the emperor or of the effect of his ideas on reform-minded contemporaries. Leo had become an almost legendary figure of righteousness.[65] George Palaeologus believed that it was a miraculous appearance of the famous metropolitan who provided him with the horse that he used to make his escape from the battlefield of Dristra. The Patzinak victory there in 1087 over a Byzantine army financed by the second round of requisitions must have seemed to pious contemporaries the judgment of God.

THE BEGINNINGS OF PATRIARCHAL REFORM ACTIVITY

While public attention fixed upon the activities of Leo of Chalcedon, the patriarchs of Constantinople were working quietly to effect a comprehensive limitation of the powers of the *charistikarioi* over ecclesiastical institutions.[66] The work of the patriarchs of Alexius Comnenus' reign, particularly Nicholas III Grammaticus, ultimately proved more significant than anything Leo and the Chalcedonians were able to achieve by themselves. The patriarchal reform of the *charistike* proceeded independently of Leo's battle against the requisitions, yet hardly without influence and inspiration from the more radical reformers.

Indeed, it was the much-maligned Eustratius Garidas who actually initiated this program of limitation, although admittedly only toward the very end of his reign when the pressure from the Chalcedonians for his removal was clearly very intense. Perhaps to show that he, too, was concerned about recovering the lost property of the church, Eustratius obtained the cooperation of the emperor in repealing some unwise grants made by his predecessors in office.[67] Alexius issued an order on March 19, 1084, that required the return of all properties that had once belonged to patriarchal monasteries but had subsequently been given out to such non-patriarchal institutions as imperial or private monasteries. The restoration of the endowments of patriarchal monasteries accomplished by this act was a necessary preliminary step to a plan to hold the *charistikarioi* of these institutions responsible for their territorial integrity.

[65] Note his appearance to George Palaeologus in the vision recorded by Anna Comnena, *Alexiad* 7.4; and the miraculous vision of Thomas in Leo's church of St. Euphemia, ed. Lauriotes, "Historikon zetema," 365B, with commentary by Grumel, "Documents athoniotes," 127); see also a dialogue by Eustratius, metropolitan of Nicaea, ed. A. Demetrakopoulos, *Ekklesiastike bibliotheke* (Leipzig, 1866), 127–51, a piece of government propaganda intended to discredit Leo.

[66] Documentary evidence published by Jean Darrouzès, "Dossier," 150–65.

[67] Darrouzès, "Dossier," 159, with editor's commentary, 152, 156.

NICHOLAS III GRAMMATICUS (1084–1111)

Eustratius' abdication in July, 1084 brought a temporary halt to the patriarchate's program of administrative reform of the *charistike*. The new patriarch, Nicholas Grammaticus, took up the matter again later, probably sometime in 1085. He recognized the gravity of the problem of illegal alienations of ecclesiastical property carried out by unscrupulous *charistikarioi*. He apparently decided that this was the most patent evil of the *charistike*. It was nearly impossible, however, to detect these alienations because the *charistikarioi* ignored Alexius Studites' requirement that all beneficiaries should register their grants along with inventories of dependent properties in the office of the *chartophylax*.[68] In the preceding winter of 1083–84, the Chalcedonians had demonstrated the usefulness of *brevia* for detecting alienations. Following their lead, Nicholas Grammaticus instructed his *chartophylax* to insert a clause in all documents donating ecclesiastical institutions that would nullify the grant automatically if the beneficiary did not submit within six months a list of the properties attached to the foundation he had received.[69]

Very soon after the crucial final session of Leo of Chalcedon's trial, at which he had announced his opposition to all *ekpoieseis* (alienations) of ecclesiastical property, Nicholas Grammaticus took the next step in the regulation of the *charistike*. The patriarch ordered his *megalos sakkelarios* (great treasurer) not to accept, as of January 28, 1086, any grants of ecclesiastical institutions for registry without an attached *praktikon engraphon* (written inventory) of the foundation's immovable properties.[70]

Nicholas Grammaticus thus declined to endorse Leo of Chalcedon's rigorist position on the inalienability of church property. He preferred to work to correct the worst problems inherent in the church's reliance on laymen for the management and exploitation of its institutions and properties. By insisting on obtaining an inventory of the properties of religious institutions granted in *charistike*, the patriarch extended to the *charistikarioi* a control that had bound the traditional private proprietors of these institutions since 861. The idea of a formal registration of endowed properties had worked well in this first instance, so the patriarch might reasonably have hoped for similar success in the case of the *charistikarioi*.

A very troubled period followed this latest decree. As we have seen, the resident synod deposed Leo of Chalcedon in early 1086. The Patzinak invasions began, and Alexius Comnenus resorted to the second round of requisitions. In the spring of 1087 disaster struck the Byzantine army at

---

[68] Darrouzès, "Dossier," 156, paraphrased in 158–59.
[69] Darrouzès, "Dossier," 158–59, with editor's commentary, 153, 156.
[70] Darrouzès, "Dossier," 159–60, with commentary, 153, 156.

Dristra. The patriarch held a steady course and did not allow himself to become embroiled in the renewed controversy over the legality of the government's requisitioning powers.

In May 1087 Nicholas Grammaticus decided to make his property registration requirement effective for beneficiaries who held unregistered *hypomnemata* granted (either by himself or his predecessors) before 1086, the date of the routine insertion of the clause of nullity.[71] These beneficiaries had to obtain a new patriarchal *prostaxis* (codicil), in which the chancellery was free to insert new restrictions, before they could obtain registry of their old *hypomnemata*. The patriarch's officials were still trying to enforce this requirement as of January 18, 1090.

The patriarch's reforms had the effect of encouraging vocal opposition to the *charistike* for the first time in over sixty years. Niketas, the metropolitan of Athens, took advantage of the growing official hostility toward the *charistikarioi* to bring an important case before the patriarchal synod on April 20, 1089.[72] Greedy laymen and subordinate bishops had taken advantage of the senility of Niketas' predecessor John, encouraging him to disperse the see's churches, monasteries, and landed property on the favorable terms customarily accorded to *charistikarioi*. Niketas sought the synod's authorization to overturn his predecessor's grants and to compel restorations. He appealed for justification to existing legislation of Alexius Studites, specifically the first *hypomnema* of 1027, rather than (as one might have expected) the second of 1028. This decree held that wealthy bishoprics should return the monasteries they had received in *epidosis* from their metropolitans if the latter had need of their revenues.[73]

Patriarch Nicholas Grammaticus and his fellow bishops were eager to do all that they could to assist Niketas in his difficulties. They ordered that the metropolitan had the right to expel those who had misused the oratories and monasteries, particularly if they had driven away the monks who as parish priests had performed the liturgical services and managed the estates.[74] The synod had a copy made of the relevant passage from Alexius Studites' *hypomnema* so that Niketas could bring it to the local thematic court and obtain the assistance of the government in enforcing the decision.[75] Niketas had the option of retaining some of the incumbents for a year or two, provided that they made provision for the officiating monks and compensation for any diminution in the value of

[71] Darrouzès, "Dossier," 153, 156.

[72] Grumel, *Regestes* No. 952; text edited by Th. Uspenskii, "Mneniya i postanovleniya konstantinopolskikh pomestnikh soborov XI i XII vv. o razdache tserkovnikh imuschchestv (charistikarii)," *IRAIK* 5 (1900), 1–48: Doc. No. 2, pp. 30–37.

[73] Uspenskii, "Mneniya," p. 39, line 14–p. 40, line 11.

[74] Uspenskii, "Mneniya," 34, lines 3–11.

[75] Uspenskii, "Mneniya," p. 34, line 11–p. 35, line 5.

ecclesiastical property. With respect to the grants of land to laymen, the synod declared that the tenants must understand that they had no rights of ownership in these properties, but had to observe the usual canonical prescriptions for the rental of church property.

The decision demonstrated that Nicholas' synod was prepared to rule favorably on cases of abuse of ecclesiastical property by unscrupulous laymen. Moreover, the reformers were beginning to rediscover old canonical precedents that they could employ to overthrow the *charistike*. The decision shows the synod taking an active role in disseminating the important legislation of Alexius Studites long held in contempt or completely forgotten during the age of the *charistike*. The rediscovery of canon law continued through the twelfth century and contributed to the discrediting of the *charistike* as well as to a radical revision in the constitutional structure of privately founded religious institutions.

For the time being, however, Patriarch Nicholas Grammaticus was unwilling to attempt the outright abolition of the *charistike*. The Athens decision of 1089 may provide the clue to the reason for this disinclination. The patriarchate, lacking the resources to restore thousands of ruined foundations itself, may have hoped to compel the *charistikarioi* to make amends for their own depredations during strictly supervised continuances of their tenures of office.

In September 1089, shortly after the announcement of the Athens decision, John, soon to be famous as the great opponent of the *charistike*, appeared as patriarch of Antioch at a meeting of the resident synod in Constantinople on the question of church reunification.[76] The exact date and the circumstances of his elevation to the see of Antioch (then still under Muslim rule) are unknown.[77] It is not certain, therefore, whether his reformist sympathies were known at the time of his selection. In any case, it soon became clear to contemporaries that John had assumed the exiled Leo's role as spokesman for the Chalcedonians. As patriarch of Antioch, John's opinions gained commensurate influence. He did not hesitate to use his prestige to champion Leo's old campaign of opposition to the government requisitions.

In the dark days of February and March 1091, an alliance of the Patzinaks and Tzachas, the emir of Smyrna, posed another grave threat to the empire. Alexius Comnenus summoned a council to decide on appropriate responses. He apparently hoped that the council would permit him to undertake another requisition of ecclesiastical property. John of Antioch boldly opposed this plan in an impassioned tract addressed to the

[76] Grumel, "Patriarches grecs," 294.
[77] Paul Gautier, "Diatribes de Jean l'Oxite contre Alexis Ier Comnène," *REB* 28 (1970), 5–55, esp. 6, n. 7. According to Grumel, "Patriarches grecs," 283–84, the patriarch of Constantinople had consecrated the newly elected patriarchs of Antioch since 996.

emperor.[78] He followed up this protest with a memorandum that restated his objections to the emperor's intentions.[79]

John's famous tract *De monasteriis* also dates from this period. Historians have not been able to assign a specific date to this document, yet it must have been composed after a great earthquake that occurred on December 6 (perhaps in the year 1090) since John alludes to the calamity in the text.[80] John's opposition to the requisitions, and his acceptance of Leo's doctrine condemning all alienations of ecclesiastical property, led him naturally to his extremely hostile view of the *charistike*. His strict definition of the consecrated status of monasteries and all their properties was also a logical extension of Leo's campaign against profane employment of consecrated vessels, icons, ornaments, and landed possessions.[81]

It is equally important not to discount the influence of Nicholas Grammaticus' reforms of the *charistike* upon the thinking of the patriarch of Antioch. As a moderate reformer himself, Nicholas had taken advantage of the growing hostility toward the role of the laity in the economic exploitation of the church to curb the truculent *charistikarioi*. His example surely suggested to John the next problem that deserved the attention of the reformers. Yet insofar as John's own program exceeded the patriarch's plans by calling for the complete abolition of the *charistike*, we must note the radical ideas which he probably received from Leo of Chalcedon.

During Leo's exile (1086–94), the deposed metropolitan's prestige increased substantially.[82] Eventually the climate of opinion was to change further so as to allow not only his return from exile, but also his reinstatement as metropolitan of Chalcedon. Tensions, moreover, relaxed appreciably after Alexius crushed the Patzinaks at the battle of Levunion on April 29, 1091.[83] Pressures mounted for Leo's recall. Such influential personalities as Empress Irene and her mother, the *protovestiaria* Maria,

---

[78] John of Antioch, *Logos eis ton basilea kyr Alexion ton Komnenon* (ed. Gautier, "Diatribes," pp. 19–49); cf. commentary by Grumel, "Documents athonites," 132–34.

[79] John of Antioch, *Symboule pros ton basilea* (ed. Gautier, "Diatribes," pp. 49–55); cf. commentary by Grumel, "Documents athonites," 134.

[80] For John's allusion to the earthquake, see *De monasteriis* Ch. 18, lines 588–90; for the earthquake itself, see Michael Glykas, *Annales* (CSHB 620), and John Zonaras, *Epitome historiarum* 18.22. Grumel, *La chronologie* (Paris, 1958), 480, proposes to date the earthquake to 1090, but see Gautier, "Réquisitoire," 80–86, for the difficulties in determining a precise date for *De monasteriis*.

[81] John of Antioch, *De monasteriis* Ch. 11, lines 306–15; cf. lines 322–24, and comments by Gautier, "Réquisitoire," 78.

[82] As indicated by Leo of Chalcedon, *Epistole pros [Marian] ten Protovestiarisan* (ed. Lauriotes, pp. 404–5) and Nicholas, metropolitan of Adrianople, *Epistole* (ed. Lauriotes, p. 413); cf. commentary by Glavinas, *Eris*, 146–50, and Grumel, "Documents athonites," 118–21.

[83] Anna Comnena, *Alexiad* 8.3.

were now among Leo's supporters.[84] Even the emperor himself could not suppress a grudging admiration for his irrepressible rival.

There are indications that this period also saw a growing rapprochement between the original Chalcedonians and the new group of reformers in the patriarchal administration. Patriarch Nicholas Grammaticus had never been central to the controversy over the requisitions, and his recent labors for the regulation of the *charistike* demonstrated his enthusiasm for moderate reform. The hierarchy's tolerance (and perhaps also its promotion) of John of Antioch also indicates that they would tolerate a diversity of opinion on the pace and extent of reforms that all parties now acknowledged were necessary. Leo also had important supporters in the hierarchy, notably his nephew Nicholas, metropolitan of Adrianople, who were working effectively on his behalf at the court.[85] Leo's nephew reported to his uncle that Basil of Euchaita had disassociated himself from the tome of deposition and once again had become a supporter of the Chalcedonians.[86]

At first Alexius Comnenus would agree to an end to Leo's exile only if he would promise to take monastic vows.[87] Leo, however, was adamant about maintaining his claims to his see of Chalcedon. The emperor eventually capitulated and dropped all preconditions except that Leo must retract his allegedly heretical views on the worship of icons. This did not prove to be an insuperable difficulty, for Leo agreed to renounce any unorthodox views he might have propounded in the past.[88]

The great reconciliation that followed took place in a memorable synod at Blachernai in Constantinople in the latter half of 1094.[89] Many who had played important parts in the controversies of the past decade were present: the emperor, the patriarch Nicholas, the *sebastokrator* Isaac, Basil the metropolitan of Euchaita, Niketas the metropolitan of Athens, George Palaeologus, and John Metaxas. The continued prominence of Metaxas, the very first critic of the requisitions, shows the continuity of Leo's support within the patriarchal administration throughout

[84] So Leo of Chalcedon, *Epistole pros [Marian] ten Protovestiarisan* (ed. Lauriotes, 404A), with commentary by Grumel, "Documents athonites," 127–30; cf. Anna Comnena, *Alexiad* 5.2.

[85] Nicholas of Adrianople, *Epistole* (ed. Lauriotes, p. 413), and Leo's reply, *Epistole* (ed. Lauriotes, pp. 414–16), with commentary by Glavinas, *Eris*, 151–55 and Grumel, "Documents athonites," 118–23.

[86] Nicholas of Adrianople, *Epistole* (ed. Lauriotes, p. 413), with commentary by Grumel, "Documents athonites," 119.

[87] Leo of Chalcedon, *Epistole pros [Marian] ten Protovestiarisan* (ed. Lauriotes, p. 404B, lines 37–40).

[88] Grumel, *Regestes* No. 967.

[89] *Acta synodi Constantinopolitanae* (1094) (PG 127, cols. 972–84), with Glavinas, *Eris*, 180–93 and Polyzoides, *Vasileus*, 98; for dating employed here, see Gautier, "Blachernes," 280–84 in preference to Grumel, *Regestes*, Vol. 1, No. 968.

the decade. In the presence of these and many other dignitaries of the court and the church, Leo renounced his doctrinal errors and was reconciled with Basil of Euchaita. Soon afterwards Leo regained his metropolitan see.[90]

The synod at Blachernai marks the triumph of the Chalcedonian reform party, although in a context that preserved appearances for the emperor and the patriarch. The synod enabled the emperor to commit himself gracefully to moderate reform.[91] As the union of all parties that had worked for an end to lay exploitation of ecclesiastical property, the synod resolved purely personal differences and allowed concentration on the greatest outstanding problem, the reform of the *charistike*.[92] The reconciliation reached here between the reformers and the emperor was soon to prove of great value toward that goal.

It is not hard to imagine the uproar that Nicholas Grammaticus' registration requirement and his annulment of the grants at Athens in 1089 caused in the ranks of the *charistikarioi*, whose economic status was bound up with the traditional acceptance of the inviolability of private property rights in ecclesiastical institutions. Some beneficiaries, upset at what they saw as abrogations of their traditional rights, took their cases to the emperor himself.[93]

The emperor did not allow himself to be swayed by their appeals. In a critical decision of May 16, 1094, he ruled that even *charistikarioi* who had received imperial *prostagmata* (diplomas) could not use these as pretexts for defying the patriarch's registration requirement.[94] Encouraged by the emperor's support, Nicholas Grammaticus moved six days later to set a deadline of three months within which the reluctant *charistikarioi* had to fulfill the requirements of his previous legislation.[95] These individuals, who for six years had managed to fight the patriarchal reforms, now faced the most serious challenge yet to their dominance of the empire's ecclesiastical institutions.

At this point the patriarch decided upon the bold project of a visitation and census of all of the nominally patriarchal monasteries managed by

[90] Grumel, *Regestes* No. 968; cf. Niketas Choniates, *Synopsis ton dogmaton* (ed. Tafel, p. 7, lines 12–13).

[91] Note Goudas, "Byzantiaka engrapha," Doc. 4, p. 128, Alexius Comnenus' reversal of an earlier confiscation of monastic property carried out by his government; also this emperor's novel of 1106 reforming the clergy of the public churches, ed. Paul Gautier, "L'édit d'Alexis Ier Comnène sur la réforme du clergé," *REB* 31 (1973), 165–201, esp. lines 325–42; on this novel see also Dölger, *Regesten* No. 1236.

[92] Note the work of subsequent patriarchs such as John IX Agapetus (1111–34), Cosmas II Atticus (1146–47), Nicholas IV Muzalon (1147–51), and Luke Chrysoberges (1157–70) discussed below in Chapters 7 and 8.

[93] Darrouzès, "Dossier," 157, cited at 159.

[94] Darrouzès, 153–54, 157.

[95] Darrouzès, 157, with commentary, 154–55.

laymen under the *charistike*.[96] A direct visitation by patriarchal function-
aries would enable Nicholas to establish the veracity of the inventories
that had been submitted and to deal with those *charistikarioi* who had
refused to register their grants.

The census appears to have begun in 1095 or early in 1096. The patriarchal archons had instructions to visit each patriarchal monastery,
enroll it in a register, and examine its operation in the presence of its
charistikarios. The archons met with fierce resistance from many of the
charistikarioi. Some of the lay beneficiaries denied entrance to the patriarchal archons, asserting that their original documents of donation
had guaranteed them freedom from ecclesiastical interference. In some
of those institutions where they did manage to gain admittance, the archons discovered grave abuses such as the secularization of monastic
buildings and the sale of consecrated property. Confronted by the formidable array of documents brought forward by the *charistikarioi*, the
archons were unable to complete their census as the patriarch had
planned. They composed, therefore, a memorandum of inquiry addressed to the emperor in order to determine the actual extent of the
patriarch's rights over these institutions.[97]

This *hypomnesis* of the archons probably dates to 1096, certainly before December of that year, when Alexius Comnenus composed his reply.
In this document the archons posed some of the most fundamental questions concerning the rights of the patriarch over institutions held in *charistike*. That the patriarchal bureaucracy should have needed these determinations now, after the *charistike* had been in existence for a century,
helps us understand how the abuses that characterized this program had
been able to flourish.

First of all, the archons asked the emperor whether the patriarch and
his officials had a right to enter any of the monasteries no longer directly
administered by the patriarchate. The archons had in mind here both
those institutions granted to laymen in *charistike* and those given to
other ecclesiastical jurisdictions in *epidosis*. Second, if they did have a
right to make visitations, the archons wanted to know if they could investigate the condition of these institutions, denounce abuses, and compel restitutions for ruined and dispersed properties. Third, the archons
asked the emperor about the legality of the *charistikarioi* compelling postulants to pay *apotagai* on reception into monastic communities. Finally,
the archons asked whether the documents that the *charistikarioi* pos-

---

[96] The only firmly dated event in this sequence is the issuance of Alexius Comnenus' reply
to the inquiry of the patriarchal archons, his novel *De jure patriarchae circa monasteria*
(1096) (*JGR* 3.407–410), issued in December 1096.

[97] *Hypomnesis ton theophilestaton diakonon kai archonton*, ed. J. Darrouzès, "Dossier,"
160–61, esp. 160, lines 10–13.

sessed entitling them to appoint monks and nuns as well as to correct their spiritual faults could be considered valid in spite of contrary provisions in canon law.

ALEXIUS COMNENUS AS REFORMER

Alexius Comnenus provided detailed responses to these inquiries in his novel of December 1096, *De jure patriarchae circa monasteria*.[98] He upheld the patriarch's rights of *epiteresis* (oversight) and *diorthosis* (correction) in all monasteries within his jurisdictional boundaries regardless of the status of their foundation or their current form of administration.[99] The law specifically includes independent (*eleuthera*), imperial (*basilika*), public (*demosia*), private (*kosmika*), and patriarchal (*patriarchika*) monasteries as well as those granted out in *epidosis*, *dorea* (that is, in *charistike*), and *ephoreia* as being among those institutions properly subject to the patriarch's oversight and correction.

As far as visitation rights were concerned, the patriarch was to have an unrestricted right to enter all of his own patriarchal monasteries except for those that had been given to other ecclesiastical authorities in *epidosis*.[100] Monasteries granted to laymen in *charistike*, therefore, were subject to patriarchal visitation. In the case of free (*eleuthera*) and self-governing (*autexousia*) monasteries, the patriarch could make a visitation only when he had learned of a spiritual fault occurring in one of these institutions.[101] No patriarchal or imperial document could prevent a visitation for the purpose of spiritual correction, but the patriarch could not exploit the occasion to alter established customs or to exact money for his own expenses (*dapane*).[102]

In the case of monasteries granted out in *epidosis*, those granted to laymen (as ephors) for *ephoreia* or (as *charistikarioi*) for *oikonomia*, and the independent monasteries, the patriarch could compel the possessors to make restitution for dimunition of their properties, or to restore buildings if they had been ruined or completely destroyed under their administrations.[103] The possessors could not claim their own improvements and enlargements of the foundations as credits against the damages they had inflicted.

The emperor absolutely forbade the exaction of *apotagai* or bequests

---

[98] *De jure patriarchae* (*JGR* 3.407–410); Dölger, *Regesten* No. 1076; commentary by Lemerle, "Charisticaires," 20, n. 3, and by Herman, "Ricerche," 324–29.

[99] *JGR* 3.408.7–14.

[100] *JGR* 3.408.14–18.

[101] *JGR* 3.408.18–24; for these institutions, see discussion below in Chapter 8.

[102] *JGR* 3.408.29–33.

[103] *JGR* 3.408.33–409.8; for ephors and the *ephoreia*, see the discussion below in Chapter 8.

of land from postulants to monastic vocations.[104] A *hegoumenos* appre-
hended in this practice would be deposed, while a *charistikarios* would
be expelled from his office. Alexius was willing to permit the traditional
free-will offerings (*prosenexeis*) of postulants, but he directed that they
should be recorded in the *brevion* of the monastery with a notice of the
gifts then being supplied to the patriarch.[105]

The emperor next took up the matter of who had the right to make
appointments to *adelphata*, the Byzantine equivalent of monastic pre-
bends.[106] We have seen earlier how some monasteries employed the sale
of annual shares of *siteresia* as a means of gaining supplementary income. When the *charistikarioi* took over monasteries, they assumed control over the sale of *siteresia* to *exomonitai*, non-resident laymen.[107]
Somehow the patriarch had also come to depend upon the awarding of
positions, both within and without the monasteries, as an important
source of patronage.[108] Perhaps the patriarch (or the emperor, in the case
of imperial monasteries) would reserve a certain number of appointments for his own use before turning over a monastery to a *charistikarios*. Whatever the actual origin of the patriarch's rights in this instance,
his insistence on the exercise of his perquisites led to conflicts with the
charistikarioi, who wished to reserve this lucrative source of income for
themselves.

The emperor upheld the patriarch's right to make appointments of
individuals as *esomonitai* who were going to embrace monastic life.[109]
The *charistikarioi* could also exercise the right of making monastic appointments, but only if they had a memorandum from the patriarch specifically delegating this authority.[110] The emperor would not allow the
patriarch to place *exomonitai* on the payroll of a monastery in *charistike*,
which meant that the patriarch could not grant an *adelphaton* to a layman who was not taking monastic orders, or to a monk transferred to
this institution from another under direct patriarchal administration.[111]
The emperor decided such appointments would place an unfair burden
on the resources of the monasteries in *charistike*. If such monasteries
already labored under the burden of paying an excessive number of *adelphata* to various *exomonitai*, the emperor enjoined the patriarch to refrain from exercising his usual right to appoint *esomonitai* in these institutions.

---

[104] *JGR* 3.409.16–20.
[105] *JGR* 3.409.20–27.
[106] See Herman, "Armut," 439–49; Lemerle, "Charisticaires," 20, n. 3.
[107] See *Hypomnesis* (ed. Darrouzes, p. 161).
[108] *Hypomnesis*, 160.
[109] *De jure patriarchae* (*JGR* 3.409.29–33).
[110] *JGR* 3.409.33–35.
[111] *JGR* 3.409.35–410.1.

The emperor did not take up the matter of the right of *charistikarioi* to appoint *exomonitai*, but his strict prohibition of a role for the patriarch in these appointments must have left them to the discretion of the lay directors. Overall, however, the law strengthened the position of the patriarch as the ultimate overlord of all patriarchal institutions held in *charistike*, and as the spiritual overseer of all foundations (including private monasteries) regardless of origin or current administrative status.

In its precise definitions of the rights of the patriarch, the emperor's law incidentally illustrates the variety of legal jurisdictions that controlled the monasteries of the Byzantine Empire in the late eleventh century. Although there are no figures to indicate the significance of each category, it appears that private foundations of the traditional sort no longer held the overwhelming position of dominance once observable in the early history of the Byzantine Empire. Yet, in spite of the multiplicity of overlords characteristic of the eleventh century, laymen still held a predominant position as the administrators of institutions and their annexed properties thanks to the *charistike*.

CONSOLIDATION OF THE REFORM MOVEMENT

Another important test case of the conflicting claims of the *charistikarioi* and the ecclesiastical hierarchy arose in 1116 during the patriarchate of Nicholas Grammaticus' successor, John IX Agapetus (1111–34).[112] Constantine, the metropolitan of Kyzikos, appealed to the patriarchal synod for assistance in regaining monasteries once dependent upon his cathedral church but presently under the administration of *charistikarioi*. Unlike Niketas of Athens' case before Nicholas Grammaticus in 1089, Constantine did not attempt to prove that the *charistikarioi* had obtained these monasteries through illegal means. He did follow Niketas' example in appealing to the legislation of Alexius Studites, alleging that his see's loss of these sources of income made it impossible for him to restore his own church, meet the expenses of its operation, or pay government taxes.

The quarter century that had elapsed since the Athens decision had been characterized by official hostility to the *charistike*. It is not surprising, then, that the patriarch's synod rendered a decision as unfavorable to the *charistikarioi* as the earlier decision of 1089. Basing its resolution strictly on the *hypomnemata* of Alexius Studites, the synod ruled that the metropolitan could reclaim any monasteries that *charistikarioi* had ille-

---

[112] Grumel, *Regestes* No. 1000 (1116); text edited by Th. Uspenskii, "Mneniya," 15–29; Grumel's attribution of this document to Patriarch John IX Agapetus is a correction of Uspenskii's original attribution to John VIII Xiphilinus (1064–1075).

gally converted into *kosmika katagogia* (secular dwellings).[113] The synod also allowed Constantine to reclaim the monasteries whose revenues had previously supported the metropolitan's see as well as any other institutions granted to bishops, monasteries, or private individuals if he now had need of them. According to a venerable canon of the Second Council of Nicaea (787), it was illegal for a bishop to alienate part of the essential property (the *autourgion*) meant for the support of his diocese.[114] The synod cited this canon in conjunction with Alexius Studites' legislation to allow Constantine maximum latitude in reclaiming monasteries and diocesan properties currently in the hands of various laymen.

The canon cited had allowed the ecclesiastical hierarchy to grant out certain unprofitable lands to clerics and neighboring peasants. Perhaps this provision became, over the course of time, an important loophole that mitigated the effectiveness of the prohibition on alienation of an institution's *autourgion*.[115] The need to support the rural clergy also probably helped to encourage a broad interpretation of the canon.

An inevitable consequence of supporting clerics with grants of church land was that the tracts would sometimes fall into the hands of lay descendants who would not themselves seek ordination.[116] In the twelfth century these laymen resisted the efforts of the metropolitans of Athens and Mesembria to oust them and appoint new tenants who would be clerics as originally intended.[117] The present tenants, however, claimed the right to propose clerics who would perform religious duties for them while they themselves retained possession of their traditional family leases. In their attempts to revive the ancient rights of episcopal appointment of clerics, the metropolitans discovered that centuries of lay domination of the church had reduced these rights to meaningless formalities.

The right of the private patrons to nominate candidates for the clerical posts in their foundations dated back to late Roman times. Eventually this right of nomination became tantamount to actual appointment. The holders of these appointments, particularly in the case of rural private churches, came to constitute a hereditary clergy.[118] Finally, the clerical families assimilated the founder's right of nomination to themselves. Confusion between mere possession of property and outright ownership

---

[113] Uspenskii, "Mneniya," p. 17, line 13–p. 18, line 7.

[114] *C. Nicaen. II* (787), c. 12 (R&P 2.592–93); Niketas the metropolitan of Athens also cited this canon in his case before the patriarchal synod in 1089 (see Uspenskii, "Mneniya," p. 36, line 19).

[115] Note the canonist Theodore Balsamon's insistence on a strict limitation of the types of ecclesiastical property that could be leased to laymen under the provisions of *C. Nicaen. II*, c. 12 (as discussed below in Chapter 8).

[116] Cf. the inheritance of shares in churches by the lay descendants of clerics in Coptic Egypt as discussed above in Chapter 3.

[117] Balsamon, *Commentaria ad C. Trull.*, c. 33 (R&P 2.380, lines 19–26).

[118] See the discussion above in Chapter 4; cf. *C. Nicaen. II* (787), c. 14 (R&P 2.615).

of it, as well as an inability to distinguish an individual's tenancy of an office from the hereditary enjoyment of its perquisites, was characteristic of the attitudes of these old clerical families. Had they chosen to rescue the ailing private religious foundations directly in the late tenth century, the ecclesiastical authorities would have had to deal with the problem of the loss of control of clerical appointments much earlier. As it was, the resort to the *charistike* obscured the problem for another century. Only with the demise of the *charistike* did the hierarchy come to realize how powerless it had become in the face of gradual lay incursions of its traditional rights.

The problem was not limited to rural churches. The late twelfth-century canonist Theodore Balsamon observed that laymen held *klerikata offikia*, the later Byzantine equivalent of ecclesiastical benefices, in various churches and monasteries of Constantinople in his day.[119] Although such traditional practices as the sale of shares of *siteresia* to laymen and the award of *adelphata* to non-resident *exomonitai* must have helped to prepare the way for this development, it stands, nevertheless, as another indication of the confounding of tenancy of office with hereditary rights.

Niketas, the metropolitan of Athens, had already called the attention of the patriarchate to the problem of regulating the leases of lay renters of church property as part of his appeal against the *charistikarioi* in 1089.[120] This was a long-standing problem, but it was Constantine of Kyzikos who first associated it with the special difficulties posed by tenancies held by lay descendants of the clergy. As part of its decision, the patriarchal court determined that Constantine could revoke such leases after two consecutive tenancies of the usual duration.[121] This meant that a cleric could pass a tenancy down to an heir, even a layman, but that (theoretically at least) the family of a cleric did not have a hereditary right to rent his former landholding. As Balsamon's testimony from the end of the twelfth century shows, this safeguard did not always prove effective.

DEMISE OF THE *CHARISTIKE*

The decisions of the patriarchal synods of 1089 and 1116 did not go beyond providing the metropolitans of Athens and Kyzikos with the authority to abolish the *charistike* within their respective spiritual jurisdications. Unfortunately the sources do not indicate how the institution

---

[119] Balsamon, *Commentaria ad C. Trull.*, c. 33 (R&P 2.380–81).
[120] Uspenskii, "Mneniya," 36–38.
[121] Uspenskii, "Mneniya," 26–27.

that had dominated the Byzantine church for more than a century met its final demise outside of these particular localities. Neither the emperors nor the church ever formally abolished the *charistike* throughout the empire.[122] Perhaps zealous reforming metropolitans suppressed it as they gained authorization to do so from patriarchal decisions like the ones preserved for Athens and Kyzikos. It is also possible that wary *charistikarioi* averted the loss of all of their rights by redefining their positions as ephors.[123] Then again, since the office of *charistikarios* was never fully hereditary, and the grants had now become distinctly unpopular, the emperor and the hierarchy may simply have stopped making new donations while allowing existing grants to lapse without renewal.

The case of the famous monastery of St. Mamas in Constantinople is instructive in this respect.[124] Originally a private foundation, this institution had become an imperial monastery under Emperor Maurice (582–602). By the late tenth century it was in need of extensive repairs. Symeon the New Theologian devoted himself to meeting these needs, but, after his departure in 1005, the monastery fell under the control of *charistikarioi*. The monastery lacked a disinterested patron in the tradition of Symeon until 1147, when the mystic George of Cappadocia obtained permission from Patriarch Cosmas II Atticus (1146–47) to rebuild it. The rapacity of the *charistikarioi* had deprived the institution of its properties, so George had to work to restore its economic base. When his labors at last proved successful, he petitioned Patriarch Nicholas IV Muzalon (1147–51) to grant an independent constitution for the monastery so that it would never again be subject to such "benefactors" as the *charistikarioi* of recent memory. Upon obtaining the patriarch's assent, George appointed Athanasios, the *oikonomos* of the monastery of Christ Philanthropenos, as the *hegoumenos*. Athanasios composed an extant *typikon* in 1159 for the reconstituted foundation which announced its status as an independent monastery.

Thus did one monastery escape the *charistike*. This particular case makes it even less likely that there was a systematic attempt by the patriarchs to stamp out the *charistike* throughout the empire. Now that the patriarchal synod had established grounds for abolishing the *charistike* in individual cases, reformers could apparently rely on the patriarchate for support for suppression whenever there was evidence of abuse. Since many institutions under the *charistike* appear to have had patriarchal

[122] This seems clear from a judicial decision of 1169 regulating *charistikarioi*; see discussion below in Chapter 8.

[123] For the transition from *charistike* to *ephoreia*, see Herman, "Ricerche," 338–39, and the discussion below in Chapter 8, but there is need for more work on this problem.

[124] *Typikon tes Mones tou hagiou megalomartyros Mamantos*, ed. Sophronios Eustratiades, *Hellenika* 1 (1928), 245–314, esp. 256–57; for the history of this foundation, see J. Pargoire, "Les Saint-Mamas de Constantinople," *IRAIK* 9 (1904), 304–12.

charters of foundation (a legacy of an earlier age when the original private benefactors sought exemption from scrupulous local episcopal control), a reliably friendly court could be assumed as well.

Yet even in the twelfth century, the *charistike* had some defenders among conservative ecclesiastics. Perhaps a continued appreciation for the benefits that might accrue from a properly supervised tenure of a *charistike* caused such a respected authority as the canonist Balsamon to hesitate to condemn the institution outright. Still, the conservative viewpoint that Balsamon espoused was a distinct minority opinion by the twelfth century. The charismatic leadership of Leo of Chalcedon, the administrative reforms of Nicholas Grammaticus, and the devastating critique of John of Antioch had accomplished the considerable task of completely reversing the government's and the ecclesiastical hierarchy's attitude toward lay exploitation of property. Henceforth, the institutional church had no patience with lay "benefactors" who exploited their positions to appropriate the incomes of religious foundations or sought to detach them from their proper subordination to the ecclesiastical hierarchy.[125] In this sort of climate the *charistike* could hardly flourish, and in fact it soon withers away from the view of our sources.

[125] Cf. Uspenskii, "Mneniya," 23–24.

CHAPTER EIGHT

The Rise of the Great Independent
Monasteries

PRIVATE churches and monasteries administered by their founding families as fully proprietary institutions continued to exist through-out the duration of the Byzantine Empire. While lay participation in the foundation and support of religious institutions remained critically im-portant, the old proprietary form of organization never regained the pop-ularity it had enjoyed before the *charistike*. By the end of the eleventh century, private benefactors, reacting to the abuses of the *charistike*, be-gan to search for an alternative form of institutional organization that would be more conducive to the religious purposes of their foundations. They had not far to seek. As in the medieval West, a slowly developing monastic reform based on new forms of organization actually preceded the more broadly based ecclesiastical reform of the late eleventh century and anticipated the needs of these new conscientious benefactors.

HISTORICAL DEVELOPMENT OF INDEPENDENT MONASTERIES

As we have seen, the *charistike* had an important impact on individuals like Eustathios Boilas and Michael Attaliates who erected private foun-dations in the third quarter of the eleventh century. The most astute ben-efactors realized that only a radical break with the traditions of private philanthropy would solve the old dilemma of assuring protection for their foundations from outside predators while simultaneously insuring against subsequent financial exploitation by their own descendants. The solution was to set up monasteries that were intended from the start (and not just in the event of the decease of the family line) to be independent (*autodespota*) and self-governing (*autexousia*) institutions.[1]

The road to this innovation was neither easy nor self-evident, although

[1] For these monasteries, see Herman, "Ricerche," 361–72; J. Moutzourès, "Ta charistika kai eleuthera monasteria," *Theologia* 35 (1965), 87–123, 271–87; and my own "The Rise of the Independent and Self-governing Monasteries as Reflected in the Monastic *Typika*," *GOTR* 30 (1985), 21–30.

the independent monastery as such was not an entirely new feature of the organizational structure of the Byzantine church. The earliest monasteries of Christian Egypt and elsewhere in the Orient were, in a sense, the "independent" foundations of their monastic directors. Yet, as we have seen, a monastery might be both "independent" and also the private, transmittable property of its *hegoumenos*. Only strict precautions could ensure that potential heirs not themselves in religious life would be excluded from the ownership of these monasteries.

The Council of Chalcedon's decision that every monastery should be subject to the authority of the local bishop brought all monasteries under theoretical episcopal control. Justinian consistently upheld the local bishop's powers of oversight and spiritual correction in his laws on private foundations. Despite this support, the powers of the episcopacy over the monasteries located in their jurisdictions became more nominal than real. As early as the reign of Maurice (582–602), the emperors had granted individual monasteries exemption from episcopal supervision by subordinating them directly to the patriarch of Constantinople.

For the next three hundred and fifty years, private monasteries and churches were in practice, if not in theory, largely independent of the ecclesiastical hierarchy. Yet when the Council of Constantinople (861) imposed a more rigorous subordination of monasteries to the local bishops and laid down a requirement for property registration, it must have become somewhat more difficult for private benefactors to maintain their old independence. The sudden renewal of interest on the part of these benefactors in obtaining patriarchal *stauropegia* to assure the independence of their foundations from the local hierarchy thus was hardly disinterested or concidental. This time the benefactors confronted an energetic episcopacy especially interested in playing a role as the restorers of dilapidated private monasteries. As we know, the fathers of the Council of Constantinople refused to allow these bishops to spend diocesan funds to restore these institutions. Though this was a considerable obstacle to arranging for structural renovations, enterprising bishops found ways to circumvent the prohibition. Other bishops, motivated by the example though not the spirit of their colleagues' activities, sought to impose a tax called the *kanonikon* on all of the monasteries in their dioceses. They also required special offerings called the *synetheiai* for their consecration of *hegoumenoi*. In some cases these bishops even seized control of monasteries to which they had no legal title. Patriarch Sisinnius II (996–998) had to restrain them from these practices in a special decree.[2]

Among the influential private benefactors who sought to ward off

---

[2]Ed. Sp. Troianos, "Ein Synodalakt des Sisinios zu den bischöflichen Einkünften," in *Fontes Minores*, Vol. 3, ed. Dieter Simon (Frankfurt, 1979), 211–20 = Grumel, *Regestes* No. 808.

these episcopal incursions by securing patriarchal *stauropegia* for their monastic foundations was John Lampardopoulos, a relative of Nicephorus Phocas. In his charter Patriarch Polyeuctus (956–970) specifically exempted Lampardopoulos' monastery of the Theotokos in the Peloponnesus from taxes paid to the local metropolitan or to the bishop of Lacedaemon (964).[3] The revival of interest in patriarchal *stauropegia* was an important step in the development of truly independent and self-governing monasteries. As things actually transpired, however, the essential conceptual innovation occurred within the mileu of imperial monasteries. The precedent was the chrysobull that Nicephorus Phocas had given to St. Athanasios for the monastery of Lavra on Mount Athos (964).[4] According to Athanasios, it was at his own request that the emperor inserted into the charter language that exempted Lavra from patriarchal control and gave it the claim to be the earliest monastery to hold the actual title (as opposed to the de facto status) of an independent and self-governing foundation. By freeing the Lavra monastery not only from episcopal control but also from that of the patriarch as well, Nicephorus Phocas made a further break from the principle of hierarchical subordination established by the Council of Chalcedon.

The innovation was timely, for the peril to the well-being of private foundations increased significantly with the institution of the *charistike* in the late tenth century. Ostensibly designed to rescue deteriorating and ruined monasteries (many of which were doubtless private in origin), the *charistike* soon came to encompass wealthy, well-managed institutions as well. Sisinnius II's opposition to the aggressive policies of the local hierarchy was quite consistent with his opposition to the *charistike*. This was because, by his time, any private monasteries taken over by the bishops were probably destined for the *charistike*, as Basil II's novel of 996 demonstrates.

Subsequent emperors followed the lead of Nicephorus Phocas in the patronage of the Lavra monastery and of the other monasteries that developed on Mount Athos in the course of the tenth and eleventh centuries.[5] In 978 Basil II and his brother Constantine VIII made a donation to Lavra of an annual income (called an *adiakopton*, that is, an "uninterrupted" *siteresion*) of 10 talents of silver in consideration of their be-

---

[3] MM 5.250–252 (964), esp. 251.24–30; cf. Alexius Studites, *Hypomnema B'* (1028) (R&P 5.31.26–32.5).

[4] For this foundation, see Paul Lemerle, *Actes de Lavra* Vol. 1 (Paris, 1970), 13–55, esp. 33–39; Denise Papachryssanthou, *Actes du Prôtaton* (Paris, 1975), 69–83; I. P. Mamalakes, *To Hagion Oros (Athos) dia mesou tou aionon* (Thessalonica, 1971), 48–63; Herman, "Ricerche," 361.

[5] *Actes de Lavra*, Vol. 1, No. 7 (978), No. 32 (1057), ed. Lemerle; *Actes de Prôtaton* No. 7 (972), No. 8 (1045), and No. 9 (1046), ed. Denise Papachryssanthou (*Archives de l'Athos*, Vol. 7) (Paris, 1975).

lief that the prayers of the monks were efficacious for the empire in its struggles with barbarian peoples. In 1057 Emperor Michael VI (1056–57) made another annual income available to Lavra, in addition to the gifts made by his predecessors. Nor was this imperial patronage limited to financial assistance, for both John Tzimisces (972) and Constantine IX Monomachus (1045) intervened to settle serious disciplinary disputes among the Athonite monks.

Some founders, such as St. Lazaros of Mount Galesion (d. 1043), continued to try to follow the old principle of Chalcedon by subordinating their monasteries to local episcopal control, but they found that individual jealousies and the meddlesomeness of the bishops made cooperation impossible.[6] Now, however, there was a suitable alternative model of organization available. St. Lazaros finally appealed to Constantine IX Monomachus (1042–55) for exemption from episcopal control. The emperor granted the request, but followed the example of Nicephorus Phocas in preference to that of Maurice by making St. Lazaros' monasteries completely independent foundations.

After Sergius II had reversed his predecessor Sisinnius' opposition to the *charistike* in 1016, even a patriarchal *stauropegion* was no guarantee that a monastery would escape donation to a *charistikarios* at some time in the future.[7] This no doubt provided an additional stimulus for founders to make their monasteries independent not only of the local episcopacy, but of the patriarchate as well.

The concept of truly independent and self-governing monasteries was hardly pleasing to the unreformed hierarchy of the eleventh century. These prelates could hope neither to exact taxes from these monasteries nor to grant them out to personal favorites in *charistike*. The concept was also irreconcilable with many of the traditional perquisites, especially financial ones, that patrons had come to expect as their due from their foundations. An independent monastery had to have its own endowment, mananged by its own officials without interference from members of the founder's family. The financial sacrifice involved in the erection of a monastery, which had always been considerable, now increased greatly. While it would still be possible for founders to insist on such traditional rights as memorial masses, burial sites, and consideration for family members as postulants, direct financial exploitation such as that

---

[6] *De sancto Lazaro monacho in Monte Galesio*, Ch. 238, *AASS*, November, Vol. 3 (Brussels, 1910), with O. Lampsides, "Anekdoton keimenon peri tou hagiou Lazarou Galesiotou," *Theologia* 53 (1982), 158–77. For St. Lazaros, see Rosemary Morris, "The Political Saint of the Eleventh Century," in *The Byzantine Saint*, ed. Sergei Hackel (Birmingham, 1981), 43–50.

[7] Note, for example, Nicholas III Grammaticus' grants of patriarchal monasteries under the *charistike* and his references to earlier grants made by his predecessors.

envisioned by Attaliates was not compatible with true institutional autonomy.

THE CONCEPT OF *EPHOREIA*

Patrons who set up monastic foundations with self-managed endowments freed these institutions from dependence upon the goodwill of their heirs and the continuance of their family lines. Yet in this troubled age no institution could be entirely without protectors, so it was still necessary to designate some sort of guardian who could look after the interests of the monastery without becoming involved in its day-to-day administration. Out of this need grew the *ephoreia*.[8]

Some founders met this need by designating local *strategoi* and other government officials as ephors or *epitropoi* (trustees).[9] Toward the close of the tenth century the monk Nikon Metanoites chose the *strategos* (military governor) and *krites* (judge) of the Peloponnesus as the protectors of his religious foundation at Lacedaemon. In 1027 the monk Nikodemos would turn to the same officials to assume the *ephoreia* of his monastery. Even St. Athanasios' faith in the ability of his Lavra monastery to fend for itself after his death failed him, for in his *diatyposis* (testamentary disposition) he designated the patrician Nikephoros, the *epi tou kanikleiou* of Basil II, as *epitropos* (trustee), *prostates* (protector), and *antileptor* (helper) of his foundation.[10] In 1052 Constantine IX would confirm this arrangement under which Lavra stood under the *prostasia* (guardianship) of the *epi tou kanikleiou*, at that time the *praepositos* and *epi tou koitionos* John.[11] In 1060 Emperor Constantine X Ducas (1059–67) added his endorsement to the sponsorship of Lavra by the office of the *epi tou kanikleiou*; by this time the arrangement bore the formal title of *ephoreia*.[12]

This marriage of the *ephoreia* to the independent monastery did not prove an entirely satisfactory solution in every case. Some ephors behaved in practice little better than the worst of the *charistikarioi*, a risk that might have been foreseen. In his *diataxis* of 1077, Attaliates damned anyone who dared to impose either an ephor or a *charistikarios* on his foundation, yet in the end it was the title of ephor that he bestowed on his son Theodore as the foundation's protector.[13] The terminological

---

[8] For the *ephoreia*, see Herman, "Ricerche," 335–39, and "Charisticaires," col. 616.

[9] S. P. Lampros, "Ho bios Nikonos tou metanoeite," *Neos Hellenomnemon* 3 (1906), 129–228, esp. 227; D. A. Zakythinos, "Kastron Lakedaimonos," *Hellenika* 15 (1957), 97–111, esp. 100.

[10] Athanasios the Athonite, *Diatyposis*, ed. Meyer, *Haupturkunden*, 123–40, esp. 125.

[11] *Actes de Lavra*, Vol. 1, No. 31 (1052), ed. Lemerle.

[12] *Actes de Lavra*, Vol. 1, No. 33 (1060), ed. Lemerle.

[13] Michael Attaliates, *Diataxis*, ed. Gautier, lines 247–62, cf. 348–51.

confusion evident in the writings of founders of religious institutions toward the end of the eleventh century indicates the uneasy transition from old forms of organization to the new. Attaliates, who was aware of the concept of the independent monastery, chose, as we have seen, to adopt the traditional private form of organization instead. This choice did not prevent him from calling his *ptochotropheion* (in occasional moments of confusion) "independent and self-governing," nor from providing that the foundation would become truly independent in the event of the decease of his family line.[14]

Unlike Attaliates, the famous ascetic Christodoulos, founder of a monastery of St. John on the island of Patmos, undoubtedly intended his foundation to have an independent constitution under the direct rule of its *hegoumenos* when he drew up his *hypotyposis* (constitution) for it in 1091.[15] Yet his *diatheke* (testament) of 1093, introduces Theodosios Kastrisiou, the *epi tou kanikleiou* of Alexius Comnenus, as *charistikarios*.[16] In fact, this is not the bizarre combination of old and new forms of organization that it might appear to be, since the conditions imposed on Theodosios clearly limit him to the status (if not the title) of ephor on the analogy of existing arrangements with the Lavra monastery on Mount Athos.[17]

By the turn of the century, the concept of the independent monastery matured under the impact of the Chalcedonian reform. The terminology became more consistent and ideologically charged. For example, no respectable ephor in the twelfth century would have wanted to bear the title of *charistikarios*. This is not to say that the lines of distinction among the various types of religious institutions were ever hard and fast.[18] In another era to come, a single monastery could accurately be described as "imperial, patriarchal, *and* independent" in reference, respectively, to its principal patronage, its *stauropegion*, and its constitutional organization. This is a reflection of the complex origins of the independent monastery in the Byzantine world. That independent monasteries were in no sense public (that is, diocesan) institutions was well understood (if not appreciated) by nearly everyone. That they were fundamentally different from traditional private foundations was a point less easy to grasp and subject to occasional confusion.

[14] *Diataxis*, ed. Gautier, lines 392–94, 1617.

[15] Christodoulos, *Hypotyposis* (1091), ed. MM, Vol. 6 (Vienna, 1890), 59–80, esp. Ch. 18, pp. 71–72.

[16] Christodoulos, *Diatheke* (1093), ed. MM, Vol. 6 (Vienna, 1890), 81–85, esp. 84.

[17] For the *ephoreia* of the monastery of Christodoulos on Patmos, see M. G. Nystazopoulos, "Ho epi tou kanikleiou kai he ephoreia tes en Patmo mones," *Symmeikta* 1 (1966), 76–94, and Ahrweiler, "Charisticariat," 5, n. 31.

[18] See *Actes de Lavra* (= *Archives de l'Athos*, Vol. 8), ed. Paul Lemerle (Paris, 1977), No. 70 (1240) in which a monastery is termed "independent, free, and ancestral"!

The revival of the *ephoreia* in the twelfth century is a surprising development that concluded the evolution of the independent monastery. It must have been with some reluctance that founders turned to it once again as an expedient for obtaining powerful protectors for independent monasteries, but this time happier results were obtained. Perhaps this was because the institutional autonomy of the foundations had been strengthened considerably since the early eleventh century and the threat posed by the *charistike* had begun to wane.

INDEPENDENT MONASTERIES AND THE ECCLESIASTICAL REFORM MOVEMENT

So by the early twelfth century the essential features of the independent monastery were in place. The new category of monasteries emerged out of more than a century and a half of creative experimentation. These foundations represent the response of private individuals to the evils of the *charistike* and the shortcomings in the proprietary form of organization that the *charistike* had failed to resolve. Thus the private benefactors who developed the earliest of these foundations actually anticipated many of the concerns of the reformers within the church, such as Leo of Chalcedon, John of Antioch, and Nicholas Grammaticus. Their successful foundations, the "easily counted, most recent *koinobia*," which John of Antioch numbered among the few monasteries that had escaped the *charistike*, demonstrated that it was possible for the church to enjoy the benefits of lay financial assistance without risking the hazards of private profiteering in these institutions. It is surely no coincidence that John of Antioch's *De monasteriis* shows indebtedness to the magnificent library of ascetic literature kept at one of these new independent institutions, the monastery of the Theotokos Evergetis, founded in Constantinople in 1049.[19] In due course a new generation of reformers would find ample reason to criticize these foundations also, for by definition they were set up to be as independent of clerical as of lay control. The future difficulties, however, were not apparent in the initial stages of the evolution of independent monasteries; only the obvious and welcome contrast to the discredited *charistike* impressed most of the reformers of the late eleventh century. A notable exception was Nikon of the Black Mountain, founder of several monasteries and a contemporary of John of Antioch.

---

[19] So Paul Gautier, "Le typikon de la Théotokos Evergétis," *REB* 40 (1982), 5–101, at 7, n. 9. For this foundation see also J. Pargoire, "Constantinople: Le couvent de l'Evergétès," *EO* 9 (1906), 228–32, 366–73, *EO* 10 (1907), 155–67, 259–63, and Janin, *Géographie*, Vol. 3, pp. 178–83.

His *Mikron Biblion*, dated to 1087/88, insists upon the subordination of monasteries to the local bishop and actually cites the relevant fourth canon of the Council of Chalcedon.[20]

TYPIKON OF GREGORY PAKOURIANOS

It is our good fortune that the independent and self-governing monasteries are especially well documented. While they were no longer proprietary monasteries, they continued to have their origins in private acts of foundation. Most of the surviving *typika* (regulatory foundation documents) for monasteries and philanthropic institutions adopted the new form of organization.[21] One of the earliest and most instructive is the *typikon* of Gregory Pakourianos, dated to 1083, for the monastery of Theotokos Petritzionitisse.[22] Although Pakourianos was a Georgian by birth who served as Grand Domestic of the East, he chose to found this monastery at Stenimachos near Philippopolis, where he owned a number of estates. He built the monastery out of his personal resources without, he claims, maltreatment or exploitation of his peasants. Pakourianos' decision to employ an independent constitution for his foundation is a clear indication of his sympathies with the sentiments of his reformist contemporaries.

Pakourianos' *typikon* sets up his foundation as an independent and self-governing monastery in perpetuity.[23] Thanks to the tax exemptions that Pakourianos had managed to obtain, the monastery was freed of all financial obligations to the emperor, the patriarch, and local ecclesiastical and governmental authorities. The *typikon* also bars all relatives of the founder from financial privileges in the monastery.[24] It explicitly censures Pakourianos' contemporaries who erected foundations of the traditional proprietary form of organization.[25] From his personal experi-

---

[20] Irénée Doens, "Nicon de la Montagne Noire," *Byzantion* 24 (1954), 131–40, at 137; V. Grumel, "Nicon de la Montagne Noire et Jean IV (V) l'Oxite: Remarques chronologiques," *REB* 21 (1963), 270–73.

[21] For *typika ktetorika*, see K. A. Manaphes, *Monasteriaka Typika—Diathekai* (Athens, 1970); Herman, "Ricerche," 312–15; I. M. Konidaris, *Nomike theorese ton monasteriakon typikon* (Athens, 1984); and R. Janin, "Le monachisme byzantin au moyen âge: Commende et typica (Xe–XIVe siècle)," *REB* 22 (1964), 5–44. The Byzantine monastic *typika* are currently being collected into a volume of English translations in a project under my direction sponsored by Dumbarton Oaks and the National Endowment for the Humanities.

[22] Ed. Paul Gautier, "Le typikon du sébaste de Grégoire Pakourianos," *REB* 42 (1984), 5–145, with important commentary by Lemerle, *Cinq études*, 115–91; see also Ostrogorsky, "Aristocracy," 30–31. For Pakourianos' career, see Skoulatos, *Personnages*, 112–15.

[23] *Typikon*, Ch. 28 (ed. Gautier, pp. 89–93).

[24] Cf. Michael Attaliates, *Diataxis*, ed. Gautier, lines 602–18.

[25] *Typikon*, Ch. 18 (ed. Gautier, p. 91).

ence Pakourianos observed that a founder who attempted to keep an institution as an integral part of the family patrimony was condemning his foundation to bitter litigation among his heirs over the rights of ownership. The courts that resolved such disputes, moreover, could not be depended upon to prefer worthy heirs to worthless ones, who might happen to have better legal claims to the foundation.

Pakourianos intended that the *hegoumenos* was to be the real master of the monastery.[26] He was to control the distribution of salaries (*rogai*) to the monks in the community. Two monks with the title of *epitropoi*, who were stationed at the most important clusters of endowed properties, were to assist the *hegoumenos* with estate administration. This was an important break with the traditional reliance upon laymen as estate managers. The *hegoumenos*, moreover, enjoyed security of tenure. He could only be expelled for failure to observe the *typikon* or for embezzlement of funds.

Pakourianos reserved only a few traditional perquisites for himself as founder's rights.[27] He named the first *hegoumenos*, his friend Gregory, but he did not retain the right of appointment for his family. He and his brother Aspasios were to receive the usual privilege of burial in the monastery's church. Pakourianos also enjoined the monks to offer commemorative masses for his brother's soul and his own. He disapproved of the usual practice of soliciting endowments from the laity at large, ordering that the monks should do this only if it did not provide a pretext for innovation or harm to the monastery.[28] Perhaps this traditional means of raising extra revenue had led to law suits like that over the payment of *siteresia* recorded in the *Meditatio de nudis pactis*. Finally, Pakourianos directed that the community should give preferential consideration to relatives of his family who applied as postulants. Incidentally, the monastery was limited to Georgians, with Greeks explicitly excluded because Pakourianos feared that otherwise they would seize control and make the foundation their personal property.[29] Always apprehensive of possible threats to his monastery, the founder made even the preferential treatment for his relatives conditional on the understanding that they would obey the *hegoumenos* as usual and not attempt to attenuate the independence of the foundation.

[26] For the *hegoumenos*' authority, see the *Typikon*, Ch. 5 (ed. Gautier, pp. 51–57); security of tenure, Ch. 19 (p. 95); distribution of the *rogai*, Ch. 9 (pp. 67–69); *epitropoi*, Ch. 6 (p. 59).

[27] For Pakourianos' appointment of Gregory, see *Typikon*, Ch. 30 (ed. Gautier, p. 115); burial of the founder and his brother, Ch. 1 (p. 31) and Ch. 2 (p. 39); commemorative services, Ch. 21 (pp. 97–103).

[28] *Typikon*, Ch. 20 (ed. Gautier, pp. 95–97).

[29] *Typikon*, Chs. 24–25 (ed. Gautier, pp. 105–7).

GENERAL ACCEPTANCE OF THE CONCEPT OF THE
INDEPENDENT MONASTERY

Pakourianos composed his farsighted *typikon* while serving Alexius Comnenus in the war against Robert Guiscard. He perished in battle against the Patzinaks in 1086, just at the time when the reformers from within the ecclesiastical hierarchy were beginning to deal with the abuses of lay control of the church for which he had already offered some solutions.[30] The concept of the independent and self-governing monastery thus had reached maturity at precisely the time when the reformers launched their ultimately successful challenge to the *charistike*.

In the twelfth century this new constitutional form of organization became the rule rather than the exception for the most important foundations of monasteries and philanthropic institutions. Even the members of the ruling Comnenian dynasty adopted the new form of organization as they abandoned the *charistike* and other discredited practices of the eleventh century. Alexius Comnenus' wife, Irene, already notable as a supporter of Leo of Chalcedon, drafted an independent constitution for her nunnery of Theotokos Kecharitomene in Constantinople.[31] The empress designated her daughter Eudokia as *antilambanomene* (corrector) in the role of an ephor. Her son, Emperor John II Comnenus (1118–43), adopted the same form of organization for the monastery of the Pantokrator which he founded in Constantinople in 1136.[32] He designated his son Alexius as overseer without title. Both Irene and John Comnenus emphasized the independent status of these institutions by stating that they were not to be considered private or imperial monasteries by virtue of their own roles in the foundations.[33]

The use of the independent form of organization was not restricted to new foundations. Athanasios, for example, had employed it in his *typikon* for the monastery of St. Mamas in 1159 after the patriarchs had freed that institution from the *charistike*. John Comnenus, in subordinating six existing imperial monasteries to the new Pantokrator monastery, also added to the number of institutions with independent gov-

[30] For Pakourianos' death, see Anna Comnena, *Alexiad* 6.14.

[31] Irene Comnena, *Typikon tes sebasmias mones tes hyperagias Theotokou tes Kecharitômenes*, ed. Paul Gautier, "Le typikon de la Théotokos Kécharitômenè," *REB* 43 (1985), 5–165, esp. Ch. 1 (pp. 29–31); for Eudocia's role as ephor, see Ch. 80 (pp. 143–45); for this foundation, see L. Oeconomos, *La vie religieuse dans l'empire byzantin au temps des Comnènes et des Anges* (Paris, 1918), 169–82, and Janin, *Géographie*, Vol. 3, pp. 188–91.

[32] John II Comnenus, *Typikon*, ed. Paul Gautier, "Le typikon du Christ Sauveur Pantocrator," *REB* 32 (1974), 1–145, esp. 127; for this foundation, see Janin, *Géographie*, Vol. 3, pp. 515–23.

[33] Irene Comnena, *Typikon* Ch. 1 (ed. Gautier, pp. 29–31); so also John II Comnenus, *Typikon* (ed. Gautier, p. 127, lines 1613–20).

ernment.[34] Even some reformist bishops embraced the independent constitution for their own foundations. Manuel, bishop of Stroumitza (1085–1106), used it for the monastery he dedicated to Theotokos Eleousa.[35] Manuel evidently had little confidence that his episcopal successors would share his piety, for he restricted the traditional rights of the local bishop to a voluntary donation of 3 *nomismata* at the time of the enthronement of a new *hegoumenos* in the institution.[36] Leo, bishop of Nauplia, followed Manuel's example in 1143 by adopting an independent constitution for his nunnery of Theotokos tes Areias.[37] Only in the late twelfth century did the hierarchy come to realize how inconsistent the idea of the independent monastery was with the maintenance of their own episcopal rights.

For the moment, the concept of the independent and self-governing monastery had found favor with the broad spectrum of individuals who traditionally founded the ecclesiastical institutions of the empire. A considerable amount of private resources, such as those of Gregory Pakourianos, went into the foundation of these independent monasteries which might otherwise have been devoted to traditional proprietary institutions. Of course, the extent to which strictly private foundations declined in numbers in the twelfth and subsequent centuries cannot easily be determined, but undoubtedly the popularity of independent monasteries among benefactors occurred largely at their expense.[38]

The generous disposition of benefactors toward granting independent charters of foundation prevailed only in the erection of monasteries and philanthropic institutions. No similarly drastic change occurred in the constitutional organization of churches and oratories. These continued their traditionally close association with the estates of their benefactors in the twelfth and succeeding centuries.

POLICY OF MANUEL COMNENUS TOWARD PRIVATE RELIGIOUS FOUNDATIONS

This new phase in the institutional history of private religious foundations proceeded with the blessings of the Comnenian dynasty, though one more emperor, Manuel Comnenus (1143–80) was to formulate his own

[34] John II Comnenus, *Typikon* (ed. Gautier, pp. 69–73, lines 685–727).

[35] Manuel of Stroumitza, *Diataxis*, ed. L. Petit, "Le Monastère de Notre-Dame de Pitié en Macédoine," *IRAIK* 6 (1900), 69–153.

[36] *Diataxis*, Ch. 16 (ed. Petit, p. 88); cf. Herman, "Abgabenwesen," 455.

[37] Leo of Nauplia, *Hypomnema*, ed. G. A. Choras, *He "Hagia mone" Areias Naupliou* (Athens, 1975), 239–44, esp. 242–43.

[38] Among the many examples, one finds the six monasteries that John II Comnenus subordinated to his new imperial monastery of the Pantokrator and the conversion of the monastery of St. Mamas to an independent constitutional status.

policy on the foundation of religious institutions by private individuals. This was to be the last time a Byzantine emperor would do so. After his reign the patriarchate would stand unassisted in its efforts to regulate what had become an exceedingly complex problem of balancing the rights of patrons and religious foundations.

Perhaps the emperor's greatest achievement was his judicious use of tax immunities to ease the shortage of clergy in the countryside. The better endowed foundations in the cities had always attracted clerics from poorly paid positions in rural churches. This development worked to the disadvantage of nearly all rural churches, whatever their origins or current status. Since the time of Basil I (867–886), the emperors had attempted to support certain favored institutions by granting their properties tax exemption.[39] These grants of immunity (*exkousseia*) were in effect indirect government subsidies. Until Manuel's reign, the emperors awarded immunity on a case-by-case basis, doubtless in response to appeals of influential individuals. Now Manuel chose to use this tool in a more general way to deal with this problem.

The emperor's original concern was with the economic status of clergy living on imperial estates serving in imperial proprietary churches. In 1144 he decided to allow the *demosiakoi*, the clergy resident on these estates, personal exemptions from some services and taxation to make their lot more bearable.[40] These clerics no longer had to perform compulsory labor services (*demosiake epereia*) or pay the cattle tax (the *zeugologion*). Later the emperor decided to extend the liberality of immunity from the *demosiake epereia* to clergy on the estates of public and private monasteries.[41] Thus the clergy of both public and traditional private churches, as well as those belonging to the new independent monasteries, came to join the imperial clergy in the enjoyment of the exemption.

Manuel was simply making general the exemption from compulsory labor services that many clerics already enjoyed as tenants of monasteries possessing imperial chrysobulls of tax immunity.[42] With an eye to his own interests, Manuel restricted the number of clergy on imperial estates who could benefit from the exemptions. He decided against placing a similar restriction on the clergy of public and private churches.

The emperor's remisssion of these obligations led to a rapid increase in the number of clerics in the countryside. The numbers of the imperial

[39] *Actes de Prôtaton* No. 1 (883), with commentary by George Ostrogrosky, "Pour l'histoire de l'immunité à Byzance," *Byzantion* 28 (1958), 165–254, at 174–75.

[40] Dölger, *Regesten* No. 1334, preserved by Balsamon, *Commentaria ad C. Nicaen. II*, c. 4 (R&P 2.570); = *JGR* 3.432.

[41] Dölger, *Regesten* Nos. 1335–36.

[42] E.g., the exemptions that Michael Attaliates obtained for his foundation from Michael VII (1074) and Nicephorus III (1079), ed. Gautier, *REB* 39 (1981), 100–122.

clergy soon rose beyond the statutory limits for exemptions, and Patriarch Luke Chrysoberges (1157–70) sought the emperor's permission for his synod to decide whether the supernumeraries should also enjoy immunity from compulsory labor services.[43] It seemed unfair that these clerics should have to render such services as the reconditioning of naval vessels when all the clergy of private institutions enjoyed exemption. Once it secured the emperor's consent in 1168, the synod ruled that these clerics should also enjoy exemption from the labor services.

The canonist Theodore Balsamon, commenting at the close of the twelfth century on the fifteenth canon of the Second Council of Nicaea which had tolerated rural pluralism, observed that a complete reversal of the eighth-century situation had occurred thanks to Manuel's grant of *exkousseia* to the clergy.[44] In Balsamon's day there were now more rural clerics than churches in which they could serve, making pluralism in the countryside unnecessary. Rarely had such a definitive solution to a persistent problem ever been found in Byzantine history, and at small cost to the state, since the government did not have to undertake a program of direct subsidization of rural clerics.

Manuel Comnenus was less successful in attempting to reverse the arrangements for organizing ecclesiastical foundations that had found favor with private benefactors since the late eleventh century.[45] The emperor was disturbed, as his distant predecessor Nicephorus Phocas had been, to find his wealthy subjects bestowing extensive properties on monastic foundations. He considered the administration of these properties a distracting burden and an obstacle to a life of monastic piety and seclusion. That his father, John II Comnenus, as well as his grandfather, Alexius Comnenus, had set the example in founding large, well-endowed independent monasteries did not sway Manuel's own judgment that supporting religious institutions with landed properties was inappropriate.

The emperor's chrysobull of 1158 embodies these attitudes in a new government policy toward private foundations.[46] The measure affected all the monasteries of the capital, the islands of the Propontis, and Ni-

---

[43] Grumel, *Regestes* No. 1082 (July 1168), mentioned by Balsamon, *Commentaria ad C. Nicaen. II*, c. 4 (R&P 2.571).

[44] Balsamon, *Commentaria ad C. Nicaen. II*, c. 15 (R&P 2.261).

[45] For Manuel's ecclesiastical policy, see Nicolas Svoronos, "Les privilèges de l'Eglise à l'époque des Comnènes: Un rescrit inédit de Manuel Ier Comnène," *T&M* 1 (1965), 325–91; Charanis, "Monastic Properties," 81–85; Jean Darrouzès, "Décret inédit de Manuel Comnène," *REB* 31 (1973), 307–17; Paul Magdalino, "The Byzantine Holy Man in the Twelfth Century," in *The Byzantine Saint*, ed. Sergei Hackel (Birmingham, 1981), 51–66, esp. 62–65.

[46] Manuel Comnenus, *Aurea bulla de possessionibus monasteriorum* (1158) (*JGR* 3.450–454) = Dölger, *Regesten* No. 1419, with commentary by Svornos, "Privilèges," 330–33. Cf. the more stringent policy in his *De possessionibus monasteriorum* (1176) = Dölger, *Regesten* No. 1537.

comedia and vicinity. This limited geographical area included many of the empire's wealthiest monasteries, though not others, such as those on Mount Athos which were also of considerable importance.[47] The law forbade the monasteries in this area to acquire further property or peasants. To encourage these institutions to swallow this bitter medicine, the emperor confirmed all of their present properties, even those for which their title was uncertain or worse, and forbade government tax collectors to intrude on the lands of monasteries that enjoyed immunity.

Unlike Nicephorus Phocas, Manuel Comnenus did not impose an outright ban on the establishment of new monasteries. Instead, he held up a foundation of his own, the monastery of St. Michael at Kataskepe, as an example of the proper way for benefactors to provide financial support.[48] The emperor had chosen to provide a cash grant from the treasury to support the monastic community of this foundation instead of the usual endowment of fields and vineyards. In so doing, he was attempting to return to earlier endowment practices common before the Council of Constantinople (861), when many benefactors provided annuities and cash subsidies to maintain their foundations. The emperor hoped once again to popularize this means of financing monasteries. Had he been successful, he would surely have dealt a severe blow to the flourishing system of independent, self-governing monasteries that had become so popular among wealthy philanthropists since the late eleventh century.

A generation later, Eustathios, metropolitan of Thessalonica (d. 1198), agreed with Manuel Comnenus that the wealth of the monasteries was a scandal, and denounced their insatiable appetite for new acquisitions of property.[49] Protests of this sort demonstrate that the independent, self-governing monasteries had in fact achieved the goals of their originators. They had gained unparalleled financial security while unburdening themselves of lay control. So much had the balance of power changed that it was now possible for a reactionary clergyman like Eustathios to comment favorably even on the thoroughly discredited *charistike* and to look back with admiration on the era when laymen administered monasteries directly for their personal profit.

Of course, in an empire of shrinking territorial resources, the prosperity of the monasteries came at the expense of classes (such as the military and the peasantry) whose services were more critical to the survival of the state. Property that came under the control of the independent mon-

---

[47] On the limited scope of this legislation, see Charanis, "Monastic Properties," 84.

[48] For this foundation, see Niketas Choniates, *Historia*, ed. J. A. Van Dieten (Berlin, 1975), p. 207; cf. John Kinnamos, *Historia*, ed. A. Meinke, *CSHB* (Bonn, 1836), p. 276; Janin, *Géographie*, Vol. 3, p. 342.

[49] Eustathios of Thessalonica, *De emendanda vita monachica* (*PG* 135, cols. 729–910, esp. 825). On Eustathios, see Kazhdan, *Studies*, 115–95, esp. 150–54.

asteries of the twelfth century lost much of its usefulness to the state, certainly to a much greater extent than in the time of Nicephorus Phocas, when tax immunities for individual monasteries were hardly known.

These monasteries finally secured the administrative and financial independence that had been so conspicuously absent under the traditional proprietary form of organization. Manuel Comnenus' attempt to return to the old means of financing private foundations did not succeed, probably because of the very success that independent monasteries had achieved in less than a century of popular acceptance. The disappearance of Manuel's own foundation of Kataskepe, probably in 1204 with the fall of the imperial government, was a vindication of the wisdom of private benefactors who preferred the independent form of organization. Many of their foundations did survive the collapse of the government, aided in no small measure by their financial autonomy.

THEODORE BALSAMON AND HIS VIEWS ON THE ROLE OF PRIVATE RELIGIOUS FOUNDATIONS IN THE BYZANTINE CHURCH

As it happened, Theodore Balsamon, the greatest of Byzantine canon lawyers, commenced his ecclesiastical career early in the reign of Manuel Comnenus, just as the conservative reaction to the growth of the independent monasteries was forming.[50] The canonist's own generally conservative views thus were in keeping with the times. He held the post of patriarchal *chartophylax* in 1179, then served briefly as titular patriarch of Antioch under Isaac II Angelus (1185–95). Although he was still living in 1195, the date of his death is unknown.

Balsamon's greatest work, his canonical commentaries, were composed in the last quarter of the twelfth century.[51] They provide a thorough explication of the canons of the ecumenical councils as well as other canons recognized as authentic and orthodox by these councils. His commentaries quote or refer to many of the important documents already discussed in this study, such as Nicephorus Phocas' ban on new religious foundations and Basil II's law repealing it, the decrees of Sisinnius II and Sergius II on the *charistike*, Alexius Comnenus' *De jure patriarchae*, and Manuel Comnenus' laws on clerical tax exemptions. It would be nearly impossible to study the internal history of the Byzantine church without the evidence Balsamon has preserved in his canonical commentaries.

[50] For Balsamon's career and works, see G. P. Stevens, *De Theodoro Balsamone. Analysis operum ac mentis iuridicae* (Rome, 1969), and Emil Herman "Balsamon," DDC, Vol. 2, cols. 76–83.

[51] Theodore Balsamon, *Commentaria in Canones SS. Apostolorum Conciliorum et in epistolas canonicas SS. Patrum*, ed. R&P 2 and 3 (Athens, 1852–53).

Since it is through Balsamon's eyes that we view a great deal of what is known about the controversies concerning private religious foundations in Byzantium, it is important to determine his own opinions and prejudices. Fortunately, Balsamon does not distort the evidence to conform to his own biases, and he readily discloses his own views on important controversies. Therefore, once allowance is made for the considerable distance he stood from many of these controversies, there is much to be learned from him about the attitudes of the ecclesiastical hierarchy toward private foundations.

Although he has nothing to say about the origin of private religious institutions in Byzantium, Balsamon was astute enough to realize the connection between early oratories (*eukterioi oikoi*) and heretical sects.[52] His commentary on a canon of a council held at Antioch in 326 indicates that he believed that certain private chapels evolved from private residences of sectaries who had been expelled from the public churches of the empire.[53]

Balsamon, who had followed in the sources the long controversy about the legality of chapels in private houses, was well aware of the distinctions between oratories and *katholikai ekklesiai*, the public churches. He knew that the distinguishing marks of the latter were that they served as repositories of relics and continued to receive the episcopal dedications that private benefactors had now dispensed with for their oratories.[54] Nevertheless, Balsamon upheld the right of patrons to have regular liturgies and baptisms, citing in support Leo VI's decision on the sacramental capacities of chapels in private houses.[55] In Balsamon's opinion, the emperor's verdict on this matter took precedence over the earlier canonical legislation to the contrary.

Not all of the canonists of the twelfth century shared this view. Alexios Aristenos, who was perhaps nearer to the opinion of the reformist party on this issue, preferred to follow the canons of the Synod in Trullo which allowed the divine liturgy in these private chapels only with episcopal consent and reserved all baptisms for public churches.[56]

Balsamon was also interested in the question of what amount of money constituted the "sufficiency" that all prospective founders since the time of Justinian had been expected to have ready before undertaking

---

[52] Balsamon, *Comm. ad C. Ant.* (ca. 326), c. 2 (R&P 3.127, lines 17–16).

[53] Cf. Balsamon, *Comm. ad C. Gang.* (ca. 362), c. 6 (R&P 3.105).

[54] Balsamon, *Responsa ad interrogationes Marci*, ed. R&P 4 (Athens, 1854), No. 4 (R&P 4.458–59).

[55] See above, note 54, with Balsamon, *Comm. ad C. Laod.*, c. 58 (R&P 3.224).

[56] Alexius Aristenus, *Commentaria ad C. Laod.*, c. 58 (R&P 3.224); for this canonist, see M. Krasnozhen, "Kommentarii Alekseya Aristina na kanonicheskii Sinopsis," *VV* 20 (1913), 189–207.

the construction of a church or monastery.[57] Balsamon did not think it necessary for a benefactor to spend thousands of *nomismata* (as in the cases of the great independent monasteries) in order to endow a monastery properly. He referred once again to a novel of Leo VI, which encouraged benefactors to undertake foundations that would support as few as three monks. It would be enough, then, Balsamon thought, to have sufficient money to complete the construction of the building and to provide for its administration and the support of the minimum number of monks. Balsamon therefore gave encouragement to small foundations in an age when public opinion favored the erection of larger independent monasteries.[58] He was even less specific in his requirements for the benefactor who wanted to erect an *eukterios oikos*. Balsamon held that Leo VI's law on monastic foundations did not apply in this case, so he only required the benefactor to advance the sum he had already agreed upon after consultation with the local bishop.[59] Balsamon admitted that in actual practice benefactors simply suited themselves, and rarely even informed the local bishops of their plans.

The canonist drew from his own experience as *chartophylax* to warn future incumbents of that office that they should not grant a patriarchal *stauropegion* (and thus an exemption from episcopal control) to a benefactor for a monastery outside Constantinople unless they had received an accounting of all the funds devoted to the proposed foundation.[60] This precaution would prevent benefactors from evading the strict property registration requirement of the Council of Constantinople (861) by appealing directly to the patriarch for a charter of foundation. The unscrupulous employment of patriarchal *stauropegia* by lay benefactors had already become a serious problem before Balsamon composed his canonical commentaries. Yet Balsamon did not sympathize with the reformist bishops and metropolitans who petitioned the emperors and patriarchs for a complete halt to the award of patriarchal *stauropegia*. In Balsamon's opinion, the awards were sanctioned by ancient unwritten custom which overrode the Chalcedonian prescription subordinating all monasteries to their diocesan bishops.[61]

Balsamon was not entirely unsympathetic to the need for striking a proper balance between the rights of the founder and those of the local bishop. Many founders of religious institutions in the twelfth century were deeply committed to reformist principles excluding all lay interests

---

[57] Balsamon, *Comm. ad C. Nicaen. II*, c. 17 (R&P 2.626).
[58] Compare with John II Comnenus' Pantokrator monastery in Constantinople, which was itself master of six smaller dependent monasteries.
[59] Balsamon, *Comm. ad C. Nicaen. II*, c. 17 (R&P 2.627.13–16).
[60] *Comm. ad C. Nicaen. II*, c. 17, lines 16–26.
[61] Balsamon, *Comm. ad Canones Apostolorum*, c. 13 (R&P 2.30.28–2.31.10).

in their foundations. They bitterly distrusted both the local hierarchy and the patriarchs. Considering the readiness with which the ecclesiastical hierarchy had handed over the foundations of their ancestors as personal favors during the century of the *charistike*, these benefactors had legitimate grounds for their distrust. These new founders preferred, therefore, to exempt their independent monasteries from both episcopal and patriarchal control. The extant founders' *typika* nearly always incorporate such an exemption or at least severely curtail the rights of the hierarchy.[62] Balsamon would have none of this, declaring that the hierarchy should pay no heed to such provisions because they were simply uncanonical.[63]

The reformist hierarchy of the twelfth century must have thought that the founders of the independent monasteries had unfairly associated them with their eleventh-century predecessors. While the benefactors had reacted to the *charistike* in a spirit of extreme distrust of the hierarchy, those bishops who considered themselves in the reformist tradition became bitterly hostile to any lay preemptions of their authority.[64] That the founders routinely appointed *hegoumenoi* and ephors without consulting them seemed particularly outrageous, a blatant disregard for their traditional rights.[65]

The reformers varied in the degree of their hostility to the founders' *typika*.[66] The extremists went so far as to declare all *typika* invalid, even when they contained nothing uncanonical. According to their way of thinking, all the privately founded monasteries in any given diocese properly belonged to the bishop as an episcopal right. This group of reformers therefore was antagonistic to the very idea of a private or independent monastery. A second group approved only of those *typika* drawn up in conformance with the canons and imperial laws. A third group accepted this premise, but required imperial ratification of each *typikon*. The majority of the extant *typika* would not have met the approval of any of these critics.

The reformers found their strongest support in the first canon of the Council of Constantinople (861), which enacted the property registration requirement and restored the local bishop to his traditional role as overseer of construction and as consecrator of the *hegoumenos*. In preparing his commentary on this canon, Balsamon diligently searched the *Basilika* to determine the legal basis for these episcopal rights. His dis-

---

[62] Janin, "Commende and Typica," 34–36.
[63] Balsamon, *Comm. ad C. Chalc.*, c. 8 (R&P 2.236.15–24).
[64] E.g., Theophylact of Ochrida, Demetrios of Bothrotos, and Demetrios of Domokos, whose reform activities are discussed below in this chapter.
[65] For founders' behavior in the late twelfth century, see Balsamon, *Comm. ad C. Const. I et II*, c. 1 (R&P 2.650.30–34); extant *typika*, e.g., those of Pakourianos and Irene Comnena, confirm the complaint of the anonymous reformer quoted here by Balsamon.
[66] Balsamon, *Comm. ad C. Const. I et II*, c. 1 (R&P 2.651.1–8).

covery of the mutilated extract of Zeno's original law on private foundations must have convinced him (if indeed he had any doubts) of a
founder's legal right to draw up a *typikon*. Balsamon did not believe,
however, that a founder's right to legislate for his foundation permitted
him to set provisions that were uncanonical or illegal. Moreover, Balsamon's research convinced him that the bishops did indeed have the right
to oversee these foundations, to expel the founders' nominees if they
proved unsuitable, and to name new appointees to replace those expelled.[67]

Balsamon thus aligned himself with the moderate reformers on the
issue of the legality of the founders' *typika*. He also rejected the claims
of the extremists by maintaining that a local bishop did not hold an
automatic right of ownership (a *kyriakon dikaion*) over a monastery
founded in his diocese.[68] He defined the bishop's rights (*dikaia episkopika*) as the traditional perquisites of inquiry (*anakrisis*) into spiritual
faults, oversight (*epiteresis*) of the foundation's administration, mention
(*anaphora*) of the prelate's name in the liturgy, and consecration (*sphragis*) of the *hegoumenos*. To assure anxious founders, Balsamon maintained that an independent monastery should continue to enjoy self-
government and not be liable to episcopal donation or lease to anyone
else.

Despite this understandable concern to reassure the benefactors whose
personal generosity made the foundations of the later empire possible,
Balsamon was no reactionary supporter of private benefactors. He
thought that the patriarch had a right to override a founder's *typikon* if
the existence of an institution was at stake. He therefore approved Patriarch Luke Chrysoberges' (1157–70) decision to appoint outsiders as *hegoumenoi* in monasteries with serious shortages of monks, even though
the *typika* of these foundations ordered *hegoumenoi* selected from
among the residents.[69] Balsamon also disapproved of burials within
churches, even though both traditional and more reform-minded patrons
had considered these interments as ordinary and fitting perquisites.[70] Not
surprisingly, he strongly condemned laymen who used their positions to
make clerical appointments.[71]

It was characteristic of Balsamon's thinking that he was hostile to the
very idea of anyone employing a religious institution for his personal

---

[67] *Comm. ad C. Const. I et II*, c. 1, R&P 2.651.8–27.
[68] *Comm. ad C. Const. I et II*, c. 1, R&P 2.651.27–652.6.
[69] Grumel, *Regestes* No. 1091 (n.d.), reported by Balsamon, *Comm. ad C. Const. I et II*, c. 4 (R&P 2.662).
[70] Balsamon, *Responsa* No. 41 (R&P 4.479).
[71] Balsamon, *Comm. ad Nomocanoni [Ps]-Photii*, ed. R&P 1 (Athens, 1852), Title 1, Ch. 24 (R&P 1.63.14–18).

financial advantage. Nevertheless, he could easily appreciate the distinction between a monastery that a bishop might erect out of diocesan funds and one paid for out of a bishop's personal fortune.[72] He knew, in other words, the difference between a diocesan institution erected in the bishop's official capacity and a proprietary institution founded by the bishop as a private individual. Although not antagonistic to the idea of private institutions, Balsamon was certainly not immune to the spirit of his age, which emphasized the consecrated status of an ecclesiastical foundation at the expense of the founder's claim to arbitrary employment of his property.[73]

It was in his attitude toward the traditional practices of the monasteries to sell shares of *siteresia* or appointments as lay brothers (*adelphata*) to non-resident laymen that Balsamon showed himself most sympathetic to the ideas of the extremist reformers. While some canonists defended the practices against charges of simony on the ground that the recipients did not receive tonsure, Balsamon refused to grant that this distinction made any difference.[74] This common thinking notwithstanding, Balsamon's basic disagreement with the more radical reformers is evident in his views on that touchstone of controversy, the *charistike*. Balsamon condemned John, his distant predecessor as patriarch of Antioch, for his opinion that the granting out of a monastery to private individuals was ipso facto impious and uncanonical.[75] Balsamon regarded the decree of Patriarch Sergius II as the definitive vindication of both the *charistike* and (more important for the hierarchy's own vested interests) its ecclesiastical counterpart, *epidosis*.

Balsamon's distance from the era of the worst abuses of the *charistike* is not in itself an adequate explanation for his defense of that embattled and now moribund institution. Some of his contemporaries evidently had a sufficiently vivid knowledge of the evils of lay domination under the *charistike* to lead them to oppose even the comparatively beneficent independent monasteries of their own day. Perhaps Balsamon, as a student of the historical development of canon law, recognized better than his contemporaries the requirements that had called the *charistike* into being and the beneficial role that it had played on occasion. Balsamon affirms that the granting out of monasteries under the *charistike* or *epidosis* still occurred on occasion in his own times.[76] Patriarch Luke Chrysoberges had declared in a synodal decision of 1169 that a *charistikarios* could

---

[72] Balsamon, *Comm. ad C. Const. I et II*, c. 7 (R&P 2.675.29–2.676.7).
[73] *Comm. ad C. Const. I et II*, c. 7, R&P 2.675.25–29.
[74] Balsamon, *Comm. ad C. Nicaen. II*, c. 19 (R&P 2.633).
[75] Balsamon, *Comm. ad C. Nicaen. II*, c. 13 (R&P 2.614.29–2.615.2).
[76] *Comm. ad C. Nicaen. II*, c. 13, R&P 2.614.24–29.

not give away a monastery to his daughter for her dowry.[77] Since this
patriarch, like his predecessor John IX Agapetus and Balsamon himself,
was apparently associated with the moderate reform tradition initiated
by Nicholas III Grammaticus, his decision typically did not condemn the
charistike outright. For the time being this faction was unwilling to join
the extremists in a campaign against all lay influence in the direction of
ecclesiastical foundations.

A more pressing concern in Balsamon's own times was the persistent
problem of the secularization of monasteries, this time under new circumstances. The ecclesiastical authorities were discovering many laymen
in possession of buildings that had once housed monastic communities.[78]
Balsamon blamed hostile invaders (actually the Seljuk Turks) for the de-
population of these monasteries. The current occupants were quick to
assert that the misfortunes of the monasteries were hardly their fault.
The forces of Turkish invaders that flowed over Anatolia in the late eleventh century had ebbed somewhat by the mid-twelfth century. Thanks to
the early crusaders and the efforts of the Comnenian emperors themselves, the empire had managed to recover a substantial portion of its
lost Anatolian dominions. Some eastern metropolitans had then been
successful in reclaiming their episcopal residences and some monasteries
from the laymen who had occupied these sites in the interim. The successful recovery of monasteries let out in *charistike* by the metropolitans
of Athens (1089) and Kyzikos (1116) could only have assisted the claims
of the Anatolian metropolitans in the latter half of the twelfth century.
Balsamon nevertheless thought that the generally recognized forty-year
statute of limitations on claims should apply, after which innocent laymen should enjoy uncontested ownership of these abandoned *episkopeia*
and monasteries.[79]

Balsamon's characteristic respect for private property rights is also evident in his pronouncements on clerical income. He mentions the case of
clergy who entered the service of laymen as children's tutors, calligra-
phers, and household secretaries.[80] Over the course of time, these clerics
might acquire great wealth, but Balsamon took the position that they
were not under obligation to share any part of it with their churches. We
are reminded again of the continued attractiveness of secular service, especially for educated members of the clergy. In contrast to Balsamon's

[77] Luke Chrysoberges, *Semeioma synodikon* (1169), ed. Jean Oudot, *Patriarchatus Constantinopolitani acta selecta* (Vatican City, 1941), Doc. No. 5, p. 34 = Grumel, *Regestes*
No. 1086.

[78] Balsamon, *Comm. ad C. Nicaen. II,* c. 13 (R&P 2.613.6–17).

[79] Balsamon, *Comm. ad C. Nicaen. II,* c. 13 (R&P 2.613.17–30).

[80] Balsamon, *Comm. ad C. Carth.* (419), c. 32 (R&P 3.389).

tolerant attitude, the conservative canonist and historian John Zonaras thought clerics should decline secular administrative positions as estate administrators (*pronoetai*) and accountants (*logaristai*).[81] Balsamon, however, was willing to allow even monks to serve as administrators not only of ecclesiastical property but also of private and government lands, provided that they did so under episcopal supervision.[82] According to his thinking, the emperor had even more of a right than the bishops to override existing canonical prohibitions in order to allow monks to assume government positions.

On this issue Balsamon was at odds with Patriarch Luke Chrysoberges' decree of 1157 which condemned the heavy involvement of certain members of the secular clergy in secular affairs.[83] According to the patriarch, clerics illegally held positions as *kouratores* and *pronoetai* in the households and on the estates of lay magnates. Other clerics collected taxes for the state, kept public records, and served in other government offices. Luke Chrysoberges tried to ban all such employment in the future, but the Byzantine clergy had long disregarded the canons, as the evidence from sixth-century Egypt makes clear. Even the canonists of the church clearly were not of one mind in opposing outside employment for clerics, which economic pressures must have made both attractive and necessary.

Balsamon's tolerance of ecclesiastical employment in lay and governmental service indicates that he appreciated the difficulties clerics might face in securing a livelihood solely from ecclesiastical sources. Given the Byzantine church's traditional commitment to the inalienability of ecclesiastical property and the new scruples against individual profiteering from religious foundations, it is no wonder that clerics and monks turned to the magnates and the state for supplementary employment.

The exaction of fees for the conferral of the sacraments and attempts to secure multiple clerical appointments were two other ways that enterprising clerics of the twelfth century eased their financial difficulties. The institutional church had fought for centuries to keep the distribution of the sacraments, particularly clerical ordination, free from mandatory fees. Now, late in Byzantine history, Balsamon agreed to permit clergymen to accept voluntary "stole fees" upon conferral of baptism, communion, and ordination.[84] In so doing, Balsamon was recognizing the

[81] John Zonaras, *Comm. ad C. Nicaen. II*, c. 10 (R&P 2.588).

[82] Balsamon, *Comm. ad C. Chalc.*, c. 4 (R&P 2.228–29).

[83] Luke Chrysoberges, *Semeioma* (1157) (R&P 3.345–49, esp. 346.28–347.4) = Grumel, *Regestes* No. 1048; cf. Herman, "Professioni vietate," 37–38.

[84] Balsamon, *Responsa* No. 31 (R&P 4.471–73); for details on these fees, see Herman, "Niederklerus," 429–31.

established but unofficial custom of collecting *eulogiai*, "sacramental gifts," though he warned against demands for very valuable gifts that might be construed as simony.

Balsamon was much more intolerant of clerical pluralism. This was another problem that had persisted through the centuries in the Byzantine church, at least since the reign of Heraclius. Thanks to the tax immunities of Manuel Comnenus, pluralism was no longer the bane of churches in the countryside where there was now a surplus of clergy. The traditional pattern had now reversed itself, and in the late twelfth century there was a shortage of clerics in Constantinople.[85] Balsamon attributed this to the great number of churches in the capital and the financial distress they suffered as a result of inadequate endowments. He nevertheless did not consider these circumstances critical enough to warrant dispensation from the canonical legislation against pluralism. His own opinion did not find general acceptance, for, as he himself admitted, the clergy generally ignored the prohibition with impunity.

Balsamon shared the general opinion of the Byzantine church that laymen should not benefit by any alienations of church properties. Accordingly, he ruled that not only the *autourgion* (protected earlier by legislation of the Second Council of Nicaea and of Patriarch Alexius Studites), but all properties yielding an income (the *euprosoda*) should be withheld for the support of the endowed institution and not subject to lay exploitation through rental or outright donation.[86]

In summary, then, it seems fair to say that Balsamon tried to steer a middle course between the extreme reformers, who demanded that the church purge itself of all lay influences, and the traditionalists, who were reluctant to do anything that might jeopardize the continuance of the considerable benefits of private philanthropy. Balsamon's attempts to strike balances on the issues give the impression of a skilled canonist not easily led into one-sided support of any position. Balsamon distinguished public from private foundations, but emphasized the consecrated status of all ecclesiastical institutions. He held that the founders' *typika* were legal and canonical in concept, but allowed the patriarch to override their provisions in critical cases. Moreover, he thought that a founder's *typikon* could not exempt a foundation from episcopal control. He allowed the celebration of the liturgy and the administration of baptism in the chapels of private houses, but he deplored the independence of founders in erecting chapels without episcopal consent. He took a lenient position on minimum requirements for endowing private foundations, yet

[85] Balsamon, *Comm. ad C. Nicaen. II*, c. 15 (R&P 2.261.16–27).
[86] Balsamon, *Comm. ad C. Nicaen. II*, c. 12 (R&P 2.594–95).

he took a very hard line against any layman's gaining a personal profit from these benefactions.

Balsamon would not tolerate the sale of ordinations, clerical appointments, shares of *siteresia*, or lay brotherhoodships (*adelphata*). Nevertheless, he supported the *charistike* in principle, although he did deny bishops the right to subordinate the new independent monasteries to laymen under this program. He favored episcopal rights of oversight in private foundations, but he denied the bishops any claim to property rights in these institutions. He was very strict on prohibiting the alienation of church property, yet he favored a statute of limitations on episcopal efforts to reclaim abandoned monasteries. He looked favorably upon clerics in state and private employment, considering the income they earned to be their own. He even tolerated the collection of modest "stole fees." Yet he abhorred clerical pluralism.

In evaluating Balsamon's work, it is important to realize that the legal and canonical tradition from which he drew his frequently ambiguous conclusions was hardly a coherent and consistent unity. Some elements of Justinian's regulatory legislation had managed to survive Leo VI's revisions and found inclusion in the *Basilika*. Yet the steady undermining of Justinian's regulations, particularly with respect to the subordination of all ecclesiastical foundations to local bishops, had also left its impact on the sources that Balsamon surveyed. The subsequent efforts of the various reformers to curtail or surpress the *charistike* resulted in the creation of a new body of canonical precedent, analogous to, but largely independent of, Justinian's original legislation. The demise of the *charistike* itself left the church divided on what role, if any, laymen should continue to play in the foundation and direction of religious institutions.

Certain problems, such as institutional secularization, pluralism, clerical employment in the service of the magnates and the state, and lay exploitation of ecclesiastical property, had plagued scrupulous authorities within the church for centuries. Despite repeated condemnations, these problems periodically reemerged, often in new guises or under altered circumstances, to trouble a new generation of concerned authorities. By the late twelfth century, canonists must have realized that neither the state nor the church could eradicate these problems entirely. Therefore, a certain amount of compromise and toleration seemed to be in order.

The political circumstances of the empire at any given time naturally had an important effect on the policies that the government set for private religious foundations. Even more than the policies of the church, the legislation introduced by the emperors lacked a consistent approach to the problems spawned by the existence of these foundations. It is no wonder, then, given this diverse heritage, that Theodore Balsamon found it difficult to determine a consensus of historical opinion on the important problems of his day. His achievement is nonetheless remarkable in summarizing this heritage so well and in offering cogent resolutions to its many contradictions.

PRIVATE BENEFACTORS AND STAUROPEGIAL FOUNDATIONS

Increasingly, benefactors' exploitation of patriarchal *stauropegia* to escape the authority of local bishops became a troubling issue for the institutional church. Ever since Theodore of Sykeon's appeal to Emperor Maurice for exemption for his monasteries from episcopal control, the patriarchal *stauropegion* was liable to be employed for enabling benefactors to circumvent Justinian's regulatory legislation, based as it was on the vigilance of the bishops. The willingness of patriarchs like Polyeuctus (956–970) to lend a sympathetic ear to requests by influential benefactors for grants of *stauropegia* also undercut the financial perquisites of their subordinate bishops. Of course it is usually not possible to determine whether it was the desire to escape the avariciousness of the local hierarchy or the unscrupulousness of the lay benefactors themselves that lay behind these requests for patriarchal *stauropegia*.

Considerations of distance naturally made patriarchal oversight less effective than that of a nearby bishop, and alert benefactors must have realized the weakness of the patriarchate in this respect. Indeed, as we have seen, the patriarch's traditional rights of visitation and spiritual correction in all the institutions located within his vast jursisdiction had suffered such severe erosion that by the end of the eleventh century he was unable to insist on these rights even in those institutions nominally under his direct control (that is, those with patriarchal *stauropegia*). It should hardly be surprising, therefore, that the traditional private benefactors of the twelfth century preferred to seek patriarchal charters for their foundations over those of the reformist episcopal hierarchy. The bishops who so bitterly opposed the new independent monasteries would not have been likely to allow a free hand to private patrons to direct their foundations as they pleased.

As early as Nicholas Grammaticus' reformist patriarchate, Theophylact, archbishop of Ochrida, had raised protests against the use of patriarchal *stauropegia*. The archbishop had tried to prevent an individual from erecting a monastery within his jurisdiction, but when the benefactor succeeded in obtaining a patriarchal *stauropegion*, he was able to proceed with construction in defiance of Theophylact's wishes.[87] The archbishop filed a formal protest with Peter, the patriarchal *chartophylax*, but the outcome of the complaint is unknown.[88]

Michael III (1170–78) was the first patriarch to deal with the abuse of *stauropegia*. Constantine Spanopoulos, bishop of Pyrgion, brought a complaint to this patriarch in 1176 in which he claimed that the benefactors who had rebuilt churches in his diocese had obtained patriarchal *stauropegia* for them under false pretexts.[89] Some bold benefactors expected patriarchal *stauropegia* as their just dues for undertaking the reconstruction of these churches. If the patriarch recognized these *stauropegia* as valid charters of foundation, the bishop would stand to lose his traditional rights over these institutions. Whereas Theophylact of Ochrida had confronted the establishment of new patriachal monasteries over which he had no control, Constantine faced an actual diminution of his present authority in institutions restored by these benefactors. Michael III chose to side with Constantine against the interests of his own office in this case.

Twelfth-century benefactors accustomed to ignoring the local bishops when they undertook the construction of new churches evidently saw no reason to consult them when they were restoring older foundations. The local hierarchy, for its part, still fought to bestow their own *stauropegia*, occasionally with success.[90] Clearly the old attitude of benefactors who considered that what they chose to do with their religious foundations was their own business still prevailed in many areas of the empire untouched by the spirit of the reform movement. Even the bishops were not immune from backsliding into the old ways of thinking, for Balsamon had to warn that a bishop who owned a monastery in another diocese in the capacity of a private benefactor should not usurp the traditional rights of that institution's diocesan bishop.[91]

The great independent monasteries, richly endowed with vast lands by their generous founders, also came to play a significant role in the reduction of the spiritual jurisdiction of the local hierarchy. Mindful of the

[87] Theophylact of Ochrida, *Epistola* 27 (*PG* 126, cols. 416D–417A), cf. Herman, "Abgabenwesen," 449, and Paul Gautier, "Le chartophylax Nicéphore: Oeuvre canonique et notice biographique," *REB* 27 (1969), 159–95, esp. 164; the addressee of this letter was Michael, a successor to Leo as metropolitan of Chalcedon.

[88] This offical was present at the Council of Blachernai (1094), *Acta* (*PG* 127, col. 973D).

[89] Grumel, *Regestes* No. 1131 (April 1176), quoted by Chomatianos, *De monasteriis et stauropegiis*, ed. J. B. Pitra, *Analecta sacra et classica spicilegio Solesmensi parata*, Vol. 7 (Paris-Rome, 1891), 348, 349.

[90] See the discussion below in this chapter and V. Laurent, "Charisticariat et commende à Byzance: Deux fondations patriarcales en Epire aux XIIe et XIIIe siècles," *REB* 12 (1954), 100–113, esp. 101, a *stauropegion* granted to Nikephoros Choiriosphaktes during the reign of Manuel Comnenus.

[91] Balsamon, *Comm. ad C. Const. I et II*, c. 7 (R&P 2.675.29–676.7).

spiritual needs of the peasant cultivators resident on their endowed properties, the monks undertook ambitious programs of rebuilding ruined *eukterioi oikoi* located on these lands. They also took over the administration of functioning oratories and erected new ones as well wherever they were needed. In this way the independent monasteries were becoming the successors to the tasks that the hierarchy had formerly imposed upon the *charistikarioi* or looked to private benefactors to perform.

In the 1180s before he became patriarch, George II Xiphilinus (1191–98) heard many bishops complain that the monasteries were denying them their traditional episcopal rights in the churches that these institutions were erecting on their properties.[92] The monasteries that held patriarchal *stauropegia* justified their actions by claiming that their own exemption from episcopal control extended to their dependencies as proprietary churches.

Soon after he became patriarch, George II issued a decree on November 27, 1191, supporting the bishops. He reserved for them the perquisites of *anaphora* in the liturgy, the ordination of clergy, and the receipt of the *kanonikon*, an ecclesiastical tax that accrued to the grantor of an institution's *stauropegion*.[93] Before too long, George II was forced to amend this sweeping decree as unforeseen complexities became apparent. A second decree of January 8, 1192, made an exception for those churches that the monasteries had recently acquired but that had been patriarchal foundations from their origins.[94] The patriarch warned that this exception from the regulation of his earlier decree was not to serve as a pretext for extending exemption from episcopal control to all other churches that the monasteries were currently rebuilding on their properties. These and all future churches would be subject to the spiritual direction of the local bishops, which implies that the patriarchate would henceforth refrain from issuing new *stauropegia* for monastic proprietary churches.

The spirit of these regulations continued to guide George II when, in a decision of February 24, 1197, he upheld the right of Michael, bishop of Limne, to collect the *kanonikon* from a priest in a monastic proprietary church.[95] This was a difficult discipline for the patriarch, since he stood to benefit financially through receipt of the *kanonikon* from any expansion in the number of institutions holding patriarchal *stauropegia*. Not all patriarchal officials shared George II's scruples. Theodore Balsamon,

---

[92] See Grumel, *Regestes*, p. 182.

[93] Grumel, *Regestes* No. 1179 = text quoted in Oudot, *Acta selecta*, No. 8, Sect. 2, p. 54; cf. Herman, "Abgabenwesen," 450.

[94] George II, *Synodike apophasis* (1192), ed. Oudot, *Acta selecta*, No. 8, Sections 1–6, pp. 54–58 = Grumel, *Regestes* No. 1180; cf. Herman, "Abgabenwesen," 451.

[95] George II, *Peri enoriakon dikaion* (1197) (R&P 5.101–102) = Grumel, *Regestes* No. 1185; cf. Herman, "Abgabenwesen," 451.

himself a patriarchal *chartophylax* in the 1180s, saw nothing inherently wrong with the granting of these *stauropegia*, provided the petitioner followed established procedures designed to protect the endowments of the foundations. Here again was an issue on which the reformist bishops differed with the moderates in the patriarchal administration. Those bishops who demanded a complete halt to the issuance of patriarchal *stauropegia* had the advantage of having the unanimous backing of canonical precedent on their side.[96] Balsamon could not produce a single canonical citation to oppose them and weakly argued that the force of long-established custom ought to prevail over previous ecclesiastical legislation.

The calamity of the conquest of Constantinople by the crusaders in 1204 and their establishment of the Latin Empire had an important effect on this controversy. Political events increased the importance of the great monasteries in the remaining areas under the control of the Greek successor states of Epirus and Nicaea by weakening the central authority of the patriarchate. The incumbents of the new patriarchal line at Nicaea chose not to maintain George II's stand against the monasteries and sometimes even helped to undermine it in rivalry with the Epirot archbishop of Ochrida.

Demetrios Chomatianos, an eminent canonist and archbishop of Ochrida (from 1217), judged an important case concerning *stauropegia* which Demetrios, bishop of Bothrotos, brought against the monastery of Choteachobou. This monastery, which itself held a patriarchal *stauropegion*, encouraged the Vlachs resident on one of its properties to forsake their village church and attend services in the monastery's own chapel instead.[97] Demetrios of Bothrotos complained that his clerical appointees to the village church had not been able to exercise their proper authority over the parishioners. The bishop based his case on two points: namely, that all laymen ought to be subject to the spiritual authority of their bishop, and that it was inappropriate in any case to admit lay women into a monastery's chapel for services. The *proestos* of the monastery based his case on the property rights that his institution had over the village in which the parish was located. He claimed that the Vlachs had attended services in the monastery for fifteen years prior to the bishop of Bothrotos' complaint.

This was not the only difficulty that Demetrios of Bothrotos faced. In the village of Tzermenikon, also under the overlordship of the monastery of Choteachobou, one of his distant predecessors had erected a church

---

[96] E.g., *C. Chalc.*, c. 2, 8, 17 (as discussed above in Chapter 2).

[97] Demetrios Chomatianos, *De monasteriis*, ed. Pitra, 339–43; cf. Herman, "Niederklerus," 409.

dedicated to St. Nicholas with his own episcopal *stauropegion*.[98] A certain neighboring magnate, Taronas, who had designs on the area, had recently erected an entirely new church very near the old episcopal foundation. Taronas' church also bore the name of St. Nicholas, and he managed to obtain a patriarchal *stauropegion* for it. The bishop thought that Taronas had uncanonically sought to undermine his rights in the earlier episcopal foundation.

Demetrios Chomatianos sided with the bishop of Bothrotos on all points. He cited Patriarch Michael III's ruling of 1176 and George II Xiphilinus' guidelines as precedents for his verdict. Chomatianos was not likely to have upheld patriarchal *stauropegia* in any case, since he was a determined opponent of Michael Sarantenus (1217–22), Patriarch of Nicaea and self-proclaimed successor to the ecumenical patriarchs of Constantinople.[99] Indeed, it seems that the patriarchs of Nicaea did not hesitate to intervene in Epirus to grant their *stauropegia*, for we find Patriarch Germanus II (1222–40) issuing an extant *stauropegion* in 1238 to a certain *hegoumenos* Bartholomew for a church he had rebuilt in the vicinity of Nicopolis.[100]

In time even Nicaea came to realize the implications of irresponsible employment of patriarchal *stauropegia*. Patriarch Manuel II (1243–54) was forced to confront the problem in the course of hearing an appeal by Demetrios, bishop of Domokos (a titular see under the metropolitan of Larissa).[101] The bishop had quarreled with some private patrons of a monastery of St. Demetrios near the town of Pokobikon. Manuel's account of the incident does not indicate the reasons for the conflict, but it seems that these patrons held an old-fashioned view of their founders' rights that included free disposal of the monastery's assets. Demetrios, acting in the best reformist tradition, obstructed their plans. Not to be outdone, the enterprising patrons set about erecting an entirely new monastery with a patriarchal *stauropegion* in order to escape the meddlesome bishop's authority. When they attempted to transfer the properties that their ancestors had consecrated for the support of the first monastery so that they could provide an endowment for the new foundation, Demetrios took his case to the patriarch.

Patriarch Manuel II decided for the bishop of Domokos and delivered a stinging rebuke to the unscrupulous patrons: "Our humility wishes to cut off at the root such a miscalculated intention as entirely forbidden by

---

[98] *De monasteriis*, 343–44.

[99] See Donald Nicol, "Ecclesiastical Relations between the Despotate of Epirus and the Kingdom of Nicaea in the Years 1215–1239," *Byzantion* 22 (1952), 207–28.

[100] Ed. Laurent, "Deux fondations," 108.

[101] Manuel II, *Peri ktetorikou dikaiou* (1250) (R&P 5.119–20, esp. 119.1–16) = V. Laurent, *Les regestes des actes du patriarcat de Constantinople*, Vol. 1: *Les actes des patriarches* (Paris, 1971), No. 1314; cf. Herman, "Ricerche," 342.

the holy canons. It is ordained by this present document that the attached properties and possessions of whatever sort are to remain for all time inseparably [joined] to the episcopal monastery of St. Demetrios. These are to be managed and directed spiritually by the bishop of Domokos, for it is not possible for either the founders (*dometores*) or anyone else to tear off a possession from an episcopal monastery and subject it to a patriarchal monastery or oratory (*eukterios naos*)." [102]

Clearly the traditional disposition of patrons to regard their ecclesiastical foundations as their personal property, subject to free and arbitrary disposal, had proven remarkably persistent. Yet the Byzantine reformers, though they did not achieve the stunning successes of their contemporaries of the Gregorian reform movement in the medieval West, did manage to reverse arbitrary disposals of consecrated property whenever a case of this sort came to trial.

Even though canonical precedent was on the side of the reformers, the ability of the bishops to exercise their episcopal rights of oversight and correction had become dependent upon obliging the institutions founded in their dioceses to accept episcopal *stauropegia*. When this had occurred, the bishops could then build a very strong case when their opponents sought to disregard or circumvent these charters of foundation. Yet wherever patrons could make a successful appeal to the patriarch for his *stauropegion*, a local bishop could not hope to exercise even an effective oversight, much less actual overlordship of the foundations located in his diocese.

Here the matter stood, for the patriarchs were unwilling to abandon their right to grant *stauropegia*, despite the clear record of its abuse. In the same decision in which he announced his support of Demetrios of Domokos, Patriarch Manuel II specifically allowed further petitions for patriarchal charters for monasteries or oratories, provided the founders agreed to make a perpetual and irrevocable donation of property to support their foundations. [103] As in the case of the challenge to the *charistike*, the patriarchate desired to avoid a sweeping condemnation of powerful lay benefactors in the church, preferring instead to correct individual abuses as concerned bishops brought these cases to court. Yet while the *charistike* eventually disappeared under the attack of the reformers, patriarchal *stauropegia* continued to exist in the Byzantine church. One must assume that the patriarchate's vested financial interest in *stauropegia* played an important part in accounting for this difference.

---

[102] *Peri ktetorikou dikaiou*, R&P 5.119.16–25.
[103] *Peri ktetorikou dikaiou*, lines 25–31; cf. Laurent, *Regestes* No. 1310.

CHAPTER NINE

Private Religious Foundations in the Last Centuries of the Byzantine Empire

THE private religious foundations of Western medieval christendom had common roots with those of Byzantium in the later Roman Empire. As they did in Byzantium, these western foundations dominated the ecclesiastical landscape until the twelfth century, when the Gregorian reform movement signaled their gradual eclipse.[1] Pope Alexander III (1159–81) and his distinguished canonists had already begun the long process of attenuating the formerly absolute authority of the private patrons of the western churches into a diluted "patron's right" when the Latin crusaders captured Constantinople in 1204. The traditional Byzantine private religious foundations, which Westerners would certainly have found familiar and unobjectionable two centuries earlier, now could hardly serve as the basis for the new Latin Empire of Constantinople's ecclesiastical organization.

IMPACT OF THE LATIN CONQUEST ON THE PRIVATE RELIGIOUS FOUNDATIONS OF BYZANTIUM

The satisfaction of the greed of the various contingents of the crusader army was the prime consideration in the immediate dispersal of the wealth of the churches and monasteries of Constantinople. Even before their conquest of the city, the Venetians and the other crusaders had agreed in March 1204 to include ecclesiastical property as part of the victors' booty.[2] The treaty excepted only so much property as would allow the clergy of these institutions an honorable living. When the cru-

---

[1] For private religious foundations in Western Europe, see Hans Erich Feine, *Kirchliche Rechtsgeschichte*, 129ff, and Franz Felten, *Äbte und Laienäbte im Frankenreich* (Stuttgart, 1980).
[2] Ed. G. L. F. Tafel and G. M. Thomas, *Urkunden zur alteren Handels- und Staatsgeschichte der Republik Venedig* (Vienna, 1856), Vol. 1, p. 447; for a study of the problems encountered in creating an economic base of support for the Latin patriarchate and its churches, see Robert Lee Wolff, "Politics in the Latin Patriarchate of Constantinople, 1204–1261," *DOP* 8 (1954), 225–94, esp. 255–74.

sader army took the city a month later, they carried out the terms of their agreement promptly, and so most ecclesiastical property fell prey to secularization.

The crusaders, like the innovators of the *charistike* over two centuries earlier, evidently considered that the churches and monasteries had more than sufficient revenues which could easily stand diversion for other purposes without endangering the existence of the institutions themselves. If there had been some truth to this assumption at the beginning of the eleventh century, it had ceased to have much validity by 1204. Less than a decade earlier Balsamon had decried the pluralism all too common in Constantinople on account of the poverty of its churches. The *charistike* had seriously depleted the endowments of many of the older ecclesiastical institutions, though several rich independent foundations had been erected in the course of the twelfth century and some others had been restored and reendowed. Still, it is likely that only a few of the foundations damaged by the *charistike* had been able to regain adequate landed endowments as the monastery of St. Mamas had managed to do in the 1140s.

It is no wonder, then, that the crusaders' arrangements for the support of the capital's religious institutions proved unsatisfactory. Pope Innocent III (1198–1216) pressed for complete restitution of the lost properties, but that policy was politically impossible for the new Latin emperors to carry out. A long process of negotiation began instead, which led to an agreement in 1219 for an assessment of one-eleventh of the properties of the empire to reconstitute a landed endowment for the churches of the Latin patriarchate of Constantinople.[3] Thus, the cathedral church of Hagia Sophia and the rest of the foundations that the Latins used during their occupation of Constantinople (including at least twenty churches and fourteen monasteries) received an entirely new basis of support.[4]

Although the story of the negotiating process that led to this agreement, and a similar one reached at the Parlement of Ravennika in 1210 for the Kingdom of Thessalonica, is not important for the history of private religious foundations in Byzantium, the Latin sources do shed some light on the fate of these institutions in the Latin Empire.[5] The text of the preliminary agreement of March 17, 1206, reveals that the Latins subordinated all monasteries, both within and without the city, directly to the ecclesiastical hierarchy.[6] Whoever held jurisdiction over a monas-

---

[3] For details, see Wolff, "Politics," 256–74.

[4] For the foundations that operated under Latin rule, see R. Janin, "Les sanctuaires de Byzance sous la domination latine (1204–1261)," *Etudes byzantines* 2 (1944), 134–84, esp. 135.

[5] For the Ravennika agreement, see Wolff, "Politics," 259–61.

[6] Quoted in Pope Innocent III's confirmation of August 5, 1206 (ed. Tafel and Thomas, *Urkunden*, Vol. 2, p. 33, lines 3–4); cf. Wolff, "Politics," 257.

tery, be he the patriarch or the local bishop, had to give his consent before the government could secularize it to serve as a fortification. It
seems, then, that the Latins swept aside the complicated Byzantine system of ownership of ecclesiastical institutions. All monasteries, including
private and independent ones, became diocesan institutions.

In the final agreement of 1219, Emperor Robert (1219–28) and his
vassals declared all churches, clerics, and religious persons, whether
Greek or Latin, to be free from all lay jurisdiction, along with their families and household servants.[7] Only laymen resident in the monasteries
of Constantinople (perhaps in the capacity of *esomonitai*, as in Byzantine
times) could not employ this general exemption to escape their tax obligations. According to the language of the agreement, all monasteries and
churches, whether standing or ruined, were to be under the control of
the ecclesiastical hierarchy, "no matter to whom they belonged in the
past." The document commanded all who presently possessed a monastery or monastic property to return it to the prelates of the church, unless
they held it (probably as a fief) by award from the late emperors Baldwin
(1204–5) or Henry (1205–16). Robert and his vassals also promised to
try to restore properties taken from the churches of Constantinople at
the fall of the city in 1204.

In the Ravennika agreement of 1210, the Latins of the Kingdom of
Thessalonica likewise promised to restore all secularized ecclesiastical
property to the patriarch of Constantinople.[8] This served as a pattern for
the settlement that Pope Honorius III (1216–27) imposed on the Frank-
ish principalities of Achaea and Athens in 1223. All of these agreements
also made provision for such matters as the support of cathedral clergy,
tax exemptions for the rural clergy, and regulations for the payment of
the Latin tithe.[9]

Thanks to hard negotiating, Innocent III and his successor Honorius
III had obliged Emperor Robert and his fellow Latin rulers to establish
an ecclesiastical organization based on the principles of the Gregorian
reform. This meant that these rulers had to abandon the old Byzantine
system and the plethora of opportunities it would have offered for re-
warding faithful vassals and recruiting new supporters among the indig-
enous Greek aristocracy. Earlier on, the Latin emperors Baldwin and
Henry had exploited opportunities for patronage by awarding some
monasteries and monastic properties to their vassals. These remained
undisturbed, for Robert realized that he could not dare to upset arrange-

[7] Quoted in Pope Honorius III's confirmation of March 17, 1222 (ed. Wolff, "Politics,"
298–301, esp. 299).
[8] Wolff, "Politics," 270.
[9] Wolff, "Politics," 260–61.

ments that were critical to the military security of the empire.[10] He agreed, however, not to generalize the award of ecclesiastical institutions as the Byzantine emperors had done under the *charistike*.

Emperor Robert also exceeded the piety and generosity of his Byzantine predecessors by promising to supplement the endowments of all monasteries and churches whose present properties were worth less than 100 *hyperpera*.[11] This measure included even those foundations that were now no more than ruins. No Byzantine emperor, even those most concerned with the deteriorated condition of ecclesiastical foundations, had ever committed public funds in this way to such a substantial undertaking.

In effect, Emperor Robert's program constituted a mortgaging of the Latin Empire of Constantinople in the interests of the church. Its execution required the dispossession of both Latin and Greek magnates who, according to a report of Cardinal John Colonna, legate of Pope Honorius III, still retained ecclesiastical property as of August 1218.[12] Grants made earlier by the emperors Baldwin and Henry were specifically exempted, however. By dispossessing the proprietors of all the other ecclesiastical foundations (at least above the parish level), the Latin rulers forsook one of the traditional supports of the state and abandoned all hope of private philanthropic aid for the church.

On July 25, 1261, the forces of the Greek successor state of Nicaea recaptured Constantinople from the Latins. The Nicaean ruler, Michael VIII (1259–82), founded the Palaeologan dynasty, Byzantium's last ruling house, which held sway over a rapidly diminishing remnant of the old empire until 1453. The last two hundred years of the restored empire's existence saw Byzantium reduced to little more than a Balkan state with the intoxicating memory of former greatness. Yet, for the history of private religious foundations, this period does have real importance, since the better-preserved patriarchal archives and monastic cartularies of this era illustrate many of the traditional practices of earlier centuries.[13] This period also saw the ultimate triumph of the opinions of the Chalcedonian reformers in their hostility to all lay exploitation of ecclesiastical property.

---

[10] Wolff, "Politics," 270.

[11] Agreement of 1219 quoted in Pope Honorius III's confirmation of 1222 (ed. Wolff, "Politics," 299, lines 33–37); cf. Wolff, "Politics," 269.

[12] Robert Lee Wolff, "The Organization of the Latin Patriarchate of Constantinople, 1204–1261: Social and Administrative Consequences of the Latin Conquest," *Traditio* 6 (1948), 33–60, esp. 42.

[13] For the role of the church and monastic foundations in particular in the last centuries of the empire, see Anthony Bryer, "The Late Byzantine Monastery in Town and Countryside," *SCH* 16 (1979), 219–41, Donald Nicol, *Church and Society in the Last Centuries of*

Before 1261 the ecclesiastical institutions of Michael VIII's realm had fared quite differently, depending on whether they had been under Latin or Greek rule. In the empires of Nicaea and Thessalonica, there was a continuous development from late Comnenian times of religious institutions and their attendant problems. The growth of independent monasteries, the abuse of patriarchal *stauropegia*, the stubbornness of traditional lay patrons, and the time-honored reliance on private philanthropy that characterized the thirteenth century were all developments observable long before the Latin conquest of 1204 destroyed the empire. For those institutions under Latin rule from 1204 to 1261, the period was one of substantial change. Some monastic congregations remained in their houses, at least for a time, but in other cases Latin communities of Benedictines, Cistercians, and Franciscans displaced them.[14] Naturally, the exclusion of laymen from the management of ecclesiastical institutions and the loss of autonomy for the independent foundations had equally drastic effects on these churches and monasteries.

Unfortunately it is rarely possible to determine the impact of the Latin occupation in the case of individual churches or dioceses. In the diocese of Domokos on the Greek mainland, the turbulent times immediately following the Latin conquest left the cathedral church without sufficient resources to support its bishop. In 1208 Innocent III had to allow the combination of this bishopric with that of Calidonia. By 1210 the diocese could barely support three clerics in the cathedral chapter.[15] As we have seen, the new Greek bishop installed after the Byzantine reconquest found that private benefactors were willing to reopen their purses, but would not countenance episcopal interference with their foundations. In the capital, Michael VIII found it necessary to meet the basic needs of the patriarch and the bishops with funds from the imperial treasury.[16] Doubtless similar problems occurred elsewhere as the government and the ecclesiastical hierarchy struggled to reorganize the church on a new financial basis.

Byzantium (Cambridge, 1979), and Nicolas Oikonomidès, "Monastères et les moines lors de la conquête ottomane," *Südost-Forschungen* 35 (1976), 1–10. For Michael VIII's reign, see Deno Geanakoplos, *The Emperor Michael Palaeologus and the West* (Cambridge, Mass., 1959).

[14] Janin, "Sanctuaires," 134–38; Elizabeth R. Brown, "The Cistercians in the Latin Empire of Constantinople and Greece, 1204–1276," *Traditio* 16 (1958), 63–120; Robert Lee Wolff, "The Latin Empire of Constantinople and the Franciscans," *Traditio* 2 (1944), 213–37.

[15] Wolff, "Organization," 44–45.

[16] Pachymeres, *De Michaele Palaeologo* Ch. 26, ed. I. Bekker, *CSHB* (Bonn, 1835), Vol. 1, p. 73; cf. Herman, "Niederklerus," 385–86.

RENOVATION AND MANAGEMENT OF ECCLESIASTICAL
FOUNDATIONS DURING THE PALAEOLOGAN DYNASTY

Under the Palaeologi, the restoration and financial support of existing ecclesiastical institutions naturally had to take precedence over the erection of new foundations. Nevertheless, a few new churches and monasteries came into existence. Michael VIII himself took the lead with the construction of a monastery dedicated to his namesake St. Michael on Mount Auxentios near Chalcedon. This institution, which dates from 1280, had an independent and self-governing organization, a revival of the form popularized by the reformist benefactors and retained now to the end of the empire.[17] The emperor's wife, Theodora, built a new church dedicated to St. John the Baptist and a *xenon* next to the ancient church and monastery of Constantine Lips.[18] Sometime in the first half of the fourteenth century, Michael's niece Theodora erected another new monastery dedicated to the Theotokos tes Bebaias Elpidos.[19] This was also an independent foundation despite its origin as an imperial benefaction. The princess designated her son as hereditary ephor in this foundation while severely restricting the patriarch to his minimal canonical rights.[20]

The patriarchate itself had never played an important part in the erection of ecclesiastical foundations, and the patriarchs of the Palaeologan age were no exceptions to this rule. Even their awards of patriarchal *stauropegia* seem to have been less frequent and more responsible than in the twelfth and thirteenth centuries.[21] They were not so uncommon, however, so as to put an end to all abuses. The enterprising monks of one independent monastery in Epirus, for instance, alleged the existence of a patriarchal *stauropegion* for a church in order to avoid payment of *kanonikon* to the bishop of Caesaropolis for this institution which they

[17] Janin, *Géographie*, Vol. 2, p. 48; Michael VIII Palaeologus, *Typikon tes basilikes mones tou archistrategou Michael*, ed. A. Dmitrievsky, *Typika*, 769–94, with independent status affirmed at 773.

[18] Janin, *Géographie*, Vol. 3, pp. 307–10; Theodora Palaeologina, *Typikon tes mones tou Libos*, ed. H. Delehaye, *Deux typica byzantins de l'époque des Paléologues* (Brussels, 1921), 106–36, with independent status affirmed at 106–7.

[19] Janin, *Géographie*, Vol. 3, pp. 158–60; Theodora Palaeologina, *Typikon tes mones tes Theotokou tes Bebaias Elpidos*, ed. Delehaye, *Deux typica*, pp. 18–105, with independent status affirmed at 27–29; Theodore Macridy, Cyril Mango, et al., "The Monastery of Lips (Fenari Isa Camii) at Istanbul," *DOP* 18 (1964), 249–315.

[20] Theodora Palaeologina, *Typikon tes Bebaias Elpidos* Ch. 16 (ed. Delehaye, p. 29).

[21] For the use of patriarchal *stauropegia* in the fourteenth century, see *Actes de Zographou* No. 39 (1357) (discussed immediately below), and No. 46 (1372); *Actes de Dionysiou* No. 16 (1389), ed. Nicolas Oikonomidès (*Archives de l'Athos*, Vol. 4), (Paris, 1968); Patriarch Philotheus, *Acta patriarchatus* No. 201 (1365) (MM 1.455–56) = J. Darrouzès, *Les regestes des actes du patriarcat de Constantinople*, Vol. 1: *Les actes des patriarches* (Paris, 1977–79), No. 2477.

had actually received as an episcopal grant in *epidosis*.[22] The episcopal role in the erection of new foundations likewise appears to have been minimal in Palaeologan times, at least on the basis of our surviving evidence.[23]

Beginning in the years of the Nicaean successor state, there is documentary evidence once again of churches and monasteries founded and owned by individual clerics and monks.[24] Frequently these were family responsibilities in which a son succeeded his father as the officiating cleric for the foundation. Perhaps because it was very difficult for a family of modest means to try to maintain a church or monastery on its own, donations of these institutions to powerful independent monasteries occurred with some frequency.[25] Sometimes the recipient monastery would allow the donor's family to retain rights of usufruct in the institution that they once owned outright.

As in virtually every other age of Byzantine history, private benefactors provided the resources for most of the ecclesiastical foundations of Palaeologan times. One of the outstanding patrons of the age was the *protostrator* Michael Glabas, who erected the monastery of the Theotokos tes Pammakaristou in Constantinople during the reign of Andronicus II (1282–1328).[26] The church of this monastery still stands in modern Istanbul. An epigram of Manuel Philas commemorates Glabas' achievement as the *demiourgos* (creator) of this monastery, recalling the dedicatory inscriptions of the *Anthologia Palatina* which honored Juliana Anicia's role as benefactress nearly nine hundred years earlier.[27] Other laymen erected churches and monasteries in Constantinople and on the islands of Lemnos and Thasos throughout the mid-fourteenth century.[28]

---

[22] *Actes de Zographou* No. 39 (1357).

[23] Joachim, metropolitan of Zichnai, who refounded a monastery of St. John Prodromos near Serres in 1324, provides an exception: see his *typikon*, ed. André Guillou, *Les Archives de Saint-Jean Prodrome sur le mont Ménécée* (Paris, 1955), 161–76. So also Theodore Kerameas, archbishop of Thessalonica, who helped endow a monastery of Christ Pantodynamos at Thessalonica with the assistance of his brother Nicholas and Emperor Michael VIII: see *Actes de Lavra*, Vol. 2, No. 75 (1284).

[24] *Cartulary of Lembiotissa*, ed. MM 4 (Vienna, 1871), No. 15 (1232) (MM 4.56–57), No. 16 (MM 4.58–60), No. 118 (1246) (MM 4.203–205), No. 40 (1254?) (MM 4.97–99).

[25] E.g., *Cartulary of Lembiotissa*, No. 40 (1254?) (MM 4.97, esp. lines 14–24).

[26] For this foundation, see Hans Belting, Cyril Mango, D. Mouriki, *The Mosaics and Frescoes of St. Mary Pammakaristos* (Washington, D.C., 1978); Janin, *Géographie*, Vol. 3, pp. 208–13.

[27] Manuel Philes, *Carmina*, ed. E. Miller (Paris, 1855–56), Vol. 2, p. 241.

[28] *Actes de Zographou*, No. 19 (1321); *Actes de Kutlumus* No. 24 (1362), ed. Paul Lemerle (*Archives de l'Athos*, Vol. 2) (Paris, 1945); *Actes du Pantocrator*, No. 4 (1363), ed. Louis Petit, (*Actes de l'Athos*, Vol. 2), *VV Prilozhenie* 10 (1903); Patriarch Nilus, *Acta patriarchatus* No. 369 (1385) (MM 2.70–71) = Darrouzès, *Regestes* No. 2787; Patriarch Matthew I, *Acta patriarchatus* No. 533 (1399) (MM 2.322–23) = Darrouzès, *Regestes* No. 3082. For excellent summaries of documents attesting private churches and monasteries in the last centuries of the empire, see Herman, "Chiese private," 303–15.

A legal handbook of the mid-thirteenth century, the *Synopsis Minor*, still required benefactors to obtain episcopal *stauropegia* for monastic foundations, though it may be doubted how seriously this obligation was now taken.[29]

The great independent monasteries founded from the mid-eleventh through the mid-thirteenth centuries continued to enjoy a predominant position in the institutional church of the fourteenth century. Most of these institutions, already blessed with substantial endowments from their founders, engaged in vigorous territorial expansion. The cartularies of the independent monasteries frequently include documents recording donations of landed property on which were located churches and monasteries formerly owned by laymen, clerics, monks, or village communes.[30] Donated monasteries became *metochia*, dependent houses of the mother institution. The *ekklesiai* and *eukteria* became private monastic churches. It appears that the great monasteries sometimes sought such donations in return for memorial services for the dead.[31] In other cases, the original proprietors were simply unable to maintain or repair their foundations. Whatever the reasons for the donations in particular cases, the changes in status amounted to a considerable curtailment of the extent of individual private ownership of ecclesiastical institutions.

The growth of monastic proprietary churches also helped undermine the public system of parochial churches under the local bishops. Even the bishops themselves joined private proprietors in turning over churches to the great monasteries for *sustasis* and *beltiosis*.[32] The bishops resorted to the old institution of *epidosis* to transfer perpetual management of diocesan churches to the wealthy independent monasteries. Both the laity and the hierarchy had come to rely upon the great foundations to care for the institutions formerly under their charge. The price paid by the bishops was a partial dismemberment of an already weak diocesan

[29] *Synopsis minor*, Letter M', Sect. 114 (*JGR* 1.167–68).

[30] For examples of donations of priests' and monks' churches and monasteries, see above, note 24, also *Actes de Dionysiou* No. 12 (before 1430) and No. 19 (1420); *Actes de Kutlumus* No. 16 (1330); *Actes de Lavra*, Vol. 2, No. 78 (1285); *Actes de Lavra*, Vol. 3, No. 153 (1392), ed. Paul Lemerle (*Archives de l'Athos*, Vol. 10) (Paris, 1979); for a donation of a communal monastery, see *Cartulary of Lembiotissa* No. 169 (n.d.) (MM 4.265–66); for donations of laymen's private religious foundations, see *Lembiotissa* No. 35 (1231?) (MM 4.91–92) with Herman, "Chiese private," 303, and *Actes de Zographou* No. 19 (1321).

[31] *Actes de Kutlumus* No. 24 (1362); *Actes de Lavra*, Vol. 2, No. 117 (1326); *Actes de Dionysiou* No. 12 (before 1430); Patriarch Matthew I, *Acta patriarchatus* No. 687 (1402) (MM 2.551–56, esp. 551–52) = Darrouzès, *Regestes* No. 3253; cf. Herman, "Chiese private," 311–12.

[32] *Actes de Zographou* No. 14 (1299), and No. 39 (1357); *Actes d'Esphigmenou* No. 28 (1387), ed. Jacques Lefort (*Archives de l' Athos*, Vol. 6) (Paris, 1973); *Actes de Lavra*, Vol. 2, No. 82 (1289); *Cartulary* of the patriarchal monastery of *Nea Petra*, ed. MM 4 (Vienna, 1871), No. 39 (n.d.) (MM 4.422–23), No. 41 (n.d.) (MM 4.424–26). For a patriarchal concession, see *Actes de Lavra* Vol. 3, No. 144 (1367), ed. Paul Lemerle (*Archives de l'Athos*, Vol. 10) (Paris, 1979).

parochial structure. Bishops counted themselves lucky if they could retain the collection of the *kanonikon* from churches surrendered to the
monasteries in *epidosis*.[33] As we have seen, a bishop might have to fight
an ambitious monastic community's attempt to deprive him even of that,
despite the rulings of Patriarch George II Xiphilinus (1191–1198) which
had upheld this right.

Perhaps the most important reconstruction undertaken by a layman in
Palaeologan times was Theodore Metochites' restoration of the church
of the Chora monastery in Constantinople. Theodore, who was Andronicus II's grand logothete, spent nearly six years on the project from 1315
to about 1321.[34] The results of his labors are still visible since the Chora
church stands in Istanbul today as the mosque of Kariye Camii. Of particular interest is the mosaic over the entrance from the narthex to the
nave which depicts the patron kneeling before Christ presenting him with
a model of the restored church.[35]

The patriarchs of the fourteenth century took an active part in organizing the restoration of the capital's churches. Throughout this century,
they were receptive to petitions from members of the nobility, other laymen, clerics, and monks who sought designation as ephors or honorary
ktetores of needy institutions.[36] The two offices had distinct historical
roots. The ephor had always been a mere protector, an interested patron
in the broad sense of the term, who theoretically did not have any rights
of ownership in the institution that he supervised. The *ktetor*, on the
other hand, was originally the proprietary owner of his institution, either
as its original founder or as one of the founder's descendants.[37] By making honorary grants of *ktetoreia*, the patriarchs of this century could

---

[33] E.g., *Actes d'Esphigmenou* No. 28 (1387); cf. *Actes de Zographou* No. 39 (1357).

[34] For Theodore Metochites, see Ihor Ševčenko, *Etudes sur la polémique entre Théodore
Metochites et Nicéphore Choumnos: La vie intellectuelle et politique à Byzance sous les
premiers paléologues* (Brussels, 1962); for this foundation, see Janin, *Géographie*, Vol. 3,
pp. 531–90, and Paul Underwood, *The Kahriye Djami*, 4 vols. (New York-Princeton,
1966–75), esp. Ihor Ševčenko, "Theodore Metochites, the Chora and the Intellectual
Trends of his Times," Vol. 4, pp. 19–55.

[35] Illustrated in Underwood, *Kahriye Djami*, Vol. 1, frontispiece. For a study of donor
portraits, see Elizabeth Lipsmeyer, *The Donor and His Church Model in Medieval Art from
Early Christian Times to the Late Romanesque Period*, diss. (Rutgers University, 1981).

[36] E.g., Patriarch John XIV, *Acta patriarchatus* No. 74 (1337) (MM 1.168) = Darrouzès,
Regestes No. 2179; Patriarch Philotheus, *Acta patriarchatus* No. 311 (1344) (MM 1.568–
569) = Darrouzès, *Regestes* No. 2620; Patriarch Callistus I, *Acta patriarchatus* No. 182
(1361) (MM 1.423–25) = Darrouzès, *Regestes* No. 2433; Patriarch Matthew I, *Acta patriarchatus* No. 627 (1401?) (MM 2.467–68) = Darrouzès, *Regestes* No. 3243.

[37] Zhishman, *Stifterrecht*, 11–13; Lampe, *Patristic Greek Lexicon*, 782; Ostrogorsky,
"Aristocracy," 31 ("For the rich aristocrat, a man in the public eye, it was, in its way, a
matter of honor to found a monastery, to be its *ktitor*, and the more magnificent the foundation, the greater the prestige accruing to the founder"); Karl Krumbacher, "Ktetor, Ein
lexicographischer Versuch," *IF* 25 (1909), 393–421, with review by August Heisenberg,
BZ 19 (1910), 588–89.

advance deserving individuals to the status of the original *ktetores* as compensation for works of restoration that they promised to undertake. The patriarchs often coupled a grant of lifetime *ephoreia* with *ktetoreia*, tending thereby to equate these once very distinct offices.[38] Over time, this had the effect of diluting the greater authority of the *ktetor* with that of a mere ephor, a policy that the patriarchs also promoted by other means.

RIGHTS AND DUTIES OF BENEFACTORS OF ECCLESIASTICAL FOUNDATIONS

One of the most significant developments of the Palaeologan era was a drastic curtailment of the once very extensive and arbitrary rights of lay patrons of ecclesiastical institutions. Simply stated, this meant the conversion of *ktetoreia*, the traditional Byzantine concept of private ownership of an ecclesiastical institution, to *ktetorikon dikaion* (founder's right), just as had occurred earlier in the medieval West.

The *ktetorikon diakaion* formed the subject of the Austrian scholar Josef von Zhishman's excellent monograph, *Das Stifterrecht in der morgenländischen Kirche* (Vienna, 1888). The nature of the sources that Zhishman had at his disposal shaped his historical perspective in the development of private religious insitutions in Byzantium. He did not have the advantage of examining the Egyptian papyri, and intensive study of the Byzantine institutions was only just beginning when he wrote, late in the nineteenth century. Above all, Zhishman relied on the newly edited patriarchal documents of the fourteenth century.[39] As is now clear, these documents were the culmination of nearly a millennium of legislation of private foundations, and together with the well-known legislation of Justinian, formed the basis for Zhishman's essentially constitutionally oriented study. By chance, the sixth and the fourteenth centuries were the high-water marks in strict regulation of private religious foundations. Not surprisingly, then, Zhishman tended to overestimate the powers that the civil and ecclesiastical authorities were able to exercise over the patrons of these foundations during other periods of Byzantine history.

Zhishman's account of the "founder's right" nevertheless remains the

---

[38] Patriarch Nilus, *Acta patriarchatus* No. 369 (1385) (MM 2.70–71) = Darrouzès, *Regestes* No. 2787; Patriarch Matthew I, *Acta patriarchatus* No. 579 (1400) (MM 2.395–99) = Darrouzès, *Regestes* No. 3138; cf. Joachim of Zichnai, *Typikon* Ch. 21 (ed. Jugie).

[39] *Acta patriarchatus Constantinopolitani*, Vols. 1 and 2 of F. Miklosich and J. Muller, *Acta et diplomata graeca medii aevi sacra et profana*, 6 vols. (Vienna, 1860–90), now partially replaced (for the years 1315–31) by H. Hunger and O. Kresten, *Das Register des Patriarchats von Konstantinopel*, Vol. 1 (Vienna, 1981).

authoritative description of the much diminished powers of the *ktetores* in the fourteenth century.[40] The most important remaining right that the *ktetores* possessed was the appointment of officiating clerics in private churches and of monks in private monasteries. It was now exceptional for the *ktetor* to appoint his own *hegoumenos*.[41] On the other hand, the patriarchs consistently upheld the *ktetor*'s right to dismiss them at will for nothing more than personal grievances.[42] Some *ktetores* retained additional rights of patronage, like the authority to appoint *esomonitai* and *exomonitai* to *adelphata*, just as the *charistikarioi* and previous patrons had done in earlier eras.[43]

The *ktetor*, like ephors of this and earlier centuries, had only a few circumscribed administrative powers, unless perchance he happened to be in religious life. A lay *ktetor* had the responsibility of maintaining a foundation's *typikon* and of overseeing its administration. Theoretically, the *ktetor* could not introduce changes in the established *typikon* or alter customary practices. A *ktetor* who did happen to be a monk might enjoy the special right of spiritual *episkepsis* (inspection) of his foundations, but ordinarily this was a responsibility left in the hands of the local bishop or the patriarch.[44]

The honorary rights accorded *ktetores* in previous ages remained largely intact. The posthumous commemoration of the *ktetor*'s memory, the *mnemosynon*, was the most durable of all founder's rights, and its lapse due to the abandonment of a foundation was deemed a grave matter.[45] Bishops and private individuals who gave up churches to the great monasteries under *epidosis* or as outright gifts still reserved this honor for themselves in perpetuity. Patriarch Isaias (1323–32) ruled in 1325 that even the heir of a *ktetor* who had sold his monastery was nevertheless entitled to his customary *mnemosynon*.

Other honorary rights constituted financially insignificant but personally gratifying recognitions of the *ktetor*'s services in the erection or restoration of a religious institution. Dedicatory inscriptions and elaborate

[40] Zhishman, *Stifterrecht*, 47–64.

[41] Zhishman, *Stifterrecht*, 59–60.

[42] *Actes d'Esphigmenou* No. 28 (1387); Patriarch Isaias, *Acta patriarchatus* No. 57, Pt. 6 (1324) (MM 1.110–11) = Darrouzès, *Regestes* No. 2116; Patriarch Matthew I, *Acta patriarchatus* No. 576 (1400) (MM 391–93) = Darrouzès, *Regestes* No. 3135.

[43] Zhishman, *Stifterrecht*, 60–61.

[44] Patriarch John XIV, *Acta patriarchatus* No. 74 (1337) (MM 1.168) = Darrouzès, *Regestes* No. 2179.

[45] For reservation after a donation in *epidosis*, see *Actes de Zographou* No. 14 (1299); for reservation after outright donation, see *Actes de Kutlumus* No. 24 (1362); for retention by *ktetor*'s heir despite sale of the institution, see Patriarch Isaias, *Acta patriarchatus* No. 63, Pt. 5 (1325) (MM 1.137–39) = Darrouzès, *Regestes* No. 2126. Importance also asserted by Patriarch Philotheus, *Actes de Lavra*, Vol. 3, No. 144 (1367) = Darrouzès, *Regestes* No. 2521. *Actes de Lavra*, Vol. 2, No. 79 (1287) expresses regret at cessation of memorial services.

mosaic portraits commissioned at the *ktetor*'s expense, such as the famous mosaic in the *Chora* church honoring Theodore Metochites, are good examples of these concessions to tradition. The *ktetor* also had the right to burial within his church, the *ktetorikon dikaion ensoriastheso-menon*.[46] This honor, not generally allowed to ordinary laymen, could be transmitted hereditarily or through marriage.

By contrast, rights of economic exploitation had suffered almost complete extinction by the fourteenth century.[47] Under strictly regulated conditions, a *ktetor* or ephor might possess the right to reside on consecrated property. Ordinarily, the administrators of religious institutions had to spend all of the income from endowments for institutional needs and aggrandizement.[48] Strict legislation (for which see below) now forbade the personal profiteering that had been such a standard feature of the administration of private religious foundations until the reformist protests of the late eleventh century.[49]

The patriarchs were careful to limit most grants of *ephoreia* and honorary *ktetoreia* to lifetime tenures.[50] Yet individuals who possessed these offices by hereditary right, what contemporaries called *dikaion tes goni-kotetos*, continued to transmit their rights to their heirs or designated successors without hindrance or prior approval by the ecclesiastical authorities.[51] Because of this practice, it was not unusual for private foundations to have multiple *ktetores*, as had been the case long ago in Coptic Egypt.[52] Priests also passed down their own private churches through

[46] Zhishman, *Stifterrecht*, 63; cf. the burial of the *protovestiarios* and Grand Logothete Theodore Mouzalon (d. 1294) in the monastery of the Tornikios family at Nicaea as recorded by Pachymeres, *De Andronico Palaeologo* Ch. 31, ed. I. Bekker CSHB (Bonn, 1835), Vol. 2, p. 193.

[47] Zhishman, *Stifterrecht*, 63–64.

[48] Patriarch John XIV, *Acta patriarchatus* No. 102 (1342) (MM 1.231–232) = Darrouzès, *Regestes* No. 2234.

[49] As Herman, "Niederklerus," 425, n. 1 observed, Zhishman (*Stifterrecht*, 63) erred in maintaining that a *ktetor* was never allowed to profit financially from the offerings and other incomes of his foundation; Lemerle, "Charisticaires," 13, reaffirms the admissibility of a layman's reception of a personal profit from his administration of a religious foundation. Patriarch John XIV's ruling of 1342 (*Acta patriarchatus* No. 102) was a landmark decision in this respect, which reversed previous practice and misled Zhishman into postulating a general rule for all periods of Byzantine history.

[50] E.g., Patriarch John XIV, *Acta patriarchatus* No. 74 (1337) (MM 1.168) = Darrouzès, *Regestes* No. 2179; Patriarch Nilus, *Acta patriarchatus* No. 369 (1385) (MM 2.70–71) = Darrouzès, *Regestes* No. 2787; Patriarch Matthew I, *Acta patriarchatus* No. 627 (1401?) (MM 2.467–68) = Darrouzès, *Regestes* No. 3243.

[51] E.g., Patriarch John XIV, *Acta patriarchatus* No. 78 (1338) (MM 1.178–80) = Darrouzès, *Regestes* No. 2182, and No. 102 (1342) (MM 1.231–32) = Darrouzès, *Regestes* No. 2234.

[52] E.g., Andreas Aspietes and his mother, the *ktetores* of a church of St. Gerontius (see Janin, *Géographie*, Vol. 3, pp. 68–69) mentioned by Patriarch Matthew I, *Acta patriarchatus* No. 526 (1399) (MM 2.301–303) = Darrouzès, *Regestes* No. 3086, cf. Herman, "Chiese private," 309; the claimants in the Makrodoukas case (MM 2.322–23), as dis-

testamentary dispositions.[53] Even a layman could be the beneficiary of a priest's testament. A number of disputes among heirs arose which led to complicated litigation over the rights to *ktetoreia* before the patriarchal tribunal, the *synodos endemousa* (permanent synod).[54] These cases provide a great deal of information on the extent of founders' rights and the state of private foundations in the fourteenth century.

Unlike the *charistike* of the eleventh and twelfth centuries, a *ktetoreia* over a religious institution could be transferred as part of a *ktetor*'s dowry.[55] This probably was a survival of a traditional right of private benefactors. Yet a *ktetor* of the fourteenth century, like the *charistikarioi* and ephors of the eleventh century, could no longer sell his church or monastery to another party as had been done by his ancestors. This was an extremely important curtailment of a practice that the hierarchy of earlier centuries had tolerated if not condoned. The change in policy is further evidence of the institutional church's intent to place *ktetores* under the same restraints as those that bound ephors. Naturally, the ecclesiastical hierarchy forbade secularization of religious foundations, just as it had always done throughout the ages.[56]

The clear definition of the duties of *ktetores* stood in sharp contrast to their ambiguous and much curtailed rights in the fourteenth century.[57] Because of the nature of the evidence, we are best informed about the responsibilities that the patriarchs imposed upon petitioners for grants of *ephoreia* and honorary *ktetoreia*. Incidental evidence indicates that the

---

cussed below in this chapter; the litigants in the suit over the *ktetoreia* of the church of Theotokos Amolyntos (Janin, *Géographie*, Vol. 3, p. 157) (MM 2.455–58), also discussed below; and the lay heirs of the priest Theodore Sisinnios in the case heard by Matthew I, *Acta patriarchatus* No. 576 (1400) (MM 2.391–93) = Darrouzès, *Regestes* No. 3135, summarized by Herman, "Chiese private," 304.

[53] E.g., *Cartulary of Lembiotissa* No. 16 (1233) (MM 4.58–60) and No. 40 (1254?) (MM 4.97–98); Patriarch Matthew I, *Acta patriarchatus* No. 610 (1400) (MM 2.443–44) = Darrouzès, *Regestes* No. 3170, cf. No. 576 (1400) (MM 2.391–93) = Darrouzès, *Regestes* No. 3135, summarized by Herman, "Chiese private," 304, a case of inheritance by a layman from a cleric.

[54] For the *syndos endemousa*, see Joseph Hajjar, "Le synode permanent dans l'Eglise byzantine des origines au XIe siècle," *Orientalia Christiana Analecta* 164 (1962), 21–43; Paul Lemerle, "Recherches sur les institutions judiciaires à l'époque des Paléologues, II: Le tribunal patriarchal ou synodal," *AB* 68 (1950), 318–33; Siméon Vailé, "Le droit d'appel en Orient et le Synode permanent de Constantinople," *EO* 29 (1921), 129–46.

[55] Patriarch Matthew I, *Acta patriarchatus* No. 583 (1400) (MM 2.404–5) = Darrouzès, *Regestes* No. 3142, summarized by Herman, "Chiese private," 314, cf. Zhishman, *Stifterrecht*, 87–88; No. 677 (1401) (MM 2.551–56) = Darrouzès, *Regestes* No. 3239, summarized by Herman, "Chiese private," 311–12, cf. Zhishman, *Stifterrecht*, 77.

[56] E.g., Patriarch John XIII, *Acta patriarchatus* No. 42 (1317–18) (MM 1.76–79) = Darrouzès, *Regestes* No. 2083; Patriarch Matthew I, *Acta patriarchatus* No. 661 (1401) (MM 2.520–524) = Darrouzès, *Regestes* No. 3222, which cites C. *Chalc.*, c. 24 and C. *Trull.*, c. 49.

[57] For the duties of *ktetores*, see Zhishman, *Stifterrecht*, 64–69.

patriarchs based these requirements upon the duties customarily discharged by hereditary *ktetores* and ephors.[58]

Ktetores mentioned in the patriarchal documents shouldered the responsibility for supporting all the liturgical functions of private churches. The *ktetores* and ephors had to meet the expenses for the liturgy itself, the daily hymnody, the annual feasts, and the *mnemosyna* of founders, of the imperial family, of the patriarch, and of the Christian laity in general.[59] The patrons were also responsible for the support of the officiating clerics and the expense of lighting their churches. In a legal case adjudicated by Patriarch Matthew I (1397–1410), the *ktetores* of a private church had to support the cleric who officiated there either by paying him a sufficient *roga* (salary) or by allowing him all the *eisodema* (parishioners' offerings).[60] We may infer, then, that benefactors ordinarily made their own arrangements to compensate the clergy who served in their churches.[61]

Beneficiaries of patriarchal concessions of *ephoreia* or honorary *ktetoreia* had additional obligations.[62] They had to meet the traditional needs of aging institutions, namely, *sustasis* (maintenance) and *beltiosis* (improvement). Some concessions also obliged the beneficiaries to provide for the enlargement (*epauxesis*) of the donated foundations. In some cases the new patrons had to continue paying an institution's *kanonikon* to the local bishop or the patriarch in accordance with established custom.

To all appearances, the hierarchy of the fourteenth century had finally

---

[58] Compare the requirements for patriarchal appointees (as discussed below) with the provisions made voluntarily by Eustathios Boilas, Michael Attaliates, and Gregory Pakourianos.

[59] Patriarch John XIV, *Acta patriarchatus* No. 311 (1334) (MM 1.568–69) = Darrouzès, *Regestes* No. 2171 (summarized by Herman, "Chiese private," 310, cf. Zhishman, *Stifterrecht*, 47) is a document conferring *ktetorikon dikaion* in a church of St. Demetrios in Constantinople upon the layman George Pepagomenos; it includes a brief description of the incumbent's duties (MM 1.568.29–569.11).

[60] Patriarch Matthew I, *Acta patriarchatus* No. 576 (1400) (MM 2.391–93, esp. 393.1–12) = Darrouzès, *Regestes* No. 3135.

[61] Herman, "Niederklerus," 425.

[62] For their usual obligations, see Patriarch Matthew I, *Acta patriarchatus* No. 627 (1401?) (MM 2.467–68) = Darrouzès, *Regestes* No. 3243 (summarized by Herman, "Chiese private," 309–10), a patriarchal concession of lifetime *ephoreia* over a church of St. Michael in Constantinople (for which see Janin, *Géographie*, Vol. 3, p. 431) to the layman Hodegetrianos which incorporates the new ephor's written acceptance of the obligations imposed upon him by the patriarch (MM 2.467.18–468.2). For the obligation for *epauxesis* which bound some concessionaires, see Patriarch John XIV, *Acta patriarchatus* No. 74 (1337) (MM 1.168) = Darrouzès, *Regestes* No. 2179, and No. 78 (1338) (MM 1.178–80) = Darrouzès, *Regestes* No. 2182, in which this obligation replaces *beltiosis*; also *Actes de Zographou* No. 39 (1357); and Patriarch Matthew I, *Acta patriarchatus* No. 648 (1402) (MM 2.495–96) = Darrouzès, *Regestes* No. 3259 (summarized by Herman, "Chiese private," 309), in which it replaces *sustasis*.

succeeded where their predecessors had failed in enforcing the strict requirements of Justinian's legislation compelling benefactors to provide adequate support for their foundations. Thanks to their efforts, the *ktetoreia* of the last decades of the empire was well on its way to becoming a simple *leitourgia* (public service) instead of the patron's customary right of ownership.

NEW RESTRAINTS ON BENEFACTORS OF ECCLESIASTICAL FOUNDATIONS

The *ktetores* of the fourteenth century not only had to contend with well-defined rights and obligations, but they also faced some severe restraints on the exercise of their patronage which had never bound their predecessors. The most important of these new restraints was the prohibition of a personal financial profit derived from the administration of a private ecclesiastical institution.

Well before a consensus had formed against all forms of lay profiteering, a decision of Patriarch Isaias dated to 1325 prohibited the sale of ecclesiastical foundations.[63] The patriarch condemned the sale of a monastery that belonged by hereditary right to the father of a kinsman of the emperor. This man, a certain Monomachos, had donated the monastery to the monk Barlaam, who sold it for 72 *hyperpera* to John Philanthropenos, another relative of the emperor. Monomachos' son, John Triakontaphyllos, sued for restitution of his founder's rights. The patriarch made Barlaam return the money he had received from Philanthropenos, who in turn was to withdraw all claims to the *ephoreia* of the institution. Isaias turned the monastery over to the local bishop, and limited the plaintiff Triakontaphyllos to "the customary memorial (*mnemosynon*) of *ktetores*."

The principle behind Isaias' decision had fairly recent ideological origins. Less than fifty years before, in 1276, a layman had sold a church with its endowed properties to the imperial monastery of the Theotokos at Lembos for 10 *hyperpera*.[64] There was also a private church among the assets of a very considerable piece of property which Maria Palaeologina, a daughter of Michael VIII, had purchased (sometime in the late thirteenth century) from Maria Akropolitissa and Demetrios Contostephanos for 4,000 *hyperpera*.[65] Yet as early as the mid-thirteenth century-date of the lawbook *Synopsis Minor*, there had been an opinion (ulti-

---

[63] Patriarch Isaias, *Acta patriarchatus* No. 63, Pt. 5 (1325) (MM 1.138–39, esp. 138.22–31) = Darrouzès, *Regestes* No. 2126; cf. Zhishman, *Stifterrecht*, 11.

[64] *Cartulary of Lembiotissa* No. 97 (1276) (MM 4.174, esp. 9–16).

[65] Reported by Patriarch Callistus, *Acta patriarchatus* No. 136 (1351) (MM 1.312.11–28) = Darrouzès, *Regestes* No. 2330.

mately derived from Justinian's *Institutes*) which held that consecrated religious foundations were not subject to valuation (*adiatimeta*) and without master (*adespota*).[66] This was the interpretation that Patriarch Isaias put into practice with his decision of 1325.

Henceforth, the patriarchate was prepared to allow the sale of ecclesiastical institutions only in exceptional cases, although sales both of individual properties and of shares of *ktetoreia* continued to occur, for old habits proved hard to eradicate. The patriarchs were quick to condemn these lapses and compel restitution, particularly after the consensus against all forms of personal financial profit from ecclesiastical institutions formed in the 1340s.[67]

The reformers of the eleventh century had advocated such a prohibition long before, but their ideas did not win immediate and unqualified acceptance. Conservative opinions continued to be heard well into the fourteenth century.[68] Theodore Balsamon's immense prestige coupled with his stubborn defense of the *charistike* doubtless made it easier for the canonist Matthew Blastares to assert in his *Syntagma* (published in 1335) that there was nothing improper about private profit obtained from episcopal donation of monasteries. At the same time, the advocates of the more radical reform tradition were rediscovering Justinian's original regulations for private religious foundations, including those provisions that Leo VI and his lawyers had decided to leave out of the *Basilika*. An anonymous conservative canonist, commenting on Balsamon's own canonical commentaries, smugly rejected the reformers' citation of Justinian's novel condemning the trafficking in monasteries practiced by the Egyptians and others in the sixth century simply because this novel had been omitted in the *Basilika*. The conservative canonist was technically correct, but the reformers were marshaling the canonical and legal precedents that would soon enable them to win the consensus of ecclesiastical opinion.

It was Patriarch John XIV Calecas (1334–47) who finally endorsed the views of these reformers on the impropriety of obtaining a personal

---

[66] *Synopsis minor*, Letter I', Sect. 1 (*JGR* 2.111).

[67] E.g., Patriarch Callistus, *Acta patriarchatus* No. 136 (1351) (MM 1.312–17) = Darrouzès, *Regestes* No. 2330; Patriarch Matthew I, *Acta patriarchatus* No. 533 (1399) (MM 2.322–23) = Darrouzès, *Regestes* No. 3082, discussed below; No. 576 (1400) (MM 2.576) = Darrouzès, *Regestes* No. 3135, summarized by Herman, "Chiese private," 304; No. 621 (1401) (MM 2.455–58) = Darrouzès, *Regestes* No. 3182, discussed below; No. 661 (1401) (MM 2.520–24) = Darrouzès, *Regestes* No. 3222; No. 677 (1401) (MM 2.551–56) = Darrouzès, *Regestes* No. 3239, summarized by Herman, "Chiese private," 311–12.

[68] Matthew Blastares, *Syntagma*, Letter E', Sect. 22 (R&P 6.276–77); cf. the scholiast on Balsamon, *Comm. ad Nomocanoni* [Ps-] *Photii*, reported by J. B. Cotelerius, *Ecclesiae graecae monumenta* (Paris, 1677), Vol. 1, p. 747C (repr. in *PG* 132, col. 1115); for this canonist see V. Grumel, "Blastarès (Mathieu)," *Catholicisme* 2 (1949), 84–85.

profit from a religious institution when he rendered a decision in a case that came before his synod in 1342.[69] The metropolitan of Chios had brought a suit against a certain Constantine Prasinos, a hereditary *ktetor* of a church and monastery on this island. The metropolitan charged Prasinos with diverting the *eisodemata* of these foundations for his personal use. The validity of Prasinos' *ktetorikon dikaion* in the foundations was not in question, but rather his use of the revenues derived from them. The patriarch's decision was a stunning rebuke to the *ktetor*: Prasinos had no right to personal enjoyment of the parishioners' offerings (the *eisodema* and *karpophoria*) of these foundations. One need only recall the entirely oposite decision rendered (ca. 1025) by Eustathios Rhomaios in the case of the church of St. Auxentios to realize how completely Byzantine opinion had reversed itself on this issue since the reign of Basil II.

It seems that this change of opinion occurred at the highest level of the ecclesiastical hierarchy during John XIV's tenure as patriarch, since he had earlier made a concession of honorary *ktetoreia* (1334) in which he alluded without adverse comment to a lay woman who received a pension from a church's *eisodema*.[70] At the same time, Matthew Blastares was still defending the propriety of donations of ecclesiastical institutions for private profit. Less than a decade later, John XIV's landmark decision reversed the official attitude of the institutional church on this important question.

Henceforth, the patriarchate upheld this attitude and vigorously condemned any lapses on the part of incorrigible patrons.[71] Indeed, when the orphaned minor sons of a priest arranged to sell their father's house and a private church to the monastery of Christ Philanthropenos in Constantinople in 1400, the monks did not neglect to bring the transaction to the attention of the patriarchal synod for its approval.[72]

The hostile attitude of the patriarchate toward any sort of private profiteering in religious foundations prevented *ktetores* from disposing of these institutions in privately arranged business transactions, but they could still transmit them to heirs or even unrelated individuals by acts of donation.[73] The institutional church had always condemned the sale of

[69] Patriarch John XIV, *Acta patriarchatus* No. 102 (1342) (MM 1.231–32, esp. 231.30–232.2) = Darrouzès, *Regestes* No. 2234; cf. Zhishman, *Stifterrecht*, 40.

[70] Patriarch John XIV, *Acta patriarchatus* No. 311 (1334) (MM 1.568–69, esp. 569.17–20) = Darrouzès, *Regestes* No. 2171.

[71] E.g., Patriarch Callistus, *Acta patriarchatus* No. 136 (1351) (MM 1.312–17) = Darrouzès, *Regestes* No. 2330, and Patriarch Matthew I, *Acta patriarchatus* No. 621 (1401) (MM 2.455–58) = Darrouzès, *Regestes* No. 3182.

[72] Patriarch Matthew I, *Acta patriarchatus* No. 610 (1400) (MM 2.443–44) = Darrouzès, *Regestes* No. 3170, summarized by Herman, "Chiese private," 304.

[73] For donation by a *ktetor* to an unrelated individual, see Leo Modas' donation of a share of his *ktetoreia* in a church at Lembos to the nobleman Astras and the Evergetis monastery (MM 2.322–23), discussed below in connection with the Makrodoukas case.

private foundations when secularization resulted, but it had previously been content to allow all financial transactions that preserved the ecclesiastical character of the foundations. Even Justinian's controversial novel on the subject had left the door open for sales of the latter sort. Now the patriarchs of the fourteenth century resolved to surpass even Justinian in their regulatory rigor.

The disposition toward strict regulation of private foundations that Isaias' and John XIV's decisions had initiated continued to characterize the policies of subsequent patriarchs. Patriarch Callistus (1350–53, 1355–63), moreover, was to judge the most important case on private foundations ever to reach the patriarchal synod. The case concerned the convent of St. Mary of the Mongols, an institution that once had enjoyed an independent constitution, but had lost its autonomy to a series of ephors related to the imperial family.[74] One of these ephors, Isaac Palaeologus, the uncle of Emperor John V (1341–91), had badly neglected the convent's endowed properties and had allowed the wineries, bakeries, and rental units earmaked to support it to deteriorate. He also burdened the convent with lay appointees to *adelphata* to the amount of 2,000 *hyperpera*. Moreover, he alienated certain dwellings and joined them to his personal estate, then bequeathed what little was left of the convent's endowment to his daughter Irene Asania Philanthropena as his successor in the *ephoreia*. Since the nuns of the convent had no confidence that there would be any improvement under their new mistress, they brought an appeal to the emperor, John V, who referred them to the patriarchal synod.

Callistus' decision announced in 1351 abolished the *ephoreia* and restored the convent's previous independent constitution. The patriarch thereby made clear that he was determined to put the welfare of a religious institution above traditional concerns to preserve private property rights. His bold action provided a precedent for a later patriarch, Matthew I, who would not hesitate to threaten the deposition of an ephor or even a hereditary *ktetor* for such offenses as non-fulfillment of duties or illegal alienations of ecclesiastical property.[75] A *ktetor* of the fourteenth century thus faced the ultimate sanction of dispossession, which would have been unthinkable in previous centuries. True, the reformist patriarchs Nicholas III Grammaticus and John IX Agapetus had ventured to depose *charistikarioi*, but there were no attempts in their day to interfere

---

[74] Patriarch Callistus, *Acta patriarchatus* No. 136 (1351) (MM 1.312–17, esp. 316.6–20) = Darrouzès, *Regestes* No. 2330, mentioned by Herman, "Chiese private," 303, and discussed by Janin, *Géographie*, Vol. 3, pp. 213–14.

[75] Patriarch Matthew I, *Acta patriarchatus* No. 533 (1399) (MM 2.322–23) = Darrouzès, *Regestes* No. 3082, discussed below; No. 627 (1401?) (MM 2.467–68) = Darrouzès, *Regestes* No. 3243, cf. No. 621 (1401) (MM 2.455–58) = Darrouzès, *Regestes* No. 3182, discussed below.

with the basic property rights of the owners of private religious institutions.

Persistent scrutiny by the patriarchs was not the only new development that boded ill for patrons in the fourteenth century. The clergy officiating in private churches, encouraged perhaps by the reformist attitudes of the hierarchy, chose to make a bid for control of these churches. The uncertainty created by the death of a patron and resultant legal proceedings before the confirmation of a new *ktetor* or ephor provided an ideal opportunity for clerics to assert their own claims or at least to demand fixed salaries and security of tenure.

Here, however, the patriarchate drew the line in its attempts to diminish lay influence in private churches. Patriarch Isaias, who would rule so decisively against the sale of private foundations, issued an earlier judgment in 1324 that denied an officiating cleric any property rights in a privately owned church.[76] Subsequent decisions followed this patriarchal decree. The clergy of a church that Joannikios, the bishop of Ezova, had granted in *epidosis* to the imperial monastery of Zographou on Mount Athos attempted (with the connivance of a local government official) to prevent the transfer of administration to the monastery or, failing that, to secure for themselves tenure and half of the altar offerings.[77] The judge in this case, Manuel Xenophon, logothete of the metropolitan of Serres and patriarchal representative, chose to reject these claims and uphold the rights of the monastic community.

Patriarch Matthew I (1397–1410) also had no sympathy for officiating clerics who attempted to assert rights against the patrons of the institutions in which they served. In an important decision of 1400, Matthew went so far as to state that an officiating cleric served at the pleasure of the *ktetores* who could dismiss him for making a nuisance of himself.[78]

IMPENDING COLLAPSE OF THE EMPIRE

The importance of these decisions can distract us from the grim contemporary political situation of the Byzantine Empire. Like the *ktetores* themselves, who were once its most illustrious and influential subjects, the empire had now lost the power and prestige that once enabled it to dominate the eastern Mediterranean. By the 1350s the mighty Ottoman Empire had crossed the Dardanelles and established itself firmly in Eu-

---

[76] Patriarch Isaias, *Acta patriarchatus* No. 57, Sect. 6 (1324) (MM 1.110–11, esp. 1–12) = Darrouzès, *Regestes* No. 2116.

[77] *Actes d'Esphigmenou* No. 28 (1387).

[78] Patriarch Matthew I, *Acta patriarchatus* No. 576 (1400) (MM 2.391–93, esp. 3–12) = Darrouzès, *Regestes* No. 3135.

rope. Encirclement threatened what remained of Byzantine possessions around Constantinople.

Emperor John V recognized the mortal danger and attempted to settle soldiers on the coast between the capital and Selymbria on lands belonging to the patriarchate (1367).[79] Patriarch Philotheus (1364–76) rejected the emperor's promise to compensate the church with other lands, and declared that he had no authority to allow even a temporary alienation of church property of which he was only the official guardian. The patriarch was not even amenable to leasing out the property in question since, according to his interpretation of canon law, "the property of the church should not be rented to anyone among the powerful, not even to the emperor."[80]

The contrast with the permissive attitudes of the Byzantine ecclesiastical hierarchy in earlier eras is certainly striking. Fortified by reformist scruples and rediscovered canon law, specifically the twelfth canon of the Second Council of Nicaea, Philotheus was unwilling to make any accommodation, even to an emergency that threatened the existence of the state. John V desisted from carrying out his plans, but only until the Ottomans crushed the Serbians at Maritza on September 26, 1371. He then decided to seize half of the monastic properties of the empire and distribute them as landholdings for soldiers.

NICHOLAS CABASILAS AND HIS CRITIQUE OF GOVERNMENT REQUISITIONS OF MONASTIC PROPERTY

It appears that it was this action that stimulated the composition of one of the most fascinating documents in all of Byzantine history, the discourse of Nicholas Cabasilas on the illegal exactions of the government and the ecclesiastical hierarchy at the expense of the great monasteries.[81] The author was a learned monk and partisan of the hesychast movement, whose mystical doctrines had received the blessing of a church synod in 1351.[82] The discourse preserves the arguments of those who defended the government's confiscations, as well as Cabasilas' own detailed legal and canonical refutations. Although the institutions that Cabasilas defends in the discourse were not the traditional private monasteries but rather the independent and autonomous foundations, the tract's argu-

[79] For details, see Charanis, "Monastic Properties," 114–16, and George Ostrogrosky, *Pour l'histoire de la féodalité byzantine* (Brussels, 1954), 161.

[80] Patriarch Philotheus, *Acta patriarchatus* No. 252 (1367) (MM 1.507–8, esp. 507.15–21) = Darrouzès, *Regestes* No. 2534.

[81] Ed. Ihor Ševčenko, "Nicolas Cabasilas' 'Anti-Zealot' Discourse: A Reinterpretation," *DOP* 11 (1957), 80–171, with text at 91–125; for the historical context of the discourse, see Ostrogorsky, *HBS*, 474, n. 8.

[82] For his life, see Ševčenko, "Cabasilas," 85–87, with nn. 17–27.

ments for and against the propriety of lay exploitation of ecclesiastical property are still important for this study.

The discourse, then, preserves the final statements of the parties to the dispute that had troubled Byzantium for centuries. The views of Cabasilas' opponents may be summarized as follows: The government is the final arbiter of what is good for its subjects. It may even break its own laws in order to advance the well-being of its subjects. It is fitting for the government to confiscate part of the vast properties of the monasteries, provided it employs the wealth obtained for good purposes such as supporting the poor, compensating the clergy, decorating churches, and defending the state. When the ends accomplished by the confiscations are more or less in keeping with the intentions of the original donors of the monastic foundations, there can be no complaint that the government has disregarded testamentary dispositions. Since the state has the sole authority to validate private donations to ecclesiastical foundations, it can overturn them subsequently for good cause.

According to this line of argument, the monks who received the benefactors' donations were not full masters over them because they were only custodians and therefore lacked the capacity to dispose of them freely (cf. the argumentation of Patriarch Philotheus in his decision of 1367). The state must act to circumvent this canonical disability. When the recipients of these private donations mismanage them, the state ought to set matters straight and carry out the wishes of the benefactors by other means. The pro-government propagandists, therefore, based their case on the vaguely socialist argument of the state's obligation to determine the greater public good in preference to the traditional Byzantine respect for private property rights.[83]

Cabasilas' ingenious refutation of the government's position may be summarized as follows: A government that breaks the laws it imposes on others, particularly with respect to private property, risks undermining the personal liberty that is the basis for its subjects' respect. The good use argument is specious, for even if some benefits should chance to occur by the confiscations, that would not change their evil character. The donors who make gifts of property to the monasteries have every legal right to do so. The acts of donation remain legally binding, a fact that the state acknowledges by confirming these donations. Moreover, the documents retain their validity in perpetuity.

According to this line of argument, the monks who administered the endowed properties do in fact dispose of their revenues, even though canonical prescriptions regulate the use of these funds. Any property owner, moreover, is free to allow subordinates to manage his property

---

[83] For the views of Cabasilas' opponents, see the *Discourse*, Sects. 6, 11–14, 16, 21, 32.

without forfeiting his ultimate rights of ownership. The proper role of the state is to ensure that the monks observe the founder's instructions and do not damage the economic prospects of the monastic community through improvident management of the foundation's resources.[84]

Cabasilas' discourse makes use of traditional arguments for the respect of private property rights and the sanctity of a testator's will in order to defend the great independent monasteries against the government's requisitions. This was possible only because the great monasteries had become important private landowners themselves. Cabasilas echoes the arguments of the lay patrons for whom the cause of private property rights was so dear.

A similar respect for private property rights had motivated the judicial decisions of Basil II and Eustathios Rhomaios. The *charistikarioi* probably brought up similar arguments in response to Nicholas III Grammaticus' census takers in 1096. It had never been an easy matter for the government or the church to override private property rights, no matter how pressing the circumstances or desirable the benefits of doing so happened to be at various critical times in Byzantine history. Now, late in the empire's existence, Cabasilas could revive the old standard arguments to resist yet another attempt to divert private ecclesiastical resources for public purposes.

Cabasilas' arguments are rooted in a secular justification of private property rights. This distinguishes his ideological position from that of the eleventh-century Chalcedonian reformers and that of the patriarchs of his own day. By contrast, the reform tradition began with the personal opposition of Leo of Chalcedon and John of Antioch to what they saw as profanation of consecrated property, and turned increasingly to canon law for support.[85] Characteristically, Patriarch Philotheus resorted to the canons when he prepared his response to the requisitions planned by John V.

As the balance of his discourse amply demonstrates, Cabasilas was no friend of the bishops and metropolitans, nor of the reform principle so dear to the hierarchy: the proper subordination of all monasteries to diocesan authorities.[86] He attacked the claims of metropolitans to hold authority over dependent bishoprics, denounced the bishops who exacted fees for ordination, and challenged episcopal collection of the *ka-*

---

[84] For Cabasilas' refutation, see *Discourse*, Sects. 4, 10–13, 15–16, 20, 22, 24, 26, 28.

[85] Note the successful appeals of Demetrios of Bothrotos and Demetrios of Domokos. The hierarchy even increased its claims in the mid-fourteenth century, or so Cabasilas, *Discourse*, Sects. 32–48.

[86] Cabasilas, *Discourse*, Sects. 32–47 (fees for ordination of clergy), 38 (alienations of the property of deceased clerics), 39–41 (domination of subordinate bishops), 42–47 (collection of *kanonikon* from the laity), 48 (collection of *kanonikon* from monasteries); cf. 58 (obligation to break communion with bishops who act uncanonically).

nonikon from the monasteries. He boldly maintained that priests stood under obligation to break communion with bishops who openly transgressed the canons. On most of these points, Cabasilas argued from a highly partisan viewpoint, with only the shakiest of canonical support.[87]

The economic interests of the ecclesiastical hierarchy coincided with their commitment to the canonically prescribed subordination of traditional private as well as independent monasteries. So Cabasilas, opposed with equal vehemence to both the extraordinary requisitions of John V and the customary exactions of the ecclesiastical hierarchy, had to fall back on traditional arguments for non-interference with the rights of private property. He and Philotheus could agree in their opposition to the government's plans for requisitions, but characteristically (and predictably) the rationales of their arguments against these requistions were entirely different.

PATRIARCH MATTHEW I (1397–1410) AND HIS REGULATION OF PRIVATE RELIGIOUS FOUNDATIONS

Shortly before the complete collapse of the Byzantine Empire in 1453, there ascended to the patriarchate a remarkable man whose achievements (in a much-restricted sphere of authority) deserve favorable comparison with those of many of his illustrious predecessors. He was Matthew I, mentioned earlier in connection with the controversy over the rights of officiating clergy in private churches.[88] The future patriarch began his career as the spiritual director of the monastery of Charsianites in Constantinople. He became metropolitan of Kyzikos in 1387, then ten years later, patriarch of Constantinople. His patriarchal register, which is complete from the middle of 1399 to early 1402, contains 161 documents as evidence of his prodigious energy and concern for a wide variety of ecclesiastical issues.[89] He took an active role in supporting the restoration of deteriorating churches and welcomed the chance to adjudicate suits over *ktetoreia*.[90] He employed his role as judge in these cases to exert his influence for better management of private foundations.

[87] Ševčenko, "Cabasilas," 144–51.
[88] For this patriarch, see H. Hunger, "Das Testament des Patriarchen Matthaios I (1397–1410)," *BZ* 51 (1958), 288–309, esp. 290–94.
[89] Analyzed by Jean Darrouzès, *Le registre synodal du patriarcat byzantin au XIVe siècle: Etude paléographique et diplomatique* (Paris, 1971).
[90] Patriarch Matthew I, *Acta patriarchatus* No. 533 (1399) (MM 2.322–23) = Darrouzès, *Regestes* No. 3082; No. 627 (1401?) (MM 2.467–68) = *Regestes* No. 3243; No. 576 (1400) (MM 2.391–93) = *Regestes* No. 3135; No. 579 (1400) (MM 2.395–99) = *Regestes* No. 3138; No. 610 (1400) (MM 2.443–44) = *Regestes* No. 3170; No. 621 (1401) (MM 2.455–58) = *Regestes* No. 3182; No. 653 (1401) (MM 2.505–6) = *Regestes* No. 3214; No. 661 (MM 2.520–24) = *Regestes* No. 3222; No. 677 (1401) (MM 2.551–56) = *Regestes* No. 3239; No. 648 (1402) (MM 2.495–96) = *Regestes* No. 3259.

Two of these cases illustrate the problems of private foundations particularly well. The first of these, which came to trial in 1399, concerned a church that a certain Leo Modas had erected on the island of Lemnos.[91] In his capacity as *ktetor*, Leo consigned a half share in the rights of ownership to a monastery of the Theotokos Evergetis, most likely the famous institution of that name in Constantinople.[92] Nicholas Makrodoukas, the defendant in this case, inherited the other half share from Leo. Although their monastery had once stood in the forefront of the reform tradition, the monks of the Evergetis did not take their responsibilities toward the church seriously so the building eventually came to the verge of complete collapse. Makrodoukas became concerned and arranged to buy out the monastery's share in the church from George Synadenos Astras, a member of the imperial family who held the *ktetoreia* in the Evergetis monastery. Makrodoukas, believing that he now held clear title to the property, undertook a complete structural renovation of the building and was able to place a priest in the church to conduct services. Astras, the plaintiff in the case, was suddenly affected by fashionable reformist scruples when he observed the value of the considerable improvements that Makrodoukas had made to the property. He sought the annulment of his contract with Makrodoukas on the grounds that he had no right to sell an ecclesiastical institution in the first place.

The patriarch and his fellow bishops in synod shrewdly saw through Astras' stratagem. He was clearly posturing behind a principle dear to the reformers, but for a venal purpose that was repugnant to them. Yet the synod was now unwilling to go on record as approving of the purchase of a church, no matter how salutary the transaction had proved to be for its preservation. They resolved the difficulty by ruling that Astras and the monks of Evergetis had so seriously neglected their *pronoia* over this church that they had voided their rights. In the interpretation of the synod, Makrodoukas had acquired not the church itself, for as the synod declared "it is illegal and against the canons to alienate anything consecrated to God," but rather the *ktetorika dikaia* (founder's rights).[93]

The patriarch and the bishops thus avoided breaking the canonical prohibition that, according to the currently accepted interpretation, banned all *ekpoieseis* (alienations) of consecrated property. The synod then confirmed Makrodoukas' *ktetoreia dikaia*, with the right to transmit the church to anyone he wished. He was warned, however, not to attempt to alienate anything for his own benefit, nor to hold back a part

[91] Patriarch Matthew I, *Acta patriarchatus* No. 533 (1399) (MM 2.322–23), = Darrouzès, *Regestes* No. 3082, summarized by Herman, "Chiese private," 304–5.

[92] For this foundation, see Janin, *Géographie*, Vol. 3, pp. 178–83.

[93] Patriarch Matthew I, *Acta patriarchatus* No. 533 (1399) (MM 2.323.10–24) = Darrouzès, *Regestes* No. 3082.

of the church's revenues for his personal use, "since this is a sacrilege and not a trivial sin before God." [94]

Matthew I and his synod thus embraced Leo of Chalcedon's bold condemnation of all alienations of consecrated property, over three hundred years after that prelate first sounded the battle cry that ultimately led to the curtailment of the independence of many private religious foundations and their subordination to the ecclesiastical hierarchy. The synod announced this principle with all the authority accorded a canonical precedent that had never been in serious question. They could hardly have been aware of the striking novelty of Leo's position in his own day, and perhaps had no idea of his role in formulating it. Yet it was an idea whose time had truly come.

The second case worth particular attention concerns the church of Theotokos Amolyntos in Constantinople.[95] A princess of the imperial house, the *protovestiaria* Palaeologina, had granted some land to the eunuch Philialetes on the condition that he should erect a church there that he would give back to the princess' children at his death. The eunuch carried out his part of the contract, and the two children of Palaeologina, the monk David and his sister Theodora, inherited the church. When the latter died intestate, her two children, Andronicus Palaeologus and Irene Palaeologina, succeeded to shares of the *ktetoreia* along with Irene's son, Alexius Palaeologus. At this point the *ktetoreia* became so divided that it became difficult to provide a capable and unified management for the church. The heirs fell to squabbling among themselves, and all apparently decided to exploit their positions to obtain whatever they could from the resources of the church.

Irene Palaeologina brought suit before the patriarchal synod in 1401, seeking the removal of her uncle David and brother Andronicus from the *ktetoreia* on the grounds that they had neglected to care for the church, pay the priest's salary, or meet the expenses of illumination. The shrewd patriarch decided to send his own investigators to the church to determine the accuracy of Irene's accusations. The investigators showed that the church did have an endowment sufficient to provide for its religious services. David and Andronicus then took the offensive and charged their estranged relation with usurping a part of the property of the church to use as her garden. The patriarch condemned this alienation of consecrated property, and ordered Irene to make restitution for the damage suffered by the church.

Matthew's inquiries did not dispose him to grant Irene's request to

---

[94] *Acta patriarchatus* No. 533, lines 24–30.
[95] Patriarch Matthew I, *Acta patriarchatus* No. 621 (1401) (MM 2.455–58) = Darrouzès, *Regestes* No. 3182, summarized by Herman, "Chiese private," 305, and by Zhishman, *Stifterrecht*, 87–88.

remove her relatives from the *ktetoreia*. He also rejected her plan to entrust the services in the church to a priest who happened to officiate in another of Irene's private churches. He decided instead to favor the plans of David and Andronicus, who had shown themselves more trustworthy, and obliged them to support a priest of their own choice for the necessary services.

The case presents a rather dismal picture of the greed and contentiousness of the Palaeologan nobility in contrast to the conscientious and high-minded patriarch. As it turns out, this is also one of the last important references to traditional private religious foundations in Byzantium. We must remember, however, that both the "founder's right" and, to a lesser extent, private foundations themselves survived the fall of the empire itself in 1453.[96]

---

[96] E.g., *Actes du Pantocrator* No. 21 (1602), a confirmation by Patriarch Neophytus of a donation of a monastery at Adrianople made by two brothers, the institution's *ktetores*, to the monastery of the Pantokrator on Mount Athos (see esp. lines 12–17).

Glossary of Technical Terms

EC: Early Christian
LRE: Later Roman Empire
BE: Byzantine Egypt
MB: Middle Byzantine (602–1204)
LB: Late Byzantine (1204–1453)

adelphaton, *-a* MB, LB: monastic prebend(s)
adespotos, *-a* LB: without master(s)
adiakopton siteresion MB: uninterrupted *siteresion* (q.v.)
adiatimeta LB: not subject to valuation
aedificium, *-a* LRE: building(s)
ager LRE: farm
allelengyon MB: joint responsibility for payment of taxes
anakrisis MB: inquiry (into spiritual faults)
analomata LRE: cash allowances
anaphora MB: liturgical commemoration
angareia MB: compulsory labor service
annona MB: subsidy or wages in kind
antilambanomene MB: corrector (fem.)
antileptor MB: helper, protector
apa BE: blessed (an honorific)
apaitetai BE: tax collectors for ecclesiastical lands
apanteterion BE: hostel for pilgrims
aparchai LRE: first fruits
apokrisarios LRE: personal envoy of an ecclesiastical official
apomoirai LRE: portions (i.e., tithes)
apotage, *-ai* MB: gift(s) of property by a postulant to a monastery
archimandrite = *archimandrites* LRE: monastic superior
archon BE: magistrate; MB: ecclesiastical administrator
artabe, *-a* BE: a dry measure (e.g., of wheat)
athroisma EC: assemblage
autexousios MB: self-governing
autodespoton, *-a* MB: independent
autourgion MB: landed endowment of an ecclesiastical insitution

basilica, *-ae* LRE: imperial church(es)
basilika monasteria MB: imperial monasteries
basilikos kourator MB: imperial curator
beltiosis MB, LB: improvement
brevion, *-a* MB: inventory(-ies)

capitatio LRE: head tax
castrum NB: fortified settlement
catapan MB: provincial governor
charistike MB: (1) program for the concession of ecclesiastical institutions to benefactors unrelated to the original founders; (2) an individual concession under this program
charistikarios, -oi MB: possessor(s) of a *charistike* (q.v.)
chartophylax MB: keeper of archives
chartoularios BE: keeper of archives
choregion, -a LRE, MB: salary (-ies)
chorion, -a LRE, MB: estate(s)
chresis MB: (rights of) use
chrysika BE: government head tax payable in cash
civitas LRE: city
collatio lustralis LRE: tax on tradesmen's business activities
collegium, -a LRE: society, fraternity
colonus, -i LRE: peasant(s) attached to the land
conductor, -es LRE: short-term leaseholder(s)
conventiculum, -a LRE: place(s) of assembly
conventus LRE: assembly
copiae LRE: means, facilities
corpus Christianorum LRE: the corporate Christian church
cubicularius LRE: palace eunuch
curia LRE: town council
curopalates LRE: honorary title for court official of patrician rank

dapane, -mata LRE, BE, MB: customary expenditure(s)
decurion LRE: member of the town councillor class
defensores curialium LRE: municipal advocates
demiourgos LB: creator (i.e., founder)
demosia BE: public taxes
demosia monasteria MB: public monasteries
demosiake epereia MB: compulsory labor services
demosiakoi MB: clergy resident on imperial estates
designare LRE: to nominate (for office) = *proballein* (q.v.)
despoteia MB: overlordship
despotes BE: master
diakonia BE: estate of an ecclesiastical institution
diamone MB: (property) maintenance
diarium, -a LRE: salary (-ies)
diataxis LRE: (legal) disposition; MB: testament
diatyposis MB: testamentary disposition
dikaia episkopika MB: episcopal rights
dikaion, -a MB: (legal) right(s)
dikaion tes gonikotetos LB: hereditary right
dioikesis BE: administrative responsibility
dioiketes, -ai BE: administrator(s)
diorthosis MB: correction of (spiritual) errors
dometor, -es MB: founder(s)
dominium LRE: ownership
dominus LRE: lord, property owner

domus LRE: house
domus divina LRE: private estate of the emperor
domus ecclesiae LRE: house church
donarium, -i LRE: votive offering(s)
donatio mortis causa LRE: donation of property reserving rights of usufruct
dorea MB: = *charistike* (q.v.)
drungarios MB: admiral
dux LRE, BE: military commander of a frontier district

ecclesia EC, LRE: church
ecclesia catholica LRE: = *katholike ekklesia* (q.v.)
Eigenkirche: proprietary church
eis beltiosin MB: for (institutional) improvement
eisodema, -ta LB: parishioners' offering(s)
ek ton themelion LRE: from the foundations, "from the ground up"
ekklesia LRE, BE, MB, LB: church
ekklesiastika choria LRE: landed endowment of the public churches
ekklesiastika offikia LRE: ecclesiastical offices
ekphoria BE: produce, revenue
ekpoiesis, -eis MB, LB: alienation(s) (of property)
eleuthera monasteria MB: "free" (i.e., independent) monasteries
embole BE: tax for public wheat distributions
enapographos, -oi LRE: peasant(s) bound to the land
engraphon prostagma MB: written mandate
epauxesis LB: (institutional) enlargement
ephor = *ephoros, -oi* MB, LB: overseer(s) of a religious institution without eco-
    nomic rights of exploitation
ephoreia MB, LB: administrative charge of an ephor (q.v.)
epi tou kanikleiou MB: keeper of the imperial inkstand
epi tou koitionos LRE, MB: chamberlain
epidosis MB, LB: (1) program for the redistribution of economic assets among
    ecclesiastical institutions; (2) an individual concession under this program
epimeleia BE: responsibility, commission
epimeletes, -ai BE: property manager(s)
episkepsis LB: spiritual inspection
episkopeion, -a BE, MB: episcopal residence(s)
epistanai LRE: to propose, nominate (for office)
epiteresis MB: (administrative) oversight
epitropos, -oi BE, MB: trustee(s)
epoikion, -a BE: farmstead(s)
esomonitai MB, LB: resident recipients of *siteresia* (q.v.)
eukterion, -a LRE, MB: (private) oratory (-ies)
eukterios naos MB: (private) oratory
eukterios oikos LRE, MB: (private) oratory
eulabestatos BE: most pious (honorific)
eulogiai MB: sacramental gifts
euprosodon, -a MB: income-yielding property (-ies)
euthenia MB: (institutional) well-being
exkousseia MB: tax exemption
exomonitai MB, LB: non-resident recipients of *siteresia* (q.v.)

facultates LRE: abilities, capacities
fundus LRE: large family estate

georgos BE: farmer
gerokomeion, -a LRE, MB: old-age home(s)

hagios BE: holy, saint
hegoumene LRE: abbess
hegoumenos, -oi LRE, MB, LB: spiritual director(s), abbot(s)
horos MB: (doctrinal) definition
hyperperon, -a LB: late Byzantine gold coin(s)
hypodektes BE: estate treasurer
hypomnema, -ta MB: memorandum(-a)
hypomnesis MB: memorandum
hypothecation: mortgaging of property to produce an income
hypotyposis MB: model, constitution

idioperiorista MB: self-determined (i.e., private, non-diocesan)
illustris BE: illustrious (honorific)
inquisitor, -es LRE: investigator(s)
iudex, iudices LRE: provincial governor(s)
iuga LRE: land tax
ius corporis LRE: corporate right
ius patronatus LRE: patron's right

kaine BE: new
kalliergia MB: (institutional) restoration
kanonikon MB, LB: episcopal tax on monasteries
kapnikon, -a MB: hearth tax(es)
karpophoria LB: dedicatory offerings
kata dorean MB: as a gift (i.e., in *charistike*, q.v.)
katholike, -ai ekklesia, -ai LRE, BE, MB: public (i.e., diocesan) church(es)
katoiketerion EC: dwelling place
keimelia MB: sacred vessels
keimeliarchos LRE: custodian of sacred vessels
kellia MB: individual monastic cells
keration, -a BE: subdivision(s) of the *solidus* (q.v.) or *nomisma*
kleisurarchos MB: commander of a mountain fortress
klerikata offikia MB: ecclesiastical benefices
kleros BE: lot
koimeteria EC: burial grounds
koinobion, -a MB: coenobitical monastery (-ies)
kome, -ai EC, LRE: village(s)
kosmika katagogia MB: secular dwellings
koubouklesios MB: chamberlain
kourator, -es BE, MB: curator(s)
kouratoreia MB: curatorship
krites MB: provincial judge
ktetor, -es LB: (1) founder(s) of ecclesiastical institution(s);
          (2) heir(s) of the preceding
ktetoreia LB: rights and responsibilities of the *ktetor* (q.v.)

ktetorikon dikaion LB: rights of the *ktetor* (q.v.)

ktetorikon dikaion ensoriasthesomenon LB: right of the *ktetor* (q.v.) and his/her family to be buried within the religious institution over which *ktetoreia* (q.v.) was exercised

ktistes LRE: founder

kyriakon dikaion MB: right of ownership

kyriotes MB: dominion, overlordship

lamprotatos BE: most brillant (honorific)

latreia MB: worship

laurai MB: collections of *kellia* (q.v.)

leitourgia: public service

litra, -ai MB: measure(s) of weight

logaristes, -ai MB: accountant(s)

logos phorou BE: accounts receivable

logothetes tou genikou MB: chief financial minister

magistros MB: master of the imperial household

makarios LRE: blessed one (honorific)

martyrion, -a LRE: martyr's shrine(s)

mechanikos, -oi LRE: architectural engineer(s)

megalos sakkelarios MB: great treasurer

meizoteros, -oi MB: estate manager(s)

metochion, -a MB, LB: dependent monastery (-ies)

misthios, -oi BE: assistant rent and tax collector(s)

mnemosynon, -a MB, LB: commemorative service(s) for the dead

modios, -oi BE, MB: subdivision(s) of the *artabe* (q.v.)

moira BE: patrimony, endowment

monasteria kosmika MB: private monasteries

munera LRE: dedications, votive offerings

munera sordida LRE: compulsory labor services

naos hagios EC: holy shrine

nomisma, -ta LRE, BE, MB: = *solidus* (q.v.)

nomos, -oi LRE: law(s)

nosokomeion, -a BE, MB: hospital(s)

nosomomos BE, MB: hospital director

notarios, -oi BE: notary (-ies)

oikeioi EC: householders, kinsmen

oikia EC: house

oikodomos, -oi BE: professional contractor(s)

oikonomia MB: (financial) administration

oikonomos, -oi LRE, MB: financial steward(s)

oikos EC: house

oppidum LRE: town

oros BE: monastery

orphanotropheion, -a MB: orphanage(s)

ousia LRE: endowment

parakoimomenos MB: chief eunuch of the imperial bedchamber
paramythia, -ai MB: monetary allowance(s) from ecclesiastical revenues
patriarchika monasteria MB: patriarchal monasteries
philokalia MB: (institutional) restoration
philoponion BE: lay confraternity
philoponoi BE: members of the *philoponion* (q.v.)
philoponos BE: chief of the *philoponion* (q.v.)
photapsia, -ai MB: allowance(s) for expenses of illumination
phrontis BE: care, responsibility
phrontistes, -ai BE: guardian(s)
phrontizein BE: to take care of
platysmos MB: (institutional) enlargement
polis EC: city
possessio LRE: occupancy
possessor, -es LRE: leaseholder(s) on property
potestas, -tates LRE: power(s)
praedium, -a LRE: private estate(s)
praepositus MB: lord chamberlain
prakteon EC: decree
praktikon engraphon MB: written inventory
presbion, -a annalion, -a LRE: annuity income(s)
privata possessio LRE: occupancy of private land
privatae ecclesiae LRE: private churches
proasteion, -a LRE, MB: suburban estate(s)
proballein LRE: to nominate (for office) = *designare* (q.v.)
procurator, -es LRE: property manager(s)
proestos, -totes BE, MB: prior(s) (of a monastery); abbot
pronoetai BE: property managers; MB: property managers for a *charistikarios*
    (q.v.)
pronoetes BE: property manager; MB: = *charistikarios* (q.v.)
pronoia BE, MB, LB: care, oversight
pronomia, -ai MB: (financial) privilege(s)
prosenexis, -eis MB: free-will offering(s) of postulant(s) to a monastery
proskynesis MB: veneration
prosodon LRE, MB: income
prosphora inter vivos BE: liturgical offerings
prosphora mortis causa BE: funerary oblations
prostagma, -ta MB: diploma(s)
prostasia LRE: patronage MB: guardianship
prostasis EC: patroness
prostates MB: protector
prostaxis, -eis MB: codicil(s)
protasekretis MB: chief personal secretary
protektor LRE: property manager
protokometes BE: head townsman
protopapas MB: chief priest of an ecclesiastical college
protos MB: director of a monastery
protospatharia MB: wife of the chief of the imperial bodyguard
protostrator MB: chief imperial groom
protovestiaria MB: wife of the *protovestiarios* (q.v.)
protovestiarios MB: chief keeper of the imperial wardrobe

psychike ophelia MB: spiritual benefit
ptochotropheion MB: almshouse
ptochotrophos MB: director of an almshouse

rectores provinciarum LRE: provincial governors
res privata LRE: ministry of imperial properties
riparios, -oi BE: constable(s)
roga, -ai MB, LB: cash salary (-ies) or annuity (-ies)
ruralia obsequia LRE: a form of *munera sordida* (q.v.)

sakkelarios LRE: treasurer
sebastokrator MB: honorary title of the emperor's brother
singoularis BE: a tax official
siteresion, -ia MB: allowance(s) or dividend(s) payable in kind
sitesis, -eis LRE: (personal) maintenance
solemnion, -a MB: imperial dedicatory offering(s)
solidus, -i LRE: standard gold coin(s) of the later Roman Empire
sphragis MB: episcopal consecration of the *hegoumenos* (q.v.)
stadium, -a LRE: unit(s) of linear measurement
stauropegion, -a MB, LB: foundation charter(s) issued by an ecclesiastical official
Stifterrecht: founder's right = *ktetorikon dikaion* (s.v.)
strategos, -oi MB: military governor(s)
stratiotika ktemata MB: soldiers' landholdings
suburbanum LRE: suburban estate
sustasis MB, LB: (insitutional) support
syneisphora, -ai MB: financial contribution(s) of monasteries to ecclesiastical authorities
synetheiai MB: episcopal fees for the consecration of the *hegoumenos* (q.v.)
synkellos MB: syncellus
synodos endemousa LB: permanent synod of bishops in Constantinople

taxiarch = *taxiarchos* MB: military commander
Theotokos LRE, MB, LB: Mother of God
therapeia MB: (personal) maintenance
topos EC: place
trakteutai LRE: tax clerks
trophe MB: (personal) support
typikon, -a MB, LB: foundation document drawn up by a founder to regulate the life of a religious institution

urbs LRE: city

vicus LRE: village
villa LRE: suburban estate

xenodocheion LRE: guesthouse, hostel
xenon LRE: hostel, hospice

zeugologion MB: cattle tax

Select Bibliography

Ahrweiler, Hélène. "Charisticariat et autres formes d'attribution de fondations pieuses aux Xe–XIe siècles," *ZRVI* 10 (1967), 1–27.
———. "La concession des droits incorporels. Donations conditionnelles," *Actes du XIIe congrès international d'études byzantines* (Belgrade, 1964), 103–14.
———. "The Geography of the Iconoclast World," in *Iconoclasm*, ed. A. Bryer and J. Herrin (Birmingham, 1977), 21–27.
Alexander, Paul J. "The Iconoclastic Council of St. Sophia and Its Definition (Horos)," *DOP* 7 (1953), 35–66.
———. *The Patriarch Nicephorus of Constantinople* (Oxford, 1958).
Alivisatos, Hamilcar S. *Die kirchliche Gesetzgebung des Kaisers Justinian I.* (Berlin, 1913).
Anrich, Gustav. *Hagios Nikolaos*, 2 vols. (Berlin, 1913–17).
Antonini, Luciana. "La chiese cristiane nell'Egitto dal IV al IX secolo secondo i documenti dei papiri greci," *Aegyptus* 20 (1940), 129–208.
Armstrong, G. T. "Constantine's Churches: Symbol and Structure," *JSAH* 33 (1974), 5–16.
———. "Imperial Church Building and Church-State Relations, A.D. 313–363," *CH* 36 (1967), 3–17.
———. "Imperial Church Building in the Holy Land in the Fourth Century," *BA* 30 (1967), 90–102.

Babić, Gordana. *Les chapelles annexes des églises byzantines* (Paris, 1969).
Bachatly, Ch. *Le monastère de Phoebammon dans la Thébaide* (Cairo, 1981).
Barison, Paola. "Ricerche sui monasteri dell'Egitto bizantino ed arabo secondo i documenti dei papiri greci," *Aegyptus* 18 (1938), 29–148.
Barnard, L. W. "Athanasius and the Meletian Schism in Egypt," *JEA* 59 (1973), 181–89.
Barnes, Timothy. *Constantine and Eusebius* (Cambridge, Mass., 1981).
Bartelink, G. J. M. "'Maison de prière' comme dénomination de l'église en tant qu'édifice, en particulier chez Eusèbe de Césarée," *REG* 84 (1971), 101–18.
Bell, H. Idris. "An Egyptian Village in the Age of Justinian," *JHS* 64 (1944), 21–36.
———. *Jews and Christians in Egypt* (London, 1924).
Belting, Hans, Mango, Cyril, and Mouriki, D. *The Mosaics and Frescoes of St. Mary Pammakaristos* (Washington, D.C., 1978).
Bingham, Joseph. *The Antiquities of the Christian Church* (London, 1708–22).
Boojamra, Lawrence. *Church Reform in the Late Byzantine Empire. A Study of the Patriarchate of Athanasios of Constantinople* (Thessalonica, 1982).
Bovini, Giuseppe. *La proprietà ecclesiastica e la condizione giuridica della chiesa in età precostantiniana* (Milan, 1948).

Brand, Charles. "Two Byzantine Treatises on Taxation," *Traditio* 25 (1969), 35–60.

Bréhier, Louis. *Le monde byzantin*, 2 vols. (Paris, 1947–48).

———. "Les populations rurales au IXe siècle d'après l'hagiographie byzantine," *Byzantion* 1 (1924), 177–90.

Brown, Elizabeth R. "The Cistercians in the Latin Empire of Constantinople and Greece, 1204–1276," *Traditio* 16 (1958), 63–120.

Bruck, Eberhard F. *Totenteil und Seelgerät im griechischen Recht* (Munich, 1926).

Bryer, Anthony. "The Late Byzantine Monastery in Town and Countryside," *SCH* 16 (1979), 219–41.

Bryer, Anthony, and Herrin, Judith, eds. *Iconoclasm. Papers Given at the Ninth Spring Symposium of Byzantine Studies, University of Birmingham, March 1975* (Birmingham, 1977).

Bury, J. B. *A History of the Later Roman Empire from Arcadius to Irene*, 2 vols. (London, 1889).

———. *A History of the Later Roman Empire from the Death of Theodosius I to the Death of Justinian*, 2 vols. (London, 1923).

Cadell, H., and Rémondon, R. "Sens et emplois de *To Oros* dans les documents papyrologiques," *REG* 80 (1967), 343–49.

Campbell, J. Y. "The Origin and Meaning of the Christian Use of the Word *Ekklesia*," *JTS* n.s. 49 (1948), 130–42.

Canart, P., Cupane, C., et al. *Studien zum Patriarchatsregister von Konstantinopel* (Vienna, 1981).

Chalandon, Ferdinand. *Essai sur le regne d'Alexis Ier Comnène (1081–1118)* (Paris, 1900).

Charanis, Peter. "Monastic Properties and the State in the Byzantine Empire," *DOP* 4 (1948), 53–118.

———. "The Monk as an Element of Byzantine Society," *DOP* 25 (1971), 61–84.

Clarke, Elizabeth. "Ascetic Renunciation and Feminine Advancement: A Paradox of Late Ancient Christianity," *ATR* 63 (1981), 240–57.

Clover, Frank. "The Family and Early Career of Anicius Olybrius," *Historia* 27 (1978), 169–96.

Comfort, H. "Emphyteusis among the Papyri," *Aegyptus* 17 (1937), 3–24.

Constantelos, Demetrios J. *Byzantine Philanthropy and Social Welfare* (New Brunswick, N.J., 1968).

Crum, Walter Ewing. "A Use of the Term 'Catholic Church'," *PSBA* 27 (1905), 171–72.

Dagron, Gilbert. "Les moines et la ville: Le monachisme à Constantinople jusqu'au concile de Chalcédoine (451)," *T&M* 4 (1970), 229–76.

———. *Naissance d'une capitale: Constantinople et ses institutions de 300 à 451* (Paris, 1974).

Dalton, O. M. *Byzantine Art and Archaeology* (Oxford, 1911).

Darrouzès, Jean. "Décret inédit de Manuel Comnène," *REB* 31 (1973), 307–17.

———. "Dossier sur le charisticariat," in *Polychronion: Festschrift Franz Dölger* (Heidelberg, 1966), 150–65.

———. "Le mouvement des fondations monastiques au XIe siècle," *T&M* 6 (1976), 159–76.

————. *Recherches sur les offikia de l'église byzantine* (Paris, 1970).
————. *Le registre synodal du patriarcat byzantin au XIVe siècle: Etude paléographique et diplomatique* (Paris, 1971).
Declercq, Carlo. "Introduction à l'histoire du droit canonique orientale," *AHDO* 3 (1947), 309–48.
Deslandes, S. "De quelle autorité relèvent les monastères orientaux?" *EO* 21 (1922), 308–22.
Dölger, Franz. *Beiträge zur Geschichte der byzantinischen Finanzverwaltung, besonders des 10. und 11. Jahrhunderts*, repr. ed. (Hildesheim, 1960).
————. *Regesten der Kaiserurkunden des oströmischen Reiches von 565–1453*, 5 vols. (Munich-Berlin, 1924–65).
Doens, Irénée. "Nicon de la Montagne Noire," *Byzantion* 24 (1954), 131–40.
Dupont, Clémence. "Les privilèges des clercs sous Constantin," *RHE* 62 (1967), 729–52.
Dvornik, Francis. *The Photian Schism: History and Legend* (Cambridge, 1948).
Dyggve, Ejnar and Egger, Rudolf. *Forschungen in Salona*, 3 vols. (Vienna, 1914–39).

Falkenhausen, Vera von. "Monasteri e fondatori di monasteri a Costantinopoli tra Costantino Magno e Giustiniano I," *Corsi di cultura sull'arte ravennate e bizantina* 26 (1979), 151–55.
Fedalto, Giorgio. *La chiesa latina in oriente*, Vol. 1, 2nd ed. (Verona, 1981).
Feine, H. E. *Kirchliche Rechtsgeschichte* (Weimar, 1950).
————. "Ursprung, Wesen und Bedeutung des Eigenkirchentums," *MIÖG* 58 (1950), 195–208.
Felten, Franz. *Äbte und Laienäbte im Frankenreich* (Stuttgart, 1980).
Ferradou, André. *Les biens des monastères à Byzance* (Bordeaux, 1896).
Filson, F. V. "The Significance of the Early House Churches," *JBL* 58 (1939), 105–12.
Fitzgerald, G. M. *A Sixth Century Monastery at Beth-Shan (Scythopolis)* (Philadelphia, 1939).
Frank, Karl Suso. *Grundzüge der Geschichte des christlichen Mönchtums* (Darmstadt, 1975).
Frazee, Charles. "Late Roman and Byzantine Legislation on the Monastic Life from the Fourth to the Eighth Centuries," *CH* 51 (1982), 263–79.
————. "St. Theodore of Studios and Ninth Century Monasticism in Constantinople," *Studia Monastica* 23 (1981), 27–58.
Frend, W. H. C. "Town and Countryside in Early Christianity," *SCH* 16 (1979), 25–42.

Gamber, C. G. *Domus Ecclesiae. Die ältesten Kirchenbauten Aquilejas* (Regensburg, 1968).
Gascou, Jean. "Les grands domaines, la cité et l'Etat en Egypte byzantine," *T&M* 9 (1985), 1–90.
————. "*P. Fouad* 87: Les monastères pachômiens et l'état byzantin," *BIFAO* 76 (1976), 157–84.
Gautier, Paul. "Le chartophylax Nicéphore: Oeuvre canonique et notice biographique," *REB* 27 (1969), 159–95.
————. "Diatribes de Jean l'Oxite contre Alexis Ier Comnène," *REB* 28 (1970), 5–55.

——. "L'édit d'Alexis Ier Comnène sur la réforme du clergé," *REB* 31 (1973), 165–201.

——. "Jean V l'Oxite, patriarche d'Antioche: Notice biographique," *REB* 22 (1964), 128–57.

——. "Précisions historiques sur le monastère de *Ta Narsou*," *REB* 34 (1964), 128–57.

——. "Réquisitoire du patriarche Jean d'Antioche contre le charisticariat," *REB* 33 (1975), 77–132.

——. "Le synode des Blachernes (fin 1094). Etude prosopographique," *REB* 29 (1971), 213–84.

Geanakoplos, Deno. *The Emperor Michael Palaeologus and the West* (Cambridge, Mass., 1959).

Gedeon, Manuel. *Patriarchikoi Pinakes* (Constantinople, 1890).

Gero, Stephen. *Byzantine Iconoclasm during the Reign of Constantine V*, CSCO, Vol. 384, *Subsidia*, Vol. 52 (Louvain, 1977).

——. *Byzantine Iconoclasm during the Reign of Leo III*, CSCO, Vol. 346, *Subsidia*, Vol. 41 (Louvain, 1973).

Giovanni, Lucio de. *Chiesa e Stato nel codice Teodosiano. Saggio sul libro XVI* (Naples, 1980).

Glavinas, Apostolos. *He epi Alexiou Komnenou (1081–1118) peri hieron skeuon keimelion kai hagion eikonon eris (1081–1095)* (Thessalonica, 1972).

Goodchild, R. "A Byzantine Palace at Apollonia (Cyrenaica)," *Antiquity* 34 (1960), 246–58.

Grabar, André. *Martyrium, Recherches sur le culte des reliques et l'art chrétien antique*, 2 vols. (Paris, 1943–46).

——. "Les monuments paléochrétiens de Salone et les débuts du culte des martyrs," in *Disputationes Salonitanae* 1970, ed. Zeljko Rapanić (Split, 1975), 69–74.

Granić, B. "L'acte de fondation d'un monastère dans les provinces grecques du Bas-Empire au Ve et au VIe siècle," in *Mélanges Charles Diehl*, Vol. 1 (Paris, 1930), 101–5.

——. "Das Klosterwesen in der Novellengesetzgebung Kaiser Leons des Weisen," *BZ* 31 (1931), 61–69.

——. "Die privatrechtliche Stellung der griechischen Mönche im V. und VI. Jahrhundert," *BZ* 30 (1929–30), 669–76.

——. "Die rechtliche Stellung und Organisation der griechischen Klöster nach dem justinianischen Recht," *BZ* 29 (1929), 6–34.

Grashof, Otto. "Die Gesetz der römischen Kaiser über die Verwaltung und Veräusserung des kirchlichen Vermögens," *AKK* 36 (1876), 193–214.

——. "Die Gesetzgebung der römischen Kaiser über die Güter und Immunitaten der Kirche und des Klerus nebst deren Motiven und Principien," *AKK* 36 (1876), 3–51.

Griffe, Elie. *La Gaule chrétienne à l'époque romaine*, 3 vols. (Paris, 1947–65).

Grillmeier, A., and Bacht, H., eds. *Das Konzil von Chalkedon: Geschichte und Gegenwart*, 3 vols. (Wurzburg, 1951–54).

Grumel, V. "L'affaire de Léon de Chalcédoine: Le chrysobulle d'Alexis Ier sur les objets sacres," *Etudes byzantines* 2 (1944), 126–33.

——. "L'affaire de Léon de Chalcédoine: Le décret ou 'semeioma' d'Alexis Ier Comnène (1086)," *EO* 39 (1941–42), 333–41.

——. "Blastarès (Mathieu)," *Catholicisme* 2 (1949), 84–85.

——. *La chronologie* (Paris, 1958).

——. "Chronologie patriarcale au Xe siécle: Basile Ier Scamandrenos, Antoine Scandalios le Studite, Nicolas II Chrysobergès," *REB* 22 (1964), 45–71.

——. "Documents athonites concernant l'affaire de Léon de Chalcédoine," in *Miscellanea Giovanni Mercati*, Vol. 3 (Vatican City, 1946), 116–35.

——. "Nicolas II Chrysobergès et la chronologie de la vie de Syméon le Nouveau Théologien," *REB* 22 (1964), 253–54.

——. "Nicon de la Montagne Noire et Jean IV (V) l'Oxite: Remarques chronologiques," *REB* 21 (1963), 270–73.

——. "Les patriarches grecs d'Antioche du nom de Jean (XIe et XIIe siècles)," *EO* 32 (1933), 279–99.

——. "Les réponses canoniques à Marc d'Alexandrie," *EO* 38 (1939), 321–33.

Grumel, V., Laurent, V., and Darrouzès, J., *Les regestes des actes du patriarcat de Constantinople*, Vol. 1: *Les actes des patriarches*, Fascicles 1–3 (Chalcedon, 1932–47), Fascicles 4–6 (Paris, 1971–79).

Guillou, André. "La classe dei monaci-proprietari nell'Italia bizantina (sec. X–XI): Economia e diritto canonico," *Bulletino dell'Istituto Storico Italiano per il Medio Evo* 82 (1970), 159–72.

Haas, Christopher. "Imperial Religious Policy and Valerian's Persecution of the Church, A.D. 257–260," *CH* 52 (1983), 133–44.

Hagemann, H. R. "Die rechtliche Stellung der christlichen Wohltätigkeitanstalten in der östlichen Reichshälfte," *RIDA* 3 (1956), 265–83.

——. *Die Stellung der Piae Causae nach justinianischem Rechte* (Basel, 1953).

Hajjar, Joseph. "Le synode permanent dans l'Eglise byzantine des origines au XIe siècle," *Orientalia Christiana Analecta* 164 (1962), 21–43.

Halkin, François. *Bibliotheca hagiographica graeca*, 3rd ed. (Brussels, 1957).

Hardy, Edward, R. *The Large Estates of Byzantine Egypt* (New York, 1931).

Heisenberg, A. (Bibliographische Notizen), *BZ* 19 (1910), 588–89.

Herman, Emil. "Balsamon," in *DDC*, Vol. 2 (Paris, 1937), cols. 76–83.

——. "Les bénéfices dans l'église orientale," in *DDC*, Vol. 2 (Paris, 1937), cols. 706–35.

——. "Das bischöfliche Abgabenwesen im Patriarchat von Konstantinopel vom IX. bis zur Mitte des XIX. Jahrhunderts," *OCP* 5 (1939), 434–513.

——. "Charisticaires," in *DDC*, Vol. 3 (Paris, 1939), cols. 611–17.

——. "'Chiese private' e diritto di fondazione negli ultimi secoli dell'impero bizantino," *OCP* 12 (1946), 302–21.

——. "Die kirchlichen Einkünfte des byzantinischen Niederklerus," *OCP* 8 (1942), 378–442.

——. "Le professioni vietate al clero bizantino," *OCP* 10 (1944), 23–44.

——. "Die Regelung der Armut in den byzantinischen Klöstern," *OCP* 7 (1941), 406–60.

——. "Ricerche sulle istituzioni monastiche bizantine: Typika ktetorika, caristicari e monasteri 'liberi'," *OCP* 6 (1940), 293–375.

——. "The Secular Church," in *CMH*, Vol. 4 (2nd ed.), Pt. 2 (Cambridge, 1966), 104–33.

——. "La 'stabilitas loci' nel monachismo bizantino," *OCP* 21 (1955), 115–42.

——. "Zum kirchlichen Benefizialwesen im byzantinischen Reich," *SBN* 5 (1939), 657–71.

Herrmann, Elisabeth. *Ecclesia in re publica. Die entwicklung der Kirche von pseudostaatlicher zu staatlich inkorporierter Existenz* (Frankfurt, 1980).
His, R. *Die Domänen der römischen Kaiserzeit* (Leipzig, 1896).
Holum, K., and Vikan, G. "The Trier Ivory, Adventus Ceremonial, and the Relics of St. Stephen," *DOP* 33 (1979), 113–33.
Honoré, Tony. *Tribonian* (London, 1978).
Hussey, Joan. "Byzantine Monasticism," in *CMH*, Vol. 4 (2nd ed.), Pt. 2 (Cambridge, 1966), 161–84.

Jameson, Andrew. *The Responsa and Letters of Demetrius Chomatianus, Archbishop of Ochrida and Bulgaria*, diss. (Harvard University, 1958).
Janin, R. *La géographie ecclésiastique de l'empire byzantin*, Pt. 1: *Le siège de Constantinople et le patriarcat oecuménique*; Vol. 2: *Les églises et les monastères des grands centres byzantins* (Paris, 1975); Vol. 3: *Les églises et les monastères* [*de Constantinople*], 2nd ed. (Paris, 1969).
———. "Le monachisme byzantin au moyen âge: Commende et typica (Xe–XIVe siècle)," *REB* 22 (1964), 5–44.
———. "Les monastères nationaux et provinciaux à Byzance," *EO* 32 (1933), 429–37.
———. "Les sanctuaires de Byzance sous la domination latine (1204–1261)," *Etudes byzantines* 2 (1944), 134–84.
Joannou, P. "Psellos et le Monastère ta Narsou," *BZ* 44 (1951), 283–90.
Johnson, A. C., and West, L. C. *Byzantine Egypt: Economic Studies* (Princeton, 1949).
Jones, A. H. M. "Church Finance in the Fifth and Sixth Centuries," *JTS n.s.* 11 (1960), 84–94.
———. *The Later Roman Empire 284–602: A Social and Administrative Survey*, American Ed., 2 vols. (Norman, Oklahoma, 1964).
Jones, A. H. M., Martindale, J. R., and Morris, J. *The Prosopography of the Later Roman Empire*, 2 vols. (Cambridge, 1971–80).

Kapsomenakis, Stylianos. *Voruntersuchungen zu einer Grammatik der Papyri der nach-Christlichen Zeit* (Munich, 1938).
Kay, Richard. "Benedict, Justinian, and Donations 'Mortis Causa' in the 'Regula Magistri'," *RB* 90 (1980), 169–93.
Kazhdan, A. P. *Agrarnie Otnosheniya v Vizantii XIII–XIV vv.* (Moscow, 1952).
———. "Predvaritelnie zamechaniya o mirovozzrenii vizantiiskogo mistika X–XI vv. Simeona," *Byzantinoslavica* 28 (1967), 1–38.
———. "Vizantiiskii monastir XI–XII vv. kak sotsialnaya gruppa," *VV* 31 (1971), 48–70.
Kazhdan, A. P. (with Simon Franklin). *Studies on Byzantine Literature of the Eleventh and Twelfth Centuries* (Cambridge, 1984).
Kirsch, Johann P. "La *domus ecclesiae* cristiana del III secolo a Dura-Europos in Mesopotamia," in *Studi dedicati alla memoria di Paolo Ubaldi* (Milan, 1937–45), 73–82.
———. "Origine e carattere degli antichi titoli cristiani di Roma," in *Atti del III congresso nazionale di studi romani*, ed. C. G. Paluzzi (Bologna, 1934), Vol. 1, pp. 39–47.
———. *Die römischen Titelkirchen im Altertum* (Paderborn, 1918).
Kitzinger, Ernst. "A Survey of the Early Christian Town of Stobi," *DOP* 3 (1946), 81–162.

Klauck, Hans-Josef. "Die Hausgemeinde als Lebensform im Urchristentum," *MTZ* 32 (1981), 1–15.

——. *Hausgemeinde und Hauskirche im frühen Christentum* (Stuttgart, 1981).

Knecht, A. *System des justinianischen Kirchenvermögensrechtes* (Stuttgart, 1905).

Konidaris, I. M. *To Dikaion tes monasteriakes periousias apo tou 9ou mechri kai tou 12ou ainos* (Athens, 1979).

——. *Nomike theorese ton monasteriakon typikon* (Athens, 1984).

——. "Die Novellen des Kaisers Herakleios," in *Fontes Minores*, Vol. 5, ed. Dieter Simon (Frankfurt, 1982), 33–106.

Krasnozhen, M. "Kommentarii Alekseya Aristina na kanonicheskii sinopsis," *VV* 20 (1913), 189–207.

Krause, Martin. "Die Testamente der Äbte des Phoibammon Klösters in Theben," *MDAI Cairo* 25 (1969), 57–67.

Krautheimer, Richard. *Early Christian and Byzantine Architecture*, 3rd ed. (Baltimore, 1979).

Krüger, Gerda. *Die Rechtsstellung der vorkonstantinischen Kirchen* (Stuttgart, 1935).

Krumbacher, Karl. "Ktetor, ein lexicographischer Versuch," *IF* 25 (1909), 393–421.

Kurth, Julius. "Ein Stück Klosterinventar auf einem byzantinischen Papyrus," *BNJ* 1 (1920), 142–47.

Lampe, G. W. H. *A Patristic Greek Lexicon* (Oxford, 1961).

Lampsides, O. "Anekdoton keimenon peri tou hagiou Lazarou Galesiotou," *Theologia* 53 (1982), 158–77.

Lassus, Jean. *Sanctuaires chrétiens de Syrie* (Paris, 1947).

Laurent, Vitalien. "Charisticariat et commende à Byzance: Deux fondations patriarcales en Epire aux XIIe et XIIIe siècles," *REB* 12 (1954), 100–113.

——. "L'oeuvre canonique du concile in Trullo (691–692)," *REB* 25 (1965), 7–41.

Leclercq, H. "Alexandrie," in *DACL*, Vol. 1, Pt. 1, cols. 1098–1182.

——. "Hospices, hôpitaux, hôtelleries," in *DACL*, Vol. 6, Pt. 2, cols. 2748–70.

Lefebvre, Gustave. "Apa," in *DACL*, Vol. 1, Pt. 2, cols. 2494–2500.

——. "Deir-el-Abaid," in *DACL*, Vol. 4, Pt. 1, cols. 459–502.

Lemerle, Paul. "Un aspect du rôle des monastères à Byzance: Les monastères donnés à des laïcs, les charisticaires," *Académie des Inscriptions et Belles-Lettres. Comptes rendus des séances de l'année 1967, janvier-mars* (Paris, 1967), 9–28.

——. *Cinq études sur le XIe siècle byzantin* (Paris, 1977).

——. "Esquisse pour une histoire agraire de Byzance: Les sources et les problèmes," *RH* 219 (1958), 32–74, 254–84, and 220 (1958), 43–94, now in English translation by Gearóid Mac Nincaill as *The Agrarian History of Byzantium from the Origins to the Twelfth Century* (Galway, 1979).

——. "Recherches sur les institutions judiciaires à l'époque des Paléologues, II: Le tribunal patriarcal ou synodal," *AB* 68 (1950), 318–33.

——. "'Roga' et rente d'état aux Xe-XIe siècles," *REB* 25 (1967), 77–100.

Lenox–Conyngham, Andrew. "The Topography of the Basilica Conflict of A.D. 385/6 in Milan," *Historia* 31 (1982), 353–63.

Levchenko, M. V. "Tserkovnie imushchestva V–VII vv. v vostochno-rimskoi imperii," *VV* 27 (1949), 11–59.

Lipsmeyer, Elizabeth. *The Donor and His Church Model in Medieval Art from Early Christian Times to the Late Romanesque Period*, diss. (Rutgers University, 1981).

Lombard, Alfred. *Constantin V, empereur des Romains (740–775)* (Paris, 1902).

MacCoull, Leslie. "The Coptic Archive of Dioscorus of Aphrodito," *Chronique d'Egypte* 56 (1981), 185–93.

Macridy, Theodore, Mango, Cyril, et al. "The Monastery of Lips (Fenari Isa Camii) at Istanbul," *DOP* 18 (1964), 249–315.

Magdalino, Paul. "The Byzantine Holy Man in the Twelfth Century," in *The Byzantine Saint*, ed. Sergei Hackel (Birmingham, 1981), 51–66.

Malz, Gertrude. "The Papyri of Dioscoros: Publications and Emendations," *Studi in onore di Aristide Calderini e Roberto Paribeni*, Vol. 2 (Milan, 1957), 345–56.

Mamalakes, I. P. *To Hagion Oros (Athos) dia mesou ton aionon* (Thessalonica, 1971).

Manaphes, K. A. *Monasteriaka Typika—Diathekai* (Athens, 1970).

Mango, Cyril. "Historical Introduction," in *Iconoclasm*, ed. A. Bryer and J. Herrin (Birmingham, 1977), 1–6.

Mango, Marlia. "The Value of Donations to Church Treasures (*keimelia*) in the Patriarchate of Antioch in the Early Christian Period," *BSC* 7 (1981), 52.

Martin, E. J. *A History of the Iconoclastic Controversy* (London, 1930).

Maspero, Jean. *Catalogue général des antiquités égyptiennes du Musée du Caire: Papyrus grecs d'époque byzantine*, 3 vols. (Cairo, 1911–16).

———. "Un dernier poète grec d'Egypte: Dioscore, fils d'Apollôs," *REG* 24 (1911), 426–81.

Mathews, Thomas. *The Early Churches of Constantinople: Architecture and Liturgy* (University Park, Pa., 1971).

———. "'Private' Liturgy in Byzantine Architecture: Toward a Re-appraisal," *Cahiers archéologiques* 30 (1982), 125–38.

Meates, A. W. *Lullingstone Roman Villa, Kent* (London, 1955).

Meester, Placide de. *De monachico statu iuxta disciplinam byzantinam* (Vatican City, 1942).

Miller, Timothy. *The Birth of the Hospital in the Byzantine Empire* (Baltimore, 1985).

Modena, G. "Il Cristianesimo ad Ossirinco secondo i papiri," *BSAA* 9 (1937), 254–69.

Morris, Rosemary. "The Political Saint of the Eleventh Century," in *The Byzantine Saint*, ed. Sergei Hackel (Birmingham, 1981), 43–50.

Moutzourès, J. "Ta charistika kai eleuthera monasteria," *Theologia* 34 (1963), 536–69 and 35 (1964), 87–123, 271–304.

Nesselhauf, Herbert. "Das Toleranzgesetz des Licinius," *HJ* 74 (1955), 44–61.

Nicol, Donald. *Church and Society in the Last Centuries of Byzantium* (Cambridge, 1979).

———. "Ecclesiastical Relations between the Despotate of Epirus and the Kingdom of Nicaea in the Years 1215–1239," *Byzantion* 22 (1952), 207–28.

Nissen, Waldemar. *Die Diataxis des Michael Attaleiates von 1077: Ein Beitrag zur Geschichte des Klosterwesens im byzantinischen Reiche* (Jena, 1894).

———. *Die Regulung des Klosterwesens im Rhomäerreiche bis zum Ende des 9. Jahrhunderts* (Hamburg, 1897).

Nystazopoulos, M. G. "Ho epi tou kanikleiou kai he ephoreia tes en Patmo mones," *Symmeikta* 1 (1966), 76–94.

Oeconomos, Lysimaque. *La vie religieuse dans l'empire byzantin au temps des Comnènes et des Anges* (Paris, 1918).
Oesterle, G. "De monasterio stauropegiaco," *Il diritto ecclesiastico* 64 (1953), 450–60.
Oikonomidès, Nicolas. "Monastères et moines lors de la conquête ottomane," *Südost-Forschungen* 35 (1976), 1–10.
Ostrogorsky, George. *History of the Byzantine State* (New Brunswick, N.J., 1969).
————. "Observations on the Aristocracy in Byzantium," *DOP* 25 (1971), 3–32.
————. *Pour l'histoire de la féodalité byzantine* (Brussels, 1954).
————. "Pour l'histoire de l'immunité à Byzance," *Byzantion* 28 (1958), 165–254.

Papachryssanthou, Denise. *Actes du Prôtaton* (Paris, 1975) = *Archives de l'Athos*, Vol. 7.
————. "La date de la mort du sébastocrator Isaac Comnéne," *REB* 21 (1963), 250–255.
Pargoire, J. "A propos de Boradion," *BZ* 12 (1903), 449–93.
————. "Constantinople: Le couvent de l'Evergétès," *EO* 9 (1906), 228–32, 366–73; *EO* 10 (1907), 155–67, 259–63.
————. "Rufinianes," *BZ* 8 (1899), 429–77.
————. "Les Saints Mamas de Constantinople," *IRAIK* 9 (1904), 261–316.
Petersen, Joan. "House-Churches in Rome," *Vigiliae Christianae* 23 (1969), 264–72.
Pfanmüller, Gustav. *Die kirchliche Gesetzgebung Justinians hauptsächlich auf Grund der Novellen* (Berlin, 1902).
Pfeilschifter, G. "Oxyrhynchos: Seine Kirchen und Klöster," in *Festgabe Alois Knöpfler gewidmet* (Freiburg, 1917), 248–64.
Polyzoides, K. Th. *Ho vasileus kai hoi laikoi eis to en genei dioiketikon ergon tes ekklesias epi Alexiou Komnenou (1081–1118)* (Thessalonica, 1979).
Puza, Richard. "Gründer einer Gemeinde und Stifter einer Kirche oder eines Klosters in der christlichen Antike," *AKK* 151 (1982), 58–72.

Rémondon, Roger. "L'église dans la société égyptienne à l'époque byzantine," *Chronique d'Egypte* 48 (1973), 254–77.
————. "Le monastère alexandrin de la Métanoia était-il bénéficiaire du fisc ou à son service?" in *Studi E. Volterra*, Vol. 5 (Milan, 1971), 769–81.
Ringrose, Kathryn. "Monks and Society in Iconoclastic Byzantium," *Byzantine Studies* 6 (1979), 130–51.
Robinson, Gertrude. "History and Cartulary of the Greek Monastery of St. Elias and St. Anastasius of Carbone," *OC* 11 (1928), 270–349 and 15 (1929), 118–275.
Robinson, Olivia. "Private Prisons," *RIDA* 15 (1968), 389–98.
Rouillard, Germaine. *L'administration civile de l'Egypte byzantine* (Paris, 1928).

Santifaller, L. *Beiträge zur Geschichte des lateinischen Patriarchats von Konstantinopel und der venezianischen Urkunden (1204–1261)* (Weimar, 1938).

Sarrazin, A. *Etudes sur les fondations dans l'antiquité en particulier à Rome et à Byzance* (Paris, 1909).

Scheltema, H. J. "Byzantine Law," in *CMH*, Vol. 4 (2nd ed.), Pt. 2 (Cambridge, 1966), 55–77.

Schlumberger, Gustave. *Un empereur byzantin au Xe siècle: Nicéphore Phocas* (Paris, 1890).

Schmid, H. F. "Byzantinisches Zehtwesen," *JÖBG* 6 (1957), 45–110.

Schmitt, Th. "Kahrie-Djame," *IRAIK* 11 (1906), 1–306.

Seston, W. "Note sur les origines religieuses des paroisses rurales," *RHPR* 15 (1935), 243–54.

Ševčenko, Ihor, *Etudes sur la polémique entre Théodore Métochites et Nicéphore Choumnos: La vie intellectuelle et politique à Byzance sous les premiers paléologues* (Brussels, 1962).

——. "Inscription Commemorating Sisinnios, 'Curator' of Tzurulon (A.D. 813)," *Byzantion* 35 (1965), 564–74.

——. "Nicolas Cabasilas' 'Anti-Zealot' Discourse: A Reinterpretation," *DOP* 11 (1957), 80–171.

——. "Theodore Metochites, the Chora and the Intellectual Trends of His Times," in Paul Underwood, *Kariye Djami*, Vol. 4 (Princeton, 1975), 19–55.

Skabalonovitch, M. *Vizantiiskoe gosudarstvo i tserkov v XI veke* (St. Petersburg, 1884).

Skoulatos, Basile. *Les personnages byzantins de l'Alexiade* (Louvain, 1980).

Sokolov, Ivan I. *Sostoianie monashestva v vizantiiskoi tserkvi s poloviny IX do nachala XIII veka (842–1204)* (Kazan, 1894).

Sokolov, Platon P. *Tserkovnoimushchestvennoe pravo v greko-rimskoi imperii* (Novgorod, 1896).

Spatharakis, Ioannis. *Corpus of Dated Illuminated Greek Manuscripts to the Year 1453*, 2 vols. (Leiden, 1981).

Speck, Paul. *Kaiser Konstantin VI.: Die Legitimation einer fremden und der Versuch einer eigenen Herrschaft*, 2 vols. (Munich, 1978).

Stein, Dietrich. *Der Beginn des byzantinischen Bilderstreites und seine Entwicklung bis in die 40er Jahre des 8. Jahrhunderts* (Munich, 1980).

Steinwenter, Artur. "Aus dem kirchlichen Vermögensrechte der Papyri," *ZSR* 75, *k.a.* 44 (1958), 1–34.

——. "Byzantinische Mönchstestamente," *Aegyptus* 12 (1932), 55–64.

——. "Die Ordinationsbitten koptischer Kleriker," *Aegyptus* 11 (1931), 29–34.

——. "Die Rechtsstellung der Kirchen und Klöster nach den Papyri," *ZSR* 50, *k.a.* 19 (1930), 1–50.

Stephanou, P. "La doctrine de Léon de Chalcédoine et ses adversaires sur les images," *OCP* 12 (1946), 177–99.

——. "Le procès de Léon de Chalcédoine," *OCP* 9 (1943), 5–64.

Stevens, G. P. *De Theodoro Balsamone. Analysis operum ac mentis iuridicae* (Rome, 1969).

Stutz, Ulrich. *Die Eigenkirche als Element des mittelalterlich-germanischen Kirchenrechtes* (Berlin, 1895).

——. *Geschichte des kirchlichen Benefizialwesens von seinen Anfängen bis auf die Zeit Alexanders III.* (Berlin, 1895).

Svoronos, Nicolas. "Histoire des institutions de l'empire byzantin," *Annuaire de l'Ecole Pratique des Hautes Etudes (IVe section)* (1975–76), 455–76.

―――. "Les privilèges de l'Eglise à l'époque des Comnènes: Un rescrit inédit de Manuel Ier Comnène," *T&M* 1 (1965), 325–91.

Thomas, John Philip. "A Byzantine Ecclesiastical Reform Movement," *MH* n.s. 12 (1984), 1–16.

―――. "The Crisis of Byzantine Ecclesiastical Foundations, 964- 1025," *BF* 9 (1985), 255–74.

―――. "A Disputed Novel of Emperor Basil II," *GRBS* 23 (1983), 273–83.

―――. "The Rise of the Independent and Self-governing Monasteries as Reflected in the Monastic *Typika*," *GOTR* 30 (1985), 21–30.

―――. "Sisinnius II: A Reform Patriarch of the Reign of Basil II," *BSC* 9 (1983), 54–55.

Tiftixoglu, V. "Gruppenbildungen innerhalb des konstantinopolitanischen Klerus während der Kommenenzeit," *BZ* 62 (1969), 25–72.

Till, Walter C. "Datierung und Prosopographie der koptischen Urkunden aus Theben," *SOAW* 240, Pt. 2 (Vienna, 1962).

Troianos, Sp. "Ein Synodalakt des Sisinios zu den bischöflichen Einkünften," in *Fontes Minores*, Vol. 3, ed. Dieter Simon (Frankfurt, 1979), 211–20.

Trombley, Frank. "Monastic Foundations in Sixth-century Anatolia and Their Role in the Social and Economic Life of the Countryside," *GOTR* 30 (1985), 45–59.

Turner, Harold. *From Temple to Meeting Place: The Phenomenology of Places of Worship* (The Hague, 1979).

Uspenskii, Th. "Mneniya i postanovleniya konstantinopolskikh pomestnikh soborov XI i XII vv. o razdache tserkovnikh imuschestv (Charistikarii)," *IRAIK* 5 (1900), 1–48.

Vailé, Siméon. "Le droit d'appel en Orient et le Synode permanent de Constantinople," *EO* 29 (1921), 129–46.

Vasiliev, A. A. *History of the Byzantine Empire*, 2 vols. (Madison, 1952).

Voelkl, L. *Die Kirchenstiftungen des Kaisers Konstantin im Lichte des römischen Sakralrechts* (Cologne, 1964).

―――. "Die konstantinischen Kirchenbauten nach den literarischen Quellen des Okzidents," *RAC* 30 (1954), 99–136.

―――. "Die konstantinischen Kirchenbauten nach Eusebius," *RAC* 29 (1953), 49–66.

Volk, Robert. *Gesundheitswesen und Wohltätigkeit im Spiegel der byzantinischen Klöstertypika* (Munich, 1983).

Vryonis, Speros, Jr. "The Will of a Provincial Magnate, Eustathius Boilas (1059)," *DOP* 11 (1957), 263–77.

Vulić, N. "Inscription grecque de Stobi," *BCH* 56 (1932), 291–98.

Walke, S. C. "The Use of *ecclesia* in the Apostolic Fathers," *ATR* 32 (1950), 39–53.

Wenger, Leopold. "Eine Schenkung auf den Todesfall," *ZSR* 32, *r.a.* (1911), 325–37.

Wipszycka, Ewa. "Les confreries dans la vie religieuse de l'Egypte chrétienne," *Proceedings of the Twelfth International Congress of Papyrology* (Toronto, 1970), 511–25.

——. "L'Eglise dans la chôra égyptienne et les artisans," *Aegyptus* 48 (1968), 130–38.

——. "Les factions du cirque et les biens ecclesiastiques dans un papyrus égyptien," *Byzantion* 39 (1969), 180–98.

——. *Les ressources et les activités économiques des églises en Egypte du IVe au VIIIe siècle* (Brussels, 1972).

Wolff, Robert Lee. "The Latin Empire of Constantinople and the Franciscans," *Traditio* 2 (1944), 213–37.

——. "The Organization of the Latin Patriarchate of Constantinople, 1204–1261: Social and Administrative Consequences of the Latin Conquest," *Traditio* 6 (1948), 33–60.

——. "Politics in the Latin Patriarchate of Constantinople, 1202–1261," *DOP* 8 (1954), 225–303.

Zhishman, Josef von. *Das Stifterrecht in der morgenländischen Kirche* (Vienna, 1888).

Zorell, Stephan. "Die Entwicklung des Parochialsystems bis zum Ende der Karolingerzeit," *AKK* 82 (1902), 74–98.

Index